question. And the more we hung [about?] the [nearer?] we[?] [came to?] the sentry, (or whoever it was).

"The game's up," I said, "tell him we're escaped prisoners and get it over with". Turning towards the hidden voice my friend shouted, in his best Italian, "Prigionieri di guerra!". The hidden speaker said nothing in reply. We advanced. Some 10 yards or so further along I saw there, off to my right, a sentry box. It was on a road junction. An Italian Alpine sentry was at the post. As we approached him he said, "BORGHESI?", to which question my friend promptly replied, "Si! Si!" — "Avanti, Buona notte" said the sentry. Suiting my actions to those of my companion I moved on, passed the post, and let my friend do the talking. I felt like breaking into a gallop right there and then, but common sense told me that such action would be fatal. Straight across the road junction we went, accelerating our speed only when out of sight & hearing of the sentry. Down the first turning left at top speed; then left, right, then left again, over a wall into a field; across the field and over

The Glass Mountain

The Glass Mountain
Escape and Discovery in Wartime Italy

MALCOLM GASKILL

ALLEN LANE
an imprint of
PENGUIN BOOKS

ALLEN LANE

UK | USA | Canada | Ireland | Australia
India | New Zealand | South Africa

Allen Lane is part of the Penguin Random House group of companies
whose addresses can be found at global.penguinrandomhouse.com

Penguin Random House UK
One Embassy Gardens, 8 Viaduct Gardens, London SW11 7BW

penguin.co.uk

First published in Great Britain by Allen Lane 2025

001

Copyright © Malcolm Gaskill, 2025

Penguin Random House values and supports copyright.
Copyright fuels creativity, encourages diverse voices, promotes freedom
of expression and supports a vibrant culture. Thank you for purchasing
an authorized edition of this book and for respecting intellectual property
laws by not reproducing, scanning or distributing any part of it by any
means without permission. You are supporting authors and enabling
Penguin Random House to continue to publish books for everyone.
No part of this book may be used or reproduced in any manner for the
purpose of training artificial intelligence technologies or systems. In accordance
with Article 4(3) of the DSM Directive 2019/790, Penguin Random House
expressly reserves this work from the text and data mining exception.

The moral right of the author has been asserted

Set in Dante 12/14.75pt
Typeset by Six Red Marbles UK, Thetford, Norfolk
Printed and bound in Great Britain by Clays Ltd, Elcograf S.p.A.

The authorized representative in the EEA is Penguin Random House Ireland,
Morrison Chambers, 32 Nassau Street, Dublin D02 YH68

A CIP catalogue record for this book is available from the British Library

ISBN: 978–0–241–62259–9

Penguin Random House is committed to a sustainable future
for our business, our readers and our planet. This book is made from
Forest Stewardship Council® certified paper.

For my mother, Audrey, and my friend Domenico
with love, admiration and gratitude
and in memory of the fugitives Ralph and Charlie

'Our concern with history . . . is a concern with pre-formed images already imprinted on our brains, images at which we keep staring while the truth lies elsewhere . . . [and] when memories come back to you, you sometimes feel as if you were looking at the past through a glass mountain.'

W. G. Sebald, *Austerlitz*, trans. Anthea Bell (2001)

'There is no complete life. There are only fragments.'

James Salter, *Light Years* (1975)

Contents

Maps	xi
Prologue: The Dream	xvii

PART ONE: BECOMING

1 War Relics	3
2 A Perfect Gentleman	12
3 The Cauldron	23

PART TWO: CAPTIVITY

4 In the Bag	39
5 The Beehive	47
6 Charlie	64

PART THREE: FLIGHT

7 Flashes and Sparks	81
8 Pursued Hares	93
9 Chi Va La!	103
10 Noci	116

PART FOUR: INTERMEZZO

11 Passing Time	129
12 The Bread Palace	141
13 Amapola	154
14 Days of Hope	168

Contents

PART FIVE: EVASION

15	A Hole in the Floor	183
16	The Fig Tree	197
17	Farewell at Molina	209
18	Sega di Ala	218

PART SIX: LIBERTY

19	Rodolfo	229
20	Green Flames	244
21	A Hazardous Mission	256
22	Incipit Vita Nova	268

PART SEVEN: MEMORY

23	The South Country	281
24	Redeemed from Time	300

Epilogue: Monte Generoso	313
Acknowledgements	317
Sources	321
Notes	327
Picture Credits	373
Index	375

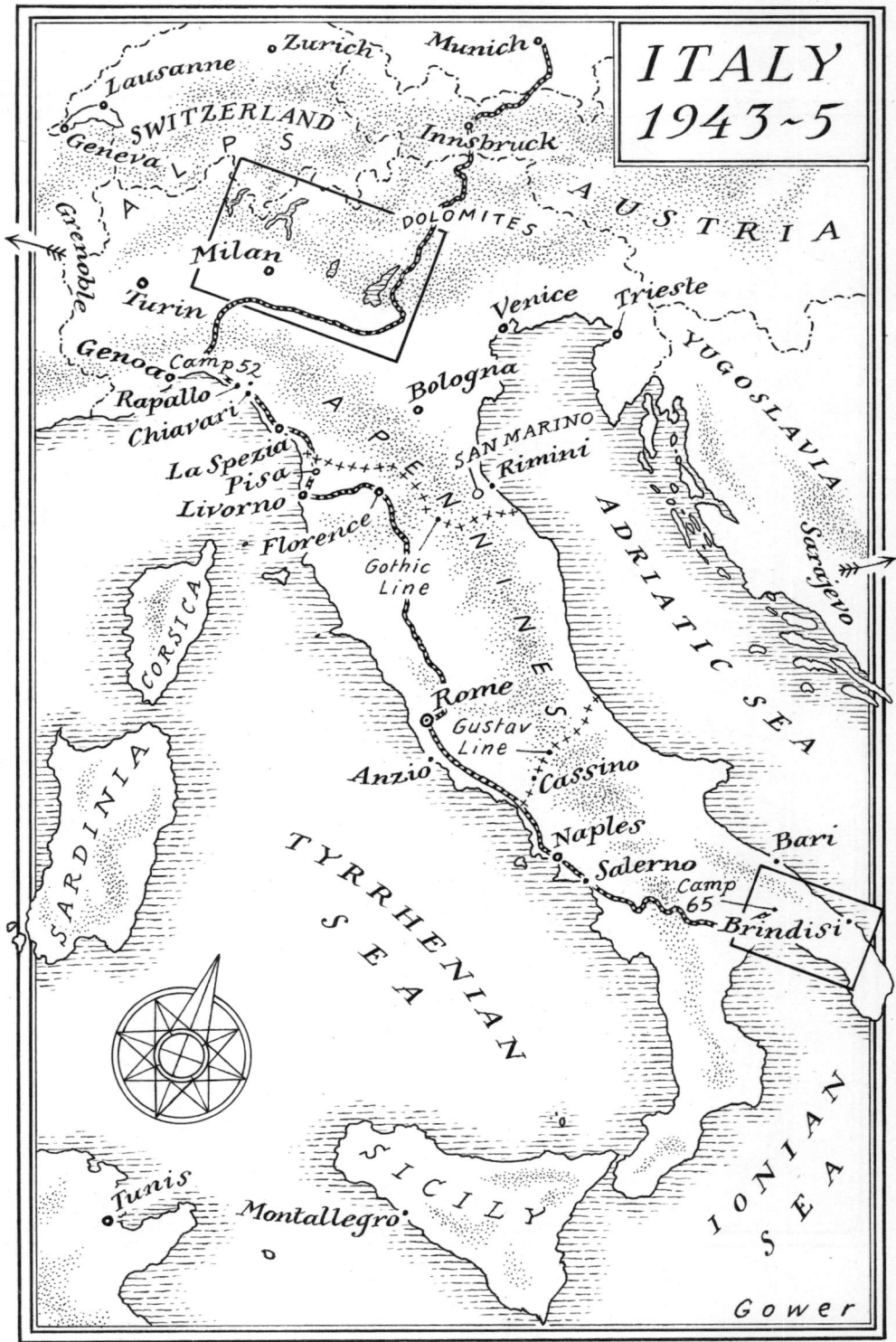

ALTOPIANO delle MURGE

P U

Bari

Gravina
Camp 65
Altamura
Escape Route
Santeramo
Gi

Matera
Laterza

BASILICATA

ION

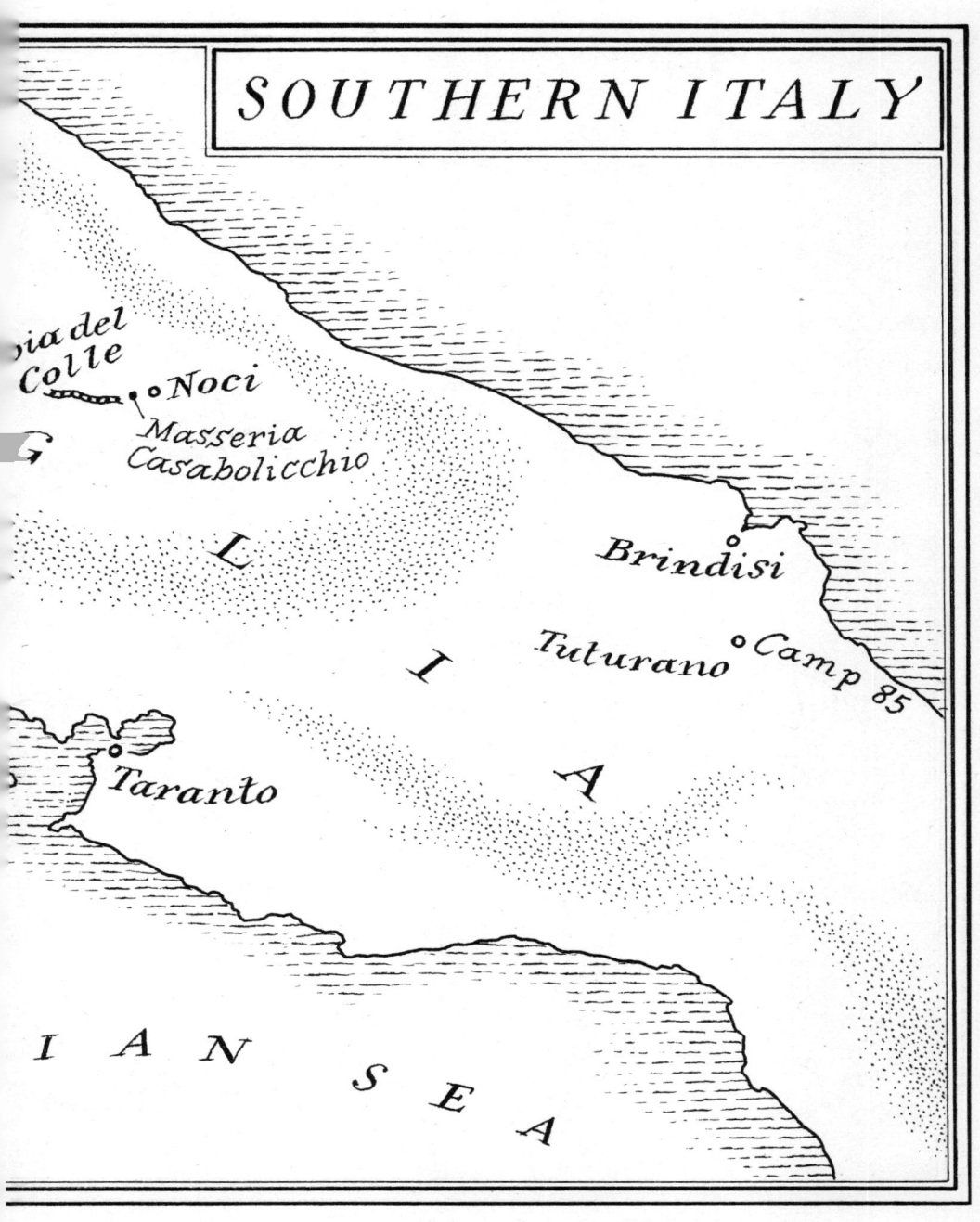

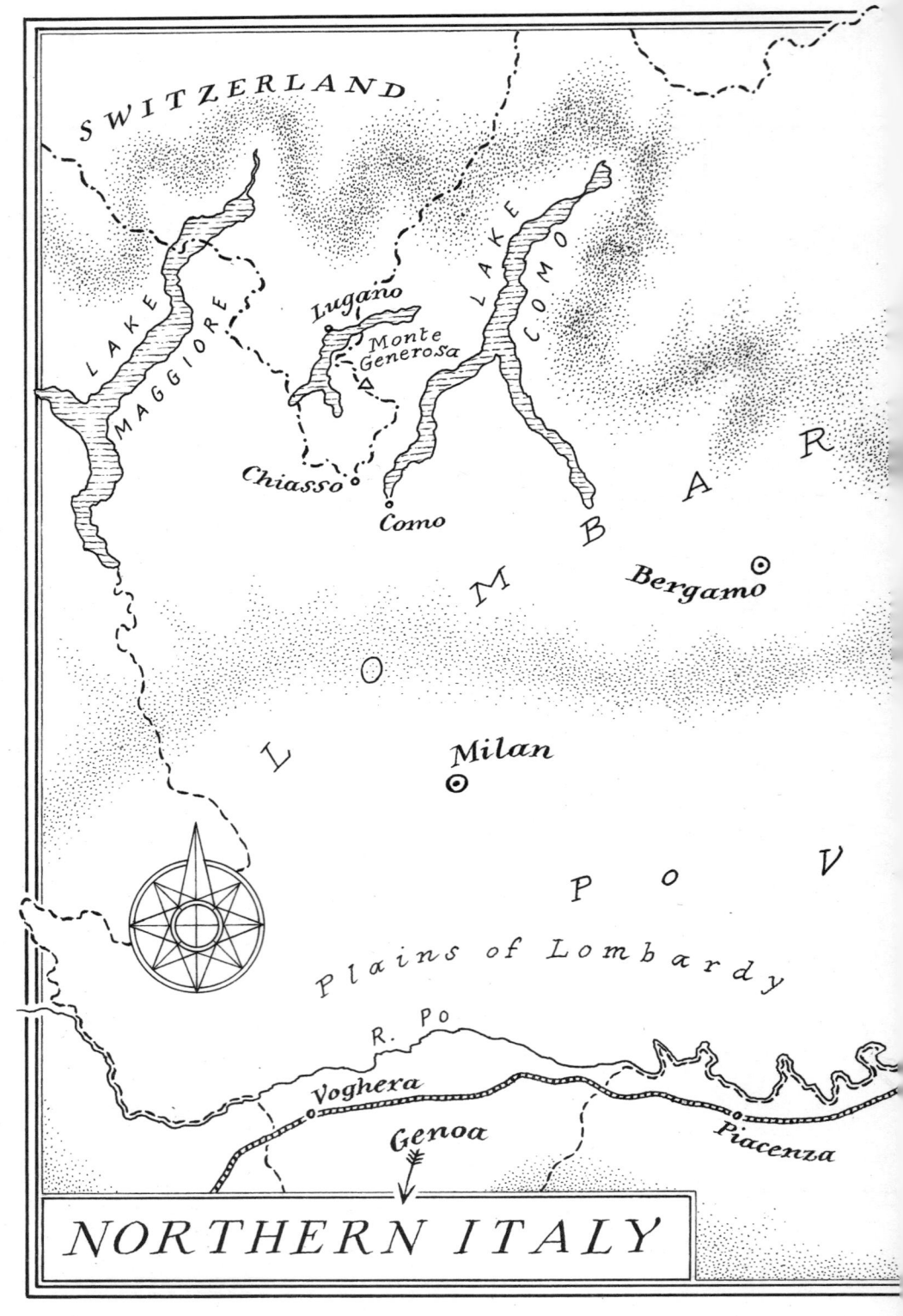

Brenner Pass
TRENTINO-ALTO ADIGE
Trento
D
Y
LAKE ISEO
Corna Blacca
Pertica Alta
Val Sabbia
Val Trompia
Gavardo
Monte Tesio
Serle
Brescia
Monte Budellone
Paitone
Prevalle
Bedizzole
Salò
Gargnano
LAKE GARDA
Garda
Monte Baldo
Brenzone
Sega di Ala
Breonio
Molina
Dolcè
Ceraino
Pescantina
Verona
Bussolengo
VERONA
R. Adige
a l l e y
Mantua
Cremona
Ostiglia

Prologue: The Dream

Late summer, 2017. We – my wife, children and I – drove from Cambridge across country to visit my elderly parents in Shropshire, a journey of a couple of hours or so. My sister, who lived nearby, invited us for tea in her spacious garden, which backed on to rolling meadows, resplendent that day under a valiant sun and cornflower sky. The warm air was tinged with eucalyptus, lavender and mown grass.

It was a perfectly ordinary occasion – but ordinary is where the uncanny creeps in, takes you by surprise. I was chatting to Mum about the usual things – kids, work, the book I was writing – when, quite abruptly, she said: 'I had a strange dream about Uncle Ralph last night.' Perplexed, she looked away, frowning to recover the memory. 'He stepped out of the shadows and held me by the arm – as if pulling me back.'

Pulling her back where, Mum wasn't sure. 'To when he was alive?' I suggested. She shrugged, as if that was all she had. But we both sensed the past had called on the present, that this wasn't just some random flotsam from the subconscious. More like a visitation, a haunting, which is how it can feel to dream of the dead.

I knew a bit about Ralph, though I'd never met him. A soldier in North Africa, a military policeman, he'd escaped from a prison camp and hidden in a farmhouse. It was all I remembered, and even that could have been wrong. I once had a couple of photos of him; perhaps they were still around somewhere.

Then, another sliver of recollection: 'Didn't he take you on holiday to Switzerland, when almost no one went abroad – and in a car?'

He did, replied Mum – but the whole thing was a virtual blank. She looked dumbfounded, which wasn't like her at all. Even in her late eighties her memory was impeccable.

Prologue: The Dream

'It must have been about 1955 or 56,' she said. 'It couldn't have been much earlier, because I was only twenty, and no later, because Dad died in 1957, and I'd never have left Mum and John on their own.'

This made sense. John, her brother, was only eight when they lost their father, after which my grandmother wore her grief heavily for the rest of her days. Her name was Charlotte; I called her 'Nan'. Nan's younger sister Florence – or Flo, as she was known – had married Ralph just before the war.

Mum's scant memories of this Swiss trip were like old photos, a scatter of silent, faded scenes. Picture-postcard chalets with wooden shutters. Sunshine and snow. Washing in a stream. Wearing white sandals by a lake. Being taught how to smoke by Flo, who, Mum noticed, was missing part of a finger. That was all.

Why did Ralph and Flo go to Switzerland? Mum had no idea. Did she like them? Not really. So why go with them? 'I expect I just thought this was my chance to go abroad and I should take it. That, and the fact they saw me as the child they'd never had. Perhaps I felt sorry for them.'

Auntie Flo was, she continued, very particular. In 1940, as little Audrey Davis, Mum had been evacuated to live with her in the Yorkshire town of Wombwell, near Barnsley. The train was full of soldiers, and they'd got off at the wrong station because the signs had been taken down to confuse German parachutists. At Wombwell, Flo wouldn't let Audrey touch her piano unless she scrubbed her hands. Mum didn't recall Uncle Ralph having been there – he was probably already away at war – but later she'd known him well. What was he like? 'Well . . . you couldn't get close to him. Stiff, he was. Stiff and cold.' Ralph's father, Thomas, who worked on the railways, used to give Audrey sweets and was a kinder soul, as was Ralph's younger brother, George.

Tea was poured and cake passed round. Swallows darted in and out of the eaves; a rook cawed. Conversation and togetherness, the now-ness of the present, tangible yet vulnerable to irruptions of the past.

Two things drifted into my mind. Hadn't Ralph kept a diary? And cut his way out of a train? Yes, Mum said, she thought both things were true.

We stared at each other expectantly. We knew no more – but we would. For that summer's day marked the start of a journey of discovery into Ralph's life and adventures in wartime Italy. Like so many of the twenty million Allied servicemen – British, Commonwealth, US and others – overseas between 1939 and 1945, he had been wrenched from the innocence of an ordinary life and thrust into terrible experience. Nearly 700,000 died; another 100,000 were never heard of again. Some who survived had epiphanies; most did not. A million men had been wounded, many maimed or weakened in body or mind.[1]

And they came home to a world familiar yet different – the old dispensation utterly changed – and to families who, in turn, found their sons and husbands and fathers transformed. And too often these men's tales of hardship and trauma were kept private within marriages or never told at all. Although often similar, each story was unique, and Ralph's was exceptional.[2]

Seven years on, recalling Mum's dream, it seemed less like he had been pulling her back into some shadowy past, and more that she'd pulled him forward into the present. For even then, at the very beginning of everything, his silent, inscrutable ghost was edging out of the gloom, daring us to know him properly.

PART ONE
Becoming

1.
War Relics

A Sunday afternoon in 1976. I'm nine years old, at home in Kent watching a war film, *Von Ryan's Express*. Ryan, a US pilot, played by Frank Sinatra, arrives in an Italian prisoner of war camp pitching the 'why bother escaping' argument against the 'it's our duty at all costs' line taken by Trevor Howard's British officer. Italy surrenders and the Germans put the POWs on a train bound for the Reich. But Ryan, who has come round to the idea of escaping, breaks through the carriage floor and leads the men out. Seizing control of the locomotive, they switch destinations from Innsbruck to neutral Switzerland.[1]

There were always old films like this shown on Sundays, full of danger and courage and swelling pride. The myths of the Second World War they played to were ingrained in British culture, a balm for economic decline and the loss of empire. Without a sense of destiny, the future was a scary place: all the country had to look forward to was the past. And there was no better past than the war: six years of finest hours, when people had proudly united to defeat Hitler. What did 1976 have to offer? Soaring inflation, terrorism and the snarl of punk, an affront to patriotism and civility. God seemed tired of being an Englishman, and that summer visited a biblical drought upon the land.

For boys like me, nostalgic rituals mattered less than the war's sheer violent excitement. We eagerly did our bit as consumers of not only films, but comics such as *Warlord* and *Victor*, and graphic novellas in the *War Picture Library* and *Commando* series. Bedrooms bristled with model soldiers, action figures and construction kits. The planes dangling from my ceiling were riddled with hot-needle bullet holes and billowed singed cotton-wool smoke. We dressed up to re-enact ghost battles that rippled benignly from another age. Dad carved me a Sten gun and a grenade with a pullable pin, while Mum made a green pullover with sergeant's stripes and an elasticated beret that sat on my head like a shower cap. A friend's brother built us a box cart painted like a German jeep, which we crashed and nearly died laughing.[2]

The same friend also had a Colditz board game. (Much later, chasing that memory, I bought a set in a charity shop only to find half the pieces, each representing a prisoner, were missing – or 'escaped', someone joked.) A TV series about the famous castle was still running in the mid-1970s, when I received an Action Man Colditz set for my birthday. I can still see him hanging from the washing line with one hand, cardboard suitcase in the other. At secondary school, I spent a fortnight of lunch breaks in the library gripped by Pat Reid's memoir on which the dramatization, game, toy, and an earlier feature film, were based.[3]

Hardcore war enthusiasts were also avid collectors. Having begged Mum to try knitting me a gas mask, I bought a real one from a junk shop in Gillingham, owned by a man known as 'Fifty-Pee Brian' owing to his inflexible pricing strategy. It took half an hour to cycle there, but I was a regular. The shop window was like some historical shore, military medals and badges washed up there – context gone, cut loose by time. Relics were props for imagining the past, with talismanic power, opening a conduit back to the war. All this spoke meaningfully to my young life. At the Queen's Silver Jubilee street party in 1977 – itself an echo of VE Day celebrations – I wore the musty gas mask and other paraphernalia for the fancy dress parade. There's cine film to prove it.

Intimacy with the war also came from family connections. Yet both my grandfathers had been in reserved occupations – Manchester lorry driver on Dad's side, electrician in Chatham Dockyard on Mum's – whereas all my friends' grandfathers seemed to have landed in Normandy, been shot down over enemy territory or torpedoed in the Atlantic. I had *some* stories. One relative had fought in France – he gave me the dog tag he'd worn – and Dad's cousin Billy had been killed in Germany in 1945, the only casualty on a day when his company commander won the Victoria Cross. Aged six, Dad himself was nearly killed in the Salford Blitz, and Mum once hid under a deckchair when a flying bomb crashed at Gillingham Strand. During an air raid, Nan had refused to let my granddad into the Anderson shelter because she was bathing in the tin tub. And this was after he'd raced home from work because incendiary bombs were falling.

The scene of this comedy was a Victorian terraced house three miles from our own, and Nan still lived there when my sister and I were small. It hadn't changed much since the war. The front room was a mausoleum of polished wood and lace doilies, where I never went except to read a book with an embossed red cover about the lives of soldiers and statesmen, explorers and inventors.[4] There was no bathroom, nor any heating except for a coal fire in the sitting room, and instead of a fridge Nan had a meat-safe in the cellar. Out in the yard, a spider-infested privy stood next to a vegetable patch, and further down the garden, among the nettles, the corrugated bomb shelter was rusting away. I remember fireside baths and fetching potatoes, which felt like digging for victory. It was the best place to hear Nan's war stories. As I listened, one relative stood out: my great-uncle, Ralph.

After the visit to Shropshire in 2017, I found myself thinking about those days, and about Uncle Ralph. Although each time Mum and I spoke on the phone she would say, 'I still can't find a little corner of my memory about going to Switzerland', more of Nan's words came back to me as I ransacked my study cupboards looking for old photos.

Soon, I'd established five things that Nan had told me back then: Ralph had been a prisoner of war in Italy; punched an Italian officer, breaking his nose; escaped from a train using, of all things, a knife and fork; hidden in a hayloft, where a family nursed him when he was sick; and written a diary. In 2017, as in 1976, I wanted everything to be true. The train escape seemed improbable, especially as this is what happens in *Von Ryan's Express*, a film about as far-fetched as war stories go. But I was convinced that Nan had told me all this, so presumably she'd got it from Ralph or Flo. Unlike the academic history from which I'd made a career, family lore doesn't insist on documentary proof. It's just a loose collection of stories, mostly unchallenged, that makes sense of the past.

I found Nan's photos, which long ago I'd put in the wooden box that once contained treasures from Fifty-Pee Brian's shop, now washed by time to another shore. One showed Ralph cross-legged at a training camp; in another he was a Guardsman in a bearskin, like a sentry at Buckingham Palace; and the third was a portrait of him wearing an unidentified uniform, complete with a row of medal ribbons, meaning it must have been taken after 1945. It dawned on me how much Ralph had tethered me to the war, and how Nan's snaps, as she called them, had lent substance to her stories, tall though they probably were. They were mine and I'd cherished them like myths.

A door shouldered ajar by Mum's dream was now fully open after

forty years. In that time, Ralph and Nan had both died, and for me the war had been displaced by music, guitars, girls and books. A longing to leave the Medway Towns propelled me to university, where, in different institutions, I hung around for the next three decades teaching the social history of the sixteenth and seventeenth centuries. My final years of research had been spent exploring historical inner lives, extracting emotion from stories in the archives. Storytelling is embedded in histories, and history a way of telling stories.

This prepared the ground for what was to come: a seed sown in the 1970s germinated decades later by a dream, then flowering into the reanimation of Uncle Ralph's life. At first, I had little sense of what lay ahead, no plan or even a clear intention. I was curious about Ralph and my childhood fascination with the war, and that curiosity led me deeper into the story.

I pulled up outside a bungalow in Warmsworth, a suburb of Doncaster in South Yorkshire. A woman in her seventies opened the door and introduced herself as Pauline, my mother's cousin. We'd never met before, but she seemed familiar, having a faint look of Mum and some of her mannerisms. Soon after the Shropshire visit, it had occurred to Mum that if anyone had Ralph's war diary it would be Pauline, since her father was Ralph's brother, George, and Ralph had had no children to inherit his effects. Thinking about Ralph had started me wondering about the diary. If it still existed, I knew I had to see it.

We chatted as the kettle boiled, but the folders and papers and albums, which Pauline had brought down from the attic and piled on the work surface, made it hard to concentrate. I was feeling the 'affective tremor' that afflicts historians, the spooky anticipation of handling documents so long imprisoned in silence yet screaming to be heard.[5]

Pauline handed me a scuffed manila envelope. Inside were three Italian school exercise books with faded illustrated covers: a skiff idling on a lake, speedboats racing, a family of rabbits. I turned the fragile pages crammed with copperplate – the remains of a life and its vanished world levelled and compressed into blue-black script. Thrillingly, the opening sentence read: 'Contrary to enemy propaganda life in a prison camp is not a happy one, and every ex-prisoner of war will, without exception, second that statement.'

I moved on to the photos. Pauline pointed to Ralph and Flo's wedding portrait from 1938, with Mum as a three-year-old bridesmaid standing just in front of the groom. Then we jumped forward to a middle-aged Ralph dressed like a British army officer, with peaked cap and Sam Browne belt. Flo, at his side, looked blithely refined in polka dots, gloves and bonnet.

I sensed that Pauline hadn't liked Ralph much. She gestured at an open box-file, in which I found letters of notification, certificates of education, a pay book, a typed document in Italian, a notelet to Flo written in a prisoner of war camp and a report in Spanish recording Ralph's death. There was also a dossier on the history of the Corps family – an old Anglo-Norman name pronounced 'Corr'.

There in front of me lay the full span of Ralph Corps' life – or as much of a life as fits in a box. Pauline lent me the diary, and on the drive back I felt its radiant presence on the passenger seat. Without my being fully conscious of it, the power of this relic in my possession had activated a quest.

Back home in Cambridge, I looked closely at the diary. The exercise books – or *quaderni* – had a distinct prewar look. 'Book No. 1', as Ralph had labelled it, was the one with the skiff on the cover. The reverse identified Lake Garda, and inside the front cover Flo had written her name three times – 'Florence E. Corps' – as if practising a signature. Beneath, she had added 'Kingolwira Prison Farm, Kingolwira, Tanganyika'; above, in a larger, curvilinear hand, was pencilled 'Chiodi Agostino, Paitone (Brescia) Italy.'

I scoured the second *quaderno* for clues – not yet the text but rather the covers. In tiny writing on the inside, Ralph had quoted someone he had thought was Disraeli, but was actually Philip James Bailey, an obscure Victorian poet: 'He most lives who thinks most, feels the noblest, acts the best'. And in spare pages at the back were scraps of poetry he'd learned at school. There was also Italian vocabulary:

Davvero? = really?; *comportarsi* = behave; *insegnare* = to teach; *mi sembra* = it seems to me . . .

The rabbits, happy on the front cover, were on the back being made into hats with the smiling approval of two elegant women. I got the gist of the text, which had a totalitarian ring to it: breeding rabbits on an industrial scale benefits the national economy by providing not only felt and fur, but delicious food for the working masses.

The third *quaderno*, with the speedboats, bore the *fascio littorio*, the Roman bundle of sticks that had been the Italian fascists' emblem. Ralph opened this notebook with a list of self-improving Latin tags relevant to his life and, as it happened, to my growing curiosity. 'Verba volant, scripta manent' (spoken words fly, written ones endure), 'Prima frons saepe decipit' (the first look often deceives) and 'Mens agitat molem' (the mind can move mountains).

Once I'd started on the text and had got used to Ralph's slanted hand, I found I couldn't stop. It was like being drawn through a rent in the fabric of time. It was immediately clear that this wasn't actually a diary, rather a memoir of POW life and an escape, which, judging by the stationery and the inscribed Italian name, must have been written soon after the event. Although the prose was mostly descriptive, Ralph hinted at deeper meanings. 'Had it not been for later events which occurred to me on Italian soil', read one statement, 'I should have returned (by God's Will) to England and hated Italy and Italians for the rest of my days.' This suggested reluctance to assume he'd ever get home – but home from where exactly? The farmhouse where Nan said he'd been? Was 'Chiodi Agostino' his host?

Paitone, I discovered, is a hamlet near the town of Prevalle, between the north Italian city of Brescia and the great open body of water that is Lake Garda, 100 miles south of the Swiss border. Paitone is small and unremarkable: there seemed almost nothing to learn about it. The memoir didn't specify what 'later events' had changed Ralph's mind about Italians, presumably something to do with the inhabitants of Paitone. I knew only what Nan told me: a family had cared for him when he was poorly.

I read on. Ralph had escaped from Campo Prigionieri di Guerra Sessanta-Cinque Gravina-Altamura – Camp 65 for short. The town of Gravina was a long way from Paitone, 600 miles south down the boot of Italy to Puglia at the top of the heel. Astonishingly, not only was the site marked on Google Maps but some buildings still remained. Even more astonishingly, a local enthusiast had just a few days earlier conducted a tour of the camp and posted footage on Facebook. His name was Domenico Bolognese. He replied to my email at once, full of excitement.

Domenico – Dom – was about my age and lived in the small Puglian city of Altamura, three miles east of the camp. He was married with teenage sons and worked as an export manager for a furniture company. His spare time was devoted to preserving Camp 65's memory through a small association, of which he was founder and president. These days, he explained, the struggle to remember was fraught. The political right was less concerned with commemorating Italy's enemies – specifically, in this case, Britain and its Commonwealth – than with the massacre of Italians by Yugoslav partisans, hundreds of whom had trained in the repurposed Camp 65 after Italy surrendered in 1943.

Dom sent pictures of the camp, adding a visual setting to the memoir. Ralph's spectral outline thickened. I worked though copies of documents and photos I'd made of Pauline's archive, often late at night and before sunrise, reading between the lines and staring at images as if to make them disclose their secrets.

There was Mum, barely twenty, posing with Flo on a snowy peak; another showed them sitting outside a café. As I pressed these relics for meaning, so the image of the mountain, a romantic metaphor of self-discovery, imprinted itself differently. In *Austerlitz*, a novel about a twentieth-century life disfigured by war and unruly memory, the German writer W. G. Sebald invokes the image of a glass mountain, a mystical symbol with the indeterminacy of dreams and their power to reveal truth. Through this cloudy prism, hopes are both raised and restrained: you can know the past, the mountain promises, but only imperfectly. Nothing on the other side remains intact, and it's up to us to find the pieces, in dim light and in darkness, and from them make a story that in good conscience feels real.

When Tolstoy once said that 'history would be an excellent thing if only it were true', he wasn't trying to be funny. By 'true' he meant 'as it really happened' – much as when his German contemporary Leopold von Ranke declared that history should be 'as it actually was', he was idealizing something that posterity cannot truly own because it's locked in time's glacier, a frozen shower of distorted fragments.[6]

The next seven years would be taken up finding these fragments and piecing them together. Propelled by Mum's dream, I found myself sitting in far-flung libraries and archives, hiking up rocky hillsides, splashing through autumn mud, sheltering from storms. I visited old barracks and remote farms, neck-hair prickling as the ghosts flared past, and met Italians with long memories who shared their stories. That sense of engagement and halting discovery mattered as much as the wartime events they revealed. These could only live again because, like the departed Ralph, they were dragged from the gloom.

Research became everything it should be: a journey into the unknown, leading to some of the most exciting discoveries of my life as a historian.[7] And along the way, I would make some incredible friends – as, it transpired, had Ralph. He may never have spoken of this intimacy; it certainly didn't colour the war stories he told his family. His feelings were but flecks and flaws in the glacier – but once they became known, as they did, they breathed life into an unexpected, absorbing story.

Having borrowed a title from Sebald, I came across a 1949 war film of the same name about an RAF observer shot down in the Dolomites and nursed by a young Italian partisan. 'Call your lover's name in the mountains', she says, 'and you will hear a mournful echo.' And that, in a way, was what I ended up doing too, gazing at the glass mountain, quietly obsessed, straining for sounds and glimpses of movement through the ice.[8]

2.
A Perfect Gentleman

For the next couple of years, Uncle Ralph's story emerged slowly yet steadily. My curiosity about him grew, but the demands of my own life kept me from satisfying it. Meanwhile, faint wraith that he was, Ralph waited patiently for my full attention.

During this time, Dom, the Italian expert on Camp 65 I'd found on Facebook, became a constant presence in my life. He sent regular messages, and more photos and documents relating to the camp; in return, I told him what I knew about Ralph's captivity and cool reserve, his buttoned-up dignity. Away in Puglia, Dom worked Ralph's story into tours of the camp ruins, which he laid on for people in Gravina and the neighbouring town of Altamura, mostly school children innocent of the events of the war that had unfolded on their doorstep. He also received visitors, mostly from South Africa and New Zealand, drawn to see the place they'd heard about from fathers and uncles. Soon Dom and I – kindred spirits, in middle age, shaped by our generation – began to talk about things other than the war. The formalities fell away, and we chatted like old friends, by email and on the phone.

All my free time, such as it was, I spent assembling what turned out to be the easiest part of the research: Ralph's backstory. Something of the man I knew from the memoir, which covered little more than a year, was surely there in his prewar past. I speculated about Ralph, fictionalized him in my head, even dreamed about him. I didn't know exactly why I was stalking him, only that he had entered my life and I was compelled to find out about him and his war. Perhaps, Dom playfully suggested, Ralph was stalking me.

I ordered birth and marriage certificates from the General

Register Office to learn more about Ralph's immediate family – my extended family – and also drew on what Mum and Pauline and other relatives knew. There had been numerous documents in Pauline's archive, some relating to Ralph's military service, and I printed copies to read by lamplight, peering closely, annotating them. Much I could do online. I subscribed to Ancestry.com, and scoured the web for local history sites, chatrooms, maps and catalogues. I contacted a man in Doncaster knowledgeable about local schools, Ralph's in particular, and read around the context of his childhood: the environment that had moulded him into adolescence.

As research progressed, I arranged my notes in narrative order, plugging or eliding gaps as I went. Whenever a new fact surfaced, I'd phone Mum, whose memory it sometimes jogged. By these means, the light cast on Uncle Ralph's expectant figure grew brighter, and the lineaments of his early years, scattered and flattened by time, were raised from dim memory and old papers into a third dimension. To my surprise, it became possible to flesh out the evasive character in the memoir, even recovering Ralph's attitudes and ambitions, and the strengths and weaknesses that the test of war exposed in him.

Ralph Corps was born on 9 May 1914 at 16 Albert Road, a terraced two-up two-down in Mexborough, near Doncaster. A centre for mining and pottery, by the mid-nineteenth century the town was also a thriving railway depot, where outsiders found work and insiders dreamed of leaving. It produced footballers and boxers and trades unionists, as well as poets and actors. Mexborough's most famous soldier was William Hackett, a miner in a tunnelling company who in 1916 won a posthumous Victoria Cross. For Mexborough's boys, Hackett was a paragon of Christian sacrifice. Methodist churches and cooperative and temperance societies taught thrift and hard work, self-discipline and self-reliance.

The Corps family were sober, law-abiding patriots, church rather than chapel, exemplars of upper-working-class respectability. Ralph's father, Thomas, had eschewed his own father's life as an agricultural labourer in the Yorkshire Dales and come to Mexborough to improve himself. Hired as a railway fireman, he met twenty-two-year-old Gladys Catherall from the Welsh town of Holywell, whom he married in 1913. Ralph was born the following summer, named after his maternal grandfather. Three months later, Britain was at war. Thomas and his younger brother George both fought on the Western Front, where George was killed. In 1918, Thomas was posted to the North-West Frontier to fight tribesmen hostile to India and the British Empire. Upon his return two years later the people of Bedale, his ancestral home, presented him with a plaque: today, Pauline has it hanging on her wall. He went back to his job on the railways, and the family moved to number 55. Ralph was six and his brother, George, born in 1916 and named after his uncle, was four.

By this time Ralph had been at Mexborough Adwick Road School for over a year. He was well-behaved and studious. Census records show that in the mid-1920s the family relocated to Bentley, north of Doncaster, where Ralph attended the village school before moving again, to the new Woodfield estate in the suburb of Balby. Weston Road was leafier, its semi-detached houses spaciously arranged near countryside for a twelve-year-old boy to explore. It must have felt like progress, the kind of upward social mobility that impressed the bright, ambitious Ralph. In September 1926, he was admitted to Oswin Avenue School, where the headmaster praised his enthusiasm for sport and trustworthy character. There was no uniform as such, but he did get to wear a cap and a striped tie.[1]

At Oswin Avenue, Ralph felt like every subject, every lesson, was an opportunity for self-advancement. Technically inclined, he also took to literature, memorizing the poetry he would later copy into his notebook. He was fond of Tennyson, Longfellow and Kipling, whose names were immortalized in streets near Weston Road – indeed, any kind of verse that spoke to the nobility of the common man, romantically masculine, dignified yet sentimental. In class, they read the *Rubaiyat of Omar Khayyam*, an epic poem meditating on life and love and death. The stiffness with which Ralph faced the world did not mean he wasn't dreamily introspective, and his love of poetry was a clue to this.

Ralph's brother, George, cheerfully followed his father onto the railways, which was not quite what Ralph had in mind for himself. Nor was there much romance in Doncaster, no exotic landscape for expanding his sense of himself and his future. His father had fought rebels in the dusty hills of Afghanistan; presumably Ralph had wanted a taste of that, not coal and steam. He was restless – but what else could he do?

Pauline believed her grandfather had scraped together the money for Ralph to finish his education at a grammar school in Doncaster – typical that he had to be different, treated specially, she scorned. But he didn't appear in any of the registers, suggesting that he must have left school and entered into an apprenticeship or work. By chance, I found buried in an archive a letter of reference indicating that between the ages of fourteen and seventeen he had been employed by the London North Eastern Railway as a 'telegraph lad', receiving and sending messages in Morse code. It was a responsible job, for which only the brightest and best employees were selected.[2]

The LNER taught Ralph a trade, one that later would prove useful – but he was biding his time. In the spring of 1932, he wrote to the Sheffield depot of the 2nd Battalion of the Coldstream Guards, the oldest and arguably most illustrious regiment in the British army. 'Nulli Secundus' was its motto. I found a recruiting poster calling for 'smart men', illustrated with a guardsman in bearskin and scarlet tunic parading in front of Windsor Castle. Pasted up in railway stations and labour exchanges, it may have caught Ralph's eye. Feeling a flush of confidence, perhaps also a sense of destiny, he handed in his notice.

On 2 May 1932, at 9.15 a.m., Ralph was called to interview, where a captain judged him to be a respectable man of sound Christian principle, eager to join the regiment. The LNER superintendent confirmed that Ralph was a decent chap who had never been in trouble with the police. Ralph's educational attainment was graded

The Glass Mountain

'very good', as was his physical fitness, albeit with a high resting pulse, raised perhaps by the fear of being rejected. But all was well. A week later, on his eighteenth birthday, Ralph returned to Sheffield, where he swore an oath of allegiance and signed a contract of enlistment, now preserved in Pauline's archive. He would serve twelve years – three in the 'Colours' (active service) and nine in the Reserve – starting on three shillings a day.[3]

At school Ralph had surely been one of the tallest boys in his class, where the growth of many was stunted by poverty and pollution. At his army medical, his height was recorded as 5 feet 11¼ inches, an inch above the minimum required for the Guards. I could see him now, walking tall, chest out, and in thick socks and army boots just reaching his own desired height of six foot. Brimful of pride, he was on his way.

Packed off to Caterham Barracks in Surrey, he trained for five months, during which time he received his Army Certificate of Education, third-class, before being transferred to Pirbright Barracks, a Victorian depot for Foot Guards. There he also studied for his second-class certificate, with classes in English, Map Reading, 'Army and Empire' and Mathematics, the last of these chosen over a foreign language. He learned writing and dictation, fractions and equations and the rudiments of regimental accounting. The qualification was awarded in March 1933 and, as a result, within four months he was promoted.[4]

To mark his becoming a lance corporal – *two* stripes in the Guards – a photographer visited the depot and immortalized Ralph in his parade uniform: the snap Nan gave me. Another photo in one of Pauline's albums, from the same occasion, showed him smiling and bareheaded, wearing a white number one mess jacket. I was to see this portrait again, stuck to a forged document from another very different time in his life.

Ralph completed his three years in the Colours on 8 May 1935 and received a glowing report from his lieutenant colonel: 'A good smart well turned out NCO. Honest, intelligent and reliable.' Moved to the Reserve and registered by the army at the Labour Exchange in

Sheffield, he considered his options. His family may have expected him to return to the railways. But Ralph was a man with a strong desire to move on.[5]

The Coldstream Guards offered to help find suitable occupations for 'all men of good character returning to civil life', which may explain how by the time he left Pirbright Ralph was already halfway to becoming a policeman. His former headmaster at Oswin Avenue, J. P. Mason, provided a second reference, which survives among Ralph's papers, describing his former pupil as 'a perfect gentleman, and thoroughly trustworthy'. Mason, who came from Bentley, where the Corps family had briefly lived, was a prominent local figure, so it may have been he who arranged for Ralph to join the West Riding Constabulary. Ralph acquired a taste for pulling strings, and for having others pull strings for him.

Unlike my usual research, available sources now included photographs. According to the American writer Susan Sontag, a photo is 'something directly stencilled off the real', not just an imitation of what the eye sees but a faithful copy of life, its captured essence. And yet, as my Italian friend Dom had warned me about the pictures he sent, a photo is also an illusion playing by its own rules. Reality is boxed in there, concealing, perhaps for ever, its surroundings and the flow of its before and after. Shorn of original truth, photos are free to deceive. When Ralph was snapped as a soldier and a policeman at this time, he was thinking and feeling something about himself, and it bothered me I might never know what it was.[6]

After a probationary period, during which he passed courses in First Aid and Lifesaving, Ralph became one of twenty-six new constables admitted on 15 December 1935.[7] He was PC 191, the silver characters pinned to the high collar of his uniform. Cut from midnight-blue serge, and worn with a crested helmet, it perpetuated the self-respect and command of deference that Ralph had enjoyed in the army. He was posted to Knaresborough, forty miles north of the WRC station in Barnsley, nearer to the Corps ancestral home of Bedale. He was given a place to live, a stone cottage with views of the Nidd Valley, allotted a beat and issued with a bicycle. Local newspapers from the time suggest there wasn't much for him to deal with: some pilfering, the odd traffic accident, drunks to be locked up. He may have felt life was happening elsewhere.

The day before Ralph qualified, the Italian leader Benito Mussolini authorized the use of chemical weapons in Ethiopia, which his army had invaded in October. The League of Nations looked increasingly toothless. In March, flouting the Treaty of Versailles, Hitler commenced rearmament, and a year later sent troops to reclaim the forfeited Rhineland. Mussolini, hitherto allied to Britain and France, drew closer to Germany. With every western submission, European politics became more polarized, and the dictators' confidence grew. Hitler and Mussolini backed the nationalists in the civil war raging in Spain, during which the bombing of civilians at Guernica in 1937 was to prove a nightmarish prophecy.

By now, Ralph had been ordered back to South Yorkshire and returned to live with his parents in Balby. There he met Florence White, who lived a short walk across the playing fields. By 1938 the Corps brothers, Ralph and George, were engaged to the White sisters, Florence and Ethel. The girls had grown up in the pit town of Rawmarsh near Rotherham, where their father, James, was a miner, their mother, Florence Mary, a housewife from Shoreditch in the East End of London. Their parents had another five children, in a tiny house on a soot-blackened hill street with shared privies and reeking pigsties. Flo worked in the Peglers factory in Doncaster making bathroom fittings, Ethel in a hardware shop.

No one seems to have thought well of my great-grandfather, James Arthur White. According to Nan – Ethel's and Flo's elder sister – he was an alcoholic like his own father, a Methodist lay preacher who whipped his children with a belt. Abuse was common in cheerless towns like Rawmarsh. James Arthur's wife, my Cockney great-grandmother (who we knew as 'Big Nanny'), detested him and waited patiently until she'd married off the last of her daughters. He lurks in the White girls' wedding photos – yet by the time their brother married in 1940 he had gone, and his long-suffering wife was a live-in housekeeper for a teacher and her elderly mother in Doncaster.

Young Flo White longed to escape this sordid world. She had already left Rawmarsh, was holding down a job at Peglers and lived in an end-of-terrace house in Balby. To progress further, she needed to marry. Ralph, the policeman from Mexborough, was not only six feet tall, give or take, used long words and had dreamy blue eyes, but came from a working-class family a shade more respectable than her own. To her, he was the perfect gentleman. She accepted his proposal, nudging her mother a step closer to leaving James Arthur.

Now engaged, Ralph and Flo spent more time alone, albeit in public. Ralph owned a camera, and they took it with them on walks. It may have been Flo who snapped Ralph in his Sunday best, trying to smile, somewhere in the countryside or in a park. The photo is undated and the context is gone. But Pauline had another from this time, one that held my gaze much longer. Ralph sits in front of a picket fence, Flo on the grass between his knees, legs crossed at the calf, his hands draped over hers. Squinting at the sun, unsmiling, the lovers stare seriously into the lens, almost as if they had an inkling of what lay ahead.

In March 1938 Hitler annexed Austria, and Mussolini was granted equal power to the king over the armed forces. In April, Britain recognized Italian control of Ethiopia, and in May, Hitler announced his designs on Czechoslovakia. These commotions were a long way from Balby, where a wedding was being planned. On 11 June, a shiny car carried Flo White in her bridal gown and veil to St John's Church, a journey of just a couple of minutes. There, she and Ralph Corps became husband and wife. Flo's sister Charlotte had made the journey from Gillingham, where five years earlier she had married an electrical wireman named Archibald Davis. Arch also attended the wedding, as did their little daughter Audrey, my mother.

Ralph, then twenty-four, and Flo, two years younger, set up home half an hour away in West Avenue, Wombwell. It was a tidy cul-de-sac near Ralph's police station, housing the better grades of railwaymen and their wives – described as 'unpaid domestics' in the census. On the continent the Munich Crisis came and went, yet contrary to assurances Hitler was not content with the Sudetenland, nor would anything stop Mussolini, whose dreams of a Mediterranean empire were voiced as demands to annex Tunisia, Corsica and Nice.

In the first half of 1939, as Ralph and Flo built a new life together in Wombwell, the wider world was sliding into war. Hitler invaded Czechoslovakia in March, then Poland in early September. War was declared. George Corps married Ethel White, but it seems Ralph was too busy to attend his brother's wedding. He spent the autumn enforcing blackout regulations and checking identity cards, anticipating the telegram that would summon him back into the Coldstream Guards. Flo, too, knew she was about to lose her husband of less than eighteen months.

On 1 December, Ralph caught a train to London. Crossing the city, with its sandbagged buildings and barrage balloons, he arrived in Westminster and made his way to Wellington Barracks, the Coldstream Guards' regimental headquarters, where he was re-enrolled. Despatched to the depot at Caterham, Ralph was medically assessed and kitted out, then posted to a training battalion in the rolling hills of the Cotswolds, in the south-west of the country. A fortnight later, he was transferred to the Corps of Military Police, which was undergoing rapid expansion after an interwar lull. As an ex-policeman, as well as a soldier with a flawless record, Ralph was an obvious candidate. What he felt about this reassignment I could only guess. The CMP had no famous victories or dashing parade uniform, and the height requirement was an underwhelming 5 feet 8 inches. Ralph did at least retain his rank of lance corporal and get to wear a pistol on his belt, conventionally the preserve of officers. And he enjoyed the kind of authority which, for all his life, was a sustaining source of self-worth. Ordinary soldiers feared Redcaps, as they were known, and loathed them too, for their arrogance and needling officiousness.[8]

Military service added an impetus to Ralph's life, lacking in his time as an LNER telegraphist and a married policeman in

Wombwell. He felt at last he really had a job to do, a calling, guided by the fervent belief, later documented in his notebook, that 'he most lives who thinks most, feels the noblest, acts the best'. Like his father and uncle in the previous conflict, he too was needed now to play his part in teaching the Germans a lesson.

War first drew men like Ralph, fit and eager, craving adventure, out into the world, then gave them almost more adventure than they could bear. In 1939, of course, all this lay ahead; but after 1945 they would look back on the epic dramas they'd performed in, romantic tragedies that had turned everything upside down. 'Fantastic, absolutely fantastic things have happened', marvelled one veteran. 'If before the war a writer had put some of these stories in a book, we would have said it was all moonshine. And now you could write a library full of such stories – and each story would be true.'[9]

3.
The Cauldron

These absolutely fantastic things were in Britain preceded by an air of unreality. Although the nation was at war, by the end of 1939 very little had actually happened. Men had been conscripted, children evacuated, buildings requisitioned, air raid precautions imposed: tense expectation was met only with mundane inconvenience. French troops had made a half-hearted bid for the German Saarland, and in November Soviet Russia attacked Finland – but otherwise anticipation fizzled into anticlimax. The British first called it 'The Bore War', then imported a better term from America: 'The Phoney War'.

Ralph came home on leave in khaki battledress, and, like other households, he and Flo celebrated Christmas modestly. Food rationing had yet to be introduced, but people were encouraged to tighten their belts anyway. Early in the New Year, Ralph kissed Flo goodbye; he had received an overseas posting, which could only mean one thing: France. On 19 January 1940 he arrived in Cherbourg as a member of the CMP provost company attached to the 50th (Northumbrian) Division. This, in turn, belonged to II Corps of what was still called the British Expeditionary Force, a quaint hangover from 1914. The division moved east and by March was preparing defences in the Lille–Loos area.[1]

The Phoney War ended on 10 May, when the Germans invaded France, triggering an Anglo-French plan to move troops to the River Dyle in Belgium. Next, Ralph's division headed towards Brussels, picking up other units along the way, reaching Vimy Ridge by the 19th. There they rested and waited. Ralph explored the town where they had camped and visited a photographer. The snap, which I found in an album, shows him with a couple of Redcap mates – Ralph on the left – at ease, whistle chains on show, suggesting a certain cocksure swagger. They were at war, out on a spree, and how the place names echoed. For this was the same blood-soaked territory over which Ralph's father and uncle had fought victoriously a quarter of a century earlier.

Their confidence was premature. German advances soon threatened to cut off the BEF around Arras, and after intense fighting the 50th Division withdrew to Ypres. Unable to break out, the British and French were steadily driven back to the coast under heavy shellfire. By 1 June, Ralph and his provost company were stranded on the beach at Dunkirk, from which throughout the night thousands of men were evacuated. Ralph made it back to the Kent coast on the 2nd, and with hundreds of other hungry, exhausted soldiers was put on a train to the transit hub at Redhill in Surrey. There he was given a mug of tea and a doorstep sandwich to sustain him during his onward journey to the West Country.[2]

British troops would not return to Europe for another three

years. Until then, the land war between Britain and the Axis powers of Germany and Italy would be fought mostly in North Africa. Not only was Libya the centrepiece of Mussolini's foreign empire, but its eastern neighbour, Egypt, was Britain's coastal stronghold for controlling the eastern Mediterranean, the security of which was vital for defending the Suez Canal and protecting the supply of oil from the Persian Gulf. Excited by German victories, on 10 June Mussolini declared war on Britain and France, ratifying the so-called 'pact of steel' with Hitler. In September Il Duce's 10th Army in Libya invaded Egypt. So began a tug-of-war for the scorching sands of the Western Desert.

The 50th Division had started re-forming as soon as it returned from Dunkirk. Ralph's provost company was sent to the Dorset town of Blandford, where in July 1940 he was promoted to corporal, then two months later acting sergeant. Throughout the summer and autumn, the division, comprising men of the East Yorkshire Regiment and the Green Howards, trained to repel a German invasion, manning pillboxes and memorizing code words and flare signals: a red rocket meant that the enemy had actually made landfall. By December, however, the danger had receded, and thoughts turned to upping the ante in the Mediterranean. Military planners were worried that the war in North Africa was already grinding to a halt. There would therefore be no more defensive tactics. The 50th Division was ordered to behave like a legion of 'storm troops' with 'a proper attitude to war'.[3]

In January 1941, while Ralph was in hospital with pharyngitis, news came that the German Afrika Korps had entered the fray, a bid to recoup Mussolini's losses over the winter. By spring, British and Commonwealth troops had been pushed back into Egypt, holding out in Libya only at the port of Tobruk, which was now besieged. In Dorset, Ralph was promoted again from acting sergeant to sergeant – a temporary 'war substantive' rank – and trained in desert warfare.[4] Most of the 50th Division's time was spent on weapons drills, field exercises, cross-country runs, parades and lectures. Meanwhile, according to war diaries in the National Archives at Kew, the provost company carried out 'normal routine duties': speed checks on military vehicles, attending accidents, collaring deserters and so on. Daily logs read 'Nothing to report', or recorded whether the weather had been 'fine' or 'wet'. It was dull work, not unlike being a bobby in Knaresborough, except for the new Norton motorcycle on which Ralph and other Redcaps practised riding up and down sand dunes. Men itching to be deployed abroad became frustrated – constantly told to stand by, then stood down again.[5]

In the end, the 50th was the first division to be posted to the Middle East. In late April 1941, the 150th Infantry Brigade and the staff of the divisional headquarters departed from Liverpool, followed a month later by the division's other units, including its CMP provost company, which sailed from Glasgow on the SS *Duchess of Bedford*, a converted ocean liner. The destination was confidential, but it had to be Egypt, and the danger was only too clear from the size of the Royal Navy escort. To the troops' alarm, however, all but one vessel was diverted to hunt for the German battleship *Bismarck* after it sank HMS *Hood* on 24 May with the loss of almost its entire crew. From Cape Town, HMS *Exeter* still at her side, the *Duchess of Bedford* skirted the east coast of Africa, past Madagascar to Mombasa and Aden, then across the Red Sea and on through the Gulf of Suez to Port Taofik, where the men disembarked on 14 June. Ten days later, Ralph's provost company received orders to travel to Cyprus. Making their way overland to Mena, they picked up their new provost officer, a lieutenant of the Green Howards, and continued north to Port Said. From there, in late July, they sailed to the eastern Cypriot port of Famagusta, where defences were hastily being reinforced after an Italian bombing raid.[6]

From Famagusta it was an hour's drive to Nicosia, which had also been bombed. There the Redcaps made themselves at home in Wolseley Barracks, its own largely self-sufficient world enclosed by barbed wire and swaying palms. Men received newspapers and post, so they knew about the air raids on England's big cities. Perhaps Flo wrote to reassure Ralph that his parents were safe. On the night of 8–9 May, the Luftwaffe dropped parachute mines on Balby, half a mile from their house – in fact in Weston Road, where they used to live. Twenty men, women and children were killed and over seventy injured.

Ralph had never before been anywhere like Cyprus. Early in October, he visited the medieval church at Lefkonico, with its imposing fresco of Archangelos Michael, and bought a souvenir photograph from a stall. It's there in his album, proof of the faraway culture he was absorbing. Nicosia was alive with cafés, bars, restaurants and concert halls. There Ralph enjoyed, possibly for the first time, some classical music. On the back of the church picture, he jotted in pencil: 'Unfinished Symphony – Schubert, Madame Butterfly – Puccini, Ave Maria – Schubert, Spring Song – Mendelssohn'. I sent it to Dom, who compared Ralph's sojourn in Cyprus to his own national service with the *carabinieri* on Sicily: 'My eyes were opened by wonder,' he recalled. 'It was an education.'

Tracing a circuitous route, by degrees Ralph was heading for the front. And yet, compared to the immediacy of his memoir, which was like listening to him tell a story, the details of his progress into battle were maddeningly vague. Although the official unit war diary in the National Archives records his every step, it still felt more like chasing Ralph on his motorbike, half-hidden by a slipstream tail of dust. Mum had said you couldn't get close to him; in a very literal way, I now felt that, too.

Ralph's military service record would surely have helped, but the file was classified until 2030, after which, it was assumed, his personal data would no longer need protecting. I applied to the Ministry of Defence under the Freedom of Information Act, attaching a copy of his death certificate to prove that the document could be safely released. Warned to expect a long wait by staff at the National Archives, where service files had been transferred, I started piecing the story together by other means.

According to its war diary, the 50th Division's provost company stayed in Cyprus until early November, then crossed the Levantine Sea to Haifa; from there they motored east in convoy between

Galilee to the north and Nazareth to the south. Averaging 100 miles a day, they continued 'into the blue', as soldiers called the desert: a daunting rite of passage. I spent an hour interpreting a photo of Ralph with men of the Transjordan Frontier Force, on the border between Palestine and Jordan, soon after his provost company had returned from a reconnaissance sortie to Al-Mafraq. Ralph, leaning in at the front, appears to be experimenting with a moustache.[7]

A scribbled note on the back of the photo suggests that from the border the provost company headed east across the Jordanian desert into Iraq, through Baghdad and north towards Kirkuk. There, Ralph attended a lecture given by his commanding officer about what to do if captured. The following month, he and his comrades returned to Haifa, a journey of a week or so, passing back through the Holy Land at Christmas time. It was snowing. Early in the New Year, in freezing weather the company set off on patrol, repeating the same looping trek through Iraq. On 19 January 1942, they arrived at Tiberias in Galilee, a mixed city of Jews and Arabs, then as snow turned to rain headed north through the mountains, accelerating between gears to prevent their engines stalling.[8]

Beyond Damascus, the convoy descended into the Lebanese Bekaa Valley, at that time part of Syria, where, through mirages rippling in the distance, they glimpsed the classical ruins of Baalbek, formerly Heliopolis. Staying in Baalbek's Grand Hotel Palmyra – a billet made less grand by the Australians they inherited it from – the military policemen patrolled the road to Beirut and performed escort duties. Ralph was one of thirty warrant officers and NCOs now under the authority of the 9th Army, a formation set up to coordinate land forces in the eastern Mediterranean. I'd been sitting in the National Archives, flicking through the unit's war diary, when his name jumped out at me.[9]

The Redcaps stayed a week in Baalbek before heading south in a column of trucks and motorcycles, through Palestine to the Gulf of Aqaba. Turning west, they crossed into Egypt, camping on the west bank of the Suez Canal at Ismailia. At sundown, the clouds of flies dispersed and the burning world gave way to cold starry silence.

They made fires by pouring petrol on tins of sand and scrub, and made a sticky porridge from biscuits crushed with bayonet hilts, tinned milk and sugar.[10]

From Ismailia it was a two-day trek through Cairo to the coast, where, at El Alamein, a lance corporal crashed his motorcycle – the provost company's first fatality. A fortnight earlier, Ralph and his comrades had been directing traffic and accusing Aussies of pilfering – but now that all seemed a long time ago.

The coast road to Mersa Matruh, with its minarets and turquoise bay, deteriorated near Halfaya Pass, a vital east–west route through a steep escarpment. Soldiers called it Hellfire Pass after a battle the previous summer. The roadside was still littered with burned-out tanks, and among the camel-thorn stood forlorn wooden crosses topped with helmets. Into the pass and beyond, Ralph would have seen a caravan of vehicles winding along the hill road, ochre and grey fading into haze.[11]

It was mid-February, and they were seven miles from the Libyan border. A fortnight earlier, a German counterattack, led by General Rommel, had reached Derna, then Gazala, recovering almost all the territory seized by the British the previous year. Now the gap between the two armies was only 100 miles of coastline, and shrinking every day. To avoid a head-on confrontation, Ralph's column veered off onto a rutted track through wind-carved hills and depressions. It was heavy going. Desert sand varied from a sifted powder to shifting grit to stone, cracked in crazy patterns.[12] Battling a sandstorm, which penetrated the tiniest gap in the trucks and reduced visibility to zero, they established a command post at Acroma Fort, an ancient baked-mud redoubt. On the 27th, a passing patrol deposited a downed German airman; the following day enemy fighters strafed the area.[13]

It began to rain, steadily then heavily, churning dust into mud and flooding slit trenches around the fort. Throughout March, the Luftwaffe raided, and between alerts Ralph's company resumed its duties: desert recces, patrolling the El Adem–Acroma road and processing prisoners. As the rain abated, so dust storms gathered, rising into an advancing wall of fury, ripping tents from their moorings and stripping paint from vehicles. During the *khamsin*, a searing desert wind, the tinted goggles that protected eyes from intense sun now saved them from howling blasts.[14]

In April, Ralph went on leave to Cairo. I read many soldiers' accounts of these jaunts, mostly in published memoirs, though Ralph himself was tight-lipped. Men pressed uniforms, found lodgings for a few piastres and had shaves and shoeshines. Everywhere a new sight – shops selling trinkets and obscene photographs, urchins crying 'baksheesh', over-burdened donkeys, clattering trams, and the scent of hookah pipes and dung. Egyptians mingled with safari-suited Europeans and an array of soldiers: Greek and French, mild-mannered New Zealanders, Australians in slouch hats, South Africans in the shortest of shorts and bearded, turbaned Sikhs. The Brits mooched around the bazaars, sipped cold beer and lounged at the YMCA or in clubs where belly-dancers sweated under greasepaint. There were horse-drawn gharry trips to the Blue Mosque and the Royal Palace, and tours up the Nile Valley, where it was obligatory to be photographed in front of the Pyramids. A snapshot captures Ralph (second from left) and his mates there, leaning nonchalantly on their motorcycles. Who knew when they'd get another chance to behave like tourists.[15]

By the late spring of 1942, the 8th Army at Gazala, 100,000 strong, was deployed in a string of defensive 'boxes' along a fifty-mile line stretching south to Bir Hakeim, a fortress occupied by the Free French. Each of these strongholds contained an infantry brigade supported by artillery and armour and was surrounded by trench systems, barbed wire and enormous minefields. The boxes seemed secure, but the distance between them meant they couldn't easily help one another. Many predicted an attack on the southern flank, where the line was weakest, and it wasn't long before they were proved right.

So far the CMP's duties had mostly involved transport logistics, maintaining discipline and dealing with Italian prisoners of war. But now the provost companies would have to fight. In May, the 50th Division was subdivided. Ralph was assigned to the 150th Infantry Brigade Provost Unit, where he took his orders from Brigadier Haydon, a veteran of the First World War. Ralph settled into life in the brigade's box, where for a while neither death nor defeat was conceivable.

The days were unvarying. Rising over the desert rim, the sun waxed quickly into a sizzling furnace, making the air hum and sapping men's energy. The heat also dulled their appetites. When they had a stomach for it, they ate bully beef and biscuits, canned sausages and pilchards, and once a week were issued with two tins of beer and a packet of lemonade powder. The daily water ration was one gallon, rank with rust and salt. After use for shaving and washing it was filtered through sand and reused. Men wore khaki-drill shirts and shorts, their skin teak brown – the sort of tan unknown in England.

Some likened the desert to an open prison whose perimeter was the edge of the world, a screen against which even familiar shapes – a lorry or a darting gazelle – were confusingly distorted. Men in fixed positions whiled away the hours squinting at the shimmering horizon or staring at white snails and pink tarantulas, scorpions and beetles. The coarse sand gave off a mineral tang tainted by sweat, woodsmoke, exhaust fumes and the reek of burning human waste. The growl of engines laid down a continuous bass to the blast of bugles, test-firing of machine guns and distant thunder of bombs. Sundown left a bitter chill that had men reaching for greatcoats and blankets. They made tea, smoked 'Victory V' cigarettes (said to be made from camel shit) and missed the comforts of home.[16]

By May, everything was in place in the brigade boxes – but they were horribly exposed, and everyone knew an attack by infantry and armour was imminent. Bravado waned. Already, persistent shelling had caused dugouts to collapse, burying men alive, and assaults by Stuka dive-bombers added to the nervous strain. Defenders cheered when Spitfires and Hurricanes swooped by, and whenever they saw the enemy twisting down, pluming black smoke. But the Messerschmitt 109s just flew higher and kept coming. Night brought dazzling displays of star shells and Verey lights, and the barrage was relentless. Bedded in holes behind tanks, trucks and gun-limbers, men tried to sleep. Many stopped eating altogether. A few went 'bomb happy' – broke down – and had to be hauled off to the rear.[17]

On 26 May, Rommel, happy that British generals used insecure radio-telephones, struck the northern part of the Gazala Line. Then, early the next morning, he led a force deep into the desert, turning at Bir Hakeim, the end of the southern flank, to attack the brigade boxes from behind. It was a supreme gamble that proved a masterstroke. The armoured column headed north-west, scattering British convoys. Four provost company vehicles joined an Italian convoy by mistake, then swerved through an enemy camp. Baffled men in the last vehicle asked directions from German soldiers, who promptly took them prisoner. Outposts were overrun, and a patrol vehicle destroyed by an anti-tank shell. A CMP officer was hit in the foot by a bullet, and others of the company captured.[18]

All the following day, the 28th, British tanks and field guns, now facing east, blasted away continuously, slowing the enemy's advance – though not for long. German shells sailed in on a low trajectory, the duds skating across the compacted sand before slithering to a halt in clouds of silver dust.

Ralph and his men were in a forward position outside the box, and stood to all night, Ralph with his sub-machine gun cocked. At 5 a.m. on the 29th, they drove three miles back towards the box, narrowly missed by shellfire. A low sun in a yellowish-pink sky cast elongated shadows, and all around explosions kicked holes in the earth. Across a wide arc, they saw German tanks put out of action, yet with more behind them.

Unknown to the defenders, Rommel was concentrating his troops in an area dubbed 'the Cauldron', until almost encircled by Allied positions and hard against the 150th Brigade's eastern flank. It was all or nothing. By a near miracle, German supply vehicles, supported by two Italian divisions, surged through the minefields, and, although strafed by RAF fighter planes, managed to hook up with Rommel's forces.[19] Ralph's brigade had been 'the cork to stop the bottle', as one officer put it, to trap the Afrika Korps; but it ended up being crushed from both sides and facing a frontal assault.[20]

Safe behind the wire that evening, Ralph scrounged ammunition from a junior officer and rested. He took a pencil and a photo from his pocketbook – a snap of Flo in the garden at Wombwell – and on the back scribbled an account of the previous night's events. On another photo of Flo, taken at the seaside with her mother, 'Big Nanny', he jotted a famous scrap of Kipling about the heat of battle: 'There's a man here with a bullet in his spleen, for God's sake get the water Gunga Din!' In the background is a café with a chalkboard. 'Today's Menu', it reads. 'Lamb, New Potatoes, Peas, Jam Tart & Custard, Tea & Coffee'. A different kind of verse – the poetry of a longed-for home.

Ralph's rest was short. That night, cut off from the rest of the division, the 150th Brigade moved north inside the box to a bare spot where men slept on the hard ground. The following afternoon, the 30th, German forces stalked the perimeter, closing in for the kill.

The defenders had lost radio contact, and a single telephone line remained open. Men began burning minefield maps and spiking their guns.[21]

At dawn the next morning, an enemy artillery barrage was followed by the thunderous rumble of tanks. The ground shook. Scores of panzers, against which anti-tank rifles were useless, surged forward, rolling over trenches full of cowering British soldiers. German anti-aircraft guns, lowered to zero elevation, tore into the defenders, infantry advancing around them, chipping away with small arms fire, seizing outlying gun pits, pushing the brigade into an ever-decreasing portion of the box. Rommel sent a message to the implacable Brigadier Haydon demanding surrender, which was ignored. Haydon had been at Dunkirk: he wouldn't have his men humiliated again.

The advance, Rommel later recalled, was won 'yard by yard, against the toughest British resistance imaginable'. As the sun went down on 31 May, and both sides fell back, the glib optimism of the

Allied high command melted away. In the stillness of the desert night, fires flickered from wrecked trucks and equipment, and men winced at the crash of igniting ammunition and the stink of flesh burning in tanks.[22]

At first light on 1 June, the assault resumed with a wave of Stukas, dive-sirens howling, and a cacophony of ear-splitting explosions. Remaining bunkers on the edge of the box were seized one by one, often after frantic hand-to-hand fighting, during which Rommel, Luger in hand, personally led an infantry platoon.

Once the Afrika Korps had overrun the British line of artillery, the brigade was powerless to resist. By midday the troops were exhausted and out of ammunition. Seeing white flags, Rommel called a ceasefire and hurried to congratulate Brigadier Haydon on his splendid defence. But like hundreds of others heaped under tarpaulins or sprawled in the sand, Haydon was dead, killed by a shell that morning.[23]

The position held so stubbornly by Haydon had fallen, later rued by Churchill as 'one of the heaviest blows I can recall during the war'.[24] For Ralph, it was two years to the day since his previous defeat, when he'd stood shivering on a dark beach at Dunkirk awaiting evacuation. He'd managed to extricate himself from that calamity, but now he and 3,000 other men of the 150th Brigade were 'in the bag'.

PART TWO
Captivity

4.
In the Bag

The ferocity of the 150th Brigade's resistance, which had so impressed Rommel's Afrika Korps, was followed by numb disbelief, then raw shock. The sun was at its apex; the men were parched and exhausted. Ralph didn't say much about this episode, but others did. It seems the Germans' war-film cliché 'For you, Tommy, the war is over' was not just real but more magnanimous than gloating: having done their bit, the defenders deserved to live. To a soldier, however, surrender was a dreadful thing. 'Never, even in the innermost recesses of my mind, had I contemplated being taken a prisoner,' wrote an officer present that day. 'I regarded it as the calamity that befell other people but never myself.'[1]

Hands raised, the men were searched while German medics treated the wounded. Some of the photos I'd seen at Warmsworth had surely passed through enemy hands. The strangeness of capture lay partly in being so close to an adversary, smelling his sweat and tobacco breath as he rummaged through your pockets. Prisoners were struck by how young these soldiers were, and how tall and blond – just as they'd imagined Teutonic warriors to be. Personal effects were returned, water and cigarettes offered. Yet however welcome, any kindness felt like pity, underlining the emasculating shame of defeat.

Whatever else was on Ralph's mind, he remembered the lecture he'd attended in Kirkuk six months earlier. Give up your name, rank and number – nothing else. If questioned, neither reveal positions nor invent information, and don't believe anything the enemy says. Men hated taking orders from Germans, and bitterly resented depending on them. Ralph had become a subordinate, a slave, no longer a subject of empire but its object. What went before now seemed a waste; what lay ahead was uncertain. But first, a worse humiliation was inflicted.[2]

Men of the Afrika Korps apologized that they had no choice but to hand the prisoners over to their Italian allies, whom the Germans themselves despised. Libya being an Italian colony, they explained, meant that Italy was responsible for enemies captured on its soil. Prisoners also felt this freed up Hitler's armies to do the real fighting.

With the exception of the Bersaglieri, an elite regiment of marksmen who wore black plumes in their helmets, Italy's soldiers struck Anglo-Saxons as peculiarly undistinguished. With baggy breeches and unravelling puttees, they resembled characters in a comic opera; their rifles with bayonets fixed were often longer than the bearers were tall. Typically, they were poorly trained peasants, who struck Allied troops – however unreasonably – as stupid, slovenly and cowardly. Even the valiant support lent to Rommel as he advanced on the Gazala Line couldn't dent the stereotype that had hardened during the Allied victories of the winter of 1940–41, when vast numbers of Italians had been captured.

But now the Italians were in charge again, and, unused to having anyone beneath them, the rank and file relished the opportunity to prod and rob their prisoners. Ralph managed to hang on to his photos and gold signet ring but lost his wristwatch. Then, with much shoving and jeering, he and his comrades were marched away from the front line. It was remarkable, the fuming captives muttered, how Italian soldiers got so much braver when their enemies were unarmed and the further they were from the fighting.

The contempt the British felt for their Italian enemies reminded me of stupid jokes from my childhood about Italian tanks with more reverse gears than forward ones, and the Italian battle flag being a white cross on a white background. It made me feel vaguely guilty, a straight line from wartime slurs about fecklessness and faint heart. 'These Italians are a rotten crowd,' General Montgomery told his troops. 'They just lie among their grapes and lemons and breed. Far too many of them. That's the trouble.'[3] I certainly didn't share any of this offensive nonsense with my friend Dom, who, like many of the Italians Ralph would meet, couldn't have been braver or kinder or nobler.

In the memoir, Ralph's silence about his capture and departure from North Africa perhaps came from reluctance to revisit what had been a painful loss of authority and agency. But like his experiences in the desert, about which he also said little, I was able to reconstruct this phase of his war from other accounts, many in the Imperial War Museum in London.

The IWM was my favourite childhood trip, usually with Dad, and though much has changed in fifty years – the emphasis shifting from military history to a more inclusive history of war – it's still full of vehicles and uniforms and guns. In pursuit of Ralph, it briefly became my place of work, and it was mildly exhilarating to sweep past tourists to the modern clinically lit room where a trolley full of archival boxes was waiting.

Dog-eared memoirs preserved in acid-free boxes, secured with white cotton tape, described how the Italians processed prisoners like Ralph early in June 1942. They were packed into fleets of open-sided trucks, Libyan guards on the cab roofs, and driven thirty miles to the coast road, where the air was cooler and fresher. After spending a night at the coastal village of Timimi, they continued westwards towards Derna. The approach road was a horseshoe cut into the escarpment, where the blasé drivers hardly braked at the hairpin bends. On one side the prisoners, rolling and clinging to their trucks, gazed up at vertical rock; on the other lay a glittering sea and a vertiginous drop. Strategically enclosed by mountains, desert and the Mediterranean, Derna had changed hands twice the previous year, Australian troops having taken it from the Italians before the Germans took it back again.

Relieved to reach the town, the men were driven through narrow streets lined with buildings bearing traces of Mussolini's slogans: 'Duce Rex' and 'Il Duce Ha Sempre Ragione', meaning that the fascist leader, like a divine emperor, was always right. Mangy dogs sniffed around, women hurried past with bundles on their heads, and townsmen offered bread and water for Egyptian pounds and gold watches. At the harbour, there was a lighthouse, palms waved, and the funnels of wrecks protruded from the water. Before the war, the Duke and Duchess of Windsor had holidayed here.[4]

The camp at Derna wasn't much: a bare compound enclosed by a high barbed wire fence. Until recently it had been an Arab cemetery, and shallow graves lay all around. There was a galvanized tank, filthy as if animals had watered there, and a standpipe where men with sunstroke, desert sores and dysentery were queueing. At one end stood a limestone warehouse and a row of square tents; at the other, where the ground sloped away, was the latrine trench. A buzzing cloud of flies hovered, and the stench was unbearable. Living space in the compound was precious, and men jostled each other not to end up right next to the open sewer. Ralph and other new arrivals were restive, the guards villainous and jumpy. Soldiers who had not already lost valuables had them stolen here, though still Ralph managed to keep hold of his signet ring. There was little discipline or order, just a short, stout captain (allegedly a former tourist guide) screaming randomly at the POWs and his own men. Italian medical officers were indifferent or brutal.[5]

Prisoners were given tins of *carne bollito* – bully beef, full of tubes and gristle – and yellow hard-tack biscuits, wolfed down so quickly they made their mouths bleed. Later came watery soup with olive oil and a few grains of rice. At dusk British officers slept in the warehouse, other ranks on rush mats in the tents or out on the stony ground. There was barely room to stretch out. The night was at least warmer than out on the escarpment, just as the day had been mercifully cooler. Some men died and were buried at the edge of the cemetery by the lighthouse.

After three days, Ralph and the men he'd arrived with were driven 200 miles further west, to the port of Benghazi. They set off early in the morning, as many as fifty crammed into each decrepit truck. The narrow, potholed road took them through deep canyon passes before climbing hundreds of feet into the mountains. The drivers went flat out, reluctant to stop even for new dysentery cases, the existing ones travelling together in the same hellish lorry known as 'the shit wagon'. The journey lasted all day, during which men begged for water and fainted from the punishing heat.[6]

Descending at last on a winding track, the wheels came within inches of the edge, and anyone foolish enough to look down saw the gullies strewn with wrecked vehicles. As at Derna, it was relief enough to make it to sea-level – which was as well because the camp at Benghazi was not much better, just another scratch-built pen with a few limestone huts to hold prisoners before they could be moved to the harbour. There, again like Derna, vessels lay half-submerged or burned out alongside the wharves.[7]

The ship Ralph boarded in the second week of June was a commercial freighter – probably the *Nino Bixio* or the *Ariosto*. Prisoners were each given a tin of bully and two dog biscuits, then made to climb down vertical ladders thirty feet into the hold, a dank, brackish iron shell with sloping sides. Several hundred men – their officers were flown out – were packed in there. They waited helplessly until the engines shuddered into life and the ship weighed anchor. No one knew how long it would take to reach Italy.

The only ventilation was through the hatches, which by day mercifully were left open. There were buckets in the corners, but these soon overflowed and men with dysentery soiled themselves where they stood. Occasionally, prisoners were allowed up on deck to fetch water and use the latrine. They noticed that the sailors wore loincloths and shoes round their necks so they were ready to swim. These ships sailed with an escort of Italian destroyers and German fighters, but once clear of the coast they were on their own and set an all-out zigzag course across the Mediterranean. If detected by patrolling RAF aircraft, their locations were relayed to Royal Navy submarines, which fired torpedoes without compunction. Many soldiers who had survived the Gazala Cauldron drowned this way.[8]

At sunset, the hatches were slammed shut. The lighting was dim, and the thudding din of the pistons relentless. After twenty-four hours, the hold was awash with seawater, urine, excrement and vomit, and many were close to breaking point, from the squalor and the terror of being sunk. A prisoner recalled 'a steamy, sickly maze of swaying forms and panic-stricken faces'. Ralph must have endured the same. There was coughing and retching, low groans and shrieks of anguish. After two days, Italian sailors threw down bread and lowered buckets of water, laughing at the fights that broke out.[9]

It took three days to reach Brindisi, an Adriatic port on the heel of Italy. Paraded through crowded streets, with filthy clothes and skin, hair and beards matted with salt and sand, they were mocked and spat at. Many of the civilians responsible had been brought in by the paramilitary policemen of the *carabinieri*, who now egged them on. The truth was that Mussolini's alliance with Hitler was never universally popular in Italy, because pro-British feeling ran strong, and had done since before the First World War. A few brave women pushed through to offer water and fruit – but, overall, the prisoners' reception reinforced their settled, even murderous loathing of Italians.[10]

Ralph was put on a train, from where, through the bars of his cattle truck, he spied a sprawl of slums and military installations. Gun batteries, barracks and airbases with German transport planes on the runway soon merged into the rippled brown-and-yellow of the Puglian countryside, with terracotta-roofed farmhouses and drystone walls. After seven miles, the train stopped at a platform whose signal box was the only visible structure on a level plain dotted with bushes and vines. Disembarking, he and the other men were marched several miles along a rough track to a wire enclosure at the edge of a small wood.

This place was Camp 85 at Tuturano, a quarantine facility intended to keep infection out of the main camps. Here were concrete sanitation blocks and wooden sheds, but the prisoners were put in tents furnished with straw bales. Most men were infested with fleas and lice. Clothes were fumigated and steamed, although, they soon discovered, at a temperature optimal for hatching parasites rather than killing them. After washing in stone troughs, and being shaved by barbers (razors were forbidden), they were fed bread rolls – *pani* – and a half a mug of soup to which existing inmates, newcomers noticed, added grass. This was the only daily meal. New prisoners were also issued with pro forma postcards, which read:

> My dear --------. I am alright. I have / have not been wounded. I am a prisoner of the Italians and I am being treated well. Shortly I shall be transferred to a prisoners' camp and I will let you have my new address. Only then I will be able to receive letters from you and to reply. With love --------.

These cards would take weeks to arrive, assuming they arrived at all.[11]

The commandant at Tuturano was a fussy middle-aged captain who owned the adjacent farm that supplied the camp. As well as cabbages, there was alfalfa, familiar to Indian prisoners – of whom there were several thousand in Italy – as cattle feed. To stave off boredom, men played cards and carved chessmen from acorns. Ralph and the new arrivals soon learned the camp song, sung to the tune of 'Roll Out the Barrel', the chorus of which addressed the bread ration:

> Roll out the pani,
> Roll out that little brown bun.
> Roll on domani,
> Let's hope we get more than one.

It was their first taste of camaraderie behind the wire. The guards, not grasping the lyric 'all who've ever been there, know the Ities are so mean there', enjoyed it too. Another song, 'The Tuturano Blues', included the lines: 'You can't get the boys of Tuturano down, / For we're all going home next year.' Of course, they had no idea.[12]

A few days later, Ralph was one of several hundred men marched back to the railway halt and again herded into closed goods wagons. It took most of the day to trundle 100 miles further inland to a station where the carriages were unbolted. Stepping giddily onto the white platform, prisoners saw a sign that read 'Gravina'.

They trudged up a winding lane, past fields where farm workers stopped and stared, then continued down a long, straight road until they could make out the distant city of Altamura and, nearer, buildings on higher ground off to their right. Still in open country, they were led up a track to the gates of what proved to be an enormous prison camp.[13]

It was 15 June 1942, a fortnight since Ralph had been captured. Having followed his tracks from Cyprus to Syria, Egypt to Gazala, I'd finally cornered him in a place where he could tell his own story – the story in the memoir I'd found at Pauline's house in Warmsworth. The picture he painted there was of a camp teeming with life and immensely socially complex. 'It was', he said, 'like living in a beehive.'[14]

5.

The Beehive

Much of what I knew about Camp 65 Gravina had been pieced together from Ralph's memoir and other first-hand accounts, published and unpublished, and some bulging files in the National Archives. Unlike for Germany, official histories were never commissioned for Italian POW camps – but even if this had happened, I doubt any formal work of record could have plumbed the strange human depths of a camp like Gravina.[1]

The essential overview came from Dom Bolognese in Altamura, the town adjacent to Gravina. I kept him posted, together with Mum, as the story unfolded. Both were keen to hear about Ralph's desert war and to read my transcription of the memoir.[2] Dom's Camp 65 Association had produced a short book, a copy of which arrived in the post. Cursing myself for being slow to learn Italian, I struggled through the text using Google Translate.[3]

Camp 65 was the largest of its kind in Italy. Designed in the spring of 1942 to be built in phases, ultimately for 12,000 prisoners, it was situated on a domed plateau between Gravina and Altamura, 150 miles east of Naples and forty south-west of the port of Bari. For most of the year, then as now, it was an arid plain surrounded by exhausted arable land and rugged pasture, rolling in dips and rises and patterned with walls and farmsteads.[4]

Even Italian officers considered it a grim posting: 'an ugly, brutal region', one adjutant confessed to a prisoner.[5] But the prisoners had it so much worse, and the opening line of Ralph's memoir, 'Contrary to enemy propaganda life in a prison camp is not a happy one', now seemed like absurd English understatement.

When Ralph arrived in mid-June 1942, the camp was still under construction – a hasty reaction to a huge influx of Allied prisoners into Italy resulting from Rommel's victories in Libya. The first contingent of 1,300 had arrived in April; within a couple of months this had risen to nearly 3,500.[6] In one of the National Archives files, I came across a report from the International Red Cross, dated May 1942. 'The treatment of the prisoners of war is in every way considerate', inspectors concluded, 'and the impression is that all that is possible is being done for their contentment.' If this was ever true, it certainly didn't last.[7]

Like all new 'Sixty-Fivers', as the prisoners called themselves, Ralph had to face the fact that lives held cheaply by the army here lost almost all value. The first step to ensure survival was getting the lie of the land. At the front of the camp, on its north side, stood the *palazzina comando*, the main administration building and its adjacent barracks, beyond which the four rectangular sectors ran in parallel down an incline. These were numbered two to five; one and six, on the wings, would in theory follow. Arranged in each sector on a perpendicular east–west orientation were six sandstone blockhouses roofed in corrugated asbestos sheeting. The kitchens and sanitation blocks were similarly constructed. Various plans and illustrations in Dom's book made sense of the scheme as it was early in 1942 and how it was intended to look when finished (which it never was).

The sectors were separated by ten-foot barbed wire fences, on either side of which were guard alleys marked off with tripwires. Enclosing the whole site was a double fence infilled with corkscrews of wire, bearing signs reading, in English: 'To pass this notice is to invite sudden death'. Guard blocks with roof platforms provided uninterrupted views of the camp, interspersed with sentry boxes and wooden towers mounted with arc lights and machine guns. In addition, mobile, battery-powered searchlights could be wheeled around the perimeter, which was patrolled day and night.[8]

Camp 65's prisoners were mostly British, but there were also New Zealanders, South Africans and Greek Cypriots, as well as a smaller number of Palestinians, Australians, Canadians,

Montenegrins and Egyptians. These nationalities did not always see eye to eye, so were segregated in their own huts and sectors. South Africans arriving after the fall of Tobruk that June were accused of surrendering without a fight, chiefly by Australians, who the previous year had held out for seven months. Nor was there much love lost between Brits and Aussies.

The overwhelming majority of POWs were soldiers, the rest downed airmen and shipwrecked sailors. Camp 65 was reserved for privates, non-commissioned officers (NCOs) and warrant officers (WOs); the only proper officers in such camps were medics and padres, who lived apart from the men – but in June 1942, this camp still had neither. Life was essentially enclosed within each sector, although it was possible to slip between the sectors if the right sentry was approached with a friendly gesture or bribe.[9]

Ralph's possessions, including his photos, were temporarily confiscated and a receipt issued for their return. His personal details were recorded, and he was given a sheet, two blankets and a canvas palliasse to fill with straw. Then he was escorted from the *palazzina comando* to Sector 2, which stood on the far eastern side of the camp overlooking the building site of the planned extension. After the ordeal of Derna and Benghazi, his first impression was broadly positive: most men's were. The buildings were solidly constructed and there was food and firewood, with felled trees being dragged in by mules for men to help themselves.

As a sergeant, Ralph was put in a blockhouse for private soldiers and NCOs, which turned out to be horribly overcrowded. Worse, he had no boots, either because they'd fallen to bits – which commonly happened – or been stolen, usually by the guards. If the latter, he never mentioned it: the shame of a copper having his boots nicked! Some men he knew or recognized from Gazala, but for the time being he led a solitary existence.

He was soon introduced to the grinding, barely changing routine. Summer days began at 5.30 with roll call, or 'check parade', which lasted about an hour while the prisoners were counted. At 7.30 a.m. hot water was brought out from the cookhouses for tea and ersatz coffee made from roasted barley or acorns; the bread ration – a 200-gram bun the size of a clenched fist – followed an hour later.

After that, Ralph spent the next four hours wandering around, sitting against the hut walls, or lying on his bunk. That's what men did. And those without boots didn't stray far, even in good weather. At midday came the cry of 'skilly up'. Bombarded by horseflies and mosquitoes, he queued with other prisoners clutching mess tins to receive half a pint of soup that was three parts water to one part rice or macaroni, in which floated cabbage stalks, chunks of marrow and, if they were lucky, morsels of fatty meat. Prisoners also received a daily ration of olive oil and sugar, a teaspoon of each, and once a week a small cube of hard cheese or rancid salami (suspected to be donkey), and a pinch of tobacco. Cigarettes were like gold – indeed, they served as currency. When none were available, men smoked straw, tea leaves, weeds, even cotton wool, rolled in pages from pocket bibles.

Another five long, tedious hours lay ahead before the next check parade and more skilly, followed by 'dangling': boiling water over embers in the cookhouse. Men were in bed by 9.30 p.m. and the dim lights switched off at ten.[10]

Ralph's hut, like its identical neighbours, was divided into an entrance area and seven bays connected by archways aligned along a central draughty corridor. The walls were whitewashed, and inside covered in prisoners' murals, cartoons and portraits. Each bay contained twenty-four double bunks. Stuffed palliasses, at first lumpy and prickly, soon went flat as the straw was crushed into chaff. The blankets were thin, coarse and meant for soldiers much shorter than Ralph. More than just a place to sleep, a bunk was a sacred space, where everything a man owned was stored. Lines were strung along the sides for drying towels and socks, spare clothing rolled into a pillow. An NCO prisoner kept each bay's forty-eight men in order and made sure the concrete floor was swept. Water was heated on campfires between the bunks, fed, when other fuel ran low, with wood chipped from bedposts and boards.

The Beehive

The air was rank with smoke and sweat and unwashed feet, and, owing to the poor diet, flatulence.[11]

Although the exterior of the camp had been photographed, and some blockhouses survived, no one had ever thought to take a picture inside. But sitting among the stacks in the Cambridge University Library I came across a book containing a sketch by a South African prisoner in Camp 65. Now I could really see Ralph there, enduring it all, planning his next move. After a cool spring, the weather had improved, and the huts were briefly bearable at night before they soon became hot and stuffy. This made it hard to sleep, as did itching caused by scabies, hunger pangs and the sound of other men farting and snoring, sobbing and mumbling deliriously.[12] Ralph came to some arrangement with another man, presumably in the next bunk, whose boots he shared so that he could answer calls of nature.[13]

To a soldier, cleanliness was self-discipline – but in Camp 65 cleanliness was impossible. The water brought into the camp in lorries was turned on and off without warning. The cry of 'water's on!' sent men running to the troughs with containers. The latrines, simple voids in the floor of the sanitation blocks, were dry and putrid; warm showers were unheard of. Ralph had an iron rule about shaving, but razor blades were scarce. Like everyone else, his uniform was full of lice, his bunk infested with bugs and fleas. Prisoners sat outside cracking nits and passing garment seams over fires.[14]

Like any unitary state, Camp 65 had its own system of governance and law enforcement – and in Sector 2 Ralph would soon play a key role. Security wasn't excessive, though, for the simple reason it didn't need to be. There was little prospect of unfit, underfed men escaping. Even if they did break out, where would they go? Switzerland, the nearest land border, was 600 miles away. The camp's insularity was reinforced by the fact that, mainly due to the foul smell, local people stayed away unless they had official business there. Drainage and telephone engineers, farmers delivering vegetables, a milk girl, a baker from Altamura and occasionally a photographer – that was it.

The guards were ordinary soldiers of the 9th Italian Army Corps and fitted the homesick 'peasants-in-uniform' model even more than the desert troops had. They were largely indifferent, occasionally friendly. Some had worked in America and had a smattering of English. On the whole their officers, too, were humane – or, at least, open to amicable overtures: one good-humoured major was thrilled when prisoners noted his resemblance to the Hollywood actor Jimmy Cagney.[15] The commandant, Colonel Vincenzo Cione, was in his fifties, plump, not much over five feet tall, and walked with a limp. His message to the camp, guards and prisoners alike, was that they were all in this together and should live and let live.[16]

There was, however, the menacing presence of the *carabinieri*, a detachment of whom lived in their own barracks outside the perimeter but were a constant presence inside. Although they were only thirty-five strong, Colonel Cione had no direct jurisdiction over them. Unlike the dull grey uniforms of the guards, the *carabinieri*, a military regiment, wore navy-blue tunics and breeches with a red stripe, and on their caps a badge of a flaming grenade. They were efficient, mostly incorruptible and had a nose for plots.[17] Their combined civil and military duties made Ralph, the peacetime constable and wartime Redcap, feel he understood them. But their ruthlessness also reminded him of what he knew of the German Gestapo. Any prisoner could on the flimsiest pretext be dragged to a cell, soaked, beaten and starved.[18] The *carabinieri* were habituated to such brutality. They also confiscated knives, compasses, civilian clothing and Italian currency – anything that might assist an escape.[19]

Most men kept their heads down and tried to stay busy. Yet there was little to do. As increasing numbers of prisoners filed through the gates, recreation space became sleeping quarters, and the exercise ground was built over, leaving only rough patches between the blockhouses and kitchens. There were hardly any books and no games. The men were saving up to buy musical instruments, but each earned only one lira per day, paid in squares of newspaper bearing the commandant's stamp, and they needed 16,000 lire to form a band.[20]

One of the most dispiriting privations was the lack of news. The commandant only allowed British newspapers that reported setbacks for the Allies. Every fortnight his officers issued an English-language bulletin full of fascist propaganda – 'a highly amusing document', recalled Ralph, much in demand as toilet paper. Scarcity of reliable news incubated rumours – in July, that the war would be over by the autumn.[21] By now, prisoners working in the camp office, with access to a duplicating machine, put together a flimsy two-page newspaper, *Domani Griff*, meaning 'tomorrow's news'. I found a copy of the first issue, dated 26 May 1942, in the archives of the Imperial War Museum – possibly a unique survival as this publication was also put to use in the latrines. The editor's mission was to quash 'the fantastic and alarming rumours which sweep Camp 65'.[22] Most 'griff' concerned Red Cross food and, voiced discreetly, suspicions that the Italians were hoarding it: national shortages and military supply problems meant the guards were hungry too.[23]

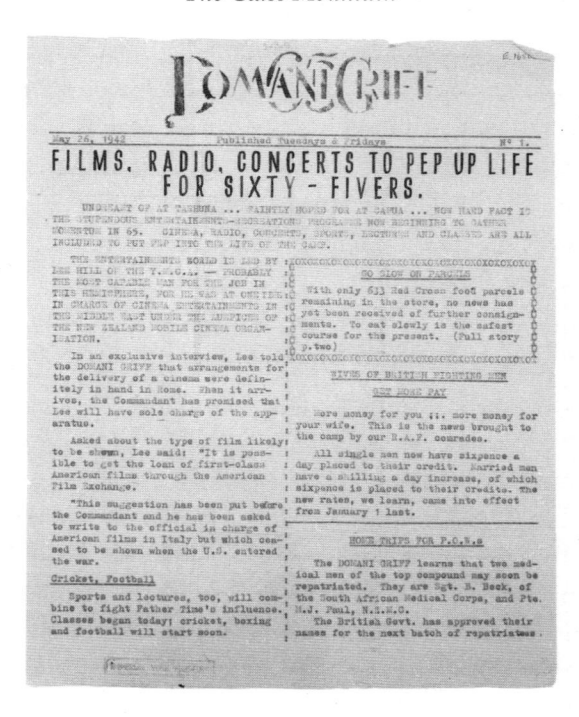

Gradually the cheese and meat ration shrank until it was minuscule; beetroot tops and dandelions were added to the skilly. Whenever supply lines broke down, men got nothing at all. The camp shop sold salted fish, eggs, vegetables, lemons and dates, but prices were astronomical. The object of men's fantasies shifted from sex to food. They tormented each other with memories of Sunday roasts and treacle puddings, and awoke from dreams of feasts to find the pillow wet with drool. A scrapbook cartoon in the IWM shows a lonely wife, her thought bubble reading: 'I wonder if he is thinking of me tonight', juxtaposed with her POW husband asleep dreaming of a roast chicken. I wondered if, in their most private thoughts, that had been Ralph and Flo.[24]

At first, only a few letters arrived in the camp, while at home a lack of information caused consternation. In June 1942, Flo had been notified that her husband was missing in action, then heard nothing for six weeks. She was sent his weekly wage of 49 shillings – worth about £150 today – and that was it. On 20 July, the International Red

Cross in Geneva finally received a telegram from Camp 65 to say that Ralph was a prisoner. Meanwhile, on the same day, Flo joined the Women's Auxiliary Police Corps – a surprise to put in a letter for her husband, and a way of being close to him by doing the work he'd done at home. Nine days later, Ralph's name appeared on a Red Cross list. Yet it would be another six weeks before he was officially classed as 'no longer missing', and Flo was probably not informed that her husband was safe until early September. Clearly the postcard Ralph sent from Camp 85 at Tuturano went astray. The first one that did make it to England came from Gravina, dated 11 July, and took several weeks. Even then poor Flo heard the news from Ralph's parents because he had, rather thoughtlessly, given them as his next of kin.[25] During that three-month wait, she could only cling to blind faith and the moonshine in the press.[26]

Based on Red Cross reports, and patriotic wishful thinking, the foreign correspondent of the *Daily Mail* viewed the camps as microcosms of the British nation in variety and coherence. POWs, he reassured readers, 'make their own barbed-wire worlds, using cheerfulness and ingenuity in adversity, that elasticity of character which has served Britain well throughout her history'. Conditions were not good, but could always be worse.[27]

The Red Cross newspaper, *The Prisoner of War*, sent to POWs' next of kin – so, in Ralph's case, his parents – preached the same sunny optimism. It published letters from men saying everything was fine – using the upbeat tone the Red Cross suggested families take when writing to loved ones in camps. People at home were advised not to mention nice dinners or air raids, which could make men homesick or anxious, and should instead talk about films and pets and children. Don't send watches or anything mechanical that could assist an escape (and so would be confiscated), the Red Cross instructed, but towels and toothpaste would always be useful. A homemade blanket of knitted squares made 'a most welcome gift'. The paper also serialized Churchill's account of escaping during the Boer War, which doubtless lifted spirits but may also have raised unrealistic expectations among civilians like Florence Corps in Wombwell.[28]

Once Flo knew where Ralph was, however, she could write to him, and also send parcels, albeit indirectly through her in-laws – yet another drawback of not being listed as next of kin. Doubtless her letters, once they got through, made Ralph feel closer to home. By now, like other prisoners, he had done what he could to recreate domesticity – sharing meals and making tea. Some men even baked cakes from biscuits, raisins and condensed milk. While women like Flo were doing men's jobs in Britain, in Italian camps these men fell into familial roles – rough imitations of spouses, mothers, fathers and even children.

As rations diminished, so the spotlight prisoners shone on one another exposed their true selves. Extremity as well as lack of privacy meant there was nowhere to hide. Under pressure, every character type manifested: introverts and extroverts, leaders and followers; men were selfish and altruistic, prudent and reckless.[29] Prisoners who eked out food parcels were called 'hoarders' or 'mossers', those who guzzled them 'scoffers' or 'bashers' – though most fell between these extremes.[30] Unlike Ralph, plenty of men relished not having to make decisions. Some even realized how civilian jobs and marriages had trapped them, and appreciated the mental detachment of prison life. One POW was only half-joking when he wrote to his mother: 'It's just the life for anybody in need of a rest.'[31]

Others felt as if they were wading through a dream, a sensation summed up in a poem accompanying the sketch of the blockhouse interior:

> For we live in a shadowland
> Like the audience at a show,
> While the play upon the stage
> Is the world we used to know.

In the end, simulacra of civilian life may have emphasized the peculiarities of this strange colony more than they compensated for them. There was no getting over the shame of being helpless and dirty and chained to one's base nature.[32]

The Beehive

Prisoners lived on top of each other, especially on rainy days – like bees, but less busy. There were many petty irritations, and most inmates grew sensitive to noise: shouting between bunks, singing and whistling, clattering mugs and mess tins, the banging of making and repairing and the scrape of hobnailed boots. A neighbour's habits could drive a man mad. Tempers flared. Jean-Paul Sartre came up with the aphorism 'hell is other people' in a prison camp.[33]

Neurosis fed into wider despair and a sense of hopelessness. Like many, Ralph was vexed to be serving an indefinite prison sentence. And after 'prisoneritis' – a morbid obsession with defeat – came 'barbed wire fever': loss of interest in everything.[34] So-called 'glumpers' sat alone watching ants or staring glassy-eyed through the wire. Some found quiet spots on the blindside of a blockhouse where they could gaze across the valley to a solitary tree on the horizon, imagining what lay beyond. Robert Lee, an artist who traded portraits for food, painted this valley obsessively.[35] Men faint with hunger would stand up quickly to make themselves black out – a blessed moment of relief.[36]

Ralph himself was resourceful and resilient, but he saw many prisoners go 'round the bend', the worst cases carted off to an asylum. This was the fate of one NCO, the only survivor of a burning tank in the Cauldron, and before the war a teacher. Men in his hut mocked his 'posh' accent and beat him up, after which he spent his days alone cross-legged reciting facts from his lessons.[37] Scapegoating and bullying were the flip side of camp camaraderie, but even popular, apparently happy, prisoners would break under the torment of confinement. A genial soldier, an accomplished saxophonist, would every now and then go berserk, hurling stones. During these episodes, one POW recalled, 'his eyes looked very strange and he seemed to be living in another world'.[38] The most disturbed hoarders gleefully watched food accumulate even as they starved.[39]

Most depressing was the spectre of illness and death, along with worry about families at home. A private of the Cheshire Regiment kept a diary, written deliriously without punctuation in a tiny pencil hand, in which he spoke only of his black mood, gnawing hunger and foot and stomach problems.[40] A minority simply gave up, neither washing nor eating, in fact never leaving their bunks, soiling themselves and repeating the same word or phrase. One man was found sprawled upon a rubbish heap, semi-conscious, crawling with lice. Exasperated prisoners dragged these poor creatures to the trough to wash them by force.[41]

Inevitably, thoughts of suicide intruded. That summer, a prisoner in Sector 3, said to be 'a rather closed and misanthropic character', grabbed a razor from a barber and cut his own throat. His life was saved by a captain of the Royal Army Medical Corps, who, along with a padre, had arrived in the camp a fortnight earlier.[42] Another prisoner, a South African gunner, gave away his rations, he claimed, on the orders of 'a higher power', the devil, who tempted him to kill himself by climbing the fence. The man died a few days later.[43]

Camp 65 was like a huge psychological experiment to see how societies formed from scratch. In this, the *Daily Mail*'s propaganda was not entirely wrong – but the reality of this evolving 'state in miniature', as one prisoner put it, was far less jolly: a Hobbesian state of nature, only loosely constrained by the leviathan of the Italian authorities. An official apparatus of control, with laws and quasi-judicial sanctions, intersected with the POWs' own divisions of labour, customs of obligation and exchange, and channels of written and spoken communication. A galaxy of clubs and committees sprang up. Prominent was the Welfare and Social Committee, which struggled to get anything done, but nevertheless symbolized a natural urge to exchange ideas and organize effort.[44]

The prevailing hierarchy did afford opportunities for self-advancement. Except for the medics and the padre in the infirmary, the absence of officers with ready-made powers and privileges only made the experiment more fascinating. Men like Ralph either tenaciously held their own or clawed their way up the ladder. One prisoner, who on arrival had felt like a scavenging wolf, described how in time he built 'a certain comfortable civilisation' for himself.[45] Others discovered the social mobility they had craved as civilians

The Beehive

during the Great Depression, a desire that Ralph Corps of Mexborough continued to nurture. The indignities he suffered in Camp 65 Gravina did not last long.

Ralph's instinct was not to seek popularity but to maintain order. Within a fortnight, he came to the attention of the camp leader of Sector 2, Regimental Sergeant Major Les Munday, who, with the approval of Colonel Cione, put him in charge of Sector 2's camp police under Munday's command. Ralph never said whether he'd actively sought this elevation of status – but it would have been like him to have done so. He was certainly glad of the position, one that put him in charge of fifteen men, mostly of his stamp: NCOs, Guardsmen, military police, ex-civilian police and a couple of tough, trusted Greek Cypriots. This authority also came with better rations and, best of all, earned him suitable footwear – no more sharing of boots. The job also earned him a nickname, 'Sleuth', which he claimed not to like, but which did confer a grudging respect for his new status.

As it happened, there wasn't much sleuthing to do, in fact little policing of any kind. Ralph held 'orderly room' at 11 a.m. each day, reporting to the Italian officers and RSM Munday, who in turn met with Colonel Cione, mostly to relay POW complaints.[46] Ralph's men were mandated to deal with infractions of discipline – insubordination, thefts and bartering with the enemy – themselves; more heinous offences were a matter for the Italians. These duties required the sector police heads to liaise with the *carabinieri*, which to prisoners looked like fraternizing with the enemy. Ralph didn't much like it, but he had a job to do. He often had to visit the office of a detested *maresciallo*, a squat, bespectacled man with bushy eyebrows, who spoke through an interpreter Ralph cared for even less.

In August, Cione was replaced by Lieutenant Colonel Attilio Coppola, a stocky, middle-aged army officer with a florid complexion and receding grey hair, who inherited his predecessor's fatalistic live-and-let-live stance. Known to the prisoners as 'Farmer Joe', perhaps owing to his rustic appearance, he quickly built a reputation for unfulfilled promises: 'oggi' (today) meant tomorrow, 'domani' (tomorrow) meant next week, and 'dopodomani' (the day after tomorrow) meant never. Imprecision irked Ralph, the punctilious sergeant, but even so he considered Coppola decent enough.[47]

Sharing a barrack block with the ordinary men must have rankled, particularly now that Ralph was the head of the Sector 2 police. But then, in August, something amazing happened. The British War Office notified the Italian authorities at Camp 65 that he had been promoted to company sergeant major.[48] No longer an NCO, he was now a warrant officer, second class, which entitled him to a bunk in the small WOs' hut at the north end of the sector.

This promotion and the perk of improved accommodation completed Ralph's elevation as a man of influence. Italian officers, who despised their own subordinates, respected rank among their enemies – besides which, it helped them run the camp on a divide-and-rule basis. This suited the WOs, too, who were not only sticklers for hierarchy but, in lieu of commissioned officers, were in charge of their men. WOs never had to work like ordinary soldiers, and if they chose to do so it was only to wield power or satisfy some special ambition.[49] And in Sector 2, after the camp leader, no one wielded as much power as Ralph Corps. Among more than 1,000 men, his was the day-to-day face of military discipline. Discovering this altered my perception of Ralph as a man – and indeed the entire top-down structure of life at Gravina.

By the late summer of 1942, Camp 65 contained over 6,000 prisoners, nearly twice as many as when Ralph arrived – but, still under construction, it was hopelessly inadequate for accommodating so many men. Newcomers were forced to sleep on the blockhouse floors. The construction of the first and sixth sectors, on the east and west flanks of the camp, was hastily approved, but work proceeded haphazardly. Some Red Cross parcels had been distributed, including an issue the day after Ralph's arrival, but each had to be shared between six men and invariably had been tampered with – robbed of tea, chocolate and soap, the tins pierced to prevent stockpiling for possible escapes. Parcels became briefly plentiful – one between four men, every two days. But this flow soon abated and by October had dried up altogether. Meanwhile, prisoner numbers soared.[50]

Hungry inmates were agitated, unruly; famished ones, however, were apathetic and easy for Ralph's men to control. In Cairo, a large part of the CMP's job had been dealing with drunk young men on leave. By late summer, such carefree high spirits were a distant memory. Instead, prisoners consuming less than 1,000 calories a day barely moved yet noticed every petty detail of existence: whose skilly ration was fractionally larger, who got the crumbs from the blanket used to carry the bread, who lost weight and who did not. The cooks, known as 'the Forty Thieves', siphoned off whatever they could. 'At Gravina honest men went hungry,' recalled one soldier bitterly, 'and each new cook took this to heart.' Hated like Redcaps, the camp police were vehemently suspected of being as bent as the cooks – a source of intense resentment towards men like Ralph.[51]

Autumn brought misery, above all to those making shift at the base of this cruel society. Malnourished men succumbed to infections; desert sores refused to heal. Dysentery was humiliating as well as debilitating. Malaria was a growing problem, and all camps lived in fear of a typhus outbreak. Back in the spring, the authorities had noted sewage flowing into nearby marshes and recorded the camp's first case of diphtheria.[52]

Even after the arrival of their British doctor, prisoners still relied on Italian medical officers who held morning sick parades. They did little good. Bandages were made of crêpe paper, and there were few medicines. A sick man might get a pill (white or black), an injection with a blunt needle, a smear of sulphur ointment for scabies or impetigo, but most patients were waved away. The camp had no dentist or dental instruments.[53]

The weakest men blacked out on parade and were taken away by horse and cart. Three days before Ralph's arrival, a young British prisoner had died from 'acute intestinal catarrh', which the leader in that week's *Domani Griff* blamed on poor hand washing and consuming dirty cabbage stalks and orange peel. Shortly before this, an emaciated New Zealander had slipped into what proved to be a terminal coma. Now, every few days, a prisoner was found stiff in his bunk. In Sector 2, RSM Munday, Ralph at his side, called the men to attention as a funeral escort carried out the balsa-wood coffins for burial in Altamura.[54]

And then, a miracle. Just as POW numbers topped 7,000, the supply of Red Cross food resumed, and parcels from home also began to arrive. They caused the most exquisite joy. 'Imagine a crowd of kiddies getting up on Christmas morning to see what's in their stockings,' a prisoner wrote home, 'and that's not a patch on what we feel like when we get them.'[55] The packaging was useful, too. Wall cupboards were fashioned from the wooden boxes – visible in the sketch I'd found, complete with red crosses – and 'tin bashers' hammered food cans into plates, cigarette cases, picture frames and brackets for shelves. String became bootlaces; cardboard, insoles. Even the cellophane from cigarette packets was woven into belts.

But the supply remained erratic.[56] Sometimes, the Italians explained, there were 'niente parcels because de aeroplano Inglese hava bombardamento'd il traino'.[57] And by the time winter set in, the miracle had evaporated into the Puglian mist. No parcels came for several weeks, and huts banned even the mention of food. Prisoners began to starve. In Sector 3, some men noticed a mongrel sniffing at the inner fence and lured it with their bread ration. It was, one recalled, 'a feast on four legs', simmered with weeds and shared among the five of them, watched hungrily by others.[58]

Cold, wet weather made things worse. People at home imagined Italy luxuriating in perpetual summer, and for Ralph at first this had been true. Days of restorative warmth were spent under azure skies. He'd seen sunrises and sunsets of maroon and orange, and luminous moons. Evening breezes carried the scent of wild herbs.[59] But Puglia in winter wasn't like this at all. Chill winds funnelled in through unglazed windows, and the stoves the Italians promised never materialized. Prisoners were allowed an extra half hour in bed, but it was better to be up and about. In November, damp crept into the huts and men's bones. Anything left on the floor was wet through by morning. Some men still had no choice: on one afternoon of driving sleet 1,000 South Africans arrived, and the floor was the only place they could sleep.[60] There were fogs and frosts and biting winds, and it rained for days. By the end of the month, the compounds were like quagmires. Roll calls were taken inside the huts, which men left only to use the latrine and collect their meagre rations.[61]

The short days of early December were spent huddled in bunks, communal activities having ceased. Even the tin-bashers fell silent. No Red Cross parcels came, and every sector was churned up into a morass of slime and puddles. Boots disintegrated, stitching rotted, soles hanging off and tied up with rags. Men still in tropical shirts and shorts were forced to wear oddments of plundered Yugoslav and Greek uniform, as well as wooden clogs.[62] Those who in the summer had traded good British clothes for food now wished they hadn't.

For all the seriousness with which Ralph treated his job, his thoughts remained fixed on escape – either to get home or back into the war. This was his obligation as a soldier, and the thought offset the shame of surrender. Escape was also an act of extreme self-possession, far exceeding the satisfaction of strutting around as a camp policeman. To achieve this, however, he ideally needed a 'mucker', a mate, a partner to plan with, to share the necessary preparations, and to rely on if he ever made it out. So, it was fortuitous that Ralph had befriended a British sergeant pilot of the RAF, a fellow warrant officer of singular ability and ambition. His name was Charlie West.

6.
Charlie

Until I read Ralph's memoir, my view of POW life was dominated by plucky British officers breaking out using tunnels, sheet-ropes, disguises, forgeries and deceptions. Escape from Colditz, enshrined in war mythology, was the standard version. But hundreds of other camp stories, retold in memoirs, dissented from this. Only a fraction were ever published, however, chiefly because most were written by soldiers like Ralph, who had little of the literary flair of their well-educated officers. Another reason is that relatively few memoirs described escapes.[1]

One Camp 65 veteran, weary of Colditz glamour, later tried to set the record straight. The typical prisoner focused on getting by, not getting out, he averred, patiently enduring a monotonous existence that was 'squalid with very little light relief or humour and . . . completely demoralizing'.[2] These men were known as 'keepers', the rank and file who regarded escaping as a dangerous waste of time. A tiny minority of 'escapers' – fewer than one in fifty – discovered that even to suggest a breakout was to be openly disdained by a quarter of the men and secretly disdained by another half. The keeper refused to take risks against what he'd convinced himself was his better judgement. Some believed they owed it to their families to stay as safe as possible.[3]

Charlie West was an 'escaper' through and through, unlike any other man Ralph met in Camp 65, and contemptuous of the excuses made by 'keepers'. He prowled around like a caged beast, constantly alert to opportunity. If keepers were short on desire, ingenuity and courage, he had all three – a magical combination – in abundance. Nor was he primarily motivated by duty. 'The true escaper', according to one commentator, 'tries to get away because he is rebellious by nature, and objects to his liberties being restricted by a lot of bastards whom he despises.'[4]

Charlie first came to Ralph's attention when he was still living in a common blockhouse and was not yet a camp policeman. It happened during check parade, when Charlie had showed up bareheaded – the sort of misdemeanour that caught the eye of a disciplinarian like Ralph. By this point, Charlie had been at Gravina for five weeks, and, seeing the RAF man improperly dressed on subsequent occasions, Ralph surmised he simply didn't own a hat. One morning Ralph introduced himself. As they talked, Charlie explained, with a wry smile, that presenting himself thus meant he was not required to salute the Italian officer taking the parade. It was an act of pure cussedness.

'Perhaps that was one of the things that attracted me, I don't know,' recalled Ralph, 'but I do know that he turned out to be the best friend I ever had in a prisoner-of-war camp.' It was unlike Ralph to be so candid. Even so, not once in 35,000 words of the memoir does he refer to Charlie by his first name.[5]

Charlie was charismatic, optimistic and naturally rebellious – qualities the straitlaced, conformist Ralph lacked yet admired. What they had in common was a blind refusal to be subjected by the enemy and cold indifference to their unpopularity among their own men. And in Ralph, Charlie saw 'Sleuth': a tough, trustworthy peeler a couple of years his senior, and a dependable partner. Ralph put up with him using the nickname – aware, perhaps, that it was not just a sardonic tease but a mark of esteem.

So they complemented one another, and soon after Ralph had moved to the WOs' block, where Charlie, as a warrant officer, was already housed, this energetic pilot, fizzing with West Country mischief, and his stiff northern mucker became inseparable. They were often to be found deep in conversation – Ralph a purveyor of stolid Yorkshire common sense, Charlie the quick-witted contrarian – or sharing the contents of Red Cross parcels and making tea. Ralph would act the scolding mother, Charlie the affable father. Ralph nodded along to his schemes, and watched him tinker with whatever he could get his hands on.

They talked mostly about escape. While stationed at RAF Kinloss on the Moray Firth in Scotland, Charlie had been lectured on conduct in captivity. 'Don't be downhearted,' advised the booklet he'd been given. 'Opportunities for escape will present themselves.' And this came with a stern injunction: 'It is the duty of prisoners to make such attempts, which in themselves have a very appreciable nuisance value.' Airmen were not, however, trained in escaping. Apart from what they'd read in novels from the First World War, most instructors had no experience to share.[6]

In contrast to Ralph's sense of military obligation, what Charlie really enjoyed about plotting to escape was precisely being a nuisance. For an escaper to reach Switzerland was unheard of – but, he reasoned, they could have fun trying.

Reading the memoir, I could tell that Charlie, who had been both foil and inspiration, was a key to unlock another hidden side of Ralph's character. Who then was he, and how did he come to be at Gravina? His early life, far more than Ralph's, was a puzzling mess. I scoured Ancestry for records – birth and marriage certificates, census returns, military attestations – and through detective work on probate records tracked down living relatives to see what they might know. Piece by piece, the story came together.[7]

Charlie West was born on 31 March 1916 in the village of Wembury, on the rocky south Devon coastline near Plymouth. His father, Archie, a wine merchant's clerk, had married his mother, Mabel, in Guildford, Surrey, when she was pregnant with his child, Charlie's elder brother Syd. This was in August 1914, a week after the outbreak of war. Archie joined the Royal Garrison Artillery and was posted to a gun battery in Plymouth. Syd was born in March 1915, and by June Mabel was expecting another baby. Charlie arrived the following spring. His father was sent to France but soon returned suffering from influenza and spent the next year in military hospitals.[8]

According to Archie West's service record, discovered in the National Archives, Mabel received her husband's sick pay; but in July 1918, this was stopped on grounds of her 'misconduct and desertion': she'd been having an affair and was pregnant. Archie was discharged as unfit and, granted a pension, took up work as a bootmaker. I found no sign that he ever again had anything to do with his ex-wife or sons.[9]

By this time Mabel had moved to Manchester with Frank Scoullar, a printer from New Zealand. They never married, but she took Frank's surname and lied on the 1921 census, meaning her sons, Syd and Charlie, also had to be renamed and re-aged as twins. Another household drama had surfaced from the archives. Their half-sisters Brenda and Olga were born in 1919 and 1920 respectively, and by 1925 Mabel was back in Plymouth, alone, where she gave birth to her fifth child, a boy she registered as a Scoullar.

Charlie attended primary school in Manchester, then, after his mother returned to Devon, Plymouth Public Secondary School for Boys between 1927 and 1931. His name appears in the register at the local archives office. Leaving school at fifteen, he became, like Syd, an RAF aircraft apprentice at Gosport, and in 1934, on his eighteenth birthday, enlisted for the usual period of twelve years.[10] He dreamed of flying, and until he could get into a cockpit settled for riding his motorcycle at full throttle. A researcher sent me a newspaper cutting from 1935 reporting his being fined at Fareham Petty Sessions for speeding in a built-up area.[11] But with an otherwise clean record, Charlie was recommended for pilot training. After a rigorous education at Cranwell and other RAF establishments, he earned his wings in November 1938, and served at various bases around Britain. Early in 1940 he was at the Operational Training Unit at Kinloss before in April being posted to 216 Squadron based at the Heliopolis aerodrome, near Cairo.

In Egypt, Charlie's skill as a pilot was rated as 'above average', but he hardly got to demonstrate his worth. He flew supply sorties in a Bristol Bombay, a lumbering transport aircraft with a fixed undercarriage. It was only ever lightly armed, but due to a shortage of tail guns some Bombays were even fitted with wooden dummies. Nicknamed 'Mother Duck' by the 8th Army, she brought the mail, but in Europe the Bombay was already obsolete.[12]

In June 1941 a new assignment changed everything for Charlie. His crew and four others from 216 Squadron were sent to RAF Kabrit on the edge of the Great Bitter Lake, near Ismailia and the Suez Canal. Their aircraft, each named after a London borough, had been put at the disposal of an eccentric Scots Guards colonel named David Stirling, commander of a shadowy unit known as 'L' Detachment. It was an untested venture, so Stirling was lucky to get them. Charlie's plane was L5847 Bermondsey. I came across a photo of a Bombay in the IWM collections, taken at Kabrit later that year. The pilot leans forward in the cockpit to watch the approach of 'L' Detachment' parachutists. My heart leaped to think I might have a picture of Charlie, however tiny. I enlarged the image – but, alas, this plane was 'Bishopsgate', the name painted on the side of the aircraft. Charlie had to be there, though, somewhere outside the frame of the photo, frustratingly hidden.

'L' Detachment were a curious bunch, not just because of their casual scruffiness and offhand indifference to rank, but because they were training for a new kind of warfare. In May, the Germans had used paratroopers to invade Crete, which had got Stirling thinking. Britain had no parachute regiment, but perhaps a small force of airborne commandos might attack Axis air bases and ammunition dumps in the Western Desert. That July, General Sir Claude Auchinleck was made commander-in-chief of the Middle East Command, and in order to relieve the siege of Tobruk planned a major offensive for November. Auchinleck agreed to give Colonel Stirling a chance to prove himself.[13]

Charlie flew 'L' Detachment on exercises, and although the men disliked his plane – it had no static parachute line and was so slow they joked about nipping out for a piss and running back in – they liked him.[14] Charlie earned their respect not only for his competence, especially during blistering sandstorms, but his good humour. Like them, he was both professional and a maverick, with nerves of steel and ice in his veins. This is how Charlie West became a founder member of the world-famous SAS – the Special Air Service.

Like Ralph, Charlie never had children, which meant no direct descendants to ask about his life. I did trace Charlie's niece Vanessa Steer and, from a list of executors on Charlie's wife's will, another niece, Emma Bassom. Both shared memories of their Uncle Charles. Emma confirmed what a generous, gentle man he'd been, and a lover of fast cars, and sent me his obituary from the SAS magazine. It was written by Ernie Bond, a member of 'L' Detachment, and later the first head of the Metropolitan Police's Bomb Squad. Miraculously, the obituary included a photo, which could only have been taken in Camp 65. Dom had sent me a very similar portrait given to him by the daughter of a POW, taken in October 1942. A diary I'd read recorded that prisoners were invited to put their names down to see the photographer, a civilian from Altamura, when he visited the camp.[15] The idea was that for a few lire men could get a nice picture to send home in a letter.

Charlie had a handsome, open face, with a wave in his side-parted hair, like the actor Kenneth More, who played RAF pilot Douglas Bader in a 1956 film about his exploits, another old Sunday afternoon favourite. Warrant Officer West was no dashing ace, but the fateful mission he flew in the winter of 1941, the first undertaken by the nascent SAS, was as dramatic as anything that happens in *Reach for the Sky*.

Auchinleck's offensive was due to begin at dawn on 18 November 1941. The plan was for 'L' Detachment, divided into five sections, one in each of the Bristol Bombays, to raid German airfields at Gazala and Timimi, destroying fighter aircraft ahead of the big push. The planes would muster at Fuka aerodrome near Mersa Matruh and prepare to depart on the evening of the 16th. Lieutenant Charles Bonington's section – No. 4 Flight – would fly in Bermondsey, piloted by Charlie West.

Stirling's fifty-four men and their aircrew gathered in the RAF mess for a hot meal, doing all they could to master their nerves. Charlie was annoyingly cheerful, celebrating the third anniversary of receiving his wings. Other airmen, however, considered this at best a 'guess-and-by-God operation', at worst a suicide mission. They waited on their proto-SAS guests at table, a final treat for men who might not be coming back.[16]

It was the worst storm for many years. At 7.15 p.m. the planes took off at intervals and flew for three hours until they reached the coast. Banking to return inland, they met a hail of Italian flak, then a sandstorm that obscured the drop zones. Undeterred, Stirling, in No. 1 Flight, dropped his men, as did three of the other flights, into a maelstrom of dust and rain. In disarray, the commands lost most of their equipment, including their bomb fuses. Lieutenant McGonigal, No. 2 Flight's commander, was killed and his men captured, and in all less than half of 'L' Detachment made it back. The mission was a disaster.[17]

Amid all the terror and confusion, Stirling hadn't even noticed that he'd lost Bonington's flight. Charlie West, trying to get his bearings at the coast but blinded by the downpour, had ducked through the cloud to 300 feet, where his plane was struck by anti-aircraft fire that damaged the instruments, fuel tanks and port engine.

'Right, it's suicide to drop here,' Charlie called to Bonington through the intercom. 'I'll take you back to Fuka.'

And with that, he steered Bermondsey westwards through skies furiously alive with flak and thunder and lightning, and in the distance the flashes of German bombers pounding the defenders at the port of Tobruk.

After fifty minutes, however, Charlie saw that he was nearly out of fuel and would have to land in the desert. This he did, in darkness, on one engine, buffeted by forty-mile-per-hour winds. Surveying the dunes, he reassured Bonington they were in Allied territory – but then discovered that a shell splinter lodged below his compass had tricked them into flying in a circle. Not only were they still behind enemy lines, they were on the edge of a German airfield at Gazala, 300 miles west of Cairo.

The SAS men considered running to the escarpment, beyond the aerodrome, but decided that the mission, even Auchinleck's entire bid to relieve Tobruk, might be jeopardized if they were caught. The rain was so heavy, though, Charlie decided to wait three hours till dawn before taking off again, with what little fuel he had left, and radioed base to get a location.

'Stand by, I will call you later' – this was Charlie's final message. A flight of Hurricanes was sent to find him and Bermondsey, but in vain.

At first light, Bonington led a patrol around the aircraft and spotted a row of tents. A figure emerged and began walking towards them. It was an Italian soldier, an astonished cook, whom they bundled into the cabin. Charlie took off, praying he had enough fuel to reach Tobruk, where he could belly flop into the harbour. But they had been spotted and gained hardly any height before they were hit by flak and had an Me-109 fighter swooping down on them, guns blazing.[18] Charlie knew they were going to crash, but kept his cool, closing the throttles, lowering the flaps and dead-sticking the plane into a shallow, level dive.[19]

Accounts of Operation Squatter, as the mission was known, focus on what happened to Stirling and his men. My interest was Charlie, flying L5847. Emma Bassom sent me a taped radio documentary about the birth of the SAS, in which Ernie Bond, Charlie's obituarist and the troop sergeant of No. 4 Flight, described vividly what happened inside Bermondsey after the Me-109 came in for the kill.[20]

They were, Bond recalled, blown apart. Cannon shells ripped through the fuselage, scattering white-hot debris. Bond felt as if 'somebody had hit me across the back of the head with a flail of nails, and down I went'. The next he knew he was lying in the sand, thirty yards from the crashed aircraft, an Italian soldier trying to twist the ring from his finger. That was the end of Ernie Bond's war. Bodies and wreckage were strewn across the sharp gravel and acacia bushes of the desert.[21]

A book about RAF escapers drew on Charles Bonington's unpublished memoir entitled 'War Is Half Luck', in which he recalled the crash that shattered his shoulder. I tried to find it through his son, the mountaineer Sir Chris Bonington, but without success. In a newspaper interview, Sir Chris did say that his father hadn't spoken much about the war, which included a spell in a POW camp from which he tried to escape. Sir Chris supposed this might be the source of his own adventuring spirit, which had led him to conquer Everest.[22]

From what I could glean at second-hand, Charles Bonington had said how well his men had known Charlie West and praised his 'marvellous three-point landing' in the desert. The memoir also described the tracer fire that had crippled the plane and how, as the Me-109 opened fire, the air gunner, Bill Humphries, collapsed. As Charlie dropped to 100 feet, the Italian prisoner started screaming, and Bonington felt a thud in his back. 'There was a flash inside the plane . . . [and] an almighty crash.' The impact threw Bonington clear of the plane, which came to a sickening halt, tipped up on its crushed nose.

All the SAS men were injured, one mortally. The co-pilot and wireless operator were dead; the flight engineer and Humphries, the air gunner, hurt but alive; and the navigator, who landed on a pile of bodies, miraculously unscathed. Charlie West lay unconscious,

Charlie

having smashed his head through the Plexiglas windscreen. In Ernie Bond's opinion, casualties would have been far worse but for 'the dedicated skill of Charles West in controlling the shattered airplane until the last possible moment before impact, and producing a violent tobogganing effect over the rough sandy ground'.[23]

It was 7 a.m. on 17 November. Italian troops began dragging bodies from the plane and robbing them, before the Germans arrived and surrounded the crash site. They were all for shooting the trembling Italian cook, suspected as a collaborator, but he was saved by the SAS men.[24] Charlie was lifted from the wrecked cockpit and stretchered into an ambulance which took him, and the others, to the field hospital at Gazala. There, still unconscious, Charlie was found to have a fractured skull, a broken shoulder and ribs, and a ruptured diaphragm. German surgeons operated, and assessed his condition to be serious but stable. He remained comatose and was fed through a tube.

In the National Archives, I found a thick Air Ministry file I'd overlooked on a previous visit. It contained notes, letters and various reports, including Charlie's own debrief, information regarding the 'army parachutists' and correspondence with the families of the deceased. After the crash, the soldiers and airmen had been reported missing, but further information had been slow to emerge after Auchinleck's offensive and the subsequent Allied advance.[25]

Bill Humphries lay in a coma at Derna for eleven days. His mother, Olive, a widow in Liverpool, worried herself sick. The Red Cross made an enquiry to the Wehrmacht High Command, who in January 1943 replied to say that he was in hospital. In fact, he had died nine days earlier, still comatose, and been buried at the lighthouse cemetery. When the news got through, Bill's sister was notified so she could tell their mother. In 1948, Bill's body was moved to Benghazi War Cemetery, where he lies today, the inscription on the headstone: 'In our thoughts you'll always be, although so far from home. Mother.' The German pilot responsible for his death was himself killed in the desert seven months later.[26]

*

It was a week before Charlie regained consciousness. He had no memory of his ordeal, but was relieved to find that except for some broken bones and a headache he was in one piece. In the next bed lay Ernie Bond, who told him about the crash.[27] The following day, the two men were separated. (Bond, too, ended up in Camp 65, but the obituary he wrote for Charlie doesn't mention it, so they must have been in different sectors.)

Charlie was flown to the hospital at Derna, and the next day put on a lorry to Benghazi, where he was kept under observation for another five days. Wounded men lay on camp beds in canvas tents, grey with shock, vomiting and excreting where they lay. Dysentery and diarrhoea were endemic, as were fevers and abscesses and cases where dust storms had embedded sand into the clear surface of men's eyes. There were aspirins and throat pastilles, but little else. POW medical officers worked long shifts on low rations (physiology training told them what was in the bully beef: blood vessels and lung tissue). A British medical officer reflected that in every way ordinary soldiers were worse off than their officers, and on ward rounds he felt 'like Elizabeth Fry visiting the prisons of old London'.[28]

On 5 December, Charlie was transferred to the main Italian-run camp near Benghazi harbour, which was divided into 'Big Pen', the main enclosure, and 'Top Pen', a holding area for embarkation. A constant din of workmen repairing bomb damage came from the harbour. By day men paced the sandy compound or rested in bivouacs and beneath palms. The latrines were cesspits carpeted with maggots; rations, the usual skilly and bully. Whenever the water tanks ran dry, there was anguished despair. Men drank their own urine. Allied air raids sent guards running in panic; the prisoners, who had no cover, stood up with kitbags on their heads against falling debris from anti-aircraft shells. The POWs were photographed for propaganda purposes, as if it had been the Italians who had captured them. Each night several hundred men were moved from the glare of the searchlights into half a dozen dark motor sheds with huge sliding doors. It was bitterly cold, and there was no bedding (officers were given mattresses).[29] Charlie's niece Emma remembered him saying he'd once had to sleep on a concrete floor. If this wasn't at Gravina, it was probably Benghazi.

In December, the Italians began emptying the camp. On the 7th, Charlie was shipped to Maleme on Crete, where he was readmitted to hospital for a month before being transferred to the prison hospital at Patras in the northern Peloponnese. It was raining and would soon be snowing. Discharged from hospital again, he was locked up in a verminous hut near the shore, where, like all POWs, he received a card from Pope Pius XII, offering his sympathies 'in your separation from distant homes at this Christmas season'.[30]

This Charlie endured until 5 March, when he was put on a boat. It took him through the Ionian Islands to Brindisi, where he was deloused and, like Ralph three months later, noticed large numbers of German transport planes lined up at an aerodrome. Then it was off to Camp 85 Tuturano, which at that time consisted solely of two wooden huts whose roofs leaked incessantly. Men there talked mostly of escape.[31]

After two months in Tuturano, on 7 May Charlie arrived at Camp 65 Gravina and was bunked in the Sector 2 WOs' block, near the *palazzina comando*. Five weeks later, he befriended Ralph and they immediately started discussing how to get out, observing the Italian officers' habits, timing the movements of the guards, examining the wire fences and surveying, as best they could, the territory beyond.

Ralph was swept along by Charlie's boundless ingenuity and enthusiasm. As all prisoners found, their best conversations were conducted over mugs of tea. Charlie built what was known as a 'blower': a charcoal-burning stove made from hammered-out Klim tins – Klim ('milk' backwards) being Canadian powdered milk – that boiled a pint of water in seven minutes, which he claimed as a record. Early models with miniature bellows had evolved into contraptions like his, which used a hand-cranked turbine to draw air into the fire chamber. Everything stopped at 4 p.m. for the tea ritual: one prisoner described smoky huddles all over the place, 'like a Red

Indian reservation'. 'The brew must go on' – that was the camp motto. And, thanks to Red Cross parcels and inventors like Charlie, it did.³²

September 2021. By now, I had a strong feeling for this camp, and needed to experience it for myself. It was time to walk the ground, projecting images onto space, imagining and feeling – 'the archive of the feet', a historian once called it.³³ I had been planning a trip to Altamura the previous spring, when the pandemic struck. As in wartime, the nation came to know the frustrations of incarceration and resulting fantasies of escape.

Through those long months of Covid my friendship with Dom, my fellow Sixty-Fiver in Altamura, grew, even though we'd still never met. I also read a lot and took the dog on long lockdown walks. Pausing on a hillside at dusk, the lighted windows of a farm below, I imagined having to knock for food there and beg a cold bed in the byre. I saw Camp 65 in the floodlights of a deserted sports ground and in barbed wire fences; every hedgerow and field drain looked like somewhere an escaper might hide.

I rewatched John Sturges's *The Great Escape*. I'd forgotten the scene where two prisoners, James Garner as 'The Scrounger' and Donald Pleasence, playing Stalag Luft III's forger, steal a German plane to fly to Switzerland. Against the swelling strings of the score, they climb unsteadily over the Alps. This never really happened, of course, but to Sturges it must have seemed an irresistible consummation of the POW's dream of freedom. I rediscovered other war films I'd not seen for forty years, all that mischievous fun masking the miserable reality of prison life.[34]

And then the pandemic was over. Restrictions were lifted, and people dusted off their plans. The Camp 65 Association arranged a three-day festival of events in Altamura, and invited me to give a talk. I made arrangements with Dom and booked a flight to Bari.

PART THREE
Flight

7.

Flashes and Sparks

Sunday morning: up at first light and out into the ancient lanes. It felt furtive, wild, as if I myself were escaping. The late-summer sky was a luminous mauve as I crossed the high road and strode down the hill, all eerily quiet and deserted except for a couple of women mopping front steps and a cat arching its back.

Turning onto Via Gravina, a long, straight road through an industrial estate, the air smelled faintly of burned rubber and ripe garbage. Behind, a white sun was peeping over the horizon, chasing away the thin cloud. There was hardly any traffic. As the road curved into the ochre terrain of the Altopiano delle Murge, the Puglian plateau at the top of Italy's heel, I wished I'd brought more water.

Joining the highway, I walked along the verge until away to the left something caught my eye: a glimpse of grey, box-like structures, like standing stones radiating power across the landscape. It made my spine tingle. Crossing over, I headed up a dirt track to the concrete posts of the main gate. Charlie and Ralph had stood right there.

I had landed in Bari on the Wednesday, full of excited anticipation. I presented my Covid vaccination certificate and had my temperature taken, then was waylaid by a customs official, who suspected me of smuggling currency. Then I was out through the sliding doors into the warm night air. And there was Dom in T-shirt and jeans, taller than I'd imagined, grinning broadly, arms wide for a hug – a brotherly reunion of physical strangers.

In the car we looked at each other for a moment – he had short hair, greying like mine, and dark, intelligent eyes – then talked enthusiastically all the way to Altamura. I gave a summary of the latest things I'd learned about Ralph and Charlie, and Dom updated me on the work of the Camp 65 Association. He also told me more about his background, and that his father, born a century earlier, had been an artillery officer during the war – but, Dom confessed, he hadn't become truly interested in his story until it was too late.

We strolled through the winding lamplit streets of Altamura's old town, bougainvillea spilling over balconies, flagstones and cobbles worn smooth by time. Dom pointed out an iron manhole cover bearing the *fascio littorio*.

Amazed, I said: 'Imagine that was a swastika in Germany!'

Dom agreed. 'But not all people here think Mussolini was such a bad man.'

We found a trattoria still open at 11 p.m. and ordered pizzas. After we'd finished, the burly chef-patron came over, and Dom explained why I'd come. Pouring glasses of digestif, the man showed us photos of the herbs he foraged to make it. During the war, he added, his father had been a fugitive POW in Albania forced to eat such things.

'La guerra è merda,' he said, with an expansive shrug – war is shit. 'But it brings people together, makes them do incredible things.' And from that, he continued, topping up our glasses, war makes 'storie incredibili'.

The next morning, in fine weather, I walked up to Monastero del Soccorso, the venue for the Camp 65 festival, which was set to last all week. I was itching to get to Gravina, but it would have to wait. In the colonnaded courtyard, Dom introduced me to many people, including an archaeologist who informed me that the site of the camp was half the size of Pompeii and every bit as interesting. He showed me a wartime architect's plan, and gave me a copy of his book. I listened to the talks – though most were in impenetrable Italian – and gave my own about Ralph and Charlie. Then, at last, Sunday came, and I was free to visit the camp, adding a strange sense of apprehension to the longing I'd been feeling. Dom had offered to drive me there – but I was determined to walk, so as to re-enter that lost world alone, at a steady pace, in quiet meditation.

Entering Camp 65 was like landing on a barren planet and discovering the ruins of some failed colony. The terrain resembled a vast upturned bowl: seventy-seven acres of dusty ground littered with bottles and rusted cans, sheep droppings and snail shells, punctuated by a scatter of dilapidated buildings. Thistles poked out among the twisted iron and rubble, and amaryllis flowers put on brave faces. It was quiet and still, the only movement lizards flitting from the scrub and a fox breaking cover. In the distance, the muffled blast of a shotgun, followed by the barking of a dog. It was a zone of haunted isolation, in time as well as space.

The silence and rising heat were oppressive. The air crackled. Past the edifice of the administration building, four storeys high and well preserved, I trudged round the perimeter, which was marked off at intervals by massive concrete watchtowers, also more or less intact. Checking the compass on my phone, I scanned the eastern horizon, a smudge of smoky haze, before turning south, where the brow of a hill met the sky and huge clouds cast shadows over the land. There, incredibly, stood the same solitary tree that the artist Robert Lee and other prisoners had stared at, wondering what lay beyond.

I stepped cautiously into a remarkably well-preserved blockhouse, with its long, echoing corridor and bays where bunks once stood and unlucky prisoners slept on the hard floor. These bays were now quite bare, although I noticed the snapped-off ends of dowel rods where cupboards made from parcel boxes had once been fixed to the wall. I called Mum using FaceTime, so she could see what I was seeing. It made her go 'all goosey', and I heard a catch in her voice. 'To think what Uncle Ralph went through!' she said.

By now the sun was ferocious, and I was being dive-bombed by insects, descendants of the creatures that had tormented Ralph. The only shade lay inside the ruins. I sat on a block of fallen masonry, took a sip of water and ate some chocolate, an emergency breakfast I'd bought from a machine on Via Gravina. It was soft and speckled white with age. I studied the maps and illustrations from the archaeologist's book, rotating the pages to align myself with what once had been there, and felt the ghostly frisson of the prisoners.

Early December 1942 was the worst time. After the influx of South Africans from Tobruk, the tally of prisoners exceeded 8,000, while packages and letters from home were taking six weeks to arrive from Britain, and three times as long from South Africa and New Zealand. If they were lucky, men received a Red Cross parcel to share once a fortnight.[1] Thoughts of Christmas with families weighed heavily. There were fevers and stomach upsets, and morale hit rock bottom. Ralph and his policemen passed on complaints to their camp leader, RSM Wilf Alderson, and were blamed by the men when nothing was done.

Alderson, who had succeeded Les Munday, did try to improve conditions. Several years older than Ralph, he was both a fellow Yorkshireman and a veteran of the 150th Brigade box at Gazala. A photograph taken in the desert, of Ralph with two comrades wearing steel helmets, had Alderson's name on the back. Ralph described him as a small man who did big things, including making sure every prisoner at least had a mattress, securing help for the sports and welfare committees, and obtaining a copy of the Geneva Convention with which to lecture the commandant. But what everyone needed was food.[2]

Then, on the 13th, their prayers were answered. A large consignment of Christmas goodies arrived, transforming the mood across the four sectors. Every man was to get his own parcel, a prospect which had them sharing visions of Dickensian table-groaning feasts.[3] While some prisoners salivated, however, others lay dangerously sick, neglected by the Italian authorities. On the 18th, a Royal Engineers sapper with diphtheria suffocated after a guard refused to fetch help. The men halted their celebrations, parading silently as his body was taken to Altamura, 1,500 miles from home on the Suffolk coast.[4]

On the 21st, prisoners drew lots for either an Indian or a Canadian parcel, the latter prized because it contained sugar.⁵ Then two days later, as if this excitement wasn't enough, the Italians began taking a few men from each hut on conducted walks up and down Via Gravina. In the evening, the curtain went up on the Sector 4 Dramatic Society's pantomime 'Aladdin and His Magic Embers' – a reference to the precious coals passed around for tea-fires. Ralph, restrained in so many ways, was full of admiration.⁶

On the morning of Christmas Eve, ordinary parcels were issued, then in the afternoon prisoners queued for the festive ones, plus a special issue from the Italians of firewood, olive oil, tomato puree, cheese and cigarettes. Each man also received an orange – a personal gift from the commandant – and a diary from the Vatican. Washing lines and food tin labels were fashioned into bunting, and a prisoner dressed up as Santa Claus. In the evening, men toured the bunks singing carols, and at midnight there was holy communion.

As the sun came up on Christmas Day, the NCOs – though not the warrant officers – brought men tea in bed, then came breakfasts of fried meat roll, toast and jam. Most parcels also contained half a pound of chocolate, biscuits, a plum pudding, a fruitcake with a snowy cottage on the label – even a sprig of holly. Many rich meals were concocted that day – tinned steak with macaroni, sardines and cheese on toast, bully beef with onions – on which prisoners made themselves merrily sick.⁷

On New Year's Eve, they stayed up till midnight to toast loved ones with mugs of tea, praying for 1943 to be the year of freedom and reunion. But men were already slipping back into the doldrums, holed up against freezing weather, living off basic rations. Supply columns to the camp were waylaid by the winter mud or suspended altogether. No parcels came for three weeks, and servings of skilly, which now contained very little fat, were reduced by a quarter. Only the warrant officers still had decent uniforms, most men having supplemented what was left of their battledress with foreign oddments. Italian army boots were issued but these soon disintegrated.⁸

At the end of January, numbers in the camp hit a new high: almost

9,000. Blockhouses intended for 336 men now housed over 350, and the South Africans still had no beds. Firewood was scarce. Light bulbs were not replaced, and the electricity supply faltered, dimming the lighting, including the perimeter arc lights, or cutting it altogether. The water supply was as erratic as ever, and now affected every part of the camp. Sector 3 had no hot water for several weeks. The cookhouses were critically overstretched. In Sector 2, where Ralph and Charlie lived, the pots and pans were worn out. Vermin abounded. The authorities promised that the two new sectors, when finished, would solve all these problems – but from what Ralph and Charlie could see through the wire little was happening. Like so much else, the project would be completed 'domani' or, worse, 'dopodomani' – never.[9]

'Everyone's nerves are on edge,' a prisoner wrote in his diary, 'and everyone is thoroughly fed up and miserable.' The most dejected men lay in the infirmaries, which were also unheated, without bedpans, let alone medicines, and overwhelmed by cases of dysentery, rheumatism, jaundice, nephritis and, increasingly, malaria.[10] Charlie West had had his first bout of malaria back in August and was given mepacrine – a quinine substitute that turned the skin yellow and was thought to cause psychosis. Mepacrine suppressed the parasite in the blood within days, but like all medicines was in short supply, meaning that Charlie's attacks recurred every few weeks. Ralph nursed him when they were mild; if severe, Charlie was hospitalized in primitive conditions: one prisoner described being left alone for a month in a vermin-infested tent. Intense chills became high fevers with a profusion of sweating and cramps lasting several hours, leaving Charlie in a state of all-consuming lethargy.[11]

By the end of February 1943 some parcels had arrived, from home as well as from the Red Cross. Like Canadian parcels with their sugar, Scottish ones were popular because they contained oatmeal to make sustaining porridge; those from Argentina (which was sympathetic to the Axis powers yet nominally neutral) were a special treat owing to their sirloin steaks, meatballs and honey. Good news also made its way into the camp. The Russians had crushed the

German 6th Army and the Italian 8th Army at Stalingrad, and Tripoli, the heart of Mussolini's Libyan empire, had fallen to the Allies.[12]

This flush of optimism, as well as better nourishment, kindled thoughts of escaping – albeit in 'escapers' rather than 'keepers'. 'Either we thought and planned and talked only about the possibilities of escape', a prisoner recalled, 'or else we . . . allowed ourselves gradually to accept our state as one which, though unpleasant, could not continue for ever.' This was not unreasonable, especially among men who had been weak with hunger.[13] Nor did Camp 65 have an escape committee, which in officer camps was a valuable source of confidence for men and coherence for their plans. In Sector 5, however, the authoritarian South African camp leader, John Rossouw, insisted on vetting all escape proposals, and censured prisoners who went ahead without his personal approval.[14]

As ever, most men cared more for escapism than escaping. A prime example was Camp 65's Anti-Boredom Committee. If, as one POW claimed, the Italians were committed to 'undermining the morale and minds of the prisoners by inflicting boredom', this group's pranks were the resistance. When the commandant showed an interest in prisoners' home lives, the committee guessed he was slyly casting about for skills to harness for the Italian war effort. Questionnaires about civilian occupations were returned with replies such as 'Snow White's personal assistant', 'Dodo hunter's arrow-maker' and 'Archbishop of Canterbury's wand holder'. There was also a professional glass-beater and a graduate of the University of Wormwood Scrubs. A few of these invented jobs were read out at check parade, until Lieutenant Colonel Coppola realized he'd been had.[15]

The motive behind the theft of a sentry box in November 1942 had been a shortage of firewood – but the comedy of it proved an even greater benefit, especially since during Coppola's outburst – he threatened to have guards sent to the Russian Front – prisoners hoisted a second sentry box over the fence, quickly destroyed it and spirited the pieces away.[16] Naturally the Allied camp police took a dim view of such antics, which was another reason the men disliked them so much.

Many men lost themselves in study, sports and handicrafts. One artisan, who had managed to keep his wristwatch and was sick of being asked the time, spent six months making a pendulum clock from Klim tins, can openers and springs from a helmet strap. It had a tick like a trip hammer, but kept such good time that the commandant, who favoured lawful anti-boredom activities, would check his watch by it.[17] Prisoners did almost anything to pass the time. There were even experiments in 'thought transference', which yielded impressive results. Perhaps inspired by a production of Noël Coward's *Blithe Spirit*, a smash-hit in the West End since 1941, men held spiritualist seances and dabbled in Ouija boards, attempting to contact dead comrades and divine when the war would end.[18]

At Gravina, escape attempts had never amounted to much. Shortly before Ralph arrived, a prisoner in an Italian army infirmary had slipped through a window, but without boots he was soon caught. A few weeks later, a Royal Artillery gunner and a Royal Navy seaman climbed onto a blockhouse roof in Ralph's sector, intending to jump the fence into the unfinished Sector 1. This bid also failed: a guard opened fire, grazing the soldier's jaw; the sailor was beaten up. Of four men who went under the fence in the summer of 1942, one was immediately recaptured, the rest a few days later.[19] In October, a pair of warrant officers in Sector 5 had arranged for Cypriot prisoners to put on a sale of goods to distract the guards while they made off. The two men had avoided check parades by pretending to be unwell, then arranged to be replaced in their beds by dummies. Everything had gone to plan, but they were apprehended sixty miles away after failing to return a peasant's *buongiorno*.[20]

Among the passive mass of 'keepers', the consensus was that 'escapers' achieved nothing except provoking the Italians into making them spend senseless hours on parade and denying them parcels as punishment. Better if everyone just sat things out until the Allies arrived. Switzerland was too far away – and even if there had been a nearer border, the Italian population was believed to be too hostile for any prisoner to reach it. The source of this hostility may have been fear of reprisal more than hatred for an enemy – but to an escaped prisoner it amounted to the same thing.

Charlie and Ralph, ardent students of failed escapes, were only too aware of the difficulty. 'To escape from inside the prison is not enough,' Charlie was given to saying. 'One must escape from those outside.' Any contact with civilians could scupper a plan – even, as the Sector 5 escapers had found, something as trivial as an unreturned greeting.[21]

All Ralph and Charlie's discussions in the second half of 1942 had hit up against this problem, then, during the winter, petered out with Charlie's malaria and the shortage of food, which precluded any being squirrelled away. By the following spring, however, things looked rosier. In better health and ebullient spirits, Charlie had been holding classes in navigation and wireless communication. Escaping was back on, and he and Ralph spoke of it often. Yet still they had no idea how to make an escape work.

One day they fell into conversation with a South African pilot familiar with German Junkers 52 transport planes. Charlie quizzed him about the Ju-52's superstructure, control panel and starting system, and solicited sketched diagrams. Ralph marvelled as the spark of an idea took flame, but for now left the pilots to talk shop.

An hour later, he was in the WOs' hut making tea when Charlie came back. Ralph handed him a mug, which he drained in pensive silence. Then suddenly, he said:

'Have you ever been to Brindisi, Sleuth?'

'Yes. Why?' This was the port through which they had both entered Italy.

'See any planes on the aerodrome there?'

'Naturally,' replied Ralph stiffly. 'Jerry transports.'

'Just so,' winked Charlie. 'And I've got the dope on 'em.'

Guessing the idea now, Ralph interjected, but Charlie carried on regardless. 'I know there are plenty of difficulties, but this idea definitely has a chance of success, more than any chance of making Switzerland ever had.'[22]

That evening, they considered the problems of getting to Brindisi.

The Glass Mountain

It was 100 miles away, they had no compass and the only available maps were unreliable. Aerodromes were heavily guarded. They had no suitable clothing. Civilians were likely to be unhelpful at best. And no one had ever tried anything like it before. In Charlie's opinion, this last objection – one of many made by Ralph – was the least off-putting. In fact, he suggested, it was the idea's madcap originality that made it so appealing.

'We'd be fools not to have a shot at it,' he grinned. Sleuth was forced to agree.[23]

They began setting aside sugar, oatmeal, biscuits and raisins – a hard yet vital act of self-denial. When dried figs went on sale in the shop, Ralph blew two weeks' wages on a two-pound block for their store. A few days later, both men received parcels from home – Charlie's from his mother, Ralph's from Flo – which between them contained six pounds of chocolate, and was also stowed away. Ralph laid hands on a simple compass and hid it. More than once the *carabinieri* searched their quarters, while Ralph and Charlie waited outside having palpitations. They began taking morning exercise to get fit, and Charlie taught Ralph everything he'd learned about the Ju-52: how to release it from its holdings, boost the engines and so on. They also worked on the part of the plan that so far had received least attention: how they were actually going to break out.

This would require help. It was known that informers within the prison community tipped off the Italians about intended escapes, so the plan was shared only with RSM Alderson and a few other warrant officers. No ordinary soldier was to be trusted. Alderson approved, and Charlie asked Ralph and an RAF flight sergeant named Hugh Owen to help with some dangerous experiments. The recurrent dipping of the electrical supply to the camp, and the consequent dimming of the lights, often for four or five minutes at a stretch, had given Charlie an idea. What if he could control this? If he subdued the lamps himself, it might cover an escape without attracting suspicion.

Initial tests were disappointing. Charlie discovered that the lighting system was on a direct circuit, which made it impossible to control. Instead, he turned his attention to the electrical cable suspended above the cookhouse, which ran down into their sleeping quarters. A homemade ladder was mounted on a table inside the hut, enabling Charlie to reach the cable where it came in through the roof. Wearing thick rubber gloves, he went to work with a knife and a pair of self-locking medical tongs. Ralph stood on the table gripping the ladder, while others kept lookout at the windows. Outside, a warrant officer was loitering in the shadows watching for any alteration in brightness.

Charlie bared two wires and, taking a breath, seized them with the tongs. Ralph, who nearly fell off the table at what happened next, picked up the story:

> There was a blinding flash of light followed by a shower of sparks and a loud crackling noise. Lights in our quarters had been switched off before the experiment so we did not know what was happening outside. The flashes and sparks continued. The cable wires grew red hot, and WO West had to release the tongs because of the heat . . . The door, which had previously been locked, was then opened and a wild looking warrant officer thrust his head inside, and said, very excitedly: 'It's a success – all the lights in the camp went dim, but for God's sake cover the windows next time, it looks like a firework display from outside.'

Ralph and Charlie went for a walk, and noticed nothing unusual among the sentries, who they guessed would assume the dipping of the lights had been caused by an outage at the power station. They went to bed in high spirits.[24]

The rest of February was spent hoarding more food and acquiring kit. Through an obliging South African, a fellow warrant officer, Ralph procured two pairs of sand-coloured overalls, the kind used by tank crews in the desert, hard-wearing with plenty of pockets. He and Charlie also cadged a new watch, a pair of wire cutters, and some rough maps from the Cypriots. The last of their biscuits were ground into powder, mixed with saved-up oatmeal, sugar and raisins, and poured into cloth food bags. There was enough now, they reckoned, for the twelve days needed to reach Brindisi.

They chose an exit point facing east, near the WOs' hut and partially hidden by the cookhouse, which between 9 p.m. and 6 a.m. was out of bounds to all prisoners except the camp police, who conveniently took their orders from Ralph. Studying the pattern of the wire, strung vertically and horizontally, they discussed where best to cut it. They also observed patrols, noting how the fences were always checked using the mobile arc light before the sentries changed over at 10 p.m. This would provide a window of forty minutes.

Then Ralph and Charlie set a date for their escape: the moonless night of 3 March.

8.

Pursued Hares

Having feigned sickness for three consecutive mornings, when 3 March dawned, Ralph felt genuinely unwell. Charlie was due another attack of malaria, but for the moment he was full of vim and vigour, tempered by a cool, focused resolve.[1]

Pretending to be ill, they knew, had been tried five months earlier as part of the camp's most promising, if ultimately doomed, escape attempt. The Italians, who were surprisingly vigilant, were certain to be wise to it – but so far there had been no hint of suspicion during check parade, probably because officers and guards feared contracting an infectious disease were they to inspect Ralph and Charlie in their bunks.

The day was spent rehearsing their self-imposed orders, which were similarly informed by previous escape bids. The most important of these were: first, to travel only by night; and second, to avoid places of habitation, likewise bridges, which were invariably guarded. They also decided on a structure of mealtimes, when their rations of the oatmeal, sugar, biscuit flour and raisin mixture – O.S.B.R. for short – would be eaten.

Ralph felt queasy and fidgeted, frequently getting up to fiddle with bits of his kit or look out of the window at the weather, which all day remained overcast but dry. Charlie just lay there, calmly meditative, ready for anything.

At 6 p.m., Ralph summoned three of his most trusted camp policemen and explained the plan. One, a former constable from Derbyshire, would at Ralph's signal alert Hugh Owen, who was in charge of dimming the lights. The second, a Scots Guards sergeant who spoke some Italian, was told to waylay any patrols approaching the cookhouse. And the third, a salt-of-the-earth Bradford man, was to remain in the cookhouse and make noise however he saw fit. He decided on loud, tuneless singing – his speciality. Ralph then asked a Greek Cypriot POW, another camp policeman and a fluent Italian speaker who had previously helped him, to engage the nearest sentry in conversation as soon as the lights went down. The Sector 2 camp leader, RSM Alderson, was also on hand to assist.

At 8 p.m. the escapers ate a good meal – Charlie with gusto, Ralph forcing it down – and an hour later began to dress. Each put on two vests, two pairs of socks, battledress blouse and trousers, well-greased boots and webbing gaiters. Pockets were stuffed with bootlaces, string, safety pins and matches, as well as their shaving kits. Ralph tucked a knife in a gaiter and made sure he had plenty of cigarettes; Charlie, a non-smoker, took an Italian dictionary and a supply of mepacrine tablets. Round their waists went towels strung with bags of O.S.B.R., after which they pinned spare socks in the armpits of their serge blouses and squeezed into the overalls, wriggling to fit them over their stuffed battledress. In breast pockets they packed the slabs of chocolate, so innocently despatched in Wombwell and Plymouth but now part of a perilous escape plan. Only then did Ralph remember his dried figs, which he wedged in the breast of his overalls before buttoning them up and tightening the belt. Charlie pocketed the compass and maps where he could most easily reach them.

Ralph could hardly inflate his lungs; Charlie had difficulty walking. They felt like balloons, and the other warrant officers, who had been watching the preparations, burst out laughing. This broke some of the tension in the hut, and even Ralph couldn't help but smile as Charlie lumbered around the room like a portly robot.

Hardly bending at the waist, they sat down. Ralph, checking his watch compulsively, found that 10 p.m. came round all too quickly. 'As the seconds ticked away,' he recalled, 'I began to get a queer feeling low down in my stomach . . . a condition, I believe, which nearly all British soldiers have experienced at some time or other during the war.'[2]

After a few minutes, the signal came from outside. Heaving themselves upright, Ralph and Charlie were helped into their greatcoats. Dummies made from spare clothes and tropical pith helmets were arranged under blankets in the escapers' bunks – the trick used in the Sector 5 escape the previous October. Charlie opened the door, and Ralph grabbed the water bottle and wire cutters from his bed. The other warrant officers wished them well, while Flight Sergeant Owen stood by with rubber gloves and tongs.

The bulb outside the hut shone a pale cone on the threshold; the only light beyond was the sickly yellow glow of the fence lamps. The air was cool, the sky a ceiling of impenetrable black. They crossed the muddy path to the cookhouse, which was in complete darkness. Nodding to the Scots Guards sergeant on watch, they hurried through the door.

Inside, with its smell of grease and huge kettles and ranges, they pulled off their greatcoats. Waiting in the stoke-room were RSM Alderson and the three camp policemen, their faces just visible by the faint light washing through the windows. Alderson reported that the guards with the mobile arc light had gone, meaning the coast was clear. They moved towards the rear of the building, where the door was already open, framing illumination from the fence just a few yards away.

It was like the curtain had lifted on a dazzling stage and this was their cue. Charlie went out first, dropping onto his front behind a mound of firewood that one of the warrant officers had helpfully stacked outside the door. Ralph followed. Pulse racing, he realized that even the Gazala Cauldron, where he'd been chased by Rommel and dive-bombed by Stukas, hadn't prepared him for this. For a moment, he wished himself elsewhere:

> Now that the moment for action was here, I didn't feel too good . . . there was a lot to be said for washing the whole thing out, withdrawing quietly, and popping back to a nice warm bed. Such things passed through my mind as I waited there during what might be termed the initial minute of my escape.

But what Ralph considered childish thoughts and feelings were swiftly chased away. He was determined to prove himself to RSM Alderson and his policemen hiding in the shadows, and to Charlie, with his unwavering composure.[3]

Behind the first fence, 100 feet to the left, loomed a watchtower mounted with a machine gun, its line of fire directly down the corridor between the two walls of wire. The sentry box to their right was much closer, barely fifteen feet away. They could see the tips of the guard's boots and couldn't move until he did. Minutes ticked agonizingly by. Then at last the guard strolled away. Passing the wire cutters to Charlie, Ralph signalled to the ex-Derby constable, who ran across to the WOs' hut to alert Hugh Owen.

There and throughout the camp, magically, the lights waned to a fuzzy pallor. The Bradford man began singing 'Roll Out the Barrel' so raucously that Ralph and Charlie barely heard RSM Alderson whisper 'good luck!' as they left the cover of the wood pile, wriggling towards the fence. They were fully exposed, albeit in a much reduced glare.

The ten-foot fence was tightly criss-crossed with barbed wire. By now, Ralph's heart was thumping in his ears like a steam hammer, palms running wet as he waited for Charlie to make the first cut. It was tougher than they'd imagined. Ralph had a go. Grasping the cutters in both hands, he just about managed to snap the down-wires near their base, as they'd planned, then propped up the cross wires with a pair of specially-made notched sticks. This allowed just enough clearance for Charlie to shuffle under on his back, pushing with his heels.

It seemed to take an age. Once Charlie was clear, Ralph repeated the manoeuvre, but the belt of his overalls snagged on a barb, snaring him there until Charlie crawled back to help. They replaced the wires as best they could, then approached the next barrier. Hearing the reassuring voice of their Greek Cypriot accomplice, Ralph tackled the second fence. But it was a tussle, and the sweat was pouring out of him.

Charlie touched his shoulder. 'There isn't time, Sleuth. It'll take too long,' he hissed. 'There's only one way now and that's over the top.'

The escapers pressed themselves against the fence, squinting back at the Cypriot, who was casually chatting with the sentry barely fifteen yards away. There was no way back now, but still Ralph's thoughts were gripped by the madness of what they were doing. They knew Hugh Owen wouldn't be able to keep the lights down much longer, and if they came back up while he and Charlie were on top of the fence, the guard operating the machine gun would knock them off like a pair of coconuts in a shy.

Charlie, who an hour earlier had barely been able to walk, was up there like a monkey, and for a split second Ralph saw him silhouetted against a shaft of dimmed lamplight. Then he was over and disappeared into the darkness.

Now it was Ralph's turn. He clambered up the same way, struggling to hold the wire cutters and water bottle. Keeping an eye on the dark shapes in the watchtower, he lowered himself down the curtain of wire into the unfinished Sector 1. Charlie was waiting. Though unfamiliar, they knew this part of the camp was routinely patrolled, so they picked their way through the building materials and equipment in a brisk yet cautious crouch.

Behind them they could hear no raised voices or alarms, only their Bradford singer who, Ralph noted, had progressed from music hall to *The Mikado* and was leading the others in a full-throated rendition of 'A Wand'ring Minstrel, I' – 'A thing of shreds and patches, Of ballads, songs and snatches . . . And dreamy lullaby.'

They scampered into a half-built blockhouse, where Ralph wiped his face and sighed with relief. Hastening along the dark central corridor, they exited at the far end. The camp lights flicked back to brightness, but already they were hidden from view on the far side of the building. They continued the short distance to the outer perimeter, a low wall at the edge of a dell. In the distance lay the town of Altamura, barely visible in the blackout, which they planned to skirt round in a wide southern arc to remain concealed in what they hoped would be sparsely populated countryside.

They tore down the hill – 'like a couple of pursued hares', Ralph recalled – and up the other side, stumbling on stones as their vision fully adjusted to the night. After negotiating this rough terrain for what felt like hours, they paused, both men blowing hard yet tingling with excitement. Out of range of the mobile arc light, they looked back on the camp with wonder. It suddenly seemed small, diminished, planted in a pool of light that illuminated a canopy of cloud drawn low across an indigo sky.

Ralph checked his watch, amazed it was only 10.45 p.m. Charlie struck a match to read the compass and maps, and predicted that in a mile they should reach a railway line. This they must put quickly behind them. Trains and stations were under strict military control, and if news had been wired from the camp, any soldiers in the area would be on high alert.

They set off again, and after another thirty minutes came to the top of a small rise. Peering over, they could just make out the railway track and a farmhouse to their left. They lay still a while, ears pricked up, then, hearing nothing unusual, descended towards the track, which cut across the open fields on a raised layer of ballast. A dog at the farm started barking, prompting the escapers to scurry forward under the loose signal wires and over the rails and sleepers.

Dom arrived at the camp at midday, by which time I was hot and thirsty and glad to see him. Like Charlie, he was the sort of charismatic man who inspired confidence, and had of course brought water and snacks. Three days earlier I'd seen him – appropriately enough, in Altamura's Piazza della Resistenza – confront a thickset shopkeeper who had called him a communist on Facebook for daring to raise awareness about Camp 65's history. The face-to-face, hand-to-hand, gesticulation made me worried I'd have to intervene. But Dom had it under control. And it was in his nature to take a stand, to do the right thing.

He showed me round the site. In what would have been Sector 2, we identified the location of Ralph and Charlie's hut, and nearby where the warrant officers' cookhouse had stood. All that remained were the outline of the walls and a tile-covered floor. In early 1943, this was the nearest building to the outer fence on the east side, overlooking the incomplete Sector 1. Crouching at the back door, now just a gap in the footprint, gave me butterflies – a soft echo through time of 'the queer feeling low down in my stomach' that Ralph had experienced on that spot in March 1943. I felt compelled to lie on my front, as he had, face in the dust, but somehow, just too close to the past, couldn't bring myself to do it.

We sat down in the shade of the camp's old main electricity box and drank some water. Dom was incredulous about Charlie causing a power cut, and without Ralph's memoir I might have been sceptical myself. After all, this is what happens in the old movie *Danger Within*, set in an Italian POW camp in 1943 – with disastrous results.[4] We talked about the differences in the friends' characters. I related how in the memoir Ralph had confessed to being nervous, which embarrassed him, not least because the perfectly composed Charlie had simply forged ahead.

'Did Ralph hold back his emotions?' Dom asked. I guessed he already knew the answer and wanted to talk about his father. Michele Bolognese was only seven years younger than Ralph, an upright army officer of the old school and similarly reserved. Dom's usual affability stiffened into seriousness – a trace of the father showing through as his son remembered him: a strict, dignified gentleman, self-possessed, restrained in manners and rock solid in his convictions. Listening to him speak, I knew if it had been the two of us planning to escape, Dom would have led the way and I would have followed.

With the sun now at its zenith, we wandered back to the site of the cookhouse to see where Ralph and Charlie had gone next. Dom pored over a copy of the Camp 65 Association's book, which contained a few contemporary photographs, some from the National Archives in Kew, others from an archive in Rome. Batting away insects, he pointed to an image of a small building, whose elevated roof section identified it as a cookhouse.

'This is Ralph's kitchen. The actual one where we are standing now.'

I looked harder at the picture. There was the extant landmark water tower. Men in greatcoats and forage caps were hanging about on the stony ground beneath pointless holiday skies – their indistinct spirits all around us. Dom showed me another photo, this time of one side of the perimeter fence, showing the gable ends of the blockhouses and on the right-hand side part of a cookhouse. With a jolt, I realized where it was. Facing south, there in the foreground was the site for Sector 1, its construction barely begun. Dom smiled as the penny dropped. Our cookhouse had to be the same one in both photos, which meant the second one gave a good view of where Ralph and Charlie had crawled out on their bellies and escaped.

Outside the foundations of the stoke-room, we identified the precise spot where they'd cut the wire. Pausing, we saw that the escape-point photo must have been taken from the watchtower under whose gaze they had climbed the fence. Of all the places the photographer might have recorded, he had by chance chosen this momentous location.

Just over a collapsed stone wall lay the valley of coarse grass through which Ralph and Charlie had made off, jinking wildly through the night. We continued down the dell to the rise on the far side. So, where was the railway track? Having earlier passed a bridge on my hike to Gravina, I thought I knew – but Dom said it made no sense for Ralph and Charlie to have gone in that direction. As history and geography realigned in his mind, a faraway, resolute look came over him. And, not for the last time, he accidentally called me Ralph.

'We'll go in the car, then we'll see,' Dom said confidently. 'But first, we eat.'

At their house on the outskirts of Altamura, Dom's wife Tina welcomed us with orecchiette and a tomato sauce in which meat had been simmering all morning. Sunday lunch, Puglia style. There was Primitivo wine – but I was parched and gulped down glass after glass of water. Once the dishes had been cleared, I asked Dom about his dramatic stand-off in the Piazza della Resistenza.

'You have to engage people you disagree with, and always stand up to fascists,' he said with a defiant nod. 'I learned it from my father.' Dom fetched a photograph of an officer in military uniform astride a horse, Michele Bolognese, bearing a striking resemblance to his son. 'Your opponents can hate truth, but without arguments of their own they will back down.'

He glanced at the clock. 'We should go.'

Since the war, the countryside surrounding Camp 65 has been confusingly criss-crossed by slip-roads and dual carriageways. Dom careered this way and that, as we tried to align ourselves with the fugitives' direction of travel. But we kept ending up on rough tracks to nowhere, and making dusty, frustrated three-point turns.

Turning off a lane onto an inclining dirt road, we continued a short distance until our way was barred by a farm gate. So we got out to survey the rolling landscape – Dom like a general preparing for battle, me his baffled adjutant. Frowning into the distance, he raised an arm and pointed.

'Look,' he said with renewed conviction. 'There's the camp, and here is the farmhouse – you remember, where they passed and the dog made a noise.'

I nodded, following the line of Dom's finger, the topography starting to match Ralph's description.

'And there,' Dom said, pointing east to a dark thread across the terrain, a note of triumph in his voice. 'There is the railway line.'

Back in the car, we crossed the rusty track and negotiated the roads until Dom was sure we were heading east, along a single carriageway, long and straight. This, Dom said, was the start of the Via Appia Antica, the Roman road between Rome and the port of Brindisi. Ruts from ancient carts scarred the roadside. Here, the land morphed from pasture to vineyards and olive groves, just as Ralph's memoir recorded. Travelling by car, though, made it hard to stay with Ralph and Charlie's progress on foot, which had been through fields and by night.

Something caught Dom's eye, and he pulled over. It was a small circular building with a conical roof, just off the road at the end of a short path. I remembered Charlie, in a postwar debrief, mentioning a dry-stone hut somewhere near here in which they had holed up. It was easy to imagine the two men there, like the scene from *All Quiet on the Western Front*, which I'd read to my son during lockdown, where Paul and Kat remake home in a ruined house by cooking a goose.

Dom explained that these shelters, known as *trulli*, were peculiar to Alta Murgia. Some had been used as cottages, but mostly as stables or field shelters. The Puglian climate was warm, but the rains could be sudden and heavy.

'A good place to hide, I think,' said Dom, adding with a wry smile: 'Also, when Charlie was sick, perhaps Ralph was in charge, yes?'

9.
Chi Va La!

It was nearly 9 a.m. when Ralph awoke, with a start, Charlie by his side. They were lying on straw in a shepherd's hut, a rough limestone construction, windowless but with light slanting through chinks in the slate roof. Except for the pitter-patter of rain, everything was quiet. Ralph was chilled to the bone, all of his clothing damp, and he'd hardly slept since they arrived there at dawn. Charlie was trembling and perspiring, his skin hot to the touch.

Tilting the water bottle to Charlie's lips, Ralph helped him take a mepacrine tablet, then went to the door. Opening it an inch, then a bit more, he watched for a full minute before venturing out into the grey morning. At the back of the hut there was a bundle of wood, which with eyes darting left and right he dragged inside:

> I told my partner I was going to build a fire. He tried to intervene, saying it was madness, that the smoke may be seen by people nearby. I took no notice; he was not in a suitable position to argue anyway, and I continued with my task. I reasoned that a good hot brew would do him good. Besides, one cannot let a man shiver himself into the grave without attempting to do something for him.

Pulling the driest sticks from the middle, Ralph kindled them in the grate with a handful of straw and soon had a blaze going. He poured water into an earthenware jar he'd found the previous evening and, tying it with bootlaces, hung it over the fire. As it came to a boil he added a half-pound block of chocolate, stirring the thickening liquid with a stick. Passing the jar between them, they felt warmth and nourishment flowing into their bodies.[1]

Ralph went out again to rig up a rainwater trap using the jar and a couple of slates, then, ignoring Charlie's murmured protests, stoked up the fire. A pleasing fug was building in the circular, nest-like room. Ralph secured the door, and lay down beside his feverish friend, who by now was still and almost asleep.

It was Saturday, 6 March 1943 – their third full day on the run. The strangest, most unexpected part of freedom was the return of responsibility. Already the trek to Brindisi had proved an ordeal, requiring constant good decision-making and, for Ralph, a tacit need to satisfy his own expectations of himself and not let Charlie down either.

So far, so good, thought Ralph – even if malaria had confined them to this hut, who knew where in the Italian countryside. There was nothing to be done but wait. In the dark silence, Ralph reflected on the previous sixty hours of freedom.

After crossing the railway line on that first night of 3 March, they had hiked across hilly terrain, leaping walls, scuttling over roads, gnawing dried figs as they went. By 2 a.m. the skies had cleared, allowing navigation by the Pole Star. Gradually the land became more cultivated, with muddy fields and untidy vineyards. Walls were a nuisance, houses a menace. At daybreak on the 4th, they were dog-tired and drained of adrenaline. The outhouses they'd planned to sleep in had not materialized. Wading into a wheat field, they saw a raised road up ahead, and hearing the rumble of iron-clad wheels ducked into a drainage culvert until an ox cart had passed over their heads.

And there, in that concrete tube, they had stayed. They slept a little, but after a couple of hours, aching and shivering, Ralph bestirred himself and banged his head. Charlie was looking quizzically at him.

'Morning, Sleuth,' he said. 'Cement pipes don't make the best of shelters, do they?' Ralph smiled weakly. 'It's nearly nine o'clock,' Charlie continued with his usual bright equanimity. 'Shall we have breakfast?'

He handed Ralph a piece of chocolate and a biscuit and measured out two portions of O.S.B.R., which they dabbed from their palms like sherbet: 'imitating children', as Ralph put it. They stayed in the drain all day, occasionally stretching their legs, unseen by workers in the wheat field. More small meals of O.S.B.R. were taken at 1 p.m. and 6 p.m., after which they studied the maps but failed to work out where they were. By 7 p.m. it was dark, so they set off again regardless, relying on the erratic compass and the heavens. The night air was mercifully cool, but they had no water, and the stream beds were dry.

Towards sunrise on the 5th, tongues swollen with thirst, they had broken a vow to avoid places of habitation and crept into a farm to drink from a steel tank. Hearing a voice, they shrank back into the night. Shortly before dawn, Charlie spotted another, larger drainage pipe. Recoiling at a pile of faeces, they moved to the other end, which they blocked with stones against the wind and carpeted with torn branches. They lay side by side, unable to settle.

At 7.30 a.m., rigid with cold, they decided to travel in daylight, another rule broken. Passing through vineyards, they found a spot among rocks and bushes, where they warmed up enough to sleep and even shave before dozing off again. The rest of the day passed in near silence, broken only by wheels on rutted tracks.

There followed a night of heavy cloud with few stars. A high, spike-topped wall forced them off course, and they ran into an old peasant. Charlie pretended to relieve himself against a wall. If the man said 'buongiorno', they were ready to return the greeting, knowing this had been the downfall of the Sector 5 escapers. But he passed by without a word.

Rattled by this, Ralph and Charlie had headed south for an hour before turning back east. They made good progress until 3 a.m., when drizzle obscured the way ahead and churned up mud that sucked at their boots. Soaked, they stumbled on through the darkness. An hour later, the heavens opened, forcing them into a *trullo*. But at dawn when Ralph opened the door, there, barely fifty yards away, stood a farmhouse. So, on they went, and soon found another *trullo*, this one with straw and a hearth.

As Ralph churned these recent memories, assessing his performance, evaluating their chances, he sank into sleep. Upon waking, he found Charlie still in the grip of sweats and shivers, though insisting they press on. Pretending to consider his objection, Ralph administered more mepacrine and lay Charlie back on the straw. At 1 p.m. he put a few sticks on the embers and in the flickering shadows made some sludgy O.S.B.R. porridge, a bit burned but the best thing they'd had yet. Ralph drowsed away the afternoon, feeding the fire while Charlie did battle with his fever.

As the sun went down, they chatted, Charlie stuttering out his words. Even by the most generous estimate, he admitted, they had covered just twenty miles, barely two-thirds of what Ralph had hoped for. With no break in the weather, they would have to spend a second night in the *trullo*. Ralph said they'd better get their heads down, and built up the fire. It was gratifying to see his friend sleeping so peacefully.[2]

Driving along the Via Appia, Dom and I pictured their isolation, yet also the *trullo*'s humble domesticity and the tenderness of Ralph's care. Looking in my notebook, I suggested they'd needed what one POW called 'the intimacy and protection of the family group against the large unfriendly outside world'.[3] Another episode, another layer to Ralph's character. The policeman, soldier, prisoner and escaper had become a nurse, and to a patient for whom he felt a kind of love, however much the word might have perplexed or offended him.

We passed more *trulli* and some *masserie*, ancient farmsteads fortified against the bandits and invaders of old. Our route – through vineyards and olive groves, limestone slopes on our left, plains on our right – had changed little since the war, indeed, since antiquity. And dotted all around, Dom said, were caves where an escaped prisoner, had he sought shelter there, might have seen frescoes of Christ and the saints, left by twelfth-century heretics fleeing persecution. Every farm we passed, every outbuilding, was somewhere Ralph and Charlie might have visited. Fixed in my head were their clothes and faces, their voices from northern and western England respectively, even their moods and motivations. And now the expansive stage for their drama was laid out before me.

Suddenly Dom braked, interrupting this reverie.

'Quick, start filming!' he said, pointing excitedly at an old man hobbling along the roadside. 'It's the old shepherd!' Apparently, this peasant-like figure was the subject of a famous documentary and lived in a cave.

Dom leaned across to speak through the window. The man was stooped with a shock of white hair and a broad smile of a few blackened teeth. In Dom's question I caught the Italian words for 'remember' and 'Germans'. The shepherd answered with a laugh, miming drawing a pistol and waving it in the air. Dom translated. As a boy the shepherd had been cheeky to a Nazi officer, who had threatened to shoot him. He'd never heard of any English POWs – but it was nonetheless astonishing that, in this unaltered landscape, we had encountered a living link to a time when Ralph and Charlie knew this place.

Saying goodbye, we continued on our way. The stony hillside on our left drew closer, narrowing its adjacent arable border: a feature that, as Dom observed, would have forced Ralph and Charlie off their intended route and across the road. Somewhere our car passed through the same volume of space the escapers had moved through as they vainly strove not to blunder into the town of Gioia del Colle. Soon, we were there ourselves.

Unlike Charlie, Ralph slept fitfully, worrying about falling behind schedule, which would mean running out of food. By the dull gleam of dawn and through a drizzly mist he crept out to hunt for vegetables. He was praying he would happen upon a chicken, even if, he thought piously, taking it would mean committing a felony. Returning empty-handed, he did at least find Charlie much recovered.

After idling away the day, they gathered their kit and set off. It was the darkest night so far, the showers torrential. Charlie checked the compass every 100 yards or so to prevent their veering off, while avoiding a path so straight they would end up in a town. Thus far they had managed to stay a good distance south, first of Altamura then Santeramo – but now the farmland beneath the higher rocky ground was tapering, funnelling them towards the main road.

A constellation of pale lights appeared in the distance. Ralph wiped his watch. It was 9.45 p.m., meaning they'd been going less than four hours.

'That will be Gioia,' said Charlie.

'I don't care if it's Timbuktu,' retorted Ralph.

They could have turned sharply south again, but atrocious weather and dwindling supplies discouraged them from making another extreme diversion.

'It's no good, Sleuth,' said Charlie. 'We'll never get round that town.'

Emerging from an olive grove, they crouched at the roadside, squinting through the wet blackness. Checking the road was clear, they crossed and rejoined the cultivated land. But they found it impossible to change course.

By 10.30 p.m. they were among houses, streetlamps and telegraph poles. Though they were drenched, the rain proved a shielding, muffling ally as they skirted along a deserted road, past a factory building with a tall chimney like a Doncaster mill. Crossing the road, they climbed over a wall and dropped down onto a railway embankment. From the left, a passenger train pulled into what had to be a station, so they turned right through a vegetable patch. Ralph pulled up a head of broccoli, which he gobbled down, soil grinding between his teeth. He stuffed more broccoli into his overalls and a piece under each arm. Charlie gathered some, too.

They continued along the embankment until a bridge loomed. They stopped and listened through the drilling of the rain. Hearing nothing of concern, Ralph took the initiative, scaling the bridge's wing wall at its lowest point. Charlie hurled up his haul of broccoli, then reached for Ralph to pull him up. They were now on the bridge itself.

'Lead the way, Sleuth,' said Charlie.

Ralph advanced in a low stoop, blinking away water to check for guards. Then they were over the bridge and in the silent, deserted town. Hugging the verge of shadow beside the buildings, they came to a main road, lit by blue lamps, which they crossed and took the first turning on the left. This was an unlit minor road where they could return to the murk, although they'd have taken any route to quit the centre.

Walking briskly, and feeling more confident, they were about to congratulate each other for having made it through an actual Italian town. But then from out of the gloom came an apparition that spoke loudly in their direction:

'CHI VA LA!'

Dom crossed the railway bridge and parked. We didn't have long before day turned to dusk. Gioia, Dom said, is well known for its beautiful women – I took his word for it: there was no one around – and also as the ancestral home of Sylvester Stallone.

We returned on foot to the main road, where Dom pointed out the tall chimney of the old Pagano mill, which Ralph and Charlie would have seen as they entered the town. The mill had been a camp for Jews in transit to the death camps.[4]

I took out Ralph's memoir, carefully opening it at the right page, but still couldn't quite make sense of what he'd described. Back on the bridge, however, frowning at a transcript, Dom soon had it all worked out, joining points in space with a finger. They entered the town there, walked here, climbed over there and up here.

It was getting dark. We returned to the car and, setting off towards Santeramo, turned our backs on Gioia. I was out of time, booked on a flight out of Bari the next morning. And yet the best of the day's discoveries was still to come. At the point where Ralph and Charlie must have found the railway track, Dom slowed so we could take a look. There in the dusk was the wall they had climbed, and spread before it, astonishingly, an acre of allotment planted with broccoli.

Charlie knew only a little Italian, and Ralph hardly any, yet both recognized this as a sentry's challenge: 'Who goes there?'

Ralph felt ice rush down his spine. Both men were rooted to the spot, unable to reply.

'What shall we do, Sleuth?' whispered Charlie.

'The game's up,' Ralph muttered. 'Tell him we're escaped prisoners and get it over with!'

Turning towards the direction of the voice, Charlie shouted: 'Prigionieri di guerra!' As Ralph raised his hands, broccoli dropped onto the glistening pavement. The sentry didn't reply. So, they moved slowly forward to find a guard box at a road junction, and a soldier wearing a cape and a helmet with a plume in it: Bersaglieri, the only regiment the Allies had respected in the desert. He presented his rifle, its long bayonet fixed.

Believing that Charlie was joking he asked if they were 'Borghesi', to which Charlie, who had an inkling the word meant 'workmen' or 'civilians', replied with an enthusiastic 'Sì, sì!'

'Avanti. Buona notte,' said the guard, lowering his gun.

Somehow they had passed as citizens of Gioia, workers home on the last train, which they'd seen pull into the station. The sentry retreated into his box.

With light heads and pounding hearts, Ralph and Charlie strolled nonchalantly across a junction, then zigzagged through dark streets before traversing a field and vaulting over a wall. Stopping to catch their breath, Ralph asked incredulously what had just happened. Charlie explained, to which Ralph replied that they'd been lucky the guard hadn't noticed their khaki overalls.

'If only he'd been intelligent enough to ask a few questions,' sniggered Ralph, 'he'd have earned himself a medal as big as a frying pan.'

Consulting their duff compass, they moved on, eager to rejoin the sodden bleakness of the *campagna*. But Gioia wouldn't let them go. It was past midnight now, and they still weren't clear of habitation. At the next main road, they took another bearing. East was straight ahead, but a high wall barred their way. To the right were buildings, some brightly illuminated, so they swung left, intending to change direction again as soon as possible.

Chi Va La!

Twenty yards down this road, Charlie touched Ralph's arm and jerked his thumb at something on their left: another sentry box, with a pair of toecaps sticking out. They steeled themselves to sneak past, but on their right was what looked like a guardroom and another sentry. Ralph asked what they should do. Charlie pointed to the kerb where roadworks were in progress: they picked their way through. On the other side, Ralph saw they were ten feet from yet another sentry and, taking Charlie's arm, quietly steered him away.

They passed into a ploughed field, crouching low. Ralph stumbled in a furrow and fell. Hurrying to his feet, he heard the double click of a rifle bolt, followed by another cry of 'Chi va la!' Torch beams criss-crossed the field, raised voices called for them to halt.

They sprinted away. After a short distance, leaping from the darkness, came a tall wire fence, which Charlie slammed into. This had to be some kind of military installation, and they were smack bang in the middle of it. After malaria, they were suddenly struck by 'barbed wire fever', the old camp malady, and made off in great haste.

For over an hour, oblivious to the rain and darkness, they ran through olive groves, over (or sometimes into) walls, across streams, down cart tracks, past outbuildings.

At last, they stopped, panting, lost to the wild night. Charlie knew the plan was failing, reality so different from theory, as with the fateful SAS mission that had started his troubles. The dream of flying to Switzerland was fading. Twelve days for 100 miles had been the objective: they'd covered less than thirty, and day five was nearly upon them.[5]

Two hours before sunrise. The escapers were weary, and a little giddy. Charlie wiped the compass, and through ground-creeping fog stepped over a low wall. There was a muffled cry and a thump, as he plummeted through six feet of inky space. Ralph guffawed; Charlie, rarely the butt of a joke, didn't find it funny.

'There you go,' he snapped, thrusting the compass at Ralph. 'Lead on.'

At 4.20 a.m., a glimmer of dawn on the horizon, they made out an undulating landscape of worked fields and woods. Overruling the compass, they found another *trullo* in an olive grove. It had a thatched roof, and the door was secured with a chain and padlock, which they broke. There were no windows, and inside it was musty and pitch dark.

Ralph struck a match. There was a small well, a fireplace and, best of all, plentiful straw and a stack of chopped wood.

'This is it,' said Ralph. 'The one place we've been looking for.'

Within a few minutes the earthenware jar was bubbling away, and the companions drew close to the hearth. Ralph glanced at Charlie, who was staring drowsily at the flames. He was plastered in mud, a pitiful sight. Ralph looked down at himself, and saw he was the same: elbows and knees caked in grime, no portion of his worn-out boots visible.

When he looked up again, Charlie was smiling. 'If only your wife could see you now, Sleuth,' he said. 'She wouldn't know you.'

'Quite true, I don't doubt it,' chuckled Ralph. 'But if your mother could see *you* now, she'd probably disclaim the relationship!'

They drank another brew of chocolate, removed their encrusted boots and laid their socks by the fire. As Ralph peeled off his overalls, some squashed broccoli fell out, which Charlie added to his own small pile. They made a washing line from string, hung out their underwear, and splashed themselves with water from the well.

Charlie found a piece of board which he positioned by the fire, and he and Ralph lay down, scooping straw around them. Charlie was soon in a deep slumber. But yet again Ralph couldn't sleep despite being bone-tired. Admitting defeat, he sat up, hypnotized by the steam rising from their overalls and the tapping of rain on tile.[6]

Dawn on Monday, 8 March, the start of the fifth full day on the run.

Charlie was snoring softly. Ralph opened the door to find it was still raining. He slipped outside – but instantly froze. In the next olive grove, 100 yards away, was parked an Italian medical truck.

Stepping back into the *trullo*, he watched for a minute or so, then crawled across the sopping ground to get a better view.

Even nearer than the truck was a pile of wooden crates covered in camouflage netting. Then Ralph saw the tents. Two long rows, green army issue, and further off some horses tethered in a field. He reckoned it must be a battalion or even brigade field headquarters. Returning to the *trullo*, he thought that if Mussolini himself had been sitting there he wouldn't have been surprised.

Charlie was up and stoking the fire. Ralph, fearful of the smoke, told him to stop. At first Charlie thought he was messing around, but soon saw for himself. They'd been lucky: had they obeyed the compass they would have ploughed straight into the encampment. This good fortune, of a sort, bred fatalistic resignation. They decided to keep the fire going, hoping the wood was dry enough to burn without much smoke.

'Better to have a fire and risk detection,' reasoned Charlie, signalling this change in attitude, 'rather than shiver away in the cold and risk pneumonia.'

Half-expecting a knock on the door, they tidied up a bit and made breakfast. After that, they slept on and off until 1 p.m., when they had their main meal of porridge and boiled broccoli. The afternoon was spent drying clothes and planning. Although Charlie was now fit and well, neither he nor Ralph relished the thought of leaving the cosy *trullo* to sally forth into the night. But around 6 p.m. they dressed and ate, then three hours later set off.

The rain had nearly stopped, and there was a fresh breeze. They stood for a while, sharpening their ears and eyes to the hushed darkness. Heading south for half an hour, to be well clear of the Italian camp, they resumed an easterly course.

Like the previous night, it was heavy going, and progress was slow. Picking stealthily through a succession of olive groves, again and again they were confronted by buildings abruptly appearing through densely packed trees. After an hour they reached a stately villa, where they shinned up a wall and landed on a lawn only to find a sentry box under a bright lamp. Charlie guessed it was a command headquarters. So back they went, over the wall, continuing south then east, feeling jaded and flippant – tents and sentries be damned. Ralph launched himself off a seven-foot wall and landed on Charlie like a sack of wet sand.

'What the devil do you think you're doing, Sleuth?' he growled. 'Couldn't you see me standing there?'

Ralph staggered to his feet. He was winded and had banged his nose on Charlie's head. Charlie, unhurt, sat against the wall, where Ralph was relieved to see his irritation had subsided into amusement.

By midnight the skies were clearer, revealing a pallid moon among twinkling stars. Olive groves soon gave way to pasture, where there were fewer walls and hardly any buildings. Picking up speed, they used roads whenever they could, abandoning the last of their self-imposed rules. They began to think they could make it to Brindisi after all.

The only problem with there being fewer farms was that, come morning, there was nowhere to hide. It was 4.30 a.m.; in half an hour they would be completely visible. Again, it started raining. Spying a farm through the saturated haze, on the very edge of a new day, they left the road and hopped over a wall into a copse. The rain grew heavier. Trees concealed them but offered little in the way of shelter. They piled stones into a coffin shape, lay in it, and pulled over a roof of branches – but the water poured through. Trying to avoid a particularly intrusive trickle, Charlie accidentally elbowed the wall, and the makeshift structure collapsed.

Shivering and dejected, they prowled around as a greenish light spread across the countryside. Then Charlie spotted something.

'There's a good hide-out in the next field!' he said, pointing at a stone hut. It was less than 100 yards away, although in full view of the farmhouse.

Choosing to walk not run, as through a minefield, they broke cover, and had almost made it when a dog barked. They kept going. Then a man's voice, shouting from the house. Still, on they went, striding across the wheat field, legs gone to jelly, one eye on their right-hand flank. A man was coming their way, then another.

Ralph and Charlie pressed on past the hut, scrambled over a rough wall, and found themselves on a cart track leading from the house. Seeing the men there, they darted left, walking briskly. The pursuers began to run and soon caught up with the escapers, who, in a semi-delirious state, stopped. Ralph felt sure now that their escape was over.[7]

10.
Noci

Altamura, September 2022. Twelve months had passed since I'd visited Gioia del Colle, with its bridge and broccoli patch, and what Ralph referred to as 'that famous Italian call': 'Chi va la!' At that point, my time in Italy had run out. On the way to Bari Airport, Dom had promised we would do the final leg of the escape the following year. And so here I was, back in the old town, where preparations were under way for Altamura's annual medieval festival – drums beating, torches blazing, summoning the dead from a deeper past.

Alone in a soft-lit cave-like restaurant, I combed through the memoir for the umpteenth time. Ralph had vividly recounted the end of the escape, but without seeing the location for myself I knew that whatever I conjured up in my mind could never be true to the event. That summer I had scanned aerial views of the landscape between Gioia and the town of Noci, twelve miles due east, swooping down to Google's ground-level views in case any farms resembled the description in Ralph's memoir. There were a few *masserie*, but their driveways were private. Google stopped at their gates and therefore so did I.

But then Dom had messaged to say that his friend Vincenzo from Noci's cultural committee had told him that a fellow committee member, a lawyer by the name of José Mottola, believed he'd cracked it. By plotting various clues of location, time and distance on a map, all forensically extracted from the memoir, José had arrived at a single conclusion: Masseria Casabolicchio. He had even driven out there to road-test his theory.

More confident with my Italian now, I ordered pasta and set about sketching my own map, guided only by Ralph – there was no signal to check Google – to reconstruct the situation. Soon I had a rough yet plausible plan of the *masseria*'s position in relation to the surrounding landscape.

Next morning it was muggy. Dom and I drove back to Gioia, where, over the bridge, on a hunch he swerved down a minor road. Startlingly, razor-wire fences stretched around a huge military air base, which, Dom said, would have been there in 1943. The fact that it was set in open countryside fitted Ralph's recollection even more precisely. This must have been their route, and they could hardly have chosen a worse one. Of course, had Charlie realized where they were, he might have tried to steal a plane here instead of Brindisi. But they had found they could barely creep past an air base unchallenged, never mind break into one. What they had attempted was virtually impossible.

'They would have been shot,' I said.

'Most probably,' agreed Dom. 'I think, yes.'

'They were lucky – for them and for us.'

'True. Otherwise, no story?'

With Gioia behind us, the landscape opened out into a plain the colour of mustard and burnt umber, pressed down by a charcoal sky. Regular patterns of olive trees were broken up by limestone walls, faded red roofs, cypresses and the odd weathered bell tower.

After fifteen minutes we arrived at the Abbazia Madonna della Scala, a Benedictine monastery hidden in wooded parkland. Waiting there were three representatives of Noci's cultural committee: Cesareo, a genially expansive ex-mayor, Dom's smiling friend Vincenzo, and José, a lean, serious man, who was impatient to get moving.

We drove out to Masseria Casabolicchio, approaching from the same direction as Ralph and Charlie, although they had arrived off-road. Rumbling up a tree-lined lane, we stopped at a corroded metal gate.

'No one is I think here,' said José, scrambling over the front wall. We followed. José explained that the current owner had inherited the house, and that the farmer there during the war had been a part-time policeman.

The *masseria* was all stuccoed boxes and pointed gables, with slate roofs, worn shutters and trailing vines, a disused pigsty and a couple of *trulli*. The points on my hand-drawn map lined up with everything there. Across the yard, by the perimeter wall, honeybees were grumbling around a hive, as if agitated by the threatening storm.

José beckoned me to the other side of the house. Ivy-clad stone steps led to a concrete platform, a roof for whatever was below. From there we surveyed fields of bare earth and forests beyond. José's English wasn't much better than my Italian, but we were looking the same way and thinking as one. He pointed down and shook his head, indicating that the platform we were standing on hadn't been there during the war, and nor had another building blocking our view on the west side of the house.

We descended to where the others were poking around the farm buildings like detectives on a case. Scrawny chickens pecked at the dust, and a pair of cats eyed us momentarily then made off. A tethered dog sprang from its kennel, yelping fretfully. We were trespassing, and now it felt as if we were being watched.

We moved down the lane, an overgrown continuation of the road on which we'd parked by the front gate. In the left-hand field stood a mound of rocks, which José assured us had been piled there by farmers. But these were evenly shaped blocks, not stones turned up by the plough. I climbed over the wall, with Dom not far behind me, and we examined what were clearly the lower courses of a collapsed hut. A hundred yards ahead lay an enclosed copse, previously obscured by the farm's postwar extension.

I hurried towards the trees, then turned to retrace the escapers' footsteps. Bang on cue the farm dog started barking. I rejoined Dom, and together we bypassed the ruins of the hut, just as Ralph and Charlie had done, and climbed back over the wall into the lane. There, strolling towards us, were Cesareo and Vincenzo, spectral echoes of the Italians who, from that exact place, had come after Ralph and Charlie in March 1943.

Charlie and Ralph stood face to face with a middle-aged Italian they took to be the farmer and a younger man, perhaps his son or a farmhand. The escapers were too tired to feel anything except a craving for sleep – and yet they hadn't completely given up.[1]

The farmer spoke too fast for Charlie to understand anything, but he was clearly hostile. Ralph responded with guttural gibberish he hoped might be taken as German.

'Carta di identità,' demanded the farmer in the rough tones, Ralph thought, of a policeman.

Ralph reached into his overalls, turning away to hide his battle-dress, and handed over his army pay book. He watched the farmer turn the pages, the man's blank expression suggesting illiteracy. He appeared unsure what to do.

Others came down from the farm, their excitement without surprise suggesting they'd been warned to look out for escaped POWs. Exploiting the hesitation, Ralph and Charlie made as if to be on their way – but the men closed in around them. The fugitives smiled sadly at each other. Their clothes were muddy and torn, their unshaven faces lined with fatigue. The game was up. The farmer jabbed a finger towards the house, and off they went. They knew instinctively it was foolish to resist – until one of the men pushed Charlie, who replied with the kind of glance that, according to Ralph, was 'full of malice aforethought and all that'. As the Italian stepped back, Ralph smiled approvingly.

Through a granite-framed doorway they entered a long, gloomy stable occupying a lower storey of the house. Two chairs were found, and the farmer gestured for Ralph and Charlie to sit. A small whispering crowd gathered at the threshold.

While the farmer went to get help, a woman they assumed to be his wife bustled in carrying a bundle and crying in great sobs. This was disconcerting: were they about to be shot? She crammed biscuits into their overall pockets, and pressed upon them a loaf of bread and some wine. All this Ralph and Charlie devoured in minutes, the fascinated spectators – labourers in fustian waistcoats, head-scarved women, barefoot children – agape at the spectacle.

This much I knew from the memoir. But where had it been? I followed Ralph and Charlie's footsteps up the lane, where the others had returned to the cars. There, in the back of the house, was a stone doorway in the shadow of the portico on which José and I had stood.

Scalp prickling, I stepped inside. It was dingy, with white grime-stained walls and a low vaulted ceiling, the air ripe with the smell of livestock. Nervous clucking and lowing came from down the corridor. My eyes adjusting, I saw the room was used for storing feed and junk – but I half expected to see two chairs and a three-pint earthenware jar.

In that moment, Ralph's story and its physical location fused like halves separated for eighty years. In my mind's eye there were Ralph and Charlie, perched warily, rapt audience at the door. And I thought about the bread and wine they'd received – an act of homespun communion, all the more poignant for being in a stable.

The wife's pity had puzzled Ralph and Charlie, but their curiosity was overwhelmed by hunger. They would understand soon enough. Many escape memoirs described Italian mothers who in their enemy saw only a mother's son in need. So many men from the town of Noci had gone to the war, mostly to Russia, and now were dead or missing.[2] This was a peasant's act of penance to earn divine protection for a son, brother or husband, who in some faraway land might receive tender care from a mother like herself.[3]

Hearing Cesareo's hearty laugh, I went outside where sunshine had broken through the menacing cover of storm clouds. We got back in our cars and drove off.

More people appeared at the stable door. The women spoke in whispers, as if, Ralph supposed, he and Charlie might object to their conversation. But this gentle lull was soon shattered by the return of the farmer, accompanied by two *carabinieri*, a soldier with fixed bayonet and a pistol-waving officer. The farmer's wife, still wiping away tears, stepped aside, and the onlookers dispersed. 'I arrest you!' shouted the excitable officer. 'You are my prisoners!' Ralph and Charlie tried to communicate with him, but soon deduced this was the only English he knew.[4]

After a cursory search, they were led out into the lane, followed by the locals, who were unhappy at this turn of events. Sighing, the officer pointed at the wall, where for the next ten minutes the prisoners sat enjoying a ferocious row. Unlike the farmer, most people seemed to want the fugitives released. Ralph unpicked the bootlaces from his now redundant earthenware jar and tossed it over his shoulder.

Three horse-drawn hansom cabs arrived. Ralph and Charlie climbed into the middle cab followed by the Italian officer. Charlie suggested he would be better off riding the horse, but instead he squeezed between the two Englishmen. Ralph thought about grabbing his gun – but then what? As the carts pulled away, the last thing he saw was the tearful farmer's wife waving farewell.

After a couple of miles, they alighted at a farmhouse, where the officer went inside and returned wearing his parade uniform, reeking of cologne. Then he marched Ralph and Charlie down the road, a procession joined by dozens of people, including other *carabinieri*. Residents called and waved from their balconies. 'It was like carnival day without the flags,' Ralph wrote in his memoir. The officer, at the vanguard, was in his element, concerned only that festivities would end too quickly. Arriving in Noci, they were shown into the *carabinieri* HQ, a large white building. The fun, however, had only just begun.

Up six flights of stairs, Ralph and Charlie entered a large, unfurnished room, which quickly filled with soldiers and civilians, women and men. Everyone spoke at once in loud, exuberant voices, but no one knew what to do. In one corner, the arresting officer was giving an entertaining account of the morning's events.

'I'd like to see his diary entry for this day,' said Charlie, not bothering to suppress his laughter. 'That would indeed be something worth seeing.'

Another *carabinieri* officer forced his way through and proceeded to speak French, which Charlie understood, yet without indicating what was happening. With the clamouring crowd in pursuit, the prisoners were taken back to the ground floor and into another room. Only a few officers were allowed in here, it seemed, together with the town council – mayor, clerk, surveyor, bell-ringer and other minor officials.

A thorough search revealed the knife tucked in Ralph's gaiter and Charlie's compass. What remained of their chocolate and cigarettes was confiscated, along with the razors, towels and soap. Overalls and battledress, which they had removed, were inspected. There was some dismay at their woollen underwear, which, Ralph and Charlie understood, belied Mussolini's insistence that Britain was on its knees economically.

Once the Italians saw from their documents that Ralph and Charlie were warrant officers, their treatment improved. Cigarettes and chocolate were returned, towels and soap likewise. Requesting permission to wash, they were taken to a trough in a public square. There, another crowd formed, saucer-eyed at their white soap. The grimy pair lathered up ostentatiously, flaunting good-quality vests. Usually averse to self-indulgence, Ralph relished this performance, which was rounded off nicely by Charlie breaking up a block of chocolate for the children, causing delight and, among the adults, much head-shaking.

Their ablutions complete, the prisoners were escorted back inside, where they were served bread, cheese and more meat than either had ever seen in Camp 65. Then, asking to sleep, they were given blankets. Visitors continued to come and go for the next five hours, but the prisoners slept obliviously until 4 p.m., when a guard woke them for interrogation.

Dom and I drove past a sand-coloured *masseria*, all squat towers and turrets, at the very modern roadside as if stranded there by time. This must have been where the *carabinieri* officer had spruced himself up. On the outskirts of Noci, we visualized the spectators and the prisoners tramping into the Piazza Garibaldi, a stately quadrangle lined with evergreen oaks. In one corner stood an ornate fountain bordered in begonias – an echo of prewar splendour.

It was nearly midday, the thick air now oppressively stormy. We wandered into the old town, looking for the former *carabinieri* HQ: no one on the Noci cultural committee knew its location. Nor had they managed to trace anyone who remembered being given chocolate by Allied prisoners. We met a stooped woman who had lived in Noci all her life, and whose brother, captured in Russia, was one of only two men from his unit to return from Siberian captivity. But she knew no more. Moments later, however, Cesareo bumped into the chief of the *carabinieri*, who directed us to a big white building.

Its four storeys had been converted into apartments. Buzzed inside – Vincenzo pressed all the buttons until an occupant answered – we found a cool vestibule with a marble floor and staircase. The building had been modified, leaving scars that hinted at the original layout. Dom said the usual arrangement was for the *carabinieri* commander to have his office at the top, beneath which would be the barracks, with the cells at the bottom. Back on the ground floor, I tried the handle of a door, which led into a spacious room, now converted into a garage, where I imagined Ralph and Charlie stretched out, sleeping off their dinner.

Back in the piazza, with Dom translating, I told Cesareo that Ralph had been brought before a bald man with a bull neck, hands on hips, looking, Ralph thought, as if he had a grudge against the world. He wasn't a *carabiniere*, rather the chief of police.

Cesareo's face lit up. He pointed at a nearby house to which as a boy he had delivered groceries. Back then, it was a barbershop belonging to the son of the wartime police chief, Onofrio Rocco Morea. I told them what Nan had told me: that Ralph had punched this Morea, breaking his nose, upon which Cesareo burst out laughing. The memoir, however, told a different story.

Morea's eyes rested coldly on his much taller prisoner. Ralph smiled and asked how he was: 'Come stai?' – one of his few Italian phrases, and provocatively informal.

> I thought he was going to choke. An angry flush overspread his features, wiping the grin from my face in an instant. Muttering something under his breath he came very close to me, placed his bald head under my chin, and started speaking in rapid Italian. He had one of those nasty, rasping voices with just a hint of a snarl – the sort of voice I have always associated with ex-Guards NCOs after having been introduced to the drill square at Caterham . . . Definitely not the voice of a friend.

Lying on the table was Charlie's Italian dictionary, at which Morea, believing it to be Ralph's, pointed as his rant gathered momentum. Gesturing 'no', Ralph appealed to an officer sitting in the corner, who refused to be distracted from his book.[5]

With Morea's clenched fist under his nose, Ralph protested: 'Non è la miei, è della mia amica', by which he meant the dictionary was Charlie's, but by using the feminine form had suggested Charlie was his girlfriend.

Snorting like a bull, Morea prodded him in the chest. Ralph took a step back, Morea a step forward. Then Ralph pushed him. Staggering upright, Morea lunged at Ralph, grabbing him by his battledress. The French-speaking officer rushed in to calm things, then brought Charlie to explain about the dictionary. Morea stormed out and everyone – Ralph, Charlie, the translator, even the reader in the corner – sighed with relief.

That evening, digesting plates of macaroni, Ralph and Charlie were questioned by the *carabinieri*. Was Protestantism England's only religion? Were British people starving? Was Churchill Jewish? Did servicemen's cigarettes contain a drug to make them aggressive? After this, once again, the captors hadn't a clue what to do. So, a *carabiniere* fetched an accordion, and soon everyone in the room was singing. A young woman plumped down next to Charlie, and they began chatting in French; Ralph, not wanting to get in the way, moved nearer to the accordionist. Morea, however, still interfering in *carabinieri* business, burst in to end the merriment and hauled the prisoners off to the town lock-up.

Pushed into a cell, Ralph and Charlie were strip-searched again, then left alone. PC 191 Ralph Corps smiled at the irony. It was almost identical to the cells in Knaresborough and Barnsley, into which he had slung countless miscreants – the same regulation wooden bed, high barred window, bell push on the wall, reinforced door.

He and Charlie made up the single bed. The blankets were ragged but didn't smell too bad. Without warning the caged light bulb went out. They rang the bell several times, but no one came. The place was deserted. Ralph climbed into bed, where

Charlie had already fallen asleep, and was himself soon dead to the world.

Dom and I spent the evening at the Chiostro di San Domenico, a convent near the Piazza Garibaldi. There we both gave talks to local people, who had ventured out in the heavy rain. Having spoken in English the previous year in Altamura, this time I read in Italian: Dom reassured me they would understand my pronunciation. They certainly listened politely enough as I laboured through my text, and applauded when I held up the *quaderni* containing Ralph's memoir. José also did a turn on the locations of Ralph and Charlie's recapture, including the trough where the men had washed. He believed the lock-up had been on the mezzanine floor of the convent, where during the war there was a *pretura*, a magistrates' court. Keys clanking, the caretaker led us through the shadows – but these rooms were not what Ralph had described, nor were they across town from the *carabinieri* HQ.

Afterwards, José took us to a pump in the piazza – the supposed water trough; but that didn't seem right either. The rain had abated, leaving a mist in which the lamplight made halos. I went over to the fountain we'd seen earlier.

'Imagine no flowerbeds,' Vincenzo said. 'They weren't here during the war.'

'Back then it was possible to go right up to the water,' added Dom, pointing to the circular trough.

It was the obvious place to take prisoners to wash – wide, accessible and a short walk from the *carabinieri* HQ. And with this sudden awareness, the spectral shades of Ralph and Charlie, the guards with their fixed bayonets, the chary locals and clamouring kids, shimmered before my eyes and were gone.

Ralph woke up around 6 a.m., daylight streaming through the high barred window. He had pins and needles, but it had been the best night's sleep in ages, and he was still tickled to be a policeman in a town lock-up.

Nudging the sleeping Charlie, he cried: 'Come on! Quick! Snap out of it!'

Charlie shot up like a jack-in-the-box, then sank back with a groan. Ralph's laughter was too much for him, and, grabbing him by the arms, he rolled him over. The wrestling match that followed made Ralph laugh all the more, and alerted the guards, who barrelled into the cell with their clothes.

Once dressed, they were taken to a guardroom full of lounging policemen. As their property was being returned, in came Chief Morea with a pair of *carabinieri*, who took Ralph and Charlie to a bus stop. Ralph saw from a clock tower it was 7.30 a.m.

Half an hour later, a crowded bus arrived. Ralph was impressed that Italians feared their policemen enough to vacate the back seat. An old man with a goose tucked under each arm wished Ralph and Charlie 'good morning' in English, to the guards' obvious disapproval. As the bus pulled away, Ralph smiled at Morea through the back window, hoping he would shake a fist like a thwarted villain – but he just stood there, watching impassively and looking for all the world like Mussolini on a podium.

They were heading back to Gravina. The bus took them to Gioia del Colle, where they caught a train that stopped at every station, bridge and tunnel, and whenever the driver spotted a friend. As they clunked along, Ralph and Charlie, confident the policemen wouldn't understand, cooked up a story to protect those who had assisted their escape.

Marched to the entrance of Camp 65, the prisoners were handed over to the Gravina *carabinieri*. The gates swung conclusively shut behind them. But while the escape had failed, they had defied their gaolers and set an example to fellow prisoners.

Ralph knew that other opportunities would arise. He liked to think that returning to captivity would be no more than an interval for him and Charlie, or, to use an Italian term he knew from opera, an *intermezzo*.

PART FOUR
Intermezzo

II.
Passing Time

Under pewter skies, Ralph and Charlie had been escorted up the hill to the *palazzina comando*, relieved the escape was over but far from glad to be back.[1]

Taking the same route today, that hulking administration block is still the first thing you see, watching over the time-scarred site of the camp. Squint, and it could be the keep of a Norman castle. Roofless, with vegetation sprouting at the windows, it remains Gravina's most complete building and its defining icon.

Heeding the *edificio pericoloso* warning signs, I'd only peered inside at the rubble and rubbish, and the graffiti on the pockmarked plaster walls. But, as in Noci, I sensed the phantoms there: the grim-faced *carabinieri* and the unkempt prisoners, fatigued yet perhaps with a hint of a smirk. They glided past me on their way to the stairs, now a crumbling ruin; in 1943 the way to the commandant's office.

Lieutenant Colonel Coppola seemed more vexed than angry as he conducted what Ralph the policeman termed a 'preliminary interrogation'. After a few basic questions, which the two prisoners answered more or less honestly, Coppola said:

'I know it is your duty to escape, but why did you take three more men with you?'

Ralph and Charlie, about to launch into their pre-prepared story, were taken by genuine surprise. 'When? How? Where?' asked Ralph.

'They left a hole in the fence big enough to drive a horse and cart through,' said the interpreter, translating the commandant's reply.

Snorting at Ralph and Charlie's baffled looks, Coppola sentenced them to thirty days' rigorous confinement. Now the real interrogation, with the *carabinieri*, would begin.

Charlie was brought before the *maresciallo*, the NCO with the eyebrows, while Ralph waited in a cell. After leaving the commandant's office, they had snatched a few words, agreeing that although the other escape must have been on the south-west side they wouldn't pretend to have got out there themselves. That would make no sense: why leave from the sector furthest from their own, requiring them to traverse three fences between compounds?

After Charlie had been grilled and taken away, a guard pushed Ralph into the office, which, as camp policeman, he had visited often. The *maresciallo* was at his desk, flanked by five *carabinieri* and the interpreter Ralph disliked. Ordered to strip, he stood there shivering while the *maresciallo* returned to his papers.

At length, the Italian rose from his chair, removed his spectacles and began to question Ralph exhaustively about the escape, which he answered as per the agreed story.

The *carabinieri* knew he was lying, just as he, a fellow policeman, would have known. The interpreter prefaced many remarks with 'Your friend says this' or 'Your friend says that'. But Ralph trusted that Charlie would only have said: 'I don't know', 'Perhaps you're right' and 'It was dark and I couldn't see.'

Unimpressed, the *maresciallo* allowed Ralph to dress, which made him think it was all over, but then he was informed that Charlie had revealed where they had crossed over from Sector 2 to Sector 3. Would he, Sergeant Major Corps, care to do the same?

Outside, Ralph paced the patrol corridor, frowning as if trying to remember. The *maresciallo* watched attentively, the guards restraining an audience of prisoners to prevent them alerting Ralph to whatever fictitious place Charlie had pointed at.

Just then, Ralph heard the Bradford man whose singing had distracted the guards from the escape.

'Keep gooin, lad, till tha sees Owd Moore. Hold on when tha's theer.'

Ralph tipped his cap. The *maresciallo* spun round, but the stooge had gone. The interpreter was nonplussed by his dialect.

'Old Moore' was outside his hut smoking casually. Drawing level, Ralph gestured towards a tiny rip in the fence.

'Impossible!' cried the interpreter. 'Show us how it was done!'

Ralph smiled. 'Ah, that would be a military secret.'

The *maresciallo* waved towards the front of the camp. The warrant officers cheered as Ralph was frogmarched away.

The *carabinieri* cells were airless and damp, with a bucket in the corner and a board for a bed. There was nothing to do, and time dragged painfully. It was a welcome distraction for Ralph, then, when statements, in Italian, were brought to him – statements, which, to make things even more interesting, he refused to sign. So, the Italians brought pen and paper for him to write his own account of the escape. Ralph agreed, knowing instinctively that Charlie would be doing the same, and that their stories were bound to tally.

Ralph described the near-psychic connection that by now he'd formed with Charlie, and the part this played in what happened next:

> I got into communication with my friend (sounds queer like that) but nevertheless I did. We had a really good medium of communication, in fact I might even say that we had a pretty complete system of intercourse. The statements made (W.O. West also made one) were almost identical, the one with the other. Needless to state, both did full justice to our imagination.

The Italians didn't even pretend to believe them. A couple of days later, Ralph and Charlie were back before the *maresciallo*. The interpreter handed them a translation of what they had written, to be sent to the International Red Cross. Still, they refused to sign, suggesting instead that the *maresciallo* pin their original to the translation and send it to Geneva. It may have gone in the bin: there's no trace of it in the Red Cross's archives.

The pair were returned to the cells. After a week, just as Ralph was starting to wonder if he could last thirty days of such extreme isolation, a guard took him and Charlie back to Sector 2. To the dismay of the *carabinieri*, the commandant had commuted their sentences from thirty days to seven, which, however much autonomy the paramilitary policemen enjoyed, still lay within his power.

Ralph lost his job in the camp police – Sleuth no more – but this didn't bother him too much. He had traded a valuable pastime and the authority it conferred for the glamour of an escaper. Soon he and Charlie, his telepathic companion, were back in their hut where the warrant officers gathered round to hear their tale. 'It was', Ralph recalled, 'a great day.'

Escapes added spice to the dull routines of captors and captives alike, however much men on both sides disapproved. The *carabinieri* aside, the camp authorities actually didn't seem overly concerned, focusing more on their talent for recapturing escapers than their incompetence at losing them in the first place. The grief that previous escapes had caused ordinary guards was replaced by something like levity whenever men were brought back. 'They came into the camp laughing, and counted us in our beds,' a prisoner recalled. 'All they asked was that we should sit up to prove that we were not dummies.'[2]

The same prisoner also mentioned Ralph and Charlie's escape, referring to them only as 'a Royal Air Force sergeant and a British RSM'. They had, he said, got through the wire undetected but had been unlucky that another escape had occurred the same night. It was the only reference to these escapes in scores of diaries and memoirs – testimony, perhaps, to the parochial insularity of the sectors.[3]

The Sector 2 camp leader, RSM Alderson, was delighted they had stayed free for so long. He supported any activity that annoyed the enemy, reminding his men that 'one Britisher is worth fifty Italians'. Alderson explained to Ralph and Charlie that on the night they broke out, there had indeed been another successful escape, on the south-west side as they'd supposed, which had put the whole camp on high alert. During a search of the WOs' quarters, an Italian officer had shaken Charlie's bed, sending the pith helmet rolling across the floor. Pulling back the blanket, he found a pile of clothes and that was that: one escape detected during the investigation of another. It hadn't been a complete coincidence: the other escapers had exploited Hugh Owen's dimming the camp lights to cover their own getaway.

The authorities had quickly established who was missing, and the next morning sent telegrams to the supreme military headquarters and the War Ministry in Rome. Dom emailed a copy from an archive there, which gave the escapers' details (this was how I discovered that the first name of the man Ralph referred to as W.O. West was Charles). As for the other escape, only two men are mentioned – Sergeant Albert Church of the Royal Armoured Corps and Private James McBean of the Cameron Highlanders. This suggests that, while Ralph and Charlie had been playing games in the *palazzina comando*, the commandant had been playing games of his own. Had they bluffed about the other three escapers, he would have known it was a lie because there were, in fact, only two. Church and McBean had managed four days, making a beeline for the coast, until recaptured.

The authorities' softening attitude towards the inmates may also have been due to other news circulating in the camp. German industry had been pummelled by Allied bombing, and several U-boats sunk in the Atlantic. Away in the east, after their victory at Stalingrad in February, the Russians were advancing westwards. It was a similar story in the Libyan desert. Later that month, Axis forces were routed to the Tunisian border and looked unlikely to regain the advantage. Surely the Allies would soon land in Italy. And when they did, Lieutenant Colonel Coppola knew that enjoying the esteem of his prisoners might prove useful.

He was also aware that living conditions in Camp 65 breached the Geneva Convention. Two days after the escapes, Red Cross inspectors had been allowed to visit – the first time for several months. Conditions were deemed 'unsatisfactory'. Men were still sleeping on the floor, there was no heating or hot water, everything was infested, and the sick were poorly treated. The day before this inspection, a Royal Artillery gunner died.[4] Food prices had risen 75 per cent since 1939, and Mussolini could hardly feed his own armies. Red Cross parcels were looted and the supply interrupted by air raids. Coppola passed prisoners' complaints to the War Ministry in Rome, which, noting that these gripes 'generally assume a character of irony and contempt', did nothing. There was little they could do. The Italian war machine was grinding to a halt.[5]

The guards may have let up, but the *carabinieri* did not. If anything, they grew more intolerant and draconian. With typical understatement, Ralph described the relationship he and Charlie had with these zealous policemen as 'a little strained'. In truth, they were strictly supervised, like all other incorrigible 'bad boys'. For the first time, Ralph was on the wrong side of the law, something he found both uncomfortable and exhilarating. Meanwhile, more prisoners had been planning escapes – but it was hard to keep these plans from the hypervigilant *carabinieri*. For several weeks, British army sergeants John Langdon and David Kidd had been saving rations and snipping at the fence. But when the night came, the guards pounced, probably thanks to a tip-off.[6]

The attempts by Corps and West, McBean and Church, and Langdon and Kidd, provoked the *carabinieri* to rage and paranoia. They even suspected outside assistance. As winter eased off, so more reading matter had reached the camp, supplied by Penguin Books and sent by the Bodleian Library in Oxford. Works by Jewish authors and anything about secret agents or Boy Scouts were banned; but the romances men liked were permitted. Each book had its cover ripped off by the authorities, in case messages or maps or banknotes were tucked away there. Playing cards were confiscated, and chessmen sawn in half in the belief that they might contain miniature compasses.[7]

These obsessions were well founded. MI9, the branch of military intelligence dedicated to escape and evasion, had been hiding tools and papers in non-essential items – although never in Red Cross parcels, the supply of which depended on trust. Instead, they sent equipment under the cover of fake charities such as the Welsh Provident Society and the Lancashire Penny Fund. MI9 even commissioned the games manufacturer Waddingtons to manufacture special Monopoly sets. A full stop after Marylebone Station meant that a map of Italy was concealed inside the board.[8]

Nor was the *carabinieri*'s distrust of Ralph and Charlie unjustified. Since before their escape, the trouble-making pair had been working on another secret project – a means to pass time but also to help them re-engage with the war.

It had all begun one evening in November 1942, back when the weather was too grim and food too scarce even to contemplate escaping. After the evening meal in their hut, Charlie, who was bored and restless, asked Ralph: 'Do you think it would be possible to build a radio here?'[9]

Charlie possessed the know-how, but Ralph was dubious. Even if parts could be found, they would need money. Nor did they speak enough Italian to negotiate with a guard or civilian worker. Ralph at first put the idea down to one of the brainstorms that almost invariably preceded Charlie's malaria attacks. But when no such attack came, Ralph realized his mercurial friend had been serious.

That winter, Charlie befriended an electrician who not only had free passage in and out of the camp, but was interested in amateur radio. Soon Charlie knew enough Italian to hold a proper conversation, and when the electrician confided that he was a communist, Charlie pretended he was, too. And so, the attachment grew. However, after the electrician – whom Ralph thought 'a villainous specimen of humanity' – asked for a thousand lire for components, the radio idea faded away. Then early in 1943, Ralph happened to mention it to a Greek Cypriot camp policeman, the same one who in due course would help him escape. Sliding a thousand lire note from his pocket, he shrugged that Ralph could pay him back after the war. Overwhelmed by the gesture, and swearing the Cypriot to secrecy, Ralph hurried back to the WOs' quarters.[10]

Charlie was brewing tea when Ralph handed him the banknote. Leaping to his feet, he held it up to the light before stuffing it into his battledress.

'What've you done now, Sleuth?' There was, Ralph recalled, 'a twinkle in his eyes and a note of unconcealed admiration in his tone'.

After this, their only topic of conversation – morning, noon and night – was radio.

Charlie kept the reluctant electrician to his offer, perhaps by threatening to report him for his left-wing opinions, and the Cypriot who had funded the operation was brought in as a translator. Soon they had what they needed: a wire coil, two old valves, a cat's whisker (a fine wire for detecting signals), several terminals, some pocket lamp batteries and a pair of headphones. Charlie fashioned a condenser from a mess tin, dials from ink bottle lids. A bed for the coil was made from aluminium, wood and candle wax. Ralph helped out with small tasks, such as tool-making, and later, in his memoir, drew a diagram showing how it all fitted together.

The greatest problem was keeping the radio secret and hiding it from the *carabinieri*. Other WOs were brought into Ralph and Charlie's confidence, and many concealment proposals rejected.

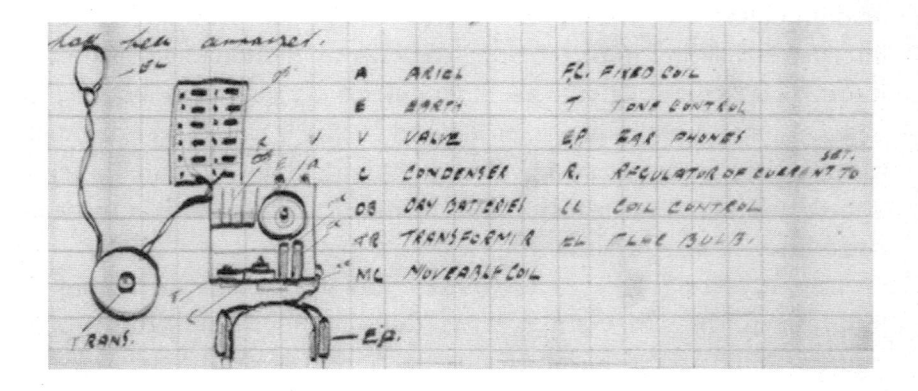

Finally, RSM Alderson arranged for a Royal Engineers sergeant major to build a wall cupboard with a sliding back. To complete the deception, another fifteen cupboards were made, one behind every WO's bunk.

By mid-February, they were ready for their first trial. Ralph likened the atmosphere of silent anticipation to that of a seance. Charlie connected a wire to a battery terminal and fiddled with the dials until, alas, a valve blew with a dull pop. Charlie needed a transformer – yet not only had the electrician refused further involvement, but Ralph and Charlie were busy with their escape, planned for a fortnight's time. After that, apprehended and back behind the wire, they were desperate to return to the radio, yet were monitored so closely by the *carabinieri* it was hard even to talk about it, never mind try to get it working. At least it was still there in its false-backed cupboard, awaiting completion.

In mid-March 1943 the *carabinieri* launched a surprise raid, a really thorough search, sector by sector. It felt like payback for the recent escapes and, in Ralph and Charlie's case, subsequent truculence. Keepers, the quiescent majority, always blamed selfish escapers for this kind of punishment. The WOs waited outside their hut in the rain while it was ransacked, fearing they'd been betrayed about the radio. Directed by the *maresciallo*, the *carabinieri* looked everywhere, including inside and behind the cupboards – but somehow the radio remained undetected.

They learned that the search was for gold watches and rings – wedding bands were exempt – which were to be confiscated, the interpreter told them, as retribution for Allied soldiers stealing from Italian POWs in Libya, of which there were now tens of thousands.

To his cold fury, Ralph lost the gold signet ring he'd kept hidden from all the thieving guards in Derna, Benghazi and Tuturano. The WOs remonstrated with the *maresciallo*, who protested unconvincingly that his orders came from Rome.

A hundred rings were taken, their owners issued with receipts. Ralph would keep his for nearly two years until he used it to roll a cigarette.[11] The commandant, Coppola, later claimed the rings had been deposited at the Banca d'Italia in Bari, then returned after Italy made peace in 1943 – but this probably never happened, not least because by then the prisoners had been moved on. Later in the war, the Germans caught Mussolini's son-in-law Count Ciano fleeing with two suitcases full of gold rings. Perhaps Ralph's was among them.[12]

The *carabinieri* may have confiscated Ralph's signet ring – but they had not beaten him up, even when, after their return to the camp, he and Charlie thwarted their investigations and made fun of them. These men half killed prisoners for less – far less. In a war crimes affidavit of 1945, RSM Rossouw, the South African Sector 5 head, testified that recaptured escapers were invariably mistreated.[13] Other prisoners, even those accused of trivial offences, had been starved, beaten, stripped, soaked, deprived of sleep and refused medical treatment.[14]

The more I looked into it, the more the anomaly seemed connected with how Ralph and Charlie had managed to escape in the first place; likewise, how they'd been able to construct a radio. As ever, the answer lay in the superior authority and privilege that set them apart from the majority of men whose memories of camp life have survived in recorded interviews and written memoirs.

When I first read Ralph's own memoir, I'd soaked up his exploits uncritically as Colditz-like tales of derring-do, typical of POW life, which like all myth-varnished history presented itself as a flat plane of simple, uniform experience. But Camp 65 had emerged as an anthropologically complex settlement, where cherished archetypes of courage and resistance mattered less than realpolitik and a uniquely introspective power structure.

Escapers, I'd learned, were special characters. Like many others, George Clifton, a New Zealander in another camp, put it down to their innate difference from the mass of 'keepers', combined with a degree of good luck. Having failed to get away by leaving a dummy in his bed, Clifton tried again and this time made it as far as Como – an extraordinary achievement. But then Clifton was a brigadier, and with senior rank came the kind of influence that made successful escapes possible.[15]

How far was Ralph and Charlie's heroic story, the one Dom had been telling visitors to Camp 65, actually rooted in the exploitation of their rank, even at the expense of others? There was another clue. Sitting in Pauline's kitchen, turning the pages of Ralph's album, I came across a pair of oval head-and-shoulder portraits of men in British uniform: Max and Tom. The style matched the photo from Charlie's obituary, reinforcing the idea that these had all been taken in Camp 65 by the visiting photographer. I guessed Charlie's portrait had once been there too. Beside Max and Tom, a space was marked by four corner mounts that once held a photo of identical size. Perhaps Charlie's obituary photo had come from that very print, borrowed and never returned.

Removing the photos from the album revealed addresses on the back. The men were Max Löw and Tom Butterworth. The photos were probably taken at roughly the same time, but had been given to Ralph several months apart. Tom, from Hull in East Yorkshire, on the right, dated his 28 August 1942; Max, a Jew from Palestine, 2 April 1943.

From records in the National Archives, an Israeli website and emails with a relative I traced in Berlin, I learned that Max had been born in 1913 in Wilhelmshaven, Lower Saxony; had farmed in Ahuza, a mountain settlement near Haifa; and in March 1940 had volunteered for the Palestine Pioneer Corps, where he rose to the rank of sergeant. He was wounded and captured in Greece in October 1941, escaped and was recaptured, then sent to Camp 65. A German POW record card from later in the war stated that he was an Australian citizen from Perth, where his wife lived on the High Street – a lie to protect him from Nazi persecution.[16]

Tom Butterworth was born in 1918, in the Hull suburb of Hessle, one of seven children. I contacted his son, Steve, in Hessle, who told me that Tom's four brothers all went into the Royal Navy – he carried their photograph throughout the war – but that Tom himself had opted for the army. As a private in the East Yorkshire Regiment, he belonged, like Ralph, to the 150th Brigade captured on 1 June 1942. It was possible, then, that the two men already knew each other from the desert.

Who Max and Tom were to Ralph would shed light on an important part of his story. Their relationships illustrated a submerged history of influence and advantage, inequality and discontent in camp life. It was a surprise to learn just how much Ralph's preferment had enabled him not only to get through captivity unharmed, but also to keep busy and, furthermore, to seize upon opportunities for escape.

12.
The Bread Palace

At the end of March, the mood in the camp continued to lighten as the Allied invasion of Italy became a matter of when, not if. Relations between the camp staff and the warrant officers – men like Ralph and Charlie, who, the *carabinieri* raid notwithstanding, had been treated leniently after their escape – were cordial. The army guards were blasé or ingratiating; Lieutenant Colonel Coppola, too, strove to be fondly remembered. The *carabinieri*, however, remained as unyielding as ever.

One morning, they were searching the Sector 2 parcels store, across the way from Ralph and Charlie's barracks, when prisoners surged forward to see that nothing was stolen. An inexperienced Italian soldier panicked and bayoneted a South African private in the stomach. Eager to cover up a crime for which they might be held responsible, the *carabinieri* informed the commandant that the prisoner, who was not mortally wounded, had pushed the hapless guard, a version Coppola was forced to accept. Ralph must have seen the bayoneting, and may have given a witness statement, although I couldn't find one in the National Archives. Although no longer in charge of the Sector 2 police, through his rank of warrant officer he continued to command authority among the prisoners.[1]

If the *carabinieri* hoped this incident would warn POWs not to be too bold, if anything it provoked them to greater defiance. Many in Sector 2, though probably not Ralph, regretted not overpowering the guard and attendant *carabinieri*. Similar resistance was seen at Foggia, eighty miles north-west of Gravina, where Camp 65 prisoners who had volunteered for agricultural labour were, contrary to the Geneva Convention, ordered to carry aviation fuel and load bombs onto aircraft. They refused, even when threatened with a sub-machine gun.[2]

As the weather improved and the Italian war effort slumped, so more POWs were sent to work on the land – at Mottola and Venosa, an hour away. Things had changed. Not only were men more likely to be incentivized with food than press-ganged, they had a better chance of escaping. Toiling in open fields, poorly supervised and housed in ramshackle outbuildings, made it much easier.[3] This enraged the *carabinieri*, who had negligent guards punished. In April, John Langdon attempted to escape for a second time, by swapping places with a man on a work party, but again did not get far. Like Ralph and Charlie six weeks earlier, he lied, claiming to have scaled the camp fence, leading the *carabinieri* to imprison two innocent army guards. Sentenced to the usual thirty days, Langdon was freed after eleven, lucky not to be lynched by the soldiers he'd framed. Nor was Langdon abused by the *carabinieri*, probably owing to the status he enjoyed as a senior NCO in this peculiar, self-contained state.[4]

I'd come to see that making a radio wasn't something just anyone could attempt: it depended on contacts, confidence, assets, privacy in the WOs' quarters and access to the cookhouse. Similarly, Ralph and Charlie's escape had required both a support network and the authority to give orders. Now, as I mulled over both projects, previously inconsequential details began to seem significant. Ralph and Charlie's overalls had been obtained from a South African of equal rank to them, but somehow this must have been transactional: possibly cigarettes or food were given in exchange, or a favour promised. Other things suddenly lifted off the page. Perhaps prior to the escape no one had checked on Ralph and Charlie in their bunks, not just from fear of infection but out of respect for two warrant officers, one of whom was a policeman. They lived charmed lives.

Many prisoners remembered Gravina as 'hell camp': Tom Butterworth even used the phrase in a list of postings, scribbled on the back of the photo of his brothers. But not Ralph, who likened the camp to a thrumming hive but actually said little about its hardships. In his account of the radio episode, he wrote: 'it grieves me even to look back on my life in that prison camp' – but his first, more honest, thought was that such recollection made him feel 'just a little feverish', a milder statement, which he crossed out.⁵ And the indignities and cruelties he did describe – bootless prisoners in winter, living skeletons, the demise of men in their prime – always seemed to be happening to someone else.

Across a sliding scale of privilege, the regular inflow of Red Cross parcels made all prisoners happier, not just Ralph, Charlie and the favoured few. Not only were men better nourished but they could trade. Parcels from home contained pyjamas, scarves and knitted sweaters, exchanged with guards for bread before they became infested. 'Quante pane una vesta?' was a phrase known by every enterprising prisoner.⁶

Bartering arrangements evolved into an 'exchange and mart' system, with cigarettes as currency and prices stabilized by notices of sales and wants. Hawkers strode through the barracks crying 'cheese for seven', which meant the standard cheese ration, a small cube, could be had for seven cigarettes. This might not be the salesman's own portion; chances were he'd bought it from a prisoner for four cigarettes, and would spend his profits with another salesman. And so, the market economy flourished.⁷

In 1945, Richard Radford, an economist and ex-prisoner, described a POW camp as 'an unusual but vital society', where economic life was regulated by supply and demand, causing inflation and deflation. Manufacture was artisanal rather than industrial, but there was a thriving service economy of tailors, cobblers, laundrymen and barbers. As specie, cigarettes were relatively stable but could be devalued by a flood of tobacco parcels or debased by tampering. In some camps, 'banks' issued paper currency backed by a 'gold standard' of tinned food. Rumours spooked markets, and speculators went bust. Hot weather pushed up the price of soap; cold weather, cocoa – although men also held to the idea of a fair price, based on custom not reason, to resist rampant profiteering.⁸

Middlemen occupied a precarious position between trusted

retailers and dishonest racketeers. Ralph would have known many men who boasted they could obtain anything; these ranged from small-time hustlers to 'barons' who cornered markets. A trooper from the Tank Corps, in cahoots with British NCOs and Italian officers, offered a night out in Gravina for 500 lire and other lavish treats that netted him a fortune. Another baron amassed thousands of cigarettes from a kindling business, which he invested in luxuries to sell on. Some prisoners found a new vocation. One man recognized a dodgy tobacco spiv as a respectable tennis player from his home town in Berkshire.[9] In the darker precincts of this world gangsters lurked. One Camp 65 cartel extorted a cut of the food cooks held back, demoralizing law-abiding prisoners and tempting them to join the cartel themselves. The Italians and the POW police knew about this but did not intervene.[10]

Such activity naturally arose from an economy of merchants, rentiers and consumers. A South African prisoner described Camp 65 in terms of a majority working class sandwiched between an underclass of beggars and a middle class who in civilian life had white-collar occupations. This middle class also included entrepreneurs, a cohort dominated by 400 Cypriots and, to a lesser extent (because there were only sixty-three of them), Palestinian Jews. Together they were the pre-eminent peddlers, salesmen, racketeers and gangsters.[11]

Most Cypriots and Palestinian Jews came from non-combatant support units captured in Greece and were based in Sector 5. But both nationalities were also represented in Sector 2. Ralph was helped to escape by a Cypriot, and I knew from his photo album he had befriended the Palestinian Jewish sergeant Max Löw. Charlie's maps were supplied by Sector 2 Cypriots, possibly Ralph's watch, the compass and wire cutters, too. The freethinking artist Robert Lee, who must have been in Sector 2 – he could see Altamura from his hut – knew many Cypriots and Palestinians, and was unbothered by their dubious reputation.[12]

Adept operators, these men had fingers in every pie. They founded the cookhouse gang and were notorious for trading 'over the wire', especially swapping Red Cross items for eggs and bread. This was forbidden, and in Sector 5 strenuously punished by RSM Rossouw. Many, like the Cypriot involved in Ralph's escape, spoke Italian – but mercantile genius made them virtuoso communicators in any language or none at all. They also had the power to fix prices for a begrudging majority outnumbering them twenty to one.[13]

Robert Lee particularly remembered one Palestinian 'godfather', who did favours in the expectation they would be returned.[14] Was this Ralph's friend, Max Löw? Ralph didn't mention Palestinians, but I knew they were part of a diffuse economy that had facilitated his escape. At the end of the war, Max completed what was known as a 'liberation report', which turned up at Kew. Under the heading 'Sabotage', he simply put: 'helping P.O.W. to escape in Italy, P65 Camp'.[15] This had to be Ralph. Max was certainly a canny, resourceful man, and had himself escaped four times while a prisoner in Greece. And he gifted Ralph his photograph on 2 April 1943, soon after Ralph was released from his cell. As prisoners often did, they probably exchanged photos – Ralph's, perhaps, given as a token of thanks.

The Cypriots were a tight-knit community, which was nonetheless outgoing, its business guided by customary Levantine hospitality and friendship. Every encounter was an occasion to close a deal or oil the wheels for some future bargain, but was invariably convivial. Cypriots pooled their food so they could eat communally and invite guests. Robert Lee ate with them in the traditional way, sitting in a circle, plates laid out on a cloth, bread passed round, and everyone encouraged to help themselves. He thought of them as friends, but then again as a portrait artist he had something to sell.[16]

Scouring books and archives, I found that Lee was almost unique in his affection for Cypriots and Palestinians. Most prisoners saw them as 'shady dealers', to be avoided if possible and certainly not trusted. A Royal Artillery gunner who admired the fair-haired, clean-limbed Afrika Korps, despised dark-skinned 'Eyeties' or 'Macaroni Men', as he called them, but reserved a special racist hatred for 'the Bloody Cyps' with their 'graft and greed' and the way they curried favour with the Italians:

A Cypriot was never hungry and could always produce a hoard of bread loaves from among his possessions. They never seemed to touch their Red Cross parcels but were content instead to sit cross-legged on their beds, unopened tins before them, while files of starving prisoners passed up and down bargaining with cigarettes, trinkets, souvenirs, clothing and anything of value to ease the pangs of hunger. It made one's blood boil to reflect that the folks back home were contributing their pennies and shillings to support this awful abuse.

Amazed by the heap of buns a Cypriot had under a blanket, one prisoner said he felt justified in helping himself. Unable to take any more, 'plundering bands' of POWs raided the Cypriots' quarters armed with knives. Huge brawls were broken up by guards with fixed bayonets.[17]

The *carabinieri* also despised Cypriots, and were less easily corrupted than the guards. In September 1942 they seized a stash of contraband money, and, always eager to divide and rule, on lines of class or ethnicity, donated it to the Welfare and Social Committee to buy musical instruments. After this the Cypriots were more careful about where they kept their wealth. It was from such a secret bank that Ralph's thousand lire note must have come.[18] That gesture – a single line in the memoir – now seemed like a gateway into a lost world, invisible behind the bland screen of familiar POW history.

For all their economic strength the Cypriots were politically marginal, and so depended on warrant officers like Ralph and Charlie. Once I'd discovered this, everything made sense. Like eastern traders, they and their fellow WOs were seen by the proletariat as an aristocracy distastefully in league with the bourgeois Cypriots and, by association, the absolutist camp authorities. After all, except for Allied padres and doctors, the WOs were the senior ranks, and so acquired the clout of de facto commissioned officers. They called the shots in every situation. Almost all escapes involved sergeants or WOs, who uniquely were sufficiently well connected to make the necessary arrangements.[19]

Location was another component of power. It dawned on me

that, unlike escapes on the south side, far from the front of the camp, Ralph and Charlie had broken out under the noses of the enemy, not as some brazen act of daring but simply because this was where they lived: just a few feet from the guardrooms and the *palazzina comando*. Although I'd long known that Ralph had been promoted and moved to the warrant officers' hut, it was only from reading memoirs in the Imperial War Museum that I realized quite what ordinary soldiers in their noisy, overcrowded barracks thought of this arrangement. Scorned as havens of comfort and plenty, it turned out that the warrant officers' half-size huts were, in each of the sectors, known as 'bread palaces'. WOs always wore pressed uniforms and polished boots, and were even said to have sprung mattresses. They had their own 'little kitchens' – *cucine piccole* – and, to many disgruntled POWs, never looked thin at times of dearth.[20]

The crux of power, and disquiet, was food. Most diaries and memoirs were obsessed with it. So, it was only after I'd been through the first-hand accounts in the IWM that it occurred to me how little Ralph said about food. He merely described the ration, which 'was very meagre to say the least, not sufficient for a boy to live on let alone a man', adding that the 'coffee' was so bad prisoners often didn't bother to collect it.[21]

Like the camp police and other POW employees, WOs received extra rations. But this wasn't their only source of additional nourishment. One POW recalled 'constant rumours of fiddles' among Camp 65's senior ranks, who were also believed to loot personal parcels – looting being the gravest camp offence, after wounding or murder. 'The general complaint amongst the prisoners was the lack of food,' a soldier reporting war crimes told Scottish police in 1946. 'Some of the prisoners blamed the Italians for this, but the majority were inclined to blame our own warrant officers and NCOs for the shortage of rations issued to the men.'[22] An army sergeant in Sector 5, trusted to ensure prisoners received their share of prepared food, was vehemently suspected to be part of a cookhouse scam.[23]

RSM John Rossouw defended this sergeant – as he might, since Rossouw, too, was a hate figure. It wasn't just that he was the Sector 5 camp leader, he was also head of its police. This was, Ralph maintained, 'an extremely difficult job though it had some compensations' – by which presumably he meant better food and other material advantages. The price was unpopularity to the point where some WOs were considered tyrants, traitors even. Among the liberation reports, I found testimony from Rossouw in which he admitted that, like all camp policemen, he punished prisoners accused of trading with the Italians by withholding food parcels. This sanction, apparently endorsed by the International Red Cross, had been imposed solely, Rossouw insisted, 'to enforce discipline to maintain my self-respect and morale'. Less plausibly, he also claimed that men approved of it as a penalty. Such strictures were universally resented. In Sector 3, the camp leader was loathed for running his own prison, 'the Clink', a tent surrounded by barbed wire and guarded by a burly South African known as 'the Hippo'. In every sector, WOs sent out police patrols and punished petty offences, mostly pilfering and illegal trading, in local 'courts'.[24]

One final hunch hardened into fact. Memoirs recorded that WOs were so absorbed by their officer-like status that they started employing batmen – servants drawn from the junior ranks, a privilege reserved for *officer* POWs – thereby redrawing class boundaries in an astonishing way.[25] I guessed what this social elevation would have meant to Ralph. If he did keep a batman in Camp 65, it's no surprise it went unrecorded. But there was a clue.

It now made sense why Ralph had a photo of Max Löw – a tough, self-possessed Palestinian sergeant, possibly one of the 'godfathers' or some other shrewd accomplice. But what of Tom Butterworth, a humble private, whose portrait was preserved alongside it? His son Steve told me that prior to demobilization his father had been stationed at Fort Widley in Portsmouth, where he had met Steve's mother, who was in the Auxiliary Territorial Service supporting officers. And what was Tom's job? He was an officer's batman. Perhaps Tom hadn't been Ralph's friend, then, more his retainer, a loyal Yorkshireman he could rely on.

Steve sent me Tom's wartime diary, in which were listed names and addresses, including – next to each other – entries for Ralph and Charlie and another warrant officer of note, W. J. Barker. Ralph is given as 'Mr Corps', which is how Tom would have addressed him: the deference of a servant to his master.[26]

When Tom gifted Ralph his photo, evidently he wrote something in the space above the portrait, presumably some kind of dedication. Before the photo was mounted in the album, however, Ralph, or perhaps Flo, trimmed it off with a pair of scissors.

By late April 1943, Gravina was blessed with brighter, drier days and a cautious warmth that gave men hope. The tally of nearly 9,000 prisoners fell to 6,500, the result of transfers and declining arrivals due to Axis military defeats. Two thousand were relocated to work camps both in Puglia and further north, and sent from there to farms and factories. On the 28th, 120 South Africans left Sector 3 for a camp south of Venice, and a similar number of British for Camp 148 Bussolengo in the province of Verona. Floor sleepers graduated to beds, rations were more plentiful, and there was a healthy supply of parcels. The guards, too, felt some *joie de vivre*. Unseen by the *carabinieri*, they cut the wire between the sectors to allow POWs free movement. Men were allowed unlimited hot showers.[27]

The Anti-Boredom Committee stepped up its campaign of practical jokes, chiefly directed at a preening Italian adjutant nicknamed the 'Corset King' owing to speculation about his trim figure. They shot pellets at him during check parade, put lice on his uniform and saluted until he grew weary of saluting back. A cistern of stagnant urine was rigged up to topple on him – now they held their noses instead of saluting – and his boots were splashed with pigswill. Their tour de force was a catapult mounted at a blockhouse window. Using stones as ammunition, tests were carried out on a donkey and the pail of the milk girl, who fell off her bike. Next they smashed the commandant's window. Guessing they might target the changing of the guard, Lieutenant Colonel Coppola, waiting with binoculars, set up a decoy so the real guard could detect the line of fire. The catapult crew were apprehended and punished, albeit leniently.[28]

Prisoners perked up. They threw themselves into hobbies, cracked jokes, swept and whitewashed their barracks. In Sector 3, a bay vacated by transfers was made over as a recreation room christened 'The Dog and Partridge', a pub with books instead of beer (membership fee: one book), where men played cards, chess and board games such as 'Attack' and 'Air Strike' sent by the Red Cross, and bingo evenings were held. In another bay, joiners built a chapel with an altar and oak beams painted using a mixture of acorn coffee and olive oil. Best of all was a newly constructed theatre, 'The Cosmopolitan', which had a stage with proper lighting and furniture made from Red Cross crates, which, by slipping through the sector fences, men from all over the camp visited.[29]

There was still no space for football, but basketball and tag rugby were popular, with tournaments, trophies and a lot of gambling. At inter-sector boxing matches, ringside seats were reserved for Italian officers and their egregious colleagues, the British warrant officers; ordinary spectators sat up on blockhouse roofs.[30]

Drama and music companies now proliferated. Sector 3 boasted a renowned concert party, Sector 2 a chamber orchestra, Sector 1 a jazz band, and so on. Instruments were provided by the Red Cross or, after much saving (supplemented by compulsory levies imposed by the WOs), bought from the Italians. The commandant also gave whatever help he could. Ralph's memoir records that the building of Sector 2's theatre was driven by RSM Alderson: 'only a little man but he certainly found a means to move the Italians'. Ralph himself got involved, sourcing wigs, costumes and props that he and others 'managed to acquire on account of our highly refined business connections'. Almost certainly this meant the Cypriots and the Palestinians. That spring, Sector 2 put on a funfair with side shows, darts challenges and other games; punters blew their lire and cigarettes, and entrepreneurs cleaned up. 'Some of the men dressed as ladies,' recalled one prisoner, 'and there was much ribaldry and teasing.' The commandant ended the fun with a check parade, just as bombers passed over and they heard distant explosions. Worried-looking Italians chased the cheering POWs back into their huts at bayonet-point.[31]

Like many who had barely glimpsed a woman, apart from the milk girl, for almost a year, Ralph was impressed by the female impersonators in theatrical productions:

> Seeing a show for the first time one would hardly realise that the ladies' parts were played by British Tommies. I've paid to see worse shows in England. And please don't get the idea that prison shows were rough and uncouth. Some of these 'ladies' were really genteel. Yes! We certainly began to get atmosphere.[32]

Some men allowed themselves to be deceived, swearing that real women had been smuggled in by some audacious baron. There was a Folies Bergère performance where a chorus line did the Can-Can, all high kicks and flipped-up skirts.[33]

This amounted to more than enthusiasm for the theatre. Now that men had more to eat, their libidos returned with no outlet except masturbatory fantasies – enthusiasts were 'bishop bashers', 'wire-pullers' and 'mutton floggers' – and suspended disbelief at cross-dressing on stage. These tableaux vivants satisfied heterosexual desire, an indulgence tinged with transgression yet entirely morally acceptable in this mixed-up social world of artifice, pretence and suspended norms.[34]

Some prisoners, naturally, were homosexual and lived the shadow life described by Dan Billany and David Dowie, prisoners in another southern camp, in their haunting 1949 book *The Cage*.[35] According to Robert Lee, there was a distinct gay community in Camp 65, although, rightly or wrongly, he believed this arose from little more than a temporary, convenient sexual orientation born of sheer privation. It's true that much sexual activity was just flirtation between straight men, among whom a few were nonetheless openly transgender or simply chose to impersonate women. The centre of temptation was Sector 5, where according to Lee the Cypriots indulged visitors:

> They must have built up quite a trade in women's clothes. They used to parade at night, dressed up. It doesn't mean every man who dressed up turned queer, or was queer already, any more than being deprived of female company automatically makes men queer . . . I went and watched them once. It was more than just drag acts, more than just song-and-dance. Dresses, handbags, stockings, everything.

Before passage between sectors was permitted, men crawled under the wire to see Cypriots dancing, kissing and cuddling. There were even reports of a brothel, and razor fights between jealous lovers. One prisoner recalled how a female impersonator became openly solicitous, and 'was eventually caught in one of the toilets misbehaving himself'.[36]

This eruption of suppressed civilian life was energized by optimistic news. Mussolini, defeated in North Africa and Russia, still hoped that when the war turned in favour of the Axis powers, it would be in the Mediterranean theatre. But this depended on peace with Stalin so that the German army could be redeployed to Tunisia. Hitler would have none of it. The future of fascist Italy looked uncertain as the Allied invasion drew nearer.

By early May, Camp 65 was buzzing with rumours that more prisoners were being moved north, starting with 'bad boys' like Ralph and Charlie. Happy to be leaving, the friends still wanted to make their radio work. As marked men, however, it would be hard for them to hide it from the *carabinieri*, both on departure and arrival at their new camp.

A week later, 700 men, including the 'bad boys', were told to pack. WOs not on the list urged Ralph and Charlie, for their own safety, to leave the radio behind. But just then the Italian electrician showed up, offering a transformer in exchange for a gold watch. They agreed. 'We hadn't a gold watch,' Ralph wrote, 'but knew where we could get one' – which again must have meant the

Cypriots or Palestinians. All Ralph said was that it was paid for by 'a sergeant who was going to the new camp with us'.[37]

There wasn't much time. The Royal Engineers made two false-bottomed cases painted in chicory essence, and the electrician came the next day, ostensibly to install a bell in the Sector 2 infirmary. The transformer and the other components were fitted into the cases.

On transfer day, Ralph arranged for two policemen whose names were on the list, but were not 'bad boys', to carry the cases as their luggage. The clothing inside was unmarked by names or badges of rank, so might belong to anyone. The men were ordered to line up in parade fashion outside the *carabinieri* search room. Ralph and Charlie hovered towards the back, the policemen five rows ahead, each holding a case. Ralph hoped that by the time the *carabinieri* got to them they would be bored and slapdash.

Only after three hours were the policemen called inside. Hearts in their mouths, Ralph and Charlie stared at the exit until they emerged, whereupon the couriers gave a prearranged signal: the cases had passed undetected.

Another couple of hours passed, by which time it was dark. Then came Ralph's turn. It was the same room where he'd been questioned after the escape, and behind the desk sat the charmless *maresciallo*. The Italian's mouth twitched at one corner, which Ralph took to be his idea of a smile and made him seem almost human. He gestured for Ralph to sit – on the floor, which was at least carpeted.

Ralph's bag, belonging to one of the stooges, was searched – but of course he had nothing to hide. The *maresciallo*, stymied again, waved him away. Ralph looked at his watch: it was 1 a.m. Outside the wire now, and under heavy guard, he lay down with Charlie and other men already asleep on the bare ground.

At first light, they were prodded awake and marched through the gate, never to return.

13.
Amapola

It was five years since Mum's dream. From knowing Ralph no better than a character in a fable or folktale, I'd begun to see the fullness of his life: its depths and detours, nuances and contrasts. He remained an Everyman, one of millions at war, but his individuality was also apparent, as in a novel or film. During hundreds of hours in archives and libraries, and out on the road with Dom, I often thought of Philip Roth's line that before we meet someone we get them wrong, then upon meeting them we get them wrong all over again.[1] Ralph, on the other hand, had received so much of my attention, I really thought I'd got him right – although what these labours said about me remained obscure. Perhaps I identified with him in some strange, secret way. Although I'd never met him, the journey of discovery had come to feel very personal, part of my own life and part of my past.

Dom called to see how I was getting on. Having been in Ralph's company for so long, I said regretfully, I felt he was slipping away. The memoir had kept me at his side in Camp 65, but soon he'd be leaving me, in the summer of 1943, which is where his memoir peters out, to recover the rest of his war on my own. I hoped the archives would finish the story, perhaps even throw in some more of his thoughts and feelings. Yet Dom wasn't sure I would ever really know Ralph – the truth of his inner life. He quoted the great Italian writer Italo Calvino, who compared this kind of reality to an infinite artichoke, the multiple, prickly layers peeled back to reveal more and more – and yet without end.[2]

The final volume of Ralph's memoir, the shortest of the three, told the story of the prison radio, not only at Gravina but subsequently.

This story would keep me with Ralph for another few weeks, before dramatic events in Italy overtook him, thinning available documentation and fading his story back to obscurity.

Ralph described how, after leaving Camp 65, he and his fellow prisoners reached a railway siding where, around 8 a.m., a train arrived pulling not the usual cattle trucks but neat civilian carriages. Ten men with baggage were crammed into each. Ralph and Charlie, who had stayed together, carefully stowed the cases containing the radio. Although forbidden to open the curtains, as the engine pulled away men rushed to the windows, returning to their seats only when an Italian officer passed down the corridor.

The westward journey lasted several hours. Ralph and Charlie naturally thought about escaping, but guards were posted all along the train, and jumping was hazardous even on slow bends. The temptation and the danger manifested together whenever the carriage doors were unlocked for men to relieve themselves.[3]

Passing through Naples in the afternoon, Ralph marvelled at the feathery plume of Vesuvius. From there the train continued up Italy's western flank, another 350 miles to the port of Livorno, where the oil depot was blazing after an RAF raid, and the men cheered until silenced by the patrolling officer. Shortly after that they reached Pisa, where they glimpsed the Leaning Tower. Into the night, the flash-and-crack of anti-aircraft batteries grew more frequent. They tried to sleep. 'You'll break your neck,' went the click-clack of the wheels, 'you'll break your neck.' Others heard: 'I must get away, I must get away.'[4]

Dawn found them trundling through Massa, the Ligurian Sea to their left, Apuan Alps on the right, after which they passed through La Spezia and hugged the coast towards Genoa for another forty miles until they reached the resort of Chiavari. There the train stopped, and the prisoners spilled onto the platform, stretching limbs. It was 9 a.m. It had been a cramped 600-mile tour of how Italy was losing the war.

Holidaymakers in light suits and tea dresses stared at the dishevelled POWs herded out of the station and wrangled into columns. There were lorries to carry kit, but the men had to walk – ten miles up a winding hill. The morning sun was searing, and many were feverish with malaria, though not Charlie. The guards kept saying it was only another few kilometres, yet by the time the road levelled out they too were staggering like drunks.[5] Even Ralph, who considered himself fit, found his legs were like rubber.

Entering the picturesque village of Pian di Coreglia, they turned off down a tree-lined path leading to a small river. Across the footbridge were a guardhouse and a gate, behind which lay a cluster of timber-framed huts, surrounded by fences and swathes of forested hillside. Welcome to Camp 52 Chiavari. Prisoners rushed to the wire to see the newcomers, but were herded back by guards. The *carabinieri* were waiting. Ralph and Charlie glanced at each other, then at the cases in their sweaty hands.[6]

Corralled outside the administration building, the new prisoners retrieved their baggage and were then made to wait in a large shed. At around 2 p.m. the first of the 700 names was called out, soon followed by Ralph's. He was ushered into an adjoining room where *carabinieri* were standing behind tables searching prisoners' bags. Ralph strode to the nearest table and set down his case.

The unsmiling *carabiniere* was young and brisk. Ralph read him as he did any fellow policeman, and helped him rummage through the clothing until he was satisfied. Ralph closed the case and raised his arms to be searched. Fifteen nerve-shredding minutes later, it was all over. Soon afterwards, Charlie was called. He too was in the clear.

Ralph and Charlie were taken to the WOs' quarters, a white bungalow constructed of chipboard panels nailed to a studwork frame. Positioned just inside the gate, Hut 16 was, like their lodgings in Camp 65, a special place of authority and privilege. A watercolour by Horace Wade, the camp's most accomplished artist, depicts it to the right of a pair of bigger two-storey huts inhabited by the rank and file.

The door, rigged to a weighted pulley, swung shut. The room was cluttered but tidy. Bunks ran either side of an aisle. The wooden headboards were decorated with pinned-up photos, clothes lines were strung across the ceiling, and the windows had shutters made from

Red Cross boxes. Wade also immortalized this interior. The warrant officers lying there smoking and reading didn't pay Ralph and Charlie much attention, except for sideways glances at their celebratory war dance. They had sneaked the radio past the *carabinieri*, who until now Ralph had considered the world's most competent police.[7]

That evening, after they had settled in and introduced themselves to their hut-mates, Ralph and Charlie discussed the failings of the *carabinieri* search. 'I hope you could do better than that at home,' joked Charlie.[8] Ralph reckoned he would have noticed had a suspect he'd arrested been carrying a wooden box full of electrical components. They did not, however, mention the radio to the other WOs – not yet anyway – supposing that Camp 52 was as infested with spies as Camp 65 had been. At lights-out they could hear newcomers still being admitted to the camp, a procedure that went on till nearly midnight. By then they were fast asleep at the end of what had been a shattering day.

★

After morning check parade and breakfast, Ralph and Charlie explored the camp, a place very different from Gravina. Consisting of forty-four wooden huts on the shallow slope of a hill, raised on stilts because this was a flood plain, it was too small to need sectors. There was a big stone kitchen, and a barn-like refectory with tables and stools for every prisoner, which also served as a common room and a theatre where a packed repertoire of plays was performed. The shop and chapel were located there, too. Fresh water was in continuous supply, and hot baths could be taken once a week. The washhouses, also solid constructions, were sited near the riverbank, and the huts furthest from there were equipped with night latrines. A house belonging to local nobility had been requisitioned as an infirmary and delousing plant. Everything smelled encouragingly of carbolic disinfectant.[9]

The buildings were set out in a rough triangle a quarter of a mile on each side, one of which ran parallel to the river.[10] A brisk stroll round the perimeter took ten minutes. On the other side of the bridge Ralph and Charlie could see a line of houses where the commandant's quarters, guards' barracks and Red Cross parcel store were.[11] The prospect was pretty, and not quite real, reminding one prisoner, the poet Robert Garioch, of a stage for an Italian opera.[12]

As for the wider setting, the camp was nestled in a tranquil enclosure of unfolding green, fragrant with orchards of peach and apple, backed by mountains and cultivated terraces, the slopes crumbling under a forest of chestnut. The higher ground looked out across the valley: fields of wheat shooting into ear, pretty, well-tended farms and the pastel towers of baroque churches. The clang of bells rose and fell on breezes from the Ligurian Riviera. As the sun went down, men listened for cuckoos, and the hillside to the rear was luminescent with the trails of fireflies.[13]

All around the wire grew tall scarlet poppies, symbols not just of sacrifice in the previous war but of Chiavari's soothing, abundant beauty. Nothing had grown in the dust of Gravina. The Italian word for poppy, some thought, was *amapola* – but it was in fact Spanish, and the title of a hit song prisoners whistled around the camp.

Having absorbed the topography, Charlie began milking prisoners for information. He and Ralph met Bert Macey, a naval petty officer in the next hut, who had been there since July 1942 after his ship, HMS *Bedouin*, was sunk off Sicily. Now, he was preparing for his part in a production of *The Mikado*. Ralph and Bert talked about their wives: Bert's was in Gillingham, Kent, where Ralph's sister-in-law Charlotte lived with her husband Arch and daughter Audrey – my mother. Yes, Ralph knew Gillingham well: summer days in the beer garden of The Three Mariners, ice creams round the bandstand at the Strand.[14]

In the days that followed, Ralph and Charlie learned everything about the history, economics and politics of Camp 52, reputedly the best in Italy.[15] Prisoners were clean and well fed, busy and amused. They numbered just 3,000 – mainly British and South Africans, the New Zealanders having been relocated in February. Hierarchy was not fiercely defended, but still the WOs, and naval petty officers like Macey, declined to mix with other ranks and, as in Camp 65, were disliked for their superiority in all matters – a privilege of rank that Ralph and Charlie had automatically acquired upon arrival.[16]

According to one prisoner, this divide was 'a case of jealousy on the one hand and a sense of guilt on the other'.[17] Presiding over everything was John Shimmin, the British camp leader, a stern, intransigent regimental sergeant major, who lived with the other WOs. There was no trace of guilt about *him*, and his judgement was never questioned. As in Gravina, there were informers among the prisoners. Macey warned Ralph and Charlie about the 'Boers' – Afrikaans-speaking South Africans – who hated the British and fraternized with the *carabinieri*.[18]

If Ralph had hoped to be made head of police, he was disappointed: the camp was so small and orderly it had no need of policemen. The ordinary guards, all of whom the POWs called 'Toni', and who in return called their charges 'Giorgio', were mostly tenderly pro-British, their sentimentality pricked when shown photographs from home. Some fussed like mothers, trying to make mad Englishmen in the midday sun take siestas: 'Prego, Giorgio, prego!' Behind the mask of his long-faced frown, the commandant, Colonel Castelli-Taddei, was fair-minded, as was his young deputy, Lieutenant Zavatteri. It was Castelli-Taddei's custom to greet new arrivals in person, offering them a home from home if they behaved. That month, the Red Cross newspaper *The Prisoner of War* published a letter describing him as 'a perfect gentleman'.[19] The camp's artisans made gifts, including woven straw shoes for his wife, and for Zavatteri a souvenir 'blower' stove complete with side oven. Castelli-Taddei admired the inmates: 'They are good soldiers, my prisoners,' he said.[20]

Red Cross parcels were plentiful in Chiavari and trading was lively. Men played a game, swapping food until the ceiling of the market had been found and an asset could no longer be improved upon. A box of Oxo cubes might be advertised as 'six square meals' by a budding investor, who hoped to end up with a tin of bully. Horace Wade captured this bartering scene in the same month Ralph and Charlie arrived.[21]

If Gravina had been Egypt, this was the Promised Land. As one prisoner remarked to his mate: 'I can remain here for the rest of the war and enjoy it after that bastard Campo 65.' But it had not always been so happy, and contrasts with Gravina were largely due to the improved supply of parcels into 1943.[22] Early in its existence, Chiavari's huts were unheated and lousy, and winds gusting down the valley tore roofs from their purlins.[23] Men had starved. Macey told Ralph and Charlie how the previous year they'd survived on less than a pound of food per day. Skilly was bulked out with weeds and even toilet paper. A Guards sergeant and his mate had eaten a cat fried with onions – one of thirty that disappeared, as well as a few dogs, including the commandant's poodle, whose pelt was made into slippers. Men also ate slugs, and smoked oak leaves and sacking.[24] Like many others, Macey, now the picture of health, had had diarrhoea and boils.

Scarcity had had the same effect as in Camp 65. A black market gang, 'The Ring', controlled the cookhouse, smuggled in potatoes and wine and intimidated rival racketeers. There had also been despair among men who, a prisoner recalled, traipsed round the perimeter, 'their faces stamped with an inexpressibly sad look of absolute boredom and personal defeat'. Others had let themselves go, wailing and soiling their bunks. A brilliant musician became indifferent to the lice hanging off his long hair 'like bunches of mouldy grapes'. There were wild delusions: one man believed he was General Montgomery; another, Winston Churchill.[25]

But that was all in the past. The Red Cross had sent uniforms, boots and toiletries, and so much food that many stopped eating skilly. Wages had gone up to ten lire a week, and the shop was stocked with cheap vegetables and fruit; even wine was available. Men were fit enough to enjoy themselves. Books and games, paper and pens, were plentiful, and there were lectures and classes in banking and bookkeeping, building and surveying, literature and music, chemistry and metallurgy, advertising and salesmanship. An Italian officer taught history of art, with special reference to Tuscany. Music – best of all, 'Amapola' – was played through loudspeakers, as in a Butlin's holiday camp at Skegness or Clacton.[26]

Chiavari's crowning glory, however, was its theatre. Early in June 1943, Ralph and Charlie enjoyed watching Bert Macey in *The Mikado*, the music for which Ralph had known since Cyprus. Rave reviews had persuaded the director to announce extra dates so it could be seen by all. This included the commandant, Lieutenant Zavatteri and other Italian officers, who, accompanied by wives and girlfriends, were seated in the front row.

The female roles were exquisitely performed in crêpe-paper dresses. Audiences were especially captivated by the secret love of Yum-Yum for Nanki-Poo.[27] A comedian from Brighton Theatre, in the role of Pooh-Bah, had everyone in stitches with ad-libbed digs at the Italians that soared over their heads. The leading tenor was an opera singer who at home in Durban had sung on the radio; some musicians hailed from the Queen's Hall Orchestra; and the costumes were made by a pair of Bond Street tailors.[28]

Most remarkable was the director Eric Huggett, a sapper in the Royal Engineers. In civvy street a musical education adviser, he had staged many plays at Chiavari, including *Charley's Aunt*, *Pygmalion*, *Hay Fever*, *Top Hat* and an adaptation of John Steinbeck's *Of Mice and Men* (dubbed 'Of Lice and Men').[29] His Christmas pantomime, he enthused in a letter home, had cast and crew 'keyed up in a terrific state of tension', yet had earned multiple curtain calls, been declared a festive sensation and left men humming his theme tune for days. An Italian photo shows the line-up for *The Importance of Being Earnest*, including Huggett seated in Edwardian hat and dress. He longed to do a Savoy opera, but the authorities had banned sheet music, fearing the notation might contain secret messages.[30]

Early in 1943 this ban was lifted, so via the Red Cross Huggett ordered *The Mikado* from the D'Oyly Carte Opera Company. Unable to wait, however, he wrote Gilbert and Sullivan's libretto and score from memory and had the bandmaster orchestrate it. It was yet another a triumph. Men laughed and cried. At the end, the Italians led a standing ovation, and Castelli-Taddei gave a speech praising the company's efforts.[31]

Humour in the camp was also provided by satirical skits, and what Bert Macey called 'the fierce joy' of tormenting the guards. Night sentries used to call to each other in operatic voices – 'Alerte Sentinella Una' followed by 'Alerte Sentinella Due' and so on – to ensure they were still awake. Prisoners delighted in breaking the chain by singing the cries out of order. Just watching the clumsy guards present arms was hilarious: the tinny bugle, rusty rifles clanking against helmets. As well as joking, there was a lot of gambling. Men placed bets on anything, including the colour of the knickers of the women who leaned over with sickles to cut the poppies and grass between the fences.[32]

Plenty more entertainment was laid on. Public debates dealt with topics as diverse as postwar universal disarmament and the abolition of fox hunting.[33] Sports included volleyball, basketball, baseball, boxing, fencing and football – league and cup – on a three-quarter-size pitch. The star player was Reg Allen, goalkeeper for Queen's Park Rangers, whose beefy physique and job in the cookhouse, prisoners muttered, were not unrelated.[34] Another prominent sportsman was the South African Percy Foster, a contender for the heavyweight wrestling championship of the British Empire, who in 1938 had competed in the first ever televised match.[35]

Like music, sport was made possible through equipment sent by the Red Cross – but, as in Camp 65, the commandant did what he could, notably providing costumes and sets for plays. He also permitted swimming in the river, and arranged walking tours to the Val Fontanabuona, the village of Calvari and Columbus's supposed birthplace of Cicagna.[36] Prisoners started calling Castelli-Taddei 'Dad'.[37] He was, one man wrote home in June, 'a trump, scrupulously fair, and nothing too much trouble for our welfare'. The same prisoner described 'ambling along a road winding through a valley with the mountains on either side, little villages perched on the top of them, clinging to their sides like eagles' eyries'. He considered the region 'a POW's dream of heaven' and hoped one day to bring his family to share in the pleasure.[38] Prisoners on these excursions also noticed with grim satisfaction the Italians' desperate measures to exploit every scrap of land for cultivation, with wheat and cauliflowers growing between vines; escape-minded men like Ralph and Charlie memorized the terrain.[39]

That summer, Castelli-Taddei extended the walks to the hills above the coastal town of Rapallo, ten miles away. Prisoners jostled for places – warrant officers like Ralph and Charlie, naturally, had priority – and dressed smartly to impress locals, who, they noticed, had given up crying 'Inglesi caput!' On one hike a contingent of prisoners was even permitted to join a church congregation.[40] From up there, Camp 52's valley appeared as a tiny spot in territory stretching far away into a belt of blue mist rising into the snow of the Maritime Alps. Trips to the Sanctuary of Our Lady at Montallegro offered sublime views across the Ligurian Sea. At this place, the guards told them proudly, Marconi had conducted early experiments in wireless communication.[41]

Whenever the river bed dried up, guards took men to a dammed-off pond so they could splash about there instead. Competition in the soccer league intensified, with bookmakers taking huge bets. There were stage performances to suit all tastes: 'Rise Above It', billed as 'an intimate review'; 'Low & Grim', a burlesque act; 'That'll Be the Day', a variety show; side-splitting madcap comedy with Jasper Miles and his Lunatics; Larry Smith's orchestra; and quizzes, mock trials, debates and talks. These included an account of an accident on HMS *Thetis*, reminiscences of the Prince of Wales's chauffeur, a masterclass in crystallizing fruit and a detailed analysis of South African soil erosion.[42]

One debate considered whether Mrs Beeton or Ginger Rogers had made the greatest contribution to Western civilization. The verdict was not recorded, but depended on whether men were more interested in food or women – in these days of plenty, the latter. In Camp 52 actors in female roles caused even more excitement than at Gravina. It was possible, remarked an avid fan, to find 'the most amazingly attractive boys . . . capable of taking the part of lovely girls'. Prisoners gasped to see 'women' in evening dresses sashay across the stage; Italian officers rubbed their eyes. One soldier, flowers and fruit piled on his head, made an enchanting Carmen Miranda – an act that especially thrilled the Italians.[43]

But there was nothing like the real thing. One hot afternoon, men were sunbathing when the lilt of female singing drifted over from the loudspeakers:

> Amapola, my pretty little poppy,
> You're like that lovely flower so sweet and heavenly;
> Since I found you, my heart is wrapped around you,
> And loving you, it seems to beat a rhapsody.

It was the tune prisoners adored, sung by the American jazz star Helen Forrest, and must have been a gramophone record because they heard it again and again. As they lay back and pictured the sultry Forrest's dark curls and eyes, it was like a collective sexual reawakening. The evenings were idyllic, warm and still, with watercolour sunsets and the song of nightingales fluting from the surrounding woodland.[44]

Whereas at Gravina it had become easier to escape while remaining as hard as ever to reach safety, at Chiavari the problem was reversed: it was closer to the Alps, but getting out was fiendishly difficult. The camp was hemmed in by hills and water, and its triple-layer fence was ten-feet high with inward-sloping posts. Sentry boxes were fitted with overhead floodlights, and at each corner of the triangular compound stood a 'tiger box' – a watchtower mounted with an arc light and a machine gun. To the rear lay a cordon of landmines. The guards were not particularly alert – but they didn't have to be, and the *carabinieri* were as thorough as they'd been in Camp 65.[45]

Ralph and Charlie continued to discuss escaping, alongside their other obsession: making the radio work. As ever, all men craved news. A rumour that Axis forces had surrendered in Tunisia was followed by tales of the intensive bombing of Sicily, Sardinia and the southern mainland. In the east, Stalin was reclaiming everything Hitler had seized since 1941. Prisoners speculated about total Italian defeat and capitulation.[46]

Once they had worked out which of their fellow WOs could be trusted, Ralph and Charlie let on that they had a radio. After all, they needed somewhere to hide it properly and try it out. The *carabinieri* searched the huts frequently, and so thoroughly that men were even made to dismantle the bunks and take them outside. A photograph from 1943, preserved in an obscure archive in New Zealand, records men doing just this.[47]

Ralph and Charlie had been in Camp 52 for three weeks when another consignment of POWs arrived. They spotted a familiar face: Bill Barker – the RSM of the Indian Army Ordnance Corps whose address Tom Butterworth had put in his diary. This was not his first time in Chiavari. A regular soldier in his mid-forties, Barker had been Camp 52's first camp leader until he and six other POWs were caught digging a tunnel under the guardhouse. As a punishment he was briefly sent to Camp 65, where he met Ralph and Charlie. Like all 'bad boys', he was put on a 'not likely to behave' list and denied privileges. He remained, however, well connected, and put the radio hams in touch with the right man.[48]

This was a South African sergeant named Ron Bates. Formerly head of Camp 52's rations, the previous summer he had given Barker bread for his escape, and soon afterwards unsuccessfully hid two other escapers in his storeroom. Bates himself had made a mad run for it through the open gate, but got no further than the footbridge. He was thrown in a cell, where the *carabinieri* beat him every three hours for a fortnight. Returned to barracks, he had to report regularly to the *carabinieri*, an arrangement which continued through the winter until March 1943, when the Italians, relenting, put him in charge of the provisions store. There, three months later, he escorted Ralph and Charlie to hide their radio. Together they created a false compartment in a crate of tinned soup, beneath a pile of junk in one corner.[49]

It was a perfect arrangement. Ralph and Charlie needed to be in the store by 9.30 p.m so that, if the radio worked, they would catch the BBC's overseas broadcast. The store was open only till 6 p.m., but Bates had all-hours access in case new prisoners arrived at night and needed bedding. Several evenings were spent trying to get a signal. Wondering whether new wire coils might help, Charlie showed Ralph how to make them. Still, nothing.[50]

They resolved to have one last go, and, in readiness for failure, went back to doing what they did best: meticulously planning another escape.

14.

Days of Hope

We drove to Calvari, near the site of Camp 52 Chiavari. Dom wasn't completely at ease: the north was too cold, he said – there had been a slight drop in temperature since we'd left the airport at Genoa – and he was wary of the people, much as northern Italians can be wary of folk from the south. Houses we passed seemed tidier, brighter and, to the tourist's eye perhaps, less Italian. It was certainly a lot greener, with climbing hill roads, upland forests and blue-grey skies hung with puffy clouds.

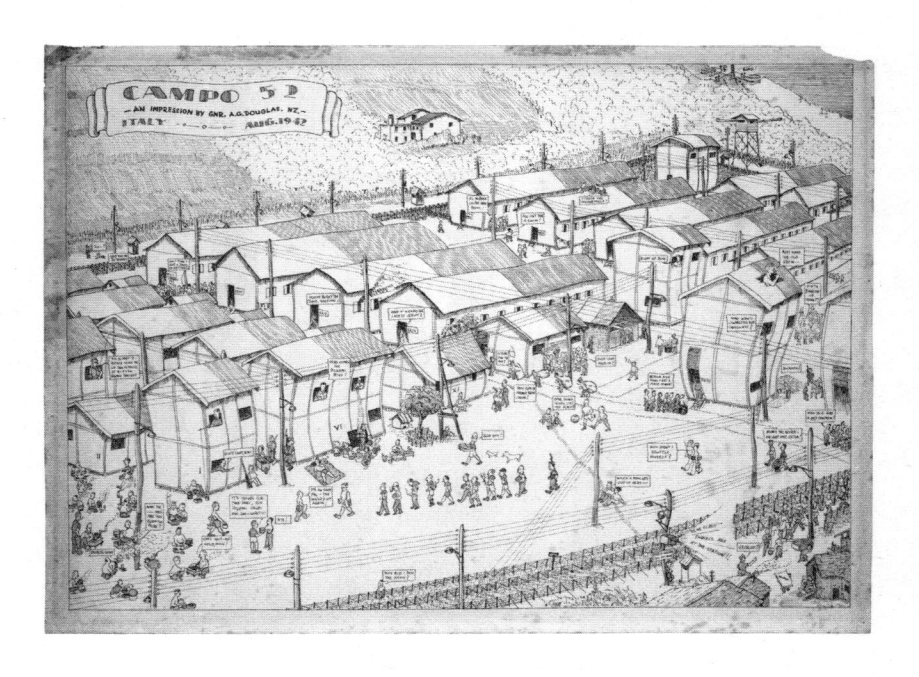

After following Ralph to Camp 65, I felt drawn here too: to be where he'd been and to visualize the next chapter of his story. Dom, loyal as ever to my quest, as well as being a much-needed interpreter, had suggested another road trip where, as in the south of the country, we could carry our present-centred lives into someone else's past. We'd heard that, unlike at Gravina, nothing remained of the camp, but excitingly that the son of the deputy commandant had a collection of relics that prisoners had left behind.[1]

Greeting us in the street, Fabio Zavatteri, a sober, courteous man in his mid-seventies, led the way to a small museum. There, spread out on a table, were boxing gloves and fencing masks once used by the POWs, a pen-and-ink sketch of a bunk by Horace Wade and a cartoon of the camp by a New Zealander, which depicted men going about their business, with speech bubbles full of jokes and sayings of the camp. Reaching into a box, Fabio produced a sepia-tinted portrait of his father, Filippo. Also there was the 'blower' stove presented to Filippo Zavatteri, alongside the straw shoes made for the commandant's wife.

Fabio remembered his father as strong-willed and stubborn, sometimes authoritarian, but always assiduously fair. He told us all about the POWs' walking and swimming privileges, and how diving had been allowed until a man broke his neck on a rock. The agreeable conditions enjoyed by the spring of 1943 had much to do with the charitable nature of Filippo Zavatteri and his benevolent boss, Dino Castelli-Taddei – something that Fabio was keen to impress upon us.

The most startling item in the collection was the original POW card index, a unique survival among Italian camps, neatly arranged in wooden trays with dividers made from Red Cross parcel boxes. Ralph's card looked like it had been typed yesterday. Charlie's didn't seem to be there, perhaps misfiled, although we did find his name typed in a register.

It was a short drive into the Fontanabuona Valley, where it was more humid. Arriving there in 1943, Ralph and Charlie had been struck by how different Chiavari was from Gravina: today, that difference is still clear from the verdant landscape of trees and hills enclosing the empty triangle of meadow where the camp once stood. Gone are the fences, the watchtowers, the huts extending up the hillside – but phantoms throng the thick air, as lively as the characters in the New Zealander's cartoon.

We made our way up a zigzag hill road to visit a British-born American named Robert, who had a house, all pink stucco and trailing rosemary, nestled in the hills above the valley. Cloud across the mountains dispersed to reveal a dazzling sun and a magnificent view, including the site of Camp 52. Over a spectacular lunch served on the veranda, conversation was only of the war. Robert's Italian grandfather had been a POW camp commandant, whose daughter – Robert's mother – had once loved a doomed Italian fighter ace. The family discovered a cache of letters: more relics imbued with haunting power. As for Camp 52, Robert said local people didn't talk about it much, doubtless because, unlike Gravina's ruins, there was nothing left of it to remind them.

We reflected on how in war many young lives had been keyed to the highest pitch, and now lingered in memory, in archives, or packed in boxes like Fabio's artefacts.

'Without us to remember,' said Dom, 'they are gone.'

Held in view for the time it took us to drink a bottle of *Insoglio del Cinghiale*, their stories were evanescent, forever slipping back into obscurity. History was the work of securing them in the present, like chemically fixing a photo.

After leaving the hills, Dom took a wrong turn, and we found ourselves back at the camp. So, with shadows lengthening, we decided to have another look. Using a plan drawn in a prisoner's diary, discovered in the Imperial War Museum, we worked out the location of Hut 16, on the corner of two perpendicular paths, and contemplated vanished walls and a line in space where the roof had been. There, Ralph and Charlie had lived and schemed. A friendly cat came over, a relative, perhaps, of the wretch fried with onions.

We were about to set off again when Dom noticed a small memorial, which we'd missed earlier. It commemorated the Jews of Genoa, the youngest a five-year-old girl, held in Camp 52 after the POWs left. They had all perished in Auschwitz. Quietly defiant, at the edge of an empty field, a plaque held out against the erasure of place and memory.²

The Tank Museum at Bovington in Dorset preserves Horace Wade's art, yet another store of affectively charged relics, which, like Wade's sketch in Calvari, survived only by chance: his mother nearly threw everything away. Among the seventy or so pictures laid out when I visited was a watercolour of two men watching the sunrise at Camp 52 Chiavari. Had it not been painted in 1942, it could easily have been Ralph and Charlie, who often conversed discreetly at the perimeter.

Never again did the escapers consider stealing a plane. For one thing they were now so much nearer to the Swiss border: Lake Como was just six days' walk away. Cutting through the wire was an option, but success at Gravina had depended on tampering with the lights. That seemed impossible here, plus surveillance was better and there were guard dogs. Frenzied barking had foiled the escape that Ron Bates, the South African sergeant, had abetted.

Ralph and Charlie preferred the idea of tunnelling, but that was hard work: the ground was boggy, they couldn't go through the floor because the huts were raised, and it didn't help that theirs was closest to the guardhouse. Tunnels also involved many men, which made it harder to keep things secret. Bill Barker's tunnel had collapsed six feet short due to heavy rain, although he was probably also betrayed. Leaving via the sewer, which ran under the wire and down to the river, was possible yet unappealing. The only other option was going through the gate, which was sometimes left open but always guarded. Even if a prisoner got through, what then? Bates hadn't even made it over the bridge before a civilian raised the alarm.

Ralph and Charlie wondered if, with more preparation, they could sneak out and stay out. Hours before they arrived at the camp, a prisoner named Bill Strachan, a Coldstream Guards sergeant, had filed into a working party fetching Red Cross parcels from across the river and, dressed as a peasant, his skin darkened with ersatz coffee, headed into the village. Seeing Castelli-Taddei and Zavatteri strolling towards him, he tore off through a vineyard and made it to the coast, where he stole a bicycle at Rapallo. From Zoagli, he took a train to Genoa, and was caught on the Rome–Turin express and carted back to Chiavari.[3]

However inspiring, Strachan's escape was another a failure – proving, as Charlie reminded Ralph, that however hard it was to break out, the greater challenge for an escaper was to remain at liberty. They had learned that lesson at Noci. Strachan's and Bates's escape bids both suggested that even if the animosity of ordinary Italians had subsided, this didn't mean they could be trusted. Strachan, moreover, received a similar punishment to Bates – one harsh enough to make any escaper think twice. Castelli-Taddei sentenced him to thirty days in solitary confinement, at which point the *carabinieri* took over. Strachan was handcuffed, starved and received what he called 'a really scientific beating up'.[4]

Although life was better than in Camp 65, the *carabinieri* were just as fastidious and, now the war's tide was turning, even more brutal. Miscreants were flogged, one prisoner recounted, 'at the slightest pretext and often for no apparent reason'. Notorious were 'the Yank', a crow-like brute who spoke English like a movie gangster, 'Pinto Pete', a squinting former Californian fruit farmer, nicknamed from a character in a radio show, and a corpulent brute known as 'the Slug'. And everyone knew about the naval rating who had spent 100 days in solitary confinement for writing to his sister that Mussolini was a fool. Similarly infamous was the story of three prisoners chained up in the rain for missing evening roll call. The camp's military authorities respected the warrant officers' rank; not so the *carabinieri*. Nor were there objections from the commandant, who shared the prisoners' fear of these zealous, sadistic policemen. When RSM Shimmin complained , Castelli-Taddei threw his hands in the air, sighing that the *carabinieri* took their orders directly from Genoa.[5]

Mid-June 1943, six weeks since Ralph and Charlie arrived at Chiavari, and their last chance with the radio. Pinning hope on a new movable coil, they arranged with Ron Bates to access the store. An unexceptional day dragged, during which Ralph thought only of the evening ahead. At 9 p.m. he and Charlie met Bates and Bill Barker, and another warrant officer, RSM Bartlett, a South African they knew from Gravina. The door was locked, and the radio set upon a crate. Charlie connected the battery and adjusted his headphones, while Ralph rigged up the aerial and earth wire.

They were ready. There was absolute silence, all eyes on Charlie's face. For ten long minutes, he tweaked and changed the coils, alternating between long wave and short wave in search of any kind of signal. Bored and frustrated, the spectators were all for giving up – but then Charlie, eyes burning with concentration, suddenly held up his hand. Everyone froze. A few more seconds passed, and then . . .

'Scottish Regional,' he said, a smile spreading across his perspiring face.

Ralph felt like shouting the news from the door. Bursting with excitement, he and the others were desperate to ask questions, but Charlie was busy listening to the Chicago blues drummer Billy Warren on a variety show. Clamouring like children, they took turns to hear some music. Then, when the news came on, Ralph took over, writing what he could in the shorthand he'd learned as a telegraphist. The RAF was doing great things over France and Germany. Train busters were getting the job done. And best of all: 'our troops in the Middle East are going from success to success'. At 10 p.m. the news ended, and the radio was packed away.

In the diffused radiance of the camp lights, the five men walked the perimeter, digesting the news in soft voices. They called in on the two New Zealand medical officers to share the news, then returned merrily to their huts, where fellow WOs were informed.

In the memoir, Ralph claimed their wireless was unique. But there had been many, in both Italian and German camps, including, I discovered, another one in Camp 65.[6] MI9 had been aware of these radio sets, which is why they arranged for the BBC to broadcast coded messages specifically for POWs. Not that this diminishes their achievement, of course, for which Ralph rightly gave all the credit to Charlie.

Close reading of the radio story revealed something else. Not only had Ralph and Charlie the right contacts to build it, but in Camp 52 they slotted naturally into the old boys' network of authority and influence, situated in their own pleasant hut near the administration buildings. Ralph may even have kept on Tom Butterworth, also sent to Camp 52, as his batman. Furthermore, the prestige that allowed Ralph and Charlie to hear the BBC in the first place was then enhanced by their ownership of the news. Once word of their dependable source of information spread, men brought rumours for consideration. Like oracles, Ralph and Charlie would express opinions, and in return received intelligence about events in the camp. As in any political state, knowledge was power.

They listened to the news every other night – and only the news, to conserve the batteries. Ralph transcribed his shorthand into a miniature loose-leaf newspaper, passed to RSM Shimmin and other WOs who vetted the sheets before circulating them hut to hut. On 10 July, prisoners applauded a report that Allied airborne and amphibious forces had landed in Sicily without meeting determined opposition.

The battle for Italy had begun.[7]

June days were full of hope, the nights warm and clear. The lice had gone, so men lay in bed discussing the news, dreaming of home and, Robert Garioch recalled, watching fireflies 'sending their strange cold light among the rafters'. In July a stifling humidity settled in the valley, making it impossible to cool off without a place on a swimming parade. Flies followed men in buzzing clouds: meals were eaten from covered mess tins, but they always got under the cloth. Most affected was the cookhouse, where the stew was full of dead insects, which men gave up trying to pick out.[8]

After the Sicily landings, a rumour raced round the camp that the

Italian king, Victor Emmanuel III, and most of his subjects wanted the war to end. This meant ousting Mussolini, which on 25 July the king duly did, causing the collapse of the fascist government. 'My dear Duce, it's no longer any good,' Victor Emmanuel told Mussolini in their final conversation. 'Italy has gone to bits.' At the king's behest, General Badoglio, Mussolini's ex-chief of staff and his replacement, entered into negotiations with the USA, during which Italian hopes for peace with honour were dashed by Eisenhower's demand for unconditional surrender.[9] Most of Chiavari's guards, however, didn't give a fig about honour. Like the prisoners, they were dreaming of home, rapturously crying: 'Benito finito!', a slogan and headline posted up in many a camp.[10]

Good news continued to raise spirits but also brought trepidation. Having been away for so long, men in Camp 52 worried about returning to a changed world. Some had prepared by studying for professional qualifications. The Red Cross's educational department, based in the Bodleian Library, had sent thousands of textbooks covering every subject from chartered accountancy to interior decorating, and arranged membership of professional bodies such as the Royal Horticultural Society.[11] The University of London sent course outlines and exam papers. With the shame of capture went the fear of being left behind. But a man who came home qualified as a bookkeeper or barrister might hit the ground running – might even feel that captivity had been a blessing in disguise.

Even so, how would they fit back in? Britain had been on the frontline since 1940, and civilians had adapted to new habits of public and private life. For the last year, Flo had been doing her husband's job in the police – a source of pride for him, no doubt, but also concern about her new horizons beyond the domestic sphere. Ralph hadn't seen Flo for three years. Like many husbands, he must have worried their love hadn't survived separation: one soldier imagined arriving home to find that 'holy wedlock' had become 'holy deadlock'.[12] Every prisoner had seen the despair inflicted by 'Dear John' letters from wives and fiancées. Now, as freedom seemed closer, men fretted about their mental and physical fitness, and wondered if their children would even recognize them, never mind love them again.[13]

Ralph and Charlie's wireless sessions continued to be profitable. Axis forces, they learned, were pulling out of Sicily, and it seemed Badoglio's government might soon surrender. By now, however, Chiavari's ordinary prisoners, who knew about the radio but not its location, had found that the flow of news had dried up. It appears that RSM Shimmin was reluctant to raise hopes unduly, which could lead to unrest, and therefore ordered that Ralph's summaries should be for the eyes of WOs and medical officers only.[14]

Even so, men wrote home buoyed by renewed optimism and an air of reconciliation blowing through the camp. Predictably, the *carabinieri* were unmoved, but army guards who had taunted prisoners with 'Molto pane Italia' now said: 'Italia kaput, England America buona.'[15] When Lieutenant Zavatteri's wife gave birth to a son – Fabio's elder brother – prisoners presented the happy couple with a picture of a baby riding a swan through hopeful sunlit skies.[16]

Among Ralph's papers, there are no letters from Flo to Ralph, and only one from him to her. Dated 16 August 1943, it thanks her for her letters of the 8th and 20th – probably, given uncertainty about his location, replies to letters that Ralph himself had sent in July.

Conversations by post were drawn out and often out of sequence, causing no end of frustration and confusion.

Who knows what Flo had said, but we might guess. Dom and I visited the town archives of Bussolengo, near Verona, to see a trunk of undelivered letters to Camp 52 and, by coincidence, Camp 65. Full of chit-chat about work and the weather, cinema visits, picnics and family gossip, they mostly end 'hope you are well sweetheart', 'cheerio to you and your pals' and the like – and yet are shot through with the pain of separation. One Doncaster woman reassured her husband that their feelings for each other would never change.[17]

Ralph's reply does contain some clues. Evidently Flo had enclosed photos, which spurred him to ask for more. She had been on holiday to Colwyn Bay in Wales with my great-grandmother and had a suntan. One of these photos survives in Warmsworth, on the back of which, in Flo's hand, is written the postal address of Camp 52. It seems she also complained about her solitary life in Wombwell, the days drifting past, making her feel old. She implied that Ralph was having more fun than she was, an opinion propagated on the home front by *The Prisoner of War*'s rose-tinted view of POW life. One of the Bussolengo letters, from a bored teenager to her fiancé in Chiavari, hints at what Flo may have said. 'I am so hungry for life sometimes and just want to be happy and laugh and have fun,' she wrote. 'You have a lot of friends there and I am sure there is always something on the go.'[18]

Among Horace Wade's sketches at Bovington is one of a Camp 52 prisoner writing home: the economical use of space, crude joinery of the bunks, handy toilet roll and photos pinned up over the beds.[19] Perhaps Ralph had Flo's face in his eyeline as he wrote:

> Your most recent letter was particularly sad . . . although you say you feel years older than 28, to me you look much younger. I'm only 29, you know Flo, and look 40 so probably that will make up for your deficiency, eh! So glad you enjoyed your holiday Flo, but I feel sure that if you saw me you'd be ashamed to say you were brown. I'm as fit as any man could be, but please don't write any more letters

telling me you're fed up Flo – just remember I'm serving a sentence in prison.

And following this reproach: 'Better look after those few remaining clothes of mine Flo, for I shall be needing them – and pretty soon, I hope.' This was Ralph saying he was coming home, a hint to sneak past the censor. And there he signed off, proud to have 'the best wife in the world' and imploring her to 'Keep smiling and remember I'm always thinking of you. Remaining ever, your loving husband, Ralph xxx.'

Letters from this time all struck the same note: one prisoner said he was 'keeping fit for when I resume my normal life!', another that 'there is certainly no lack of optimism here – maybe the end will come suddenly'. The day after Ralph wrote home – 17 August – he and Flo would have heard the same news: the Sicily campaign was over and the invasion of the mainland about to begin. POWs' letters were exuberant. On the 18th, a soldier in Hut 22, a few yards from Ralph in Hut 16, wrote to his daughter in Kent. 'I often think about the good time we are going to have together,' he said. 'Lots of love and kisses dear, from Dad xxxx.'[20]

There were men in every hut writing such things, thinking these thoughts, rereading letters from home, a pastime sensitively captured by Horace Wade. As ever, they did whatever they could to shorten the days. On 20 August, the cast of *The Mikado* performed a selection of pieces, although by now the paper costumes had disintegrated. Men pooled wages to buy wine, which was rough yet strong, and drank hooch brewed from fruit. They picked fights that had to be broken up by the *carabinieri*. After crewmen from HMS *Bedouin* went on the rampage, Eric Huggett cast – typecast – Bert Macey as a drunken sailor for his planned production of George Bernard Shaw's *Saint Joan*.[21]

Shaw had insisted there were no villains in his play, and that men who did bad things often did so with good intentions. An unforeseen twist in events meant that Huggett would never get *Saint Joan* to the stage, but this guiding idea made it a curiously apt choice. No one knew it yet, not even Camp 52's well-meaning leadership, but the days of hope were numbered.

PART FIVE
Evasion

15.

A Hole in the Floor

Those late August days were spent watching waves of sleek American B-24s, high and remote, and waiting for the far-off crump of their bombs. Hut roofs had been painted red and blue to identify it as a POW camp, but the planes' target was Genoa, twenty miles west – and, besides, excitement about liberation beat fear of air raids. It was swelteringly hot, and men lounged around in cut-off shorts or loincloths, content to sit tight. Most men, that is: not all. Ralph and Charlie had finally got their radio going. What now? Rather than wait for the Allies to reach Chiavari, they decided they would break out to meet them. Other 'bad boys', including Bill Strachan, had the same idea. A Liverpudlian prisoner wearing a fake Italian uniform strode confidently towards the gate – which, however well-guarded, still seemed like the best point of exit – but he was stopped and chucked in the cooler.[1]

As *prominenti*, Ralph and Charlie were privy to news that another tunnel, complete with ventilation system, was under way.[2] Put off by the collapse of the last one, however, they opted for the sewer. The plan was to crawl naked through the pipe from the latrine, dragging their clothes in containers to the now dry river bed. Ralph was dubious, but if Charlie was going so was he. During an evening stroll around the wire the old friends fine-tuned the details, and in following days studied guard movements and saved food from their parcels. Meanwhile, they kept an ear on the bulletins, hoping to hear that the invasion had begun.

On 3 September news came that finally Montgomery's 8th Army had landed in Reggio Calabria. Prisoners rejoiced to think that their comrades were now on the same soil, and spread wishful rumours of a second landing in the north. Spirits soared. It was surely a matter of days before Allied forces reached Genoa. More and more men spoiled to get back in the fight; others, unmoved, just wanted to go home.

The weekend passed with febrile speculation and earnest appeals for calm from Colonel Castelli-Taddei and the domineering RSM Shimmin. On Wednesday the 8th, a particularly warm and sticky day, another rumour boiled up, this time from an apparently reliable source. Ralph and Charlie hurried over to the provisions store, earlier than usual, in search of confirmation on the airwaves. This time the talk was true: Italy had surrendered.[3]

Ralph informed Shimmin, who broke the news to the camp. 'Every prisoner went virtually mad,' Ralph recalled. 'There was singing and shouting, war whoops and battle cries filled the camp from end to end. All were happy.'[4] But there was a problem. Charlie had switched to short wave, hoping to hear they were free to go, yet heard nothing. Early that evening, he tuned in to a broadcast by Rev. Selby Wright – the 'Radio Padre' – and using an MI9 cipher smuggled in on a silk square finally received instructions from London. Prisoners were to stay put, and camp leaders empowered 'to take necessary disciplinary action to prevent individual prisoners-of-war attempting to rejoin their own units'.[5]

The commandant summoned Shimmin and asked him to ensure that no prisoner left, vowing to open the gates if the Germans arrived before the British. Shimmin called a general parade. At 6 p.m. all 3,000 men assembled in the refectory, facing a picket of guards in front of the stage, where Castelli-Taddei was waiting to speak. A hush descended. Looking exhausted – a good man in a tight spot, trying to do the right thing – he made an extraordinary promise: if necessary, he would arm the prisoners. But for now, he begged them to be patient, concerned that if the POWs ran free, the Germans might advance on the area, endangering civilians.[6] Too excited to care, men spread fantastical rumours of British landings at Livorno, Rimini and La Spezia; US troops were, they said, in Milan and already guarding the Brenner Pass.[7]

Then it was Shimmin's turn. 'The Armistice was signed at two o'clock this morning,' he announced. 'You are now . . .' But before he could say another word, the cheering grew so loud he had to stop. The din continued for a full minute before he resumed – and yet what came next was unexpected. 'You are now . . . under army discipline. Nobody leaves this camp until our forces arrive. Anyone attempting to go will be court-martialled. Good night.' No one dared challenge Shimmin. Instead, everyone just sang the national anthem.[8]

Escape, never popular, was now forbidden – which did seem odd. Even Italian officers thought the POWs should be freed. Ralph and his fellow WOs reassured the men that the order had come from the War Office. They may have inferred that the top brass – actually Montgomery and the head of MI9 – feared that roaming prisoners would hinder rather than help the Allied advance, which, it was naively assumed, would not be seriously opposed by a fleeing German army.[9] Sensing unease in some quarters, guards talked tough about resisting the Germans, which caused cynical amusement among prisoners, most of whom chose to look on the bright side and let fate take its course.[10]

The Liverpudlian escaper was released from the cooler, and all restrictions were lifted. Food stores were broken out, including tins of stew saved for Christmas, and Ralph and Charlie's hoard for their escape – which Ralph was only too glad to call off.[11] Men took down the pictures over their beds, packed up kit, shook hands and exchanged photos and addresses. The tunnel was abandoned with thirty yards to go. Rehearsals for Eric Huggett's *Saint Joan* were cancelled, as was revision for civil service and bar exams. Men drank and sang and danced for most of the night. Like the ensemble finale of *The Mikado*, for one night they could pretend that 'the threatened cloud had passed away'.[12]

Except it hadn't; nor did everyone celebrate. The teetotal Bill Strachan carried on watching the gate, which now was guarded not just by *carabinieri* but also their Afrikaner stooges. A few who had made a run for it were brought back by these 'vigilantes'. What the revellers didn't know was that for some time German troops had been pouring south through the Brenner Pass, ready to disarm or fight Italian soldiers and occupy the country to halt the Allied push. Yet a minority instinctively knew things were off, and refused to passively hope for the best. Of these, 100 or so climbed over the rear fence and, picking their way through the mines, fled to the hills.[13]

Shortly after 11 a.m. on Thursday, 9 September, prisoners on the higher ground noticed movement in the trees near the river. At first they thought the British had arrived – until they saw the trucks. Another group escaped at the back of the camp and ran towards the forest. Dark figures emerged from the trees, and they hurried back again. By now the *carabinieri* were moving between the huts, where bottles and tins lay strewn after the premature festivities. Men lying in were woken by gunfire and rushed outside.[14]

German soldiers had entered the camp, shooting into the air, upon which the commandant immediately broke his promise to defend the prisoners: whatever his intentions had been, any kind of resistance was futile. Lieutenant Zavatteri felt betrayed – not just by Castelli-Taddei but by the military high command, the king, and what he called that 'Judas' Badoglio, who after signing the Armistice fled Rome, splitting the army into factions, leaving troops to the mercy of the Germans, and condemning Italy to total war. Prisoners blamed the War Office's 'stay put' order.[15] But mostly they blamed Shimmin, even if, like the commandant, he had tried to do the right thing in impossible circumstances. Were Castelli-Taddei's bungling soldiers ever really going to fight battle-hardened Germans?

In many regions, prisoners abandoned by their guards had simply walked out – more than half the total of 80,000 POWs in Italy. In camps like Chiavari, however, where the Germans were already in charge, few leaders, Italian or British, stood their ground or even voiced objections.[16] One Italian commandant who did resist was shot dead by the Germans, along with a fellow officer and a private soldier. This commandant was Colonel Vincenzo Cione, head of a camp near Livorno and formerly of Camp 65.[17]

On the back of the keepsake photo of his brothers, Tom Butterworth jotted that he had enjoyed fifteen-and-a-half hours of freedom. Some men were too stunned to speak; a few youths stifled tears. They felt they had fallen for a con trick – 'the famous double-cross', as Ralph put it. He and Charlie regretted not swimming through the sewers as soon as the gate was barred. By following the order to stay put, they had chosen their fate.[18]

A mixed unit of German infantry, panzer grenadiers and paratroopers, some from the elite Hermann Goering Division, took up positions around the camp. An officer sent Castelli-Taddei a typed note saying that because Italy had broken its alliance with Germany he must immediately surrender all weapons and vehicles or be attacked. To reinforce the point, artillery was aimed at the camp, and a Junkers 88 bomber roared low overhead. Eager to save Allied and Italian lives, the colonel agreed.[19]

By this time, the *carabinieri*, fearing captivity or reprisal, had fled. Remaining Italian guards were dismissed; senior officers, including Castelli-Taddei and Zavatteri, ordered to stay on as administrators. German soldiers set up their own machine guns in the tiger boxes, and a check parade was called. Prisoners were told to remain in their huts on pain of death and await transportation. 'Life might be a bit rough for a time until you get settled in your camp in Germany,' warned the new commandant. 'But the food is better, and you will have more opportunity for playing sports and work.'[20]

Sloping off to their quarters, men noticed that Shimmin looked sick with remorse, and had even started saying it was every man for himself.[21] In truth, like many senior WOs, he was conditioned to obey orders, and even if the gates had been opened, less obedient soldiers wouldn't have got far. This was proved by the mass walkouts throughout Italy. Although sometimes called 'the greatest escape in history', the fact is that two-fifths of the 50,000 escapees were swiftly recaptured and more than half as many again in due course.[22] But in Camp 52 none of this mattered. From their hut windows, dejected prisoners watched a stream of vehicles heading south to the advancing front, sorry that it hadn't advanced far or fast enough.[23]

German soldiers, radiating brutality, came round to make lists of names: the card index of prisoners had vanished – spirited away by the commandant. Each man received a number. While this census was in progress, the camp was searched. Men were found hiding in the woodpile, in the stores and infirmary, even up in the rafters squashed behind hardboard panels. Meanwhile, the prisoners who had escaped were rounded up and taken to Turin, where they were locked in a goods yard while the RAF bombed the city.[24]

It was a balmy evening. After several hours of confinement, the men were fed macaroni and vegetables in the refectory, after which the Germans allowed a morale-raising concert to go ahead. At the end, the whole camp forlornly sang 'South of the Border':[25]

> Then she sighed as she whispered 'mañana',
> Never dreaming that we were parting;
> And I lied as I whispered 'mañana';
> For our tomorrow never came.

Not present was Bill Strachan, who had spent the day in undergrowth outside the camp with three Royal Navy submariners. As night fell, they headed south to Rapallo, where they were helped by locals, including a woman who had befriended D. H. Lawrence in the 1920s and had his novels on her shelf. After splitting from the submariners, Strachan met another Camp 52 desperado; together they tackled a *carabinieri* officer who had challenged them and hurled him into a ravine. Strachan made it to the surrounding hills, where he joined a partisan band. In June 1944, he spotted Colonel Castelli-Taddei among fugitives there and had to be restrained from shooting him. 'He was in a very nervous condition,' Strachan admitted later, 'and broke down and wept.'[26]

The Germans kettled the prisoners in the rear half of the camp, explaining that the other huts were needed for German troops arriving from France. At 9.30 p.m., with arc lights shining and sentry boxes manned, a soldier blew the first whistle, the signal to return to the huts; then a second blast after which, they had been advised, men still at large would be shot. All doors and windows were then secured.[27]

The overcrowding was appalling, there were no slop buckets, and the lice were back. One man became hysterical and had to be gagged. In the morning, the prisoners rolled out like drunks, staggering onto the parade ground. For the next two hours, the Germans counted them, ten times, until satisfied. At the appearance of the German commander, the prisoners stood to attention as a demonstration of undiminished pride. RSM Shimmin was instructed to have several hundred men ready to leave by noon.[28]

That same evening of 10 September, a German sergeant fired a burst from his sub-machine gun to warn men still out and about after the second whistle. A bullet ricocheted into a hut and broke a soldier's arm. Later that night a sentry fired his rifle at a POW who had sneaked to the latrine, missing him but hitting two others in the arm and the chest respectively.[29]

Ralph and Charlie were scheduled to leave two days later, on the afternoon of the 12th.[30] They packed the radio into a case and were searched but again got away with it. Outside the guardroom, the sun was bright in a cloudless sky. As they filed through the gate, men waiting their turn felt a pang of melancholy. Bert Macey would remember his comrades as a 'queer, unhappy, glorious, quarrelling, generous, indomitable, scruffy family'.[31]

The column, three abreast, tramped down the hill with guards front and back and down the sides at four-yard intervals. The Germans carried sub-machine guns and, as a prisoner recalled, 'managed to convey the impression that very little provocation would be plenty'. One man nonetheless broke away, sprinting through a house, and hid in woodland before being sheltered by peasants, one of whom who had worked in California and called the enemy 'goddamn sons of bitches'.[32]

Buckling under the blistering heat, after a few miles many prisoners discarded their heavier bundles of luggage. Standing by the roadside, women in coloured dresses – their Sunday best – put out buckets of water and proffered grapes, oranges and peaches.

The Glass Mountain

Prisoners longed to stop and chat, but the Germans ordered the women back inside.[33]

By the time they arrived at Chiavari station, the men were exhausted. On the platform a steam engine stood ready, coupled to a long line of cattle trucks. As the prisoners were sorted into groups of fifty, Ralph and Charlie, like other would-be escapers, looked for possibilities. But the exits were blocked and machine gunners positioned on roofs. The men each received two small loaves and a tin of bully, and were ordered into the wagons.

With Ralph and Charlie went Bill Barker, Ron Bates and the other South African, RSM Bartlett. Everyone claimed a patch, but there was barely enough room to sit down. Nor were there any sanitary arrangements, and just one rectangular, mesh-covered window, high in a corner. 'No funny business,' warned the German guards as the doors were bolted. The prisoners knew they wouldn't hesitate to shoot.[34]

There they waited over two hours, an intense evening sun beating down on the truck. Men who had gorged themselves on fruit regretted it, as did everyone else. The air was rank with faeces, urine and sweat. It was dark when the train pulled out of the station, the beginning of a 300-mile journey across the plains of Lombardy to the Brenner Pass and beyond, deep into the heart of the German Reich.[35]

Ralph's memoir ends with the Germans arriving in Camp 52. As with his life prior to Camp 65, I would have to work out what happened next by other means. Ralph said nothing about the ghastly railway journey from Chiavari, just as he'd said nothing about the even more ghastly sea crossing from North Africa. Had it been too traumatic? Every prisoner remembered that train, including the sign that read, in French: 'eight horses or forty men'; but perhaps not everyone could bear to describe what it had been like inside.[36]

It was dark and noisy, and men suffered cramps. Suffocatingly hot by day, by night the wagons were shiveringly cold and there were no blankets. In most cases, one corner was used as a toilet, and men wrapped excrement in newspaper and wiped themselves with Italian banknotes. They pissed in bully tins, emptied through the window grille where a prisoner would invariably be straining for fresh air. A remarkable photo taken in one of these carriages, reproduced in Dom's Camp 65 book, left a powerful impression of claustrophobia and squalor.[37]

The train moved slowly, halting frequently in sidings and marshalling yards to make way for troop trains heading south. Men glimpsed flatbed wagons mounted with anti-aircraft guns, the type that at low elevation the Germans used against tanks.[38]

Prisoners struggled to keep their nerve. Besides the filth and discomfort, they knew that trains and tunnels were often bombed. Even if they survived, they now faced many months in a Nazi camp, probably working in factories or mines. Most felt utterly powerless, but as usual a few resolved to escape. Seventy miles north of Chiavari, two submariners squeezed through a wagon window. One was caught; the other, Jim Wilde, lay on the track until the train passed over him. Then he ran for his life and managed to join the partisans.[39] Sergeant Jack Knowles jumped from the same train with John Langdon, the Camp 65 escaper. Knowles was caught six weeks later, put back on a train, from which he jumped again, was caught and put in a camp, from which he escaped to Allied lines; Langdon made it to France, where he fought with the resistance until liberation.[40]

There would be more escapes. A Royal Artillery gunner named Paddy Cullen, and two other soldiers, removed the mesh from the window strand by strand. Machine-gunners had been ready at the door of the next truck – but Cullen couldn't bear another second in that noxious, fractious box.[41] Thirty miles down the line, a Welsh sergeant, Evan Llewellyn Edwards, who had once tried to get out of Camp 65 suspended beneath the water lorry, carried out a similar escape as Cullen's, together with a pair of RAF sergeant pilots.[42]

The final volume of Ralph's memoir, devoted to the radio, ends with some tantalizing words about Charlie's precious device:

> The last time I saw it, it was sitting snugly in the fake bottom of a travelling case en route for Germany. W.O. West and I said goodbye to it somewhere between Verona and Trento in the north of Italy. Another escape had been arranged.[43]

It was a promising lead – but what did these escape arrangements involve?

One of the Camp 52 men recaptured in the hills said the floor of the train that took him to Turin was made of metal, which meant 'there was no opportunity to rip up the floorboards and drop down on to the track, as in all the best war films'.[44]

Not all wagons were built the same, however. John Rossouw, the camp leader at Gravina, who was moved to Camp 52, claimed that men with axes had been successful, which implied cutting through timber. Another prisoner remembered urine draining between planks. Yet even these floors were formidably solid. I'd seen a cattle truck in the Imperial War Museum's Holocaust galleries, and making a hole with anything less than an angle grinder seemed improbable. A South African prisoner remembered one man hacking away before he 'gave up in black despondency'. Another said everyone at least had a go, but without proper tools it was futile. A British officer on a transport from a different camp told of men using a range of implements, including a set of dentists' drills.[45]

Before midnight on the 12th, Ralph and Charlie's train passed through Genoa before turning north to Voghera, then forty miles east to Piacenza, the largest terminal in northern Italy. At every stop, German soldiers jumped down from the brake van to check the bolts and grilles, followed by an almost unbearable wait. Morning saw the train rumbling on through Cremona and Mantua, where an escape bid from one carriage resulted in several men being shot and wounded by the guards.[46] From there they proceeded east of Lake Garda towards Verona, then across the River Adige at Pescantina – the start of the final 100 miles to Trento and Bolzano. This was the route that the fictional *Von Ryan's Express* would have taken had its intrepid POW passengers not seized control.

By now, Charlie was displaying malarial symptoms and had no mepacrine, nor was there much water. It was escape either now or never. Perhaps, given Ralph's size, they ruled out the slot-like window, deciding instead to go through the floor, and may have found a spot worn thin by hooves and rotted by urine. Some men on another transport had been lucky this way, but they did have an iron bar. Similarly in *Von Ryan's Express*, Frank Sinatra uses a surgical knife to cut into the degraded boards, which he then prises up with a handy stave.[47] Ralph and Charlie, however, had only table cutlery. I suspected now that Ralph had indeed escaped from his train, as Nan described all those years ago – but was that escape really achieved by cutting through the floor with a knife and fork?

The answer lay in the National Archives at Kew. Feeling the same frisson as when Pauline first handed me the memoir, I leafed through two heavy black binders of MI9 debriefs. And there, astonishingly, they were: Ralph and Charlie's liberation reports. In small block capitals, Ralph had written: 'Levered up floor boards of wagon'.

The Glass Mountain

Charlie said they 'cut a hole in the floor'. Further searching revealed Charlie's supplementary escape report, which elaborated: their tool had been a table knife.[48]

Once one plank was up, it was easier to loosen the others until there was a hole big enough to squeeze through. The train was moving slowly because this stretch of track was so often damaged – but still the thought of lowering oneself onto the rails was daunting. They would have to wait for the engine to stop. It was still dark, but sunrise was less than two hours away. They would need to be ready the moment the driver braked.

Who was coming with them? Paddy Cullen's experience of an identical situation suggests what might have been said. Not only did most men in his carriage not want to escape, some even tried to talk Cullen out of it in case it got them all shot. Cullen's companion, a South African, replied that if they were that fucking cowardly they deserved to be shot. A New Zealander who jumped near Verona said the usual excuse was that men had promised their wives not to take risks. One of Jim Wilde's submariner friends stayed behind on account of his children, which Wilde thought fair enough.[49] Of the forty or fifty men in Ralph and Charlie's carriage, not even Ron Bates, who had risked hiding the radio in his store, said yes. The only one who agreed to join them was their old 'bad boy' friend Bill Barker.

They said their farewells and entrusted the radio to the two South Africans, Bates and Bartlett. In their care, it travelled another 600 miles to Stalag VIII-A at Görlitz, east of Dresden, where thanks to Ralph and Charlie prisoners would enjoy listening to the BBC, undetected by the Germans, until the end of the war.[50]

As the train approached Dolcè, in the Adige Valley, twenty miles north-west of Verona, the locomotive slowed with much squealing of wheels and clanking of couplings; as usual, the guards alighted to make their checks. It was 5.30 a.m. Dawn was still an hour away, and the station was dark due to the blackout.

Ralph didn't say exactly what happened next, but another POW who escaped from a cattle truck near Verona, also using a table knife, possibly even from the same transport, described dangling through the hole gripping the plank in front, before descending to the track, where he lay for what felt like an eternity, paralysed with fear.[51]

Charlie was first through the hole and immediately shuffled backwards on the track to let Ralph out. He then did the same for Bill Barker, but didn't see him follow. Hearing the crunch of jackboots on ballast, Ralph and Charlie lay like funerary statues, breathing quick, shallow breaths. Once the guard had passed, they rolled between the wheels and down the embankment into a vineyard. Crouching in bushes, they heard a whistle blow and peered out as the train departed in a cloud of steam.

Of Bill Barker there was still no sign; Ralph later told MI9 they never saw him again. (Barker's liberation report reveals that he didn't leave the train for another forty miles, near Trento. He walked back south, and twelve weeks later was captured by German field security troops at Sandrà, near Bussolengo.)[52]

That long day was spent crouching in the undergrowth, watching trains passing up and down the line, servicing the German war machine. By twilight, Charlie was perspiring and trembling with malaria. As darkness covered the landscape, they prepared to leave. There is no clue as to what either man was thinking. But perhaps the submariner Jim Wilde, remembering a similar moment, can speak for them, especially the ailing Charlie:

> Looking back, I don't know how I did it. I'd come to the end of the road. I was exhausted, mentally and physically. I don't think there was a muscle or bone in my body that hadn't been strained to the absolute limit. Yet somehow I managed to climb to my feet again.[53]

Ralph and Charlie dropped down to the riverbank, lined with willows and a deep bed of reeds. It was a clear night, with a bright half-moon to guide them. For a couple of hours, they followed a footpath, creeping unsteadily in a half-crouch, taking longer and more frequent breaks as Charlie's fever possessed him.[54]

Ignoring his protests, Ralph – in charge again – decided they could go no further, even though they had covered only four miles. Charlie could hardly stand. Straining his eyes off to their left, Ralph made out a bank rising towards what looked like houses, presumably the outskirts of a village. Below this lay a sloping expanse of straggling vines, and between the frames, silhouetted by moonlight, young fig trees.

16.

The Fig Tree

Ralph and Charlie's freedom once more depended on finding somewhere to hide by sunrise. If there were no outhouses by the river, the only alternative was to go up into the village and knock on a door. They would need food anyway. There were ripe figs and grapes, but Charlie needed something warm – like their chocolate on the way to Noci.

Their last contact with Italian civilians, six months earlier, had ended in reincarceration. But some people had been on their side, like the tearful woman at the *masseria* who had felt for them and fed them. How would they be here in the north? The women in Chiavari had been sympathetic, offering refreshment in defiance of the Germans. What of their menfolk though? Even if not actively hostile they were bound to be fearful, for northern Italy was thick with Germans and fascists. And such fear was dangerous to prisoners on the run.

They passed a low bank to the left of the footpath, a bulwark against flood. Behind this, in the faintest light, Ralph spied the outline of a structure, on closer inspection a concrete shed with a flat roof. The door was unlocked. Empty save for a few tools, there were no windows and it was cobwebbed and musty. The cement floor would be their bed, as at Benghazi and, for some, at Gravina. At least they had a greatcoat – a prisoner's most precious possession – for a blanket. Ralph made Charlie as comfortable as possible, quietly closed the door, and they fell asleep.

By 7 a.m. the full glow of morning had settled on the ridge above the vineyard, but the hut remained in darkness. Ralph and Charlie were wrenched from deep sleep by a man silhouetted against a panel of daylight at the doorway. Shielding their eyes, they saw he was about their age, wearing a cloth cap and waistcoat and, if anything, more startled than they were. He introduced himself as Cirillo Fumaneri and although he spoke no English made it clear they were in a village named Ceraino, fifteen miles north-west of Verona and ten or so east of Lake Garda. He warned that the presence of a fascist in the village made it 'molto pericoloso', very dangerous, for them to be there – but Cirillo had a kind, honest face and said they could stay.

Ralph was unsure whether to trust him – but cornered in that hut, with Charlie too sick to move, he had no choice. The question was: would Cirillo return with the *carabinieri*, or a tender-hearted farmer's wife bearing bread and biscuits and wine?

I returned to Warmsworth to see Mum's cousin Pauline, who, thrillingly, had found more papers and photos in her attic. It felt different from my last visit, five years earlier. My investigation into Uncle Ralph's life had expanded dramatically from when he was still just a vague memory, a fleeting spectre in a dream, a blank face from a photo. Obscurely dead for so long, he now seemed freshly complex and vital. And, by opening up her archive, like Mum, Pauline had become part of the story. Our exchanges had fed my passion to recover Ralph's life, the substance of which had died with him, leaving only scattered pieces. Besides, no one alive had known Ralph better than Pauline.

As we chatted at her kitchen table, it was plain how much she'd disliked Ralph. Nor did she care much for Flo. She found them aloof, selfish and snobbish – 'snooty upper-crust people' who erased their northern accents and affected airs and graces. Flo owned many cigarette holders, some ivory, and when she smoked you saw her finger stump with a horrible bit of nail poking out. For all her pretensions, it was a reminder of where she came from: poverty in coal-blackened Rawmarsh and her job at Peglers in Doncaster, making brass bath taps until the accident with the machine.

They used to visit Pauline's parents done up to the nines, drawing up to the house in a shiny saloon when no one round their way had any kind of car. Ralph, the big shot, gave the kids pennies to watch it. He expected his nieces and nephews to adore him, but Pauline found him nothing like her dad, Ralph's brother. George had been kind and fun, she said – the same as Arch, my grandfather, who like George died of cancer in his forties. Pauline didn't remember the Corps brothers having had a close relationship – for one thing Ralph was 'very educated . . . poetry and English grammar and all that'.

Flo, who was not at all educated, adopted Ralph's habit of picking people up on their diction. Pauline once said something was 'smashing', only to be told: 'you smash glass, you don't smash anything else'. Small, mean reprimands, painful to recall. Pauline showed me a beautiful amethyst ring, presumably a gift from Ralph, but said that much of Flo's jewellery was made of plastic – fake, like her.

Even so, I kept thinking about the young woman who had married a man she loved, only to have him carried away by war, then living alone in Wombwell, killing time in the West Riding Constabulary. Flo received letters, at least – but these had stopped in the autumn of 1943, after Ralph escaped from the train, from which point she'd had no idea if he was even alive.

Flo's vaulting ambition, Pauline continued, was fixed in her nature from birth, and she found herself a husband who was just the same. When Pauline was a child, they used to think of Ralph as an ex-prisoner of war but not a war hero – and he didn't talk about being a POW because, she surmised, he found it humiliating, even though he had escaped.

A silence hung in the room. 'Didn't they try to get through the train floor?' Pauline asked at last. 'With a fork or something?' I showed her a copy of Ralph's liberation report – but again sensed some resistance.

'I don't think the war changed him at all,' she said. 'The character he was before the war was the character he came back with.'

How then, I wondered, would she sum him up?

'I get a sinking feeling when you ask that question,' came the reply – at which point Pauline's husband John, pottering in the kitchen, chipped in: 'A bit of a lad?'

'No,' bridled Pauline. 'Not a bit of a lad, no. He never had friends.' She turned in her chair to face John. 'We didn't ever see him with a man, did we? Always with Florence.' She looked back at me: 'I would have said he was a loner.'

And yet in September 1943, hiding in a hut in a vineyard, Ralph had the closest friend anyone could ever want, with whom everything was shared, even thoughts passing between them, like radio waves through space. For more than a year, he and Charlie had done everything together and trusted each other with their lives.

In the Ceraino hut they lived cheek by jowl, as in the *trulli* near Santeramo and Gioia, except they had no fireplace and the nights were getting colder. Nor were they there just for a day or two: they stayed five weeks. Cirillo provided straw and blankets, and jackets, trousers, shirts and a hat that were either his or came from his boss at the local quarry, where he worked to supplement his meagre income as a farmer. Needing help, Cirillo had to confide in his boss: sourcing everything for the men he called 'Rodolfo' and 'Carlo' was risky, and to do it openly in the village impossibly so. The boss was sympathetic and sent his grown-up daughter with food and quinine for Charlie's malaria. Over those five weeks the fugitives got to know Cirillo as an uncomplicated, good-humoured fellow, who treated them like sons or brothers.

Sitting in Warmsworth, however, I knew only what was contained in the MI9 debriefs. These said little about Ceraino. In his escape and evasion report, Charlie mentioned nameless civilian helpers, with only a sprinkling of details. Ralph described how Cirillo Fumaneri had sheltered them between 15 September and 25 October, providing clothing 'of poor quality' and on average two meals a day. Charlie confirmed this, adding that this indigent farmer had also given them money, 'and at great risk aided fourteen British POWs to cross the River Adige'. That was all I had to go on.[1]

After lunch, Pauline left me to go through her latest finds, mostly postwar correspondence. There were also a couple of albums, containing photos of Nan and her sister Flo, relaxing in deckchairs with their husbands, Granddad Arch and Uncle Ralph in a straw fedora. In one snap, of a picnic in 1937, my infant mother sits in a dark pram, and Flo is eating a sandwich, Ralph's head resting in her lap.

Not wanting to outstay my welcome, I took photos of everything without paying much attention to what was there. But just as I was packing up, everything changed.

On the table lay a curious informal group portrait, the size, low saturation and joyless composition of which was unlike any other photo I'd seen that day. And, even stranger, hiding beneath it was a small, square document, headed 'Salvacondotto'. Pauline had dug these things from the pile, but it felt as if they'd been teleported from another world. The *salvacondotto* bore the emblem of the Repubblica Sociale Italiana (RSI), the revanchist fascist government established after the Armistice in September 1943. On the same day that Ralph and Charlie had left Camp 52, German paratroopers

MINISTERO DELLE FINANZE
GABINETTO DEL MINISTRO

SALVACONDOTTO

Rilasciato a: Signor

RODOLFO OORPI

had rescued Mussolini, who, on the orders of the king, had been arrested by *carabinieri* pending his handover to the Allies as part of the peace settlement. The Nazis then installed the former dictator as the head of the RSI, an ignominious puppet state, in the waterside town of Salò, twenty miles from Ceraino on the other side of Lake Garda.[2] And this document was a safe-conduct pass supposedly issued by the RSI's Finance Ministry to 'Rodolfo Corpi', Ralph Corps Italianized: a forgery.

Pauline let me take it. After eight decades in an attic, the *salvacondotto*, a silent witness to war, was on the move again, hurtling south down the M1.

Back at my desk, I stared at the safe-conduct pass and a print of the group photo: salvaged scraps of ephemeral time. For now, the beguiling document refused to make sense. By a stroke of luck, however, the photo was about to prove a critical clue for my next trip to Italy, when Dom and I planned to hunt down Ralph and Charlie as they moved through the north of the country after their astonishing escape from the train.

In the line-up Ralph and Flo appeared second and third from the left, smartly dressed, he in a summer suit and striped tie, she in a sleeveless print dress, cinched at the waist. Neither is smiling – but then, except for a boy in T-shirt and shorts, no one looks pleased to be there. Behind them was a concrete wall and timber door, and on the reverse, a Kodacolor date stamp for 1958. I scoured the scene, but this photo had said all it wanted to say.

Pauline had no idea who these people were. Apart from the woman on the far left, they looked like Italians. Was Ralph returning to Italy – somewhere – after the war? I'd read how in the 1950s and 1960s, many ex-POWs were compelled to make pilgrimages, usually with wives and families in tow; others went on to visit every summer, spending time with Italians, once saviours, now friends. Some annual reunions lasted into the twenty-first century. Could this have been the Fumaneri family, who had helped Ralph fifteen years earlier? I posted the photo on a Facebook group in Ceraino, hoping that a picture sunk in memory would refloat in the world whence it came.

While waiting for a response, I learned what I could about the place. During the war, as in much of Italy, Ceraino's quasi-feudal landlords still took 50 per cent of the produce of their sharecropping tenants, the *contadini*. For centuries, their time had passed in cycles, season by season, occasionally interrupted by some foreign invading army. Peasants had long ago learned to be wary of all superiors and strangers, except itinerant beggars and stray defeated troops, who were welcomed.[3] An escaped POW summed up the mentality:

> They understood one life only – working the land, rearing a family. Birth, work, and death, divinely guided by God and the Virgin Mary. All things more complicated than this left them utterly bewildered. Their attitude to us was typical of that overflowing quality of Italian tenderness. We were human beings in distress. Therefore, we were objects of pity deserving help.[4]

Only after Ralph and Charlie experienced this in Ceraino had the anguish of the farmer's wife in Noci made sense. Memoirs described the laments of peasant women who saw missing sons in these indigent young men: 'Dio mio, mamma mia, povero figlio!' they cried. 'Poveri, poveri!', 'poverino mio!', 'poveri ragazzi . . . che brutta vita!' My God, you poor boys – my poor sons – such a terrible life![5]

This 'strange alliance', as a British ambassador termed it, was one of the most extraordinary phenomena of the Second World War. After the Armistice in September 1943, almost 18,000 Allied prisoners on the loose in northern Italy, men with no idea of what to do or where to go, were never recaptured.[6] And only the selfless courage of ordinary Italians ensured their lasting freedom. The motives of the *contadini* transcended politics, of which they knew little, and even Christian charity. To harbour a prisoner was to defy authority and resist historic adversity. The appeal was also practical: POWs could work the land, meaning that farmers actually competed to bag one. What was more, fugitives from faraway rich nations now depended on them and were deferential. Women never before thanked or smiled at by a man glimpsed in prospect an end to subordination. According to the historian Roger Absalom, caring for prisoners brought instant social elevation and 'an anticipation of an imagined golden future'.[7] It may also have been, as another historian put it, 'a way of exorcising fear, a rite that succeeded in strengthening bonds within the community at a time of great uncertainty'.[8]

In Ralph's and Charlie's liberation reports, particularly the 'Appendix A' sections, names and events were underlined in red and annotated 'A.S.C.'. This, it turned out, stood for 'Allied Screening Commission', an agency dedicated to compensating civilians for helping escapers. Money was put up by the British Treasury, staff were hired, and a headquarters established in Rome after the city was liberated in June 1944. The ASC placed advertisements in newspapers and despatched forms; claims could also be made by letter, sent directly or through local councils. These were checked against MI9's records and either approved, queried or rejected. Claimants were encouraged to attach 'chits' left by POWs; they also submitted letters, photos and military insignia.[9]

By the time the scheme was wound up in 1947, the ASC had

received 85,000 claims, of which three-quarters were settled at a cost of half a billion lire. Deemed historically worthless, the files were saved from incineration by General Eisenhower, who, supposing they might contain anti-communist intelligence, had them shipped to NARA – the National Archives and Records Administration in Maryland.[10] Declassification began in the 1970s, but at the time of writing they remain uncatalogued. However, a helpful contact at the Monte San Martino Trust, an educational charity dedicated to the memory of the 'strange alliance', told me that if I sent names from my liberation reports to NARA, they would scan any files they found. I began with Cirillo Fumaneri of Ceraino, Verona.[11]

As I waited for a reply from Maryland, I received an email saying that the photo I'd put on Facebook had indeed been taken in Ceraino. According to Stella Manzelli, her mother, born 1925, had been one of ten Fumaneri siblings, the eldest of whom, Cirillo, became the householder when their father died. Stella remembered hearing about 'due ragazzi inglesi' – two English boys – whom the family had hidden during the war, one of whom was called Carlo, thus confirming the presence of Charlie West. The woman in the middle of the photo, Stella told me, was her aunt Lisetta, another Fumaneri sibling, next to her husband, Remo Berti. Then, Stella put me in touch with her brother.

Describing himself as 'a passionate researcher of events and characters', Claudio Manzelli sent me more information relating to the Fumaneris: – Cirillo was born in 1913 and married a woman named Albina Loro. He also identified the older man, to the right of the photo. This was Giuseppe Zanoni, whose land the family worked and, in the suit jacket, his hired hand, Gino. Now I'd identified everyone except the little boy and the woman to the left of Ralph.

Ralph's return to Ceraino, as documented in this photo, was a revelation. I only wished Charlie had been there too, the fugitives reunited, but if he had, surely he'd have been in the photograph. Guessing he'd gone another time, I started digging. Charlie's niece Emma Bassom said he had indeed visited his friends in Italy every summer for the rest of his days. She sent holiday snaps from the

1960s and 1970s, showing him with a middle-aged man tending a vineyard. The Manzellis confirmed that this man was Cirillo Fumaneri. Emma also had her uncle's address book with contact details not only for Cirillo and his wife Albina but for Ralph, too: an updated sequence of PO boxes in East Africa. This proved they had stayed in touch after the war. None of Charlie's letters survived, however, so I swept through Ralph's postwar correspondence – but it was all administrative, mostly relating to employment. That stiff, unemotional man again: nothing personal.

Not for the first time, the trail had gone cold. But then some scanned ASC files arrived from Maryland. They were full of archival wonders that, like the *salvacondotto*, shed a bright light on Ralph's and Charlie's lives in northern Italy. I now knew that Charlie's helpers had become his friends. Perhaps Ralph had formed the same bond, or even some deeper, more transforming connection.

More emails arrived from Ceraino. A man named Arnaldo Testi remembered as a child seeing a British-registered car whose driver was asking for Cirillo Fumaneri. Arnaldo also identified the boy in the photo: Cirillo's son Gianni, who was still alive. Finally, the building in the background was a *casotto*, a worker's hut belonging to Giuseppe Zanoni. It was the very place where Ralph and Charlie had taken refuge in the autumn of 1943.

'It's still there,' Arnaldo informed me, 'but not visible on Google because it is hidden by an enormous fig tree.'

A fortnight later, Dom and I were standing on a deserted railway platform, buffeted by driving rain and the concussion of goods trains thundering towards the Brenner Pass. On either side dark hills were draped in mist; below us was the Adige, which flows from Trento through Verona to the Adriatic. The station was Dolcè, where Ralph and Charlie had escaped through the train floor just before dawn on 14 September 1943, seventy-nine years earlier.

We had arrived in darkness in the town of Gavardo, not far from Salò, a couple of days earlier. Dante, our jovial Airbnb host, pointed to the mountains and, arms spread like a plane, told us about the partisans the Germans had tried to bomb. The next morning, with Dom still asleep, I stared out at the dawn-lit land Ralph had known: low roofs of terracotta pantile, thick copse and scrubland, dark hills against a wash of grey-pink sky. Every new place had been a fresh challenge for him, and our arriving in each felt like cutting into a deeper layer of the sediment of who he had been.

That morning, we crossed the train track – the power cables were overhead – and peered over the fence at a bank of brambles leading down to the river, which was in spate. A growl of thunder, and the rain became insistent. I clung to the portable umbrella that Dom liked to call my *ombrellino* – a British eccentricity.

We drove back to Ceraino and into its narrow streets. By now the rain had thickened into a hailstorm, and Dom feared for the hire car's paintwork. Great white pellets clattered like buckshot, as water spouted from gutters and slid across the tarmac in sheets. Wipers at full tilt, we turned onto a dirt track through the vineyard down to the furious river, ignoring the signs warning against taking vehicles any further. I glanced at Dom, hoping he'd both watch where he was going and see that I was clenching my teeth.

Of where the *casotto* was, I had only the vaguest idea. We stopped by the river, but the downpour was so intense it prevented our getting out of the car.

As if by divine intervention – or revelation – the clouds parted and the rain ceased. Setting off along the soggy river path in the direction of Dolcè, we met a vineyard worker who had been sheltering from the storm. I showed him the 1958 photo, at which he shook his head. He regularly cycled the full length of the footpath, and there was nothing like that.

Dispirited, we pressed on. It was squelchingly muddy, and after a mile Dom seemed, unwontedly, to be running out of patience. We'd eaten nothing since the egg yolk, sugar and espresso shot Dom had made for breakfast – an acquired taste – and his suede desert boots were no longer mouse grey. With the path ending at a fence, we turned back.

I strode off ahead, scanning the riverbank foliage for fig leaves.

After fifteen minutes we were nearly back at the car; I thought I must have got it wrong. Dom was some way behind now, hidden by the bend of the river.

At the point of giving up my phone rang.

'Come back, Malcolm. Come back . . .'

Dom had cheered up and was nonchalantly eating a bunch of grapes. Beside him was the biggest fig tree I'd ever seen – so vast and sprawling we had missed it on the first pass. He gestured for me to go first. On the other side, entirely concealed from the path, was the *casotto*. The wooden doors had been replaced with metal ones, but otherwise it was unchanged, displaying the same blemishes and cracks visible in the photo.

I tried the latch and the door swung open. Inside it was dingy and damp, empty except for a rusty shovel. Scanning the walls for graffiti using the torch on my phone, I noticed rough wooden shelves either side of the doorway. They were very old, too small for any obvious agricultural purpose. Had Cirillo put them up, perhaps for shaving kit and quinine, or a candle, or as a place to stand photographs? Here, Ralph and Charlie had made a home, watching the ridge, waiting for food, washing in the river, sleeping side by side, Charlie recovering from malaria, longing to see Allied troops appear in the vineyard.

It was hard to believe I was there, within weeks of finding the mysterious photo in Warmsworth. In that musty cobwebbed shed, I felt a different kind of affective tremor: the historical power of place to rival any document. Ralph and Charlie had been there in 1943, and had both returned after the war to stalk their shadow selves, just as I was stalking them now.

I heard Dom's voice as he approached the doorway.

'Ralph? Are you there? It's me. Charlie.'

17.
Farewell at Molina

As Dom and I emerged from the *casotto*, dark clouds were drifting back and spots of rain falling. The first thunderclap made me think we should retreat to the shelter rather than be caught out in the open. Cirillo's ghost would surely be waiting there, smiling, with blankets and a snack. But we pressed on, making it to the car just before the deluge resumed.

I wanted to stay longer in Ceraino. The vine worker said that people up at the café had lived there for ever and would surely know more than him. And beyond, the mysterious hills and mountains were calling to me. But Dom and I were both tired, wet and hungry, and it was an hour's drive through worsening weather back to Gavardo. We had to call it a day, knowing of course we could return another time.

The winter of 2022–3 was spent trying to work out what Ralph and Charlie had done at Ceraino, and where they went afterwards, who else helped them, and how they survived. But more than ever, the past guarded its secrets – and what little did spill out raised new questions, which the past then refused to answer. The MI9 files were sketchy. Charlie's escape report included an account of drifting from place to place after leaving the *casotto*, but it was terse and his timeline was puzzling. Ralph was no less vague. A story that the memoir had furnished in rich detail down to their entrainment at Chiavari now faded into mountain mists until I could hardly see them at all. A friend, a writer of non-fiction with an eye for cryptic author–subject relationships, wondered if perhaps Ralph's greatest escape had been from his most tenacious pursuer: me.

The Glass Mountain

The archivist in Maryland dug out more files. I already had Cirillo Fumaneri's, which revealed that in September 1946 he had been paid 24,000 lire, without presenting a chit or any other documentary evidence, which was often destroyed in case the Germans found it. The Allied Screening Commission had, however, been able to draw upon the testimony Ralph and Charlie gave to MI9 when they were debriefed. Under the heading 'Points for further investigation' was written 'See 75614'. So, I submitted another request, and a fortnight later received a scanned claim in the name of a new character to enter the story: a young woman at Ceraino named Vittorina Radaelli.

This file concerned Charlie alone; Ralph was not even mentioned. A clue to Vittorina's identity lay in her award of 5,000 lire: this suggested strongly that she was Cirillo's 'employer's daughter', which is how Charlie, when questioned, referred to the woman who had helped him.[1] The Radaellis came from Ostiglia on the River Po, thirty miles south of Verona, but had been prominent in Ceraino as the owners of a limestone quarry employing scores of local people: there was a square in the town named after them. Cirillo had worked for Vittorina's father, whom he trusted sufficiently to tell him about the prisoners of war he'd stumbled upon in his landlord's *casotto*, and who in return, it seemed, had arranged for his own daughter, at great personal risk, to help them.[2]

People in and around Ceraino remembered Vittorina. Flavio Manzelli, a cousin of the Fumaneris, sent me a photo: his mother had been Vittorina's best friend. The photo showed Vittorina as Charlie would have known her, in her youthful prime, high in the mountains, pointing serenely into the distance. What she saw lies outside the frame, illuminated by sunglow – or perhaps this was just a symbolic gesture, an expression of happy anticipation for her life to come.

Vittorina's file confirmed something else Charlie had said: she taught him Italian. The intimacy of these lessons was easy to imagine, especially as both were young and unmarried: 'Carlo', the handsome British pilot, she with her dark hair and kind yet defiant eyes. I could see her with a covered basket, knocking at the door of the *casotto*, chatting amiably, swapping Italian terms for English ones – 'warm, generous, tough and curiously reckless', which is how one POW described every Italian woman he encountered while on the run.[3] I also pictured Ralph stretching his legs by the river during these visits, which might explain why Vittorina's ASC claim didn't mention him.

Vittorina may or may not have been in love, but she was certainly brave. She had to be careful not to be seen walking through the vineyard to the river. Ceraino was a place where people minded other people's business, and there was the fascist everyone feared. It was suspicious enough that a family might start buying more food or selling less, which could only be avoided by spreading what little they had even more thinly. Danger tainted every day. Ralph and Charlie soon learned the most important Italian phrase of all: *Alzatevi! I tedeschi vengono!* – get up, the Germans are coming![4]

For a month after the Armistice, things were not too bad. Italian soldiers of the new fascist RSI cared little about escaped prisoners, and the Germans treated them like houseflies: swat them if you can but don't go out of your way. By mid-October, however, the realization that POWs were joining the partisans changed this. Civilians sheltering Allied soldiers now risked being beaten or shot, imprisoned or exiled, their possessions confiscated and houses burned. The Germans issued martial law edicts and offered rewards of 1,800 lire for turning in a POW, advertised in radio broadcasts and on posters and air-dropped leaflets. The equivalent of a month's wages for a British manual worker was, recalled one fugitive, 'sufficient to make a poor man think seriously about taking up prisoner-of-war hunting as a profession'. In bigger towns, gangs of knife-wielding bounty hunters sprang up. Knowing that people tuned in to its Italian language programme, *Radio Londra*, the BBC broadcast that anyone who helped an evading prisoner could expect an even greater reward from the Allies.[5]

Exactly how Ralph and Charlie passed those five weeks is unknown. It may have been pleasantly disorienting. A POW in the same situation recalled how 'a strange dreamlike feeling of unreality smothered me'.[6] Men given bed and board were usually expected to do farmwork, and Emma Bassom's postwar photo of her uncle posing among the vines suggests he and Cirillo were reliving his former labours. Charlie told MI9 that he also carried out nuisance raids: rolling boulders onto roads at night, cutting telephone wires and putting sand in the fuel tanks of enemy vehicles. Nowhere was Ralph's involvement mentioned, and in his liberation report he denied ever being a saboteur. He may have refused to accompany Charlie on the grounds that such acts were dishonourable for a soldier and provoked reprisals against civilians – a common enough occurrence.

In the last week of October, the secret leaked out. Cirillo Fumaneri heard that Allied prisoners were known to be hiding in Ceraino, and the Germans and their Italian allies were searching houses and outbuildings. Perhaps ordered by his landlord or his boss Radaelli, Cirillo gave Ralph and Charlie notice. Sultry storms had turned to night frosts and freezing drizzle – but there was nothing else for it.[7]

They left grateful notes about the hospitality they'd received, and Cirillo gave them food and directions into the mountains avoiding German and RSI units. Then they were gone. We'll never know if Vittorina came to see them off.

Using what little I knew from the MI9 files, I plotted Ralph and Charlie's course on Google Maps. I wondered if they'd felt what one escaper had upon reaching the mountains: sudden exhilaration and relief, like an end to toothache or the restoration of a lost faculty.[8] Another recalled 'an inner happiness difficult to describe, and seldom experienced – until liberty has been lost no one can realise what freedom really means'.[9] The picture was blurred, but gradually a stronger outline emerged, and with added colour.

Their sights set on the Alps, Ralph and Charlie climbed steeply past the village of Monte, then ten miles along the mountain ridge to a small town named Molina. This was only fifteen miles from Ceraino, but the going was hard, and the weather rough. There, on 2 November, they were taken in by father-and-son farmers, Francesco and Battista Sega, in their house, Casa Scariotti. The archivist at NARA sent me a file in the name of Sega. It contained something remarkable: letters written by Ralph and Charlie. Ralph's, dated 19 November 1943, stated that Francesco (misnamed as Francesco *Scariotti*) had provided shelter and food, and had done the same for Charlie West, who was also seeking refuge in the mountains. Ralph indicated that the farm was a known safe house, 'notwithstanding the fact that the German commander in this area has offered a reward for any information regarding the whereabouts of any escaped prisoner'. The letter was to be presented to the provost marshal of the Military Police when British forces arrived.[10]

The Segas also provided clothes – for Charlie a shirt, socks and woollen vest, for Ralph 'un mantello usato', an old goatherd's cloak. It was much colder in these highlands, the weather was turning, and now the evaders were exposed to the elements. Thin air and the shadow of death, however, made life sweeter: other men recalled taut muscles, fellowship with danger, freedom from responsibility and an intoxicating vigour.[11]

Already planning another road trip, I longed to know where this had been. Dom drew a blank: nowhere was Casa Scariotti listed as an address. But then using Google to follow the southern road out of Molina I noticed a tinplate sign reading 'Località Scariotti'. Next to this was a rough ascending drive where Google's camera had not ventured, and 'SCARIOTI' (with one 't') cut into the rock face at the entrance.

The Allied Screening Commission had linked the Segas' claim to that of one Emilio Assogna at 'Rive di Breonio', near Molina, who said that Ralph and Charlie had stayed at his house, too. To prove it, Assogna enclosed a chit, crumpled and brown as if it had been hidden up a chimney. On this, the fugitives had written their names and, in Ralph's case, the address of the Military Police HQ in the Worcestershire town of Kidderminster. Accompanying this was a letter from a Scottish medical officer, who had also sought refuge there. Dated 14 November, it described Assogna as 'a man of strong pro-Allied sympathies', a host to many evading POWs despite being poor and having 'to overcome his natural reluctance to put his family in danger – and a very real danger it is!'[12]

An old farmhouse called 'Le Rive' still remained in Molina. I traced the current owner, Fabio Giacopuzzi, who told me that Assogna's name was on the deeds, and that he was aware of a landslide that shortly after the war had destroyed half the house, compensation for which Assogna had in vain requested from the ASC. Fabio invited Dom and me to stay at his *agriturismo*, a bed-and-breakfast popular with hikers, not far from Le Rive, and in September 2023 we were there.

After the expeditions of the previous couple of years, Dom and I were accustomed to one another's company, to long tiring days, half-living in the car, filming and planning, unwinding in bars and crashing in Airbnbs. Like Ralph and Charlie, we often found we knew pretty much what the other was thinking.

A hot, sunny day, driving from Brescia to the province of Verona. Rather than going round the southern shore of Lake Garda, we took the car ferry to appreciate this expanse of water that Ralph and Charlie had come to know so well.

Framed by lush scenery, with sunshine glittering off iron-blue ripples, the crossing was fast and exhilarating. On the other side, we drove up through densely wooded hills and meadows, fat white clouds bulking on the horizon. 'Monte' and 'Molina' read the road signs, then, a couple of miles ahead, 'Breonio'. We stopped to take in the view, munching apples and discussing how, German patrols aside, up here a prisoner might feel he'd left the war behind, even a kind of blissful contentment.

Arriving in the stone-built village of Breonio, we crossed an ancient bridge and pulled into the drive of the Giacopuzzis' farmhouse. A middle-aged man hurried out open-armed, beaming hospitably. This was Fabio. Comparing us fondly to Ralph and Charlie arriving at some place of refuge, he showed us to a twin room, while Rosangela, his wife, made lunch: tagliatelle with foraged mushrooms, fresh bread and a jug of red wine – the sort of food served to POWs. For most of the year, we learned, Fabio worked as a thermal energy consultant in Verona, but in the summer months he and Rosangela ran the *agriturismo*.

Over coffee, Fabio proposed that we go first to Casa Scariotti. I put down my glass, hardly believing what I'd just heard. Having failed to find any modern address for the house, I was convinced it no longer existed. But off we went in Fabio's car, bouncing down the hill, through Molina, and up the drive marked 'SCARIOTI'.

As the road levelled into a yard, there it was: a three-storey farmhouse of flat stone brick, with shuttered windows, the back elevation abutting a grass bank. From a neighbouring house came a tall, flat-capped man with a prominent moustache and rheumy eyes, bent with age at the knees and waist. Fabio introduced him as Fioravante Bacilieri, born 1931.

As a child, Fioravante's family had lived down in the town, but his father owned Casa Scariotti and its land, which he rented to Francesco and Battista Sega. In the autumn of 1943, he recalled, the Segas sheltered two British POWs there, and young Fioravante was sent up the hill with food for them. Only he could do this: older boys wandering around risked being press-ganged by Organization Todt, the Germans' civil and military engineering corps. The youngest of thirteen, Fioravante had several brothers whom their father spirited away for this reason. As a teenager, his father had been conscripted to fight in the First World War; his sons, he pledged, would not die for fascism.

Fioravante looked hard at my photos of Ralph and Charlie, but shrugged apologetically: they must have been the men he'd met, but he was young and it was so long ago. Nonetheless anxious to help, he pointed to the wings of the house:

'La stalla qui,' he said. 'E sopra il fienile, dove vivevano i prigionieri.'

This I understood: the stable was here and above it the hayloft where the prisoners lived. Fioravante smiled and grasped my hand as we moved to the rear of the house, where the entrance to the hayloft was at ground level. This had made it an excellent hiding place: if the Germans came through the front, an exit opened straight into the woods. Clearly no one had touched it for decades. The warped, sawn planks covered barely half the joists, so you could see down into the dusty stable. Fabio explained that straw would have been thickly layered there, so a man could sleep comfortably but also burrow into it to avoid detection.

Dom asked Fioravante whether his father had made a claim to the ASC, the file for which we could order from America. He shook his head sadly. No, his father was shot and killed by the Germans, and he himself had been hit by a bullet. Lifting a trouser leg, he pointed at a scar on his calf. We hung our heads. Looking up, I saw tears in Fioravante's eyes.

He walked a little further with us until the path began to climb the hill. We shook hands and said farewell. Then he turned and went indoors.

On 7 November 1943, after five days at Casa Scariotti, Ralph and Charlie set off again – though the date on Ralph's letter, the 19th, suggests they scouted the area for another week or so trying to find a guide or a route to Switzerland. After that, they returned to Molina, where they agreed to head off in different directions.

Why, we'll never know. Ralph said it was 'owing to fascist activity in that area', which doesn't explain much unless they felt their chances were better if they travelled alone.[13] Charlie was eager to force his way back into the war; Ralph, I felt, like so many others from Chiavari, simply wanted to go home. Such partings of the ways were not unusual. Many memoirs told of evaders splitting up, either to head south towards Allied lines or north into the Alps. The pros and cons were rarely mentioned. Sometimes men just followed a whim.

After Dom and I found Casa Scariotti, the reason for Ralph and Charlie's parting no longer seemed to matter that much. More important was that Fioravante Bacilieri's continued presence there transcended time, and meeting him had been an intimate moment of remembrance, connecting us to Ralph and Charlie on the point of separation in November 1943. Paraphrasing T. S. Eliot, history was now and Molina.[14]

After everything the two of them – the stolid, principled Sleuth and the restless, ingenious Warrant Officer West – had been through together, I pictured some heartfelt embrace, perched on an outcrop against a moody backdrop of mountains and sky. Yet I'm certain they would have kept their feelings buttoned up. They had shaken hands, for sure, and wished each other good luck. That was all they needed to do: they both knew what it meant.

18.

Sega di Ala

Fabio guided us up the hillside, sunlight filtering through an avenue of scrub oaks. The path opened into a clearing, a meadow strewn with buttercups at the entrance to a gloomy forest. He pointed at the overgrown slopes leading into the valley: during the war they had all been cultivated. Goats and deer observed us from the shade, and as the route climbed further a stag with spreading antlers stared imperiously at his unwelcome visitors.

We reached another clearing, crepuscular and cool, under a high canopy. This, Fabio explained, was *il roccolo*, a place hunters once netted birds and, he continued, where Ralph and Charlie had laid low during the day. He had asked around: apparently they only went to Casa Scariotti in the evenings, to eat and sleep.

Ahead stood a tiny two-storey hunting lodge, built in 1884 for a Bacilieri ancestor, a cardinal no less.[1] Fabio took a key from the sill of the casement window and unlocked the door. There was a sooty hearth, a few sticks of furniture, and an open staircase leading to a hatch in the ceiling. Beyond lay an identical room, whitewashed with bare rafters, but with a cast-iron balcony, which, Fabio pointed out, had a bullet hole in it. There was a lot of old graffiti. Dom fancied he could see the name 'Ralph', partly covered by render.

Afterwards Fabio took us down into Molina. With its weather-worn façade, the Bacilieri ancestral home looked out on a courtyard, which served as the outlet for a winery. The owner was Fioravante's son Marco, who received us like honoured guests and invited us to sit. There was music playing, which Dom, in a whispered aside, said was an old revolutionary folk song, a rousing anthem of the left.

Over a reviving bottle of *spumante*, Marco expanded the story of

Sega di Ala

his grandfather's death. In 1945, the Germans were trying to get home through the hills, avoiding the Val d'Adige, which was being bombed. This brought them to places like Molina, where truces were agreed with local partisans on condition the Germans proceeded unarmed. But one soldier had reneged on the deal and opened fire.

Marco took us to a terraced house where the current generation of Segas, Ralph's wartime hosts, now lived. Inviting us in, a middle-aged man in hoodie and shorts showed us through to the kitchen, where panoramas of Jerusalem and Bethlehem lined the walls. The man's mother bowed humbly; across the room on a sofa sat his elderly father, immobile and bolstered by cushions. With eyes half closed, his mouth slack, he held his face between the palms of his hands as if in quiet despair.

We sat at the table facing the old man, who was introduced as Raffaele, the ninety-four-year-old son of Battista Sega. He stared blankly at my photos, mumbling. Until recently, the son told us, Raffaele had been lucid enough to tell stories from the war, when like the Bacilieris he had gone into hiding to avoid compulsory service. The family had a photo of Battista, a face Ralph had known, freshly unearthed and restored to his story.

After half an hour, the church bell struck six, and we lined up at the sofa to say goodbye. Holding my hand tightly for a long time, Raffaele Sega looked searchingly into my eyes, as if to trying to understand who I was or what had happened to him.

Back at Fabio's farmhouse that evening, we had supper with a local historian named Francesco. Over drinks, he told us about a POW escape network in the nearby town of Fosse, run by the local priest, Don Domenico Veronesi. Although there was no direct link to Ralph or Charlie – I had Veronesi's ASC file – one of the prisoners he'd helped was the Scottish medical officer who had stayed at the safe house of Le Rive.[2]

I spread my papers on the table, including the entry for Battista Sega from Charlie's address book. Charlie had crossed out the address of Casa Scariotti when the Segas moved back into the town. Then, while Dom, Fabio and Francesco chatted away, I noticed something else: Charlie had added the names of the children, one of whom was Raffaele, the old man on the sofa. Another connection drifting purposefully out of the past.

We were waited on by Fabio's children. Nothing could have made Dom and me feel more like Ralph and Charlie, the fugitives enjoying a simple, nourishing meal at a remote farmhouse in the night-silent hills – perhaps served by a boy named Fioravante Bacilieri, sent up the hill with a food basket.

As the plates were cleared, more was added to the story of the Bacilieris. Fioravante's father had been a partisan and, according to Francesco, had provoked the Germans by shooting at them. The implication was that he was partly responsible for his own death.[3] Francesco, it seemed, didn't care for partisans – but perhaps Fioravante and his son Marco did, which would have explained the rebel music playing in the winery courtyard. Such differences of opinion, and of interpreting the past, reverberated from an Italy divided in 1943.

We retired, our stomachs, brains and senses full. It had been an incredible day. After all we'd experienced together, without shyness Dom and I climbed into our single beds.

'Fabio and his family – they're so nice,' whispered Dom, who had supposed that generous hospitality was a uniquely southern thing.

'They are indeed,' I replied, and switched off the lamp.

Awake before Dom, I went into the adjoining room and unfastened the shutters. Mist blurred the valley plain. By the time Dom surfaced, however, this had burned off, giving way to a fine, clear morning. We stood at the window inhaling country air and saw Fabio's wife Rosangela returning from the baker's.

Downstairs, the breakfast table was spread with coffee and pastries. Fabio was worried that we had come all this way for what he felt was a mundane itinerary. I hardly knew what to say. Thanks to him, I had finally caught up with Ralph and Charlie in the hills. Fabio admitted he'd been wary when I'd first written to him: what could this Englishman possibly want with us? I confessed that I hadn't been entirely sure myself.

We were finishing breakfast when a fresh-faced man in his seventies arrived. He introduced himself as Alberto Antolini – a name I recognized: a cross-reference in the priest and prisoner-smuggler Don Veronesi's ASC file had led me to a Gino Antolini, a node in Veronesi's escape network. This, Alberto said, was his father.[4]

Taking a seat at the breakfast table, Alberto recounted how his parents, not yet married during the war, had belonged to an organization helping refugees and escapers based in Pescantina, fifteen miles south of Breonio, where the town priest coordinated operations from a hotel. In 1945, at the end of the war, Pescantina became a major transit hub: thousands of Italian soldiers arrived by train from Germany and elsewhere, all trying to get home. Alberto's mother had worked in an infirmary, which had been overwhelmed with sick soldiers: the most common illness was tuberculosis.

Usually, as he listened to such stories, Dom would wink and grin at me in boyish wonder, as if to say: wow, isn't this great? But as Alberto spoke, he became attentive and serious, as if deeply drawn into what he was hearing. It was soon clear why. Dom revealed that his father had been at Pescantina in 1945, stranded for a while on his way back to Altamura after release from captivity in Hamburg. Alberto explained that, because Verona station had been bombed, many displaced persons like Michele Bolognese ended up in limbo there: trains could go no further.

It was an electrifying moment. Dom and I had spent so long finding out about Ralph and Charlie, without ever really asking why, or wondering what the desire that drove us on these endeavours said about us. But now, for Dom at least, the veil lifted. His search had led him to his father, who had died before Dom fully understood his past. The many hours he had devoted to teaching and learning about Camp 65, as well as accompanying me on my trips, now emerged as an unconscious quest for something else. All along, and by his own admission, he had been trying to access the emotional dimension of the war – the war that had been the defining factor in Michele Bolognese's life as a young man. The window Dom's inquiry had opened on the past was also a mirror.

'Why . . . ?' Dom asked hesitantly. 'Why did your parents help these men?'

Alberto spread his palms. 'From pity for them – in their suffering.'

We pored over my papers. Gino Antolini had escorted Allied evaders into the mountains, where he handed them over to a partisan leader, who took them further and higher towards the uplands of Sega di Ala: the southern border of the autonomous province of Trentino, Italy's most northerly point, and the Alpine gateway to neutral Switzerland. Don Veronesi also kept a safe house in the woods at Fosse, similar to Ralph and Charlie's hideaway at *il roccolo*. In the end, Alberto's father and the partisan were betrayed by an American POW and imprisoned in Verona. Gino was released, having protested his innocence; the partisan escaped and was decorated for his courage. These ordinary Italians, and the women who supported them at home, all took enormous risks. One Allied fugitive was so moved by Don Veronesi's steely courage and commitment that after the war he himself took holy orders and returned to Fosse to say Mass.[5]

By now, the table was covered in maps displaying the whole mountainous region. With a pen Fabio traced the winding escape route between Pescantina, Breonio and Fosse, and said we should see part of it for ourselves. Not far from there, he added, was the farmhouse of 'Le Rive', once the home of Emilio Assogna, who had sheltered fleeing Allied prisoners there, possibly including, for a while, Ralph and Charlie.

Abandoning the table with its detritus of papers and breakfast things, we drove out to a breezy field with a 180-degree view of the rooftops of Breonio, and, further along, Monte Baldo, a mountain range that runs parallel to the eastern shore of Lake Garda. The scenery was painted in great blocks of colour: ultramarine sky, emerald grass and the silver-grey of soaring titanic rock. Beyond, half-concealed by haze, stood the Dolomites, extending from the Adige to the Piave, and the Lessini Mountains, where the hamlet of Sega di Ala had once beckoned to Allied POWs. Another 100 miles through jagged Alpine heights and shining glaciers and you reach the Swiss border. Further to the right, down the hill across another meadow, lay *il roccolo* and Casa Scariotti.

Roaming between Molina and Breonio, living hand to mouth, Ralph and Charlie had seen this view and knew the chance it offered. The mountains shone like a mirage in a fairy tale, majestically inviting yet impossibly vast and deadly.

We wandered down a steep lane, covered by spreading branches, at the end of which stood a tall, whitewashed cottage. There it was: the POWs' safe house of Le Rive. A bank of trees enclosed the plot to the back and sides; in front lay the valley and far distant Apennines. It was a secluded place, perfect for hiding prisoners on the run.

A wiry man wearing outdoor work clothes appeared. This was Remo, the tenant to whom Fabio let the house. Pointing to a copy of Emilio Assogna's ASC form, Fabio explained things to him, and we were invited in.

We entered a flagstoned hallway. Rooms off to the left had been rebuilt after the landslide; on the right was the pristine nineteenth-century kitchen, where a fire crackled in the grate and Remo's tools and weapons hung from hooks. On the shelf were books on Italian fascism, including *Perché L'Italia Amò Mussolini* and *Perché L'Italia Divento Fascista*, titles that looked sympathetic to the old cause.

The hallway led to a tight curving staircase, at the top of which was a door summounted by a carved lintel. On the other side was a hayloft with mortared walls, golden shafts of light entering from a high aperture and gaps around the raised rear entrance. Nothing had changed since 1943, maybe a century before that. Except for a few rusty bed frames propped against the wall, it was empty yet teeming with ghosts.

Were Ralph's and Charlie's among them? Had they once moved through that same space, kipped on those old beds even? I felt they must have been there: dropping by as they circled the area, shovelling down a meal in that kitchen. But had they stayed?

Clearly Assogna hadn't known Ralph as well as the Segas did. Although he attached their chit to his claim, he thought Ralph's surname was 'Kidderminster'. An easy mistake, perhaps – but neither Ralph nor Charlie ever mentioned Assogna or Le Rive, which they surely would have done had they slept there even a single night, never mind the eighty days Assogna claimed for Charlie and twenty for Ralph. Emilio Assogna was desperate for money, especially after the landslide, and may have obtained the chit from the Segas. (The ASC clearly didn't buy the whole story, and awarded Assogna less than half of the 22,000 lire he put in for.)[6]

On the way back to Fabio's house, Dom was unsurprised by the reading matter I'd seen on the kitchen shelf. 'In Italy we never drew a line under fascism,' he said with a resigned sigh. 'It's still a choice.'

The author of these books, he continued, was a journalist from Abruzzo, a fervent supporter of the former prime minister Silvio Berlusconi and falsely rumoured to be Mussolini's illegitimate son. Spectres and echoes everywhere, just beneath the surface of another ordinary day, a past not past but parallel and close.

Heeding Alberto's advice to wear something warm, in the afternoon we set off in his car, rising steadily above the Val d'Adige. He and Fabio were chatting merrily; Dom and I were in the back, like children.

'Look at them,' chuckled Dom, under his breath. 'They only met properly an hour ago.'

Our destination was Sant'Anna d'Alfaedo, a plateau of bright springy grass 5,000 feet above sea level. The sky was an infinite canvas of evenly applied blue, patterned with silver clouds. Such mountain pastures, Dom explained, were known as *malghe*, traditional collectives for storing milk from Alpine cows, and making butter and cheese. As well as cattle, neck-bells clanking, there roamed wild horses with flowing manes – a place immune to modernity and time itself.

We followed a bumpy track to a homely-looking restaurant, woodsmoke scenting the ice-sharp air. To the west, across the valley, hulked the great range of Monte Baldo, solemn and sublime, and through a southerly gap in the hills a fuzzy glimpse of Verona.

Further, and mistier, lay Lessinia and other unnamed Alpine ridges and peaks.

Hikers were sitting at picnic tables, eating cold meat and cheese from wooden boards. That's what we had too, followed by *gnocchi di malga*, the house speciality, and a huge bottle of ruby-red wine poured into plastic cups.

As we ate, we spoke less of Ralph than of Charlie, who had spent a bitter winter on Monte Baldo with a partisan band. Talk of partisans prompted Dom to say more about his father, who had embodied the political chaos of 1943–5: first, the fascist invader in Yugoslavia, then the socialist guerrilla in Italy, and finally the forced labourer in Germany. In his youth, Dom had never completely appreciated what this meant – but he did now.

The meal ended with a shortbread biscuit the size of a dinner plate that Alberto broke into pieces and drenched in grappa. It had been the most basic, satisfying food, which in that company, and in that location, made for one of the best lunches of my life – an exalted moment in which, as Seamus Heaney put it, hope and history rhymed.

When Dom asked if I was ready to go home that evening, I felt a pang and said I could stay there for ever. But we had to make a move, already cutting it fine to reach the airport in Milan, two hours away, where we would go our separate ways. And first we still needed to get back down the mountain. So Alberto proposed a final toast, which he insisted should be to *amicizia e libertà* – to friendship and liberty.

PART SIX
Liberty

19.
Rodolfo

Winter 1943 – the harshest many had known. Fierce blizzards kept peasants close to their hearths, living off maize flour, smoked meat and preserves stored in summer.[1] German troops patrolled the mountain trails and passes less frequently – but snow and ice favoured neither side. Evaders and partisans found tumbledown huts and caves and hunkered down till spring. It could hardly be called liberty.

After he and Ralph parted in November, Charlie had remained in the Molina–Breonio area, sheltering wherever he could, scrounging food and indulging in petty sabotage. Returning to Casa Scariotti on 16 December, he stayed for a month; then another three weeks in the spring of 1944, after which he said a final goodbye to Francesco and Battista Sega. The letter he gave them read, cryptically: 'Owing to various circumstances I must now depart.'[2] In between, Charlie went back to Ceraino, where he and Ralph had sought sanctuary after their escape from the train. Most of February 1944 was spent there with Cirillo Fumaneri, followed in mid-April by another stay of four months, after which he joined the partisans on Monte Baldo until January 1945.[3]

What was the enduring appeal of Ceraino? Perhaps Charlie was just hungry or needed quinine; or perhaps he missed Vittorina Radaelli. If there was romance, some new love tying Charlie to this land, it was vital to the story – and yet I'd never know.

Ralph had chosen a different path. Twenty miles from Sega di Ala – a day's hike from Molina – with the promise of Switzerland beyond, he turned away, deciding instead to meet the advancing Allies. He hoped they'd already crossed the River Po – a key natural line of defence, as all soldiers knew – which seemed a reasonable assumption. Yet it proved to be 'hysterical wishful thinking', as one evader put it, a habit born of British daily 100-mile gains in Libya. In Italy, things were different. There were only three routes to the north: the Adriatic coast to Pescara, the Tyrrhenian coast to Naples, or over the central spine of the Apennines. All of these were heavily defended.[4]

November drew banks of cumulus across an already pale sun. Biting winds and freak showers turned tracks into quagmires, trickling ravines became turbulent rivers.[5] Wrapped in his goatherd's cloak, Ralph thanked the Segas, praising their courage and promising they would be rewarded. Then he set off back along the rocky ridge to Monte, where a kindly villager put him up for the night. The next day he headed down towards Ceraino, where Cirillo may have rowed him across the Adige. Skirting the city of Verona, he crossed the southern plain, begging bed and board at farms. He would also have found pumpkins, chestnuts and withered apples, and perhaps risked a few mushrooms.

Prolonged contact with Italians at Ceraino and Molina meant that Ralph had picked up even more of the language and, like most prisoners on the run, memorized life-saving phrases like *per favore, stasera posso dormire qui sulla vostra paglia, sono molto stanco* – I'm very tired, please can I sleep on your straw this evening.[6] There were farms, here and there, and he heard voices on the breeze – but in these parts people were terrified of the Germans, who had deployed agents posing as Allied servicemen to trap whoever helped them.[7] So, he was repeatedly turned away, famished, cold and afraid now he would be reported – Noci all over again – then sent to a dismal camp, this time in Germany or Poland, or suffer some worse fate. Although he looked more like a beggar than a spy, the Germans and their fascist Italian allies had been known to shoot POWs caught in civilian garb.[8]

It turned even colder. Chill winds whipped across the flatlands, and Ralph spent his nights curled up in whatever miserable hole he could find. However restrained the farewell at Molina, he must have sorely missed Charlie now. Later, he described only the bare facts – but another memoir gives a sense of what he went through. This prisoner had fled south through the fields of Verona, floundering over muddy drainage ditches, shivering in the darkness and damp morning mists, lying low whenever German patrols passed, and cursing himself for ever having decided to head south.[9]

Ralph crossed from the province of Verona into the province of Mantua, where there were many marshes, lakes, irrigation canals and tributaries to negotiate. Finally, he reached the Po itself, a high, urgent river edged by dark poplars and sheep meadows and in winter shrouded in fog. The nearest town was Ostiglia. There, Ralph found not the 8th Army's warm welcome, but grey German pillboxes and anti-aircraft batteries, the box-girder bridge laced with barbed wire and closed off with machine-gun nests.

Some escapers braved the Po's turbid waters, which at Ostiglia were only a few hundred feet wide. Ralph was a strong swimmer and might have attempted it had it not been December and he'd had more confidence and energy. Not only was the Allies' absence a huge blow to his morale, but he had walked fifty miles, a journey of two or three days for a fit, well-nourished man who didn't have to keep hiding from an enemy. It had taken him twice that long. Now, he would have to go back.

Weak sunshine ceased to thaw the ground, and snowflakes fluttered over the bleak, grey landscape.[10] Cold and confused, almost feral now, Ralph headed north-west across the plains of Lombardy, west of Lake Garda, and through a broad corridor of farmland. He crossed the River Chiese at the Ponte Clisi, or may have waded further down. His boots were tattered, and every step pained him. But still the obsessive dream burned, albeit dimly. Having once turned away at the Alps, Ralph now knew his only safety lay in Switzerland.

From an expanse of vineyard between the towns of Nuvolento and Prevalle, Ralph gaped at the foothills ahead. Crossing a minor road, he staggered on, deeper and higher, as if obeying the summons of the mountains. Snow fell steadily, then heavily. Icy squalls blasted along the gullies, stinging his hands and face. Visibility faded to zero. Creases in his clothes froze and cut into chapped skin, his feet were badly swollen, and he was suffering from cramps, headache and nausea. Progress slowed until he feared he might stumble and sleep and never wake up. It was eighteen days since he'd left Molina – nearly three weeks since he'd been warm, well fed or spoken more than a few words, and even then to unfriendly *contadini*.

Yet again, Ralph was forced into a volte-face. Finding a track, he was soon back on the main road, this time at the foot of a monumental black mountain overlooking more vineyards. Dazed after this desperate retreat, he couldn't think what to do, where to go next. The northern tough, the no-nonsense copper, the cocksure Guardsman, the defender of the Cauldron, the man of substance in the camps and intrepid escaper . . . he was broken.

The watery moonlight picked out a village some way ahead. Where Ralph was, on this settlement's northern fringe, there were just two isolated farmhouses. Pulling his sodden mantle around him, he limped to the nearest one and tapped on the door.

There followed a critical, suspended moment when a farmer in a warm, well-lit house faced a beggar trembling on his threshold. Time froze as if equivocal about the future, and then in an instant everything changed for the good. The farmer brought the stranger, limping badly, into the kitchen and sat him by the fire. Then he called his wife. The last home Ralph had been in was his own, in another life, four years earlier.

The farmer was Angelo Maccarinelli, his wife Caterina Zanola, both in their late sixties.[11] They spoke no English, but Ralph knew enough Italian to explain, once he'd had a drink and some bread, that he was *un prigioniero di guerra evaso*. This was probably obvious, likewise that he was *molto stanco* and *voracemente affamato* – very tired and ravenously hungry. His body was also seriously deprived of salt – a rare detail Mum had remembered – and combined with exhaustion the reason he was so unwell. There was a salt shortage in northern Italy, its supply cut off by the Allied advance.

Christmas was a week away, and Ralph's arrival held the Maccarinelli household to the spirit of the festival. He was hypothermic, lame and, for the first time in his life, in a state of despair. But the pity that Angelo and Caterina felt for him was like a cocoon, offering immediate assurance that under their roof he would come to no harm. He said his name was Rodolfo and, for now at least, probably little else. They told him he was in Paitone, and that their sons were away at war, which meant they had a spare room; there, a bed with mattress, sheets and pillows awaited. Caterina and Angelo helped this hunched man up the stairs, laid him down and doused the light.

Ralph slept all night and well into the next day. Rising stiffly, he removed the rest of his clothes – his tattered boots and cloak had already been taken away – and was given soap and water. Caterina dressed his raw, throbbing feet, and brought food and wine, perhaps heated with sugar and herbs to make a reviving drink.

A man about his age, maybe a little older, came to visit. He introduced himself as Doro Garletti, a factory worker married to the Maccarinellis' daughter Margherita, who lived with their three children in Brescia, ten miles west of Paitone. Ralph insisted on leaving for Switzerland as soon as possible – but Doro and Angelo would have none of it. Not only did he need to rest and recover, especially to reduce the swelling in his feet, but the winter weather had not yet done its worst. Doro, it turned out, was a communist involved with the resistance. He had a Beretta pistol. German and Italian fascists, cautioned Doro, were patrolling the hills, making it too dangerous to travel. It was a wonder Ralph hadn't already been caught.

Ralph's hosts were curious to learn everything about him, and he, more trusting now, was willing to oblige. Italians had heard some strange things about the English – that they were amoral gluttons, the women flirtatious, their husbands quick to divorce or even sell them.[12] Now they would see if it was true. Did Ralph have a mother and father? He did. What were they like? Good Christian people. And a wife? Also, yes: Florence – like the Italian city, *Firenze*. Children? He lied that he did, presumably to persuade them of his urgent need to get home. This was a dangerous stratagem. Resisters like Doro often asked POWs personal questions, not from curiosity but to flush out imposters with shaky backstories.[13]

Christmas Day was an understated affair: everyone wished each other *Buon Natale*, enjoyed a decent meal, and that was it. No work was done, and the family sat chatting by the fire. Ralph, however, spent much of the season in bed, alone with thoughts of Flo, wondering about Charlie and regaining his strength. But the Maccarinellis and Doro Garletti came up to him often, bringing food and news and good cheer. 'I was strangely moved,' wrote an evader who shared Ralph's experience. 'I had a sense of wonder at the rare beauty the simple things of life had acquired since last I had seen them; as if some subtle alchemy had been working on them in my absence, gradually transforming them into something that was rich and strange and yet old and familiar at the same time.'[14]

Ralph was not back on his feet until the first week of January 1944. He was moved to the hayloft, from whose open sides there was a commanding view of the road. Caterina's brother, a vicious fascist, had a habit of visiting unannounced. The house was also becoming overcrowded. When Ralph arrived, Angelo and Caterina's daughter-in-law Augusta, wife to their eldest son Dante, then missing in action, was already living there with her three-year-old daughter; now, the Garletti family arrived as refugees from the bombing in Brescia. (Doro made ammunition belts at the Tempini metalworks, which made the city a target: while he stayed there, his wife and two infant sons found indefinite shelter in Paitone.)

Ralph may have enjoyed more privacy in the hayloft, which was accessible only by ladder, but the nights were chilly. Angelo and Caterina's grandchildren took to bed a *monaca* – an ember-filled earthenware pot – and perhaps he did the same. Some heat did rise from livestock in the stable below, which would also have been his toilet.

Ralph's presence was a danger for the family, especially with youngsters running around the house and garden. German soldiers had been known to question children, knowing that they struggled to keep secrets. Everything was more dangerous now. The Germans had stepped up their campaign to find Italian workers and escaped POWs, the reward for information now raised to 2,000 lire, the price of a cow.[15]

Rodolfo

So in February Ralph was moved again, across the way to the home of three unmarried siblings similar in age to Angelo and Caterina. Like most peasant farmhouses, theirs was built of brick rendered in lime, with terracotta pantiles, exposed joists and shuttered casements. Inside, floors were cobbled and walls whitewashed; there was an open hearth and grain sacks were stored in the corners. Water came from a well.[16] The two men were tough, taciturn and unsmiling, their sister small yet capable of work, with patched clothes and black headscarf, hands and face creased like leather but with sympathetic eyes. Women in northern Italy carried crates and jars on their heads, marvelled a fugitive airman, 'just as if they had stepped out of an illustrated Old Testament'.[17]

Ralph was given his own room at the top of the house, and steps were taken to clothe him like an Italian *contadino*. Owing to his height, unusual in Paitone, suits and shirts had to be specially made; he was also given three sets of underwear and a pair of leather boots, when wooden clogs were the norm.[18] Warned not to march straight-backed, arms swinging – POWs had been caught because they walked in step, often dressed like sightseers with knapsacks and staves – Ralph started loping around like a peasant, hands shoved in his pockets, which did not come naturally to an ex-Guardsman.[19]

While Ralph was learning his part and getting used to his surroundings, he was visited by a neatly dressed primary school teacher from the adjacent town of Prevalle. His name was Omodeo Cantoni. Unlike Doro Garletti, he went unarmed, but like so many other ordinary people did crucial work for the resistance. They agreed that Omodeo would help Ralph with his Italian, and Ralph would teach Omodeo more English.

Doro also dropped by regularly. One fine morning he brought his camera and for posterity photographed their Rodolfo standing in the yard.

Back in January 2021, the start of the second lockdown, Pauline had sent more photographs she'd unearthed. One showed a dapper, bespectacled man by a lake; another, children in a garden. Most arresting was a tiny sepia snapshot of Ralph outside a farmhouse, dressed like a peasant. On the back, someone – at first, it looked like '*Dora* Garletti' – had written in Italian: 'A memory of Paitone for Rodolfo Corps, 1944'. I phoned Mum, who predicted that somewhere in Italy a family had a photo of Uncle Ralph in a box, possibly a print of this very exposure.[20]

Out of habit, I scanned it for clues: a barred window, the edge of a shutter; an olive tree; a clothes line; a wooden bench; trousers lengthened several inches; and the health and happiness radiating from Ralph's smile. Oh, to break that frame – to see the rest of the house, its surroundings, and the person behind the camera, adjusting the focus, fiddling with the aperture.[21]

I turned to Ralph's MI9 debrief. He said he'd arrived in Paitone on 18 December 1943, and was taken in first by Angelo Maccarinelli and his wife, and then early the following year by a man named Augusto Chiodi. With a start, I recognized this as the name inside the exercise book, one of the first things I'd seen standing in Pauline's kitchen in 2017: he and 'Chiodi Agostino' were one and the same.

The Maccarinellis and the three Chiodi siblings lived respectively at 15 and 13 Via Valletta, the road at the foot of Monte Budellone, where Ralph had begun and abandoned his foray into the hills. Both families, Ralph attested, had made great sacrifices on his behalf. Doro Garletti was not mentioned in the report. Still at that time believing Doro to be a woman, 'Dora', I wondered if this had been Ralph's lover: such relationships between evading POWs and Italian women were common enough and, thwarted in my search for Charlie's romance, I wanted it to be true.

Using available online sources, I formed an image of a valley community between Brescia to the west and Lake Garda to the east. On the edge of an already remote hamlet, Angelo, Augusto and their families led simple lives, surviving on their produce and the grape harvest. They received relatively few visitors – and yet these people were connected, through some secret purpose, to others: Doro Garletti in Brescia and, just a mile from Paitone, the teacher-turned-resister, Omodeo Cantoni.

Naturally, I ordered Allied Screening Commission files from the archives in Maryland, and waited impatiently, hoping they could be found. Meanwhile, an Italian-speaking friend emailed with a surprise: she had posted Ralph's photo on Facebook, and within twenty-four hours received a message from a Maccarinelli in Paitone. Her name was Celestina, and it had been her grandparents who had taken in Ralph – or 'Rodolfo', as she called him – on that bitter night at Christmas time 1943.[22]

Celestina also identified other photos Pauline had sent: the children were Maccarinelli and Garletti cousins posing in the garden of 15 Via Valletta, and the dapper man by the lake was Omodeo Cantoni: he had taught Celestina's husband. Known as 'Il Maestro', Cantoni was related to the Maccarinellis by having married a woman whose two sisters married Angelo Maccarinelli's brothers. Of the Chiodis almost nothing was known, except that Augusto's siblings were named Pietro and Erminia, and they were all long gone.

There was more. Not only did Celestina's brother Ugo live at 15 Via Valletta, but number 13, Augusto Chiodi's house, was still there too – though only just. An aerial view showed a hollow ruin, hemmed in by wild greenery, positioned beside a quarry, at the bend of a service road for an industrial estate. The roof had collapsed, Celestina explained, during a heavy snowfall. Today it belonged to her cousin Anna, who had salvaged a cupboard, a table and the wooden bench visible in the photograph.

Among her mother's possessions, Anna had also found a photo taken by her uncle Isodoro Garletti – the man known to everyone as 'Doro'. Uncannily, Mum's prediction had been fulfilled, and so soon after she made it, for the photo was identical to the Warmsworth snap; on the back, in Doro's hand, was Ralph's name and number, and a note that read: 'Prigioniero Inglese nascosto a Paitone (Brescia)' – an English prisoner in hiding. This suggested the photo was to have been used to support a claim to the ASC.

Soon, I had claim forms for Angelo Maccarinelli, Augusto Chiodi and Doro Garletti. Pinned to Angelo's was yet another copy of the photo of Ralph. So that made three: one in England, one in Italy and one that had made its way to the United States. The documents, meanwhile, would unlock the mystery surrounding Ralph's months in northern Italy.

I learned that the Chiodi brothers had worked in America – their names appear in the Ellis Island register for 1910 – and spent their New World savings on a house in their hometown of Corteno, north of Lake Iseo.[23] They lived there until a flood from a failed hydroelectric dam sent them eighty miles south to Paitone. As strangers from a different valley, the siblings were never fully accepted. Known locally as *gli americani*, they never married, and out on Via Valletta kept themselves to themselves. Whatever they felt about their isolation, it made their farm an ideal spot for hiding an Allied POW, helped by the fact that Augusto and Pietro spoke some English and could be trusted. Their nephew, a courageous partisan back in Corteno, had been tortured to death by *squadristi*, which made harbouring Ralph an act of quiet retaliation.[24]

The siblings lived frugally, their work was hard and pace of life slow. After a day of labouring (or hiding), Ralph's evenings were spent at the kitchen table, where Erminia gave him the best cuts, the largest portions – due, he suspected, to fascist propaganda alleging that Englishmen ate five gargantuan meals a day.[25] In this family of circumstance, he became the Chiodis' surrogate son and reciprocated with the greatest courtesy. After supper, Ralph smoked with Augusto and Pietro by the glow of the oil lamp and made halting conversation. The ticking wall clock somehow made it feel that time stood still. Now and then, for a change, Ralph wandered over to the Maccarinellis, always checking first there wasn't a lantern in their upstairs window – which meant: don't come.

So Ralph settled into a routine in which he ceased merely to act the part of Rodolfo and instead transmuted into him, without any contact or correcting influence to tether him to his old life. He cherished his photos of Flo and his memories; but that was all. He no longer even had his army pay book or anything bearing his name. And all the things a *contadino* did, Ralph did too: following the contours of his day, doing his work, eating his food and soon speaking not just fluent Italian but Brescian dialect – slouching, shrugging, gesticulating, accepting.

Dom and I parked on Via Valletta and found number 15. Celestina, an olive-skinned woman in her sixties, embraced us on the gravel drive like long-lost sons. Three generations were gathered there, Garletti and as well as Maccarinelli, including Piero and Ugo, two of the boys in Pauline's photo, now in their eighties.

The house had been remodelled in the 1960s, but Celestina led us into what was formerly the kitchen, through the same door Ralph had hobbled in December 1943. She showed us where the bread oven had been, and the pigsty. The adjoining room, she explained, had been *senza pavimento*, meaning it only had a rough floor, and was used for storing tools and bicycles. On the walls hung portraits of Angelo and Caterina and a painting of the house as it was during the war, with the old hayloft and stable – remote, ageless, enclosed by mountains and vineyards.

We sat in the new kitchen, chatting over drinks and snacks. Federico Garletti, a history student, showed me a certificate awarded to his great-grandfather Doro by the Allied Screening Commission. Celestina brought out an aluminium mess tin that Angelo and Caterina's youngest son Pietro, a soldier in North Africa, had carried throughout the war. It was engraved with a simple vow: 'Mamma ritorno' – Mum, I will return, which he did.

Celestina's cousin Anna arrived, a slight woman in silk scarf and pearl earrings. Her father Dante was the eldest Maccarinelli child, shipwrecked during the war and taken in by a family in Crete. Like his brother, he made it home, and Anna was born in 1947. She and her husband had bought the marble quarry, including the Chiodi house, which was on the same land. From her handbag she produced her photo of Ralph. I had mine, too, and she smiled as we laid them side by side on the table. Another cousin showed me an aerial photo of the Chiodi homestead: against the odds, I had broken the frame of Ralph's photo.

I also had with me a copy of the ASC file in which Angelo described Ralph turning up 'in a pitiful condition, with swollen feet, and given shelter and kept in bed for fifteen days in a state of extreme physical debilitation and moral depression'. He had stayed two months and, said Angelo, 'always maintained an impeccable demeanour and so earned our total sympathy and affection'.[26] I read the statement, aloud, in Italian, and as my voice cracked, the audience of Maccarinellis and Garlettis closed in around me with murmurs of pity, recalling the loving kindness this family had shown mine, on that spot, eighty years before.

We went into the garden, where the elderly Piero Garletti was standing alone. A smiling, tactile man, he posed for a photograph holding the picture of the cousins, which had been taken at the end of the garden. Piero, the eldest of Doro's three sons, remembered Ralph well. He was tall and wore a broad-brimmed hat, which in the children's eyes made him look like a cowboy. He came from another world, and was always polite and kind, never agitated.

Rodolfo, as Piero had known him, was also full of marvellous stories, including how he had been on sentry duty at Buckingham Palace when Edward VIII and Mrs Simpson walked past. The king, who looked drunk, put a cigarette in Ralph's mouth, then lit it from the royal lighter. Then the pair strolled off laughing. It sounded like something the king might have done. It was definitely a story Ralph had told to a ten-year-old Italian boy, who had cherished it all these years.

By now so many aunts, cousins and grandchildren had arrived, all wanting to meet Dom and me, that I started to lose track. Yet everything they said flowed back to Ralph in that place in 1944. He had been appalled, I heard, that the children were fed bread dipped in wine and sugar, warning they would never grow up tall and strong like him – which, the family later conceded, might have been true, for they did turn out quite small. Eager to please him, the kids had gathered fruit, which they left for him in the hayloft, and were told not to breathe a word.

We adjourned to a local restaurant, where Federico confided that the Maccarinellis and Garlettis rarely got together like this. I propped up Ralph's photo, seeing as he was responsible for the occasion. After lunch, Celestina took us to the cemetery in Prevalle, where the bones of many Maccarinellis lay and their ceramic portraits were set into marble memorials: Angelo and his sons Dante and Pietro, and the Zanolas: Angelo's wife Caterina and her brother Domenico, the fascist villain.

'Are the Chiodis here?' I asked Celestina, hoping to see their faces.

'Not here,' she replied, gesturing into the air. 'In Paitone.' Even in death, it seemed, they had been outsiders, excluded from the main cemetery where the Maccarinellis and Cantonis, and others from Ralph's story, were at rest.

Celestina and I left the cemetery arm in arm. In an email a few days earlier, she'd said that she and her husband were simple people, and thanked me for my 'belle parole di amicizia' – fond words of friendship. She understood why I was drawn to the war years, when there had been at least as many good folk as bad. Beneath threatening skies, I held Celestina's hands and did my best to repeat that expression of friendship. She hugged me tightly, as if we'd known each other for ever.

Next morning, through grey drizzle, Dom and I returned to Via Valletta, this time to explore the Chiodi house. Broken timbers, a few brick courses and a chimney pot poked out from a towering clump of trees and weeds – but the remains were otherwise invisible. Dom found a hole in the fence and through we went, wiping rain from our eyes. A steamy thicket of bamboo soon separated us and made it impossible to reach the ruins, even though they were less than six feet away. I could just make out a shutter hanging from a casement, recognizable from Doro Garletti's photograph. And with that I turned back.

Dom and I emerged from the jungle, soaked and defeated. Fed up with wet fieldwork, we decided to visit Celestina Maccarinelli's cousin Anna, who owned the Chiodi house and had salvaged some of its relics. She'd said we were welcome to call in.

Anna lived in a gated, porticoed mansion, a few minutes' away in Prevalle. She welcomed us into her kitchen, with its vaulted ceiling and dangling pans, and in another room showed us the walnut table saved from the old house and an elegant armoire the Chiodis had used as a tool cupboard. I ran a finger over the key, knowing Ralph had touched it too. I asked about the bench, but Anna thought it was somewhere else in the family.

Compared to her cousin Celestina, Anna seemed reserved, shy even. Over coffee, she indicated that Rodolfo had been moved not just because the Maccarinellis' house was full, nor even because of the penalty if he were discovered, but because it was deemed improper for a married man to be living first with her mother and then Doro Garletti's wife as well. Anna's father was missing in action, and during the week Doro was away working in Brescia. There was no suggestion of impropriety – but it was on their minds. Anna did wonder why her mother had kept Rodolfo's photograph, which, I noticed, was there on a sideboard, back in its porcelain frame.

Later, I asked Dom if he thought Anna's unease was because, deep down, she suspected her mother and Ralph had been lovers. He didn't – and, after my musings on Charlie and Vittorina, then Ralph and the non-existent Dora, shot me a quizzical look that said:

are you obsessed or what? As before, the truth was prosaic: forty years earlier Anna and her late husband had ploughed money from the quarry into their stately home while leaving the Chiodi house to decay. But now that the ruin had become a beacon of memory, for Ralph and for the brave people who sheltered him there, she felt a bit guilty.

It was time for us to leave the north. But before we left, there was one last thing I had to do. Running late for yet another flight, we found a small cemetery in Paitone, and searched the marble walls. With minutes to spare, Dom found the Chiodis, complete with their portraits: three stony-faced siblings who had risked everything to save a stranger, a foreign enemy and a friend in need. Hardly anyone remembered them in Paitone now, and the line of their family had died out. These may have been the only images of them in existence – perhaps *ever* to have existed, given that Ralph had not brought any photos of them back from the war.

One might have expected their British guest to leave Paitone as soon as his health, the weather and enemy activity allowed. But spring would come and go, and Ralph would still be there the following spring. In all, he stayed fifteen months. At home with the Chiodis, reborn as Rodolfo, he had found a new life.

A RICORDO DEI
FRATELLI CHIODI
PIETRO DI ANNI 74
AGOSTINO DI ANNI 81
ERMINIA DI ANNI 88

20.

Green Flames

February 1944. Winter was nearly behind them; ahead, the sweetness of spring. The war was always there – the menace of Germans and RSI troops, searching murderously for partisans and Allied fugitives – but in Paitone it didn't flood the senses. Life went on in a mostly untroubled way, and, except for the occasional lean patch, everyone had enough to eat.

Larders were stocked with pecorino, pickled fruit and turnips. Every family in Paitone kept chickens, rabbits, pigeons and a pig fattened on acorns. The slaughterman had been, and hams, sausages and blood puddings prepared.[1] There was wheat for pasta and maize for polenta. Every day at 11.30 a.m. Angelo Maccarinelli came in from the fields to simmer golden flour in a cauldron, pouring the seething liquid onto the table, where it spread like lava; when set, it was topped with tomato sauce and cheese. Each person set to with a fork, intuiting which portion was theirs. Many a fugitive knew it as 'the yellow peril' – but it was filling.[2] The Maccarinellis and Garlettis also ate soup – *minestra*, which could be thick or thin. Augusta, Angelo and Caterina's daughter-in-law, was in charge of the bread.[3]

Ralph's metamorphosis into an Italian, his manners and gait and fluency, meant he could safely take more meals at their house, which added variety and relieved pressure on the Chiodis' food stocks. If the Germans came, he could easily pass for a shabby, taciturn farmhand. Even the suspicions of Caterina's fascist brother were unlikely to be aroused: from a distance, Ralph was just another day labourer from out of town.

Ralph received visits from Doro Garletti, who each day after the factory whistle blew devoted himself to resistance work. For

Green Flames

Erminia Chiodi he brought sacks of flour and desiccated potato to feed her hungry lodger; for Ralph underground newspapers, bottles of home-brewed liqueur, and a worker's ration of tobacco.[4] Ralph and Doro, the imperial patriot and the Marxist revolutionary, became good friends. The teacher Omodeo Cantoni also cycled over from Prevalle, always smart in suit and tie, and with him, too, Ralph nurtured a close friendship. Omodeo came bearing food his wife had prepared, and the two men always looked forward to their language lessons.

In the evenings, the Garlettis and Maccarinellis listened to *Radio Londra*, another reason for Ralph to go over to their house. The news was mostly disappointing: the Allied advance was held up south of Rome at the Gustav Line, a forbidding chain of fortifications running west to east across the country.

The spirit of the Brescian resistance, in Paitone embodied by Doro and Omodeo, meanwhile burned brighter. Rebels had been carrying out gun-grabbing raids since the Armistice in September 1943, and the Fiamme Verdi partisan group was founded soon afterwards. The FFVV, as they were known, were prevalent south of the mountains, whereas on the other side the socialist Brigate Matteotti and communist Brigate Garibaldi held sway. Mainly Catholic in composition, the FFVV nonetheless united men of different persuasions around the motto 'Morte al Fascismo – Libertà all'Italia!'. Politics, they believed, bred division, whereas repentance and reconciliation were strength. Proudly wearing green neckerchiefs, they attracted new members from many walks of life. The first resistance newspaper, *Brescia Libera*, appeared around the time of the FFVV's creation.[5] Give us the weapons, they told the Allies, and we will rid Italy of fascists and Germans. In December 1943 an FFVV commander sent a list of wants so long it was said the only thing missing was General Montgomery himself.[6]

Early in 1944, the Comitato di Liberazione Nazionale Alta Italia (CLNAI) was formed, a cross-resistance organization to coordinate anti-fascist units and also lay foundations for reconstruction. In Prevalle, Omodeo Cantoni was a leading light. The following month, the first issue of the Fiamme Verdi newspaper *Il Ribelle* ('The Rebel') was printed, a copy of which Doro Garletti would surely have brought for Ralph.

The Germans and the RSI conducted frequent *rastrellamenti*, roundups, combing the hills where partisans were based. If the rebels resisted, they were crushed without mercy. Over the winter, a band of ex-army guerrillas had been captured near Lake Iseo, fifty miles from Paitone, and Brescia's resistance leaders executed or deported. Blackshirts often called at the farms on Via Valletta, usually for eggs but also to make checks. On at least one occasion that spring, German soldiers came to the Chiodi house to see if anyone was hiding there.

April brought showers, and wildflowers covered the land. Then in May came hay-cutting, the workers moving in waves, stopping only to whet their scythes or for refreshment. Later, they tossed the drying grass before building it into hayricks.[7] Carefree evenings were a time to pick figs and cherries, while all around the war continued to rage. In June, the RSI's Brigate Nere, or 'Black Brigades', were formed to terrorize ordinary Italians, and in August, a Fiamme Verdi commander was killed in the Chiodis' home town, Corteno; a fortnight later an entire detachment of resistance fighters was caught and shot.[8]

The Germans, still dominant yet under pressure, grew more ruthless. Field Marshal Kesselring, the supreme Nazi commander in Italy, ordered hostages to be taken after every instance of sabotage, and homes burned wherever his troops were fired upon. Partisans were summarily executed. Atrocities escalated into massacres. That September, a month of intense activity, over 100 civilians in three villages west of Bologna were murdered. POW partisans caught up in these actions were hanged with their Italian comrades. Such was the news that Doro Garletti, energized by rage, communicated to Ralph on his visits.[9]

As the summer days grew shorter, Ralph decided to spend the evenings writing about his escape from Camp 65. This would be a welcome pastime, perhaps also a way of recovering something of his old self. Needing paper, it seems he asked Omodeo Cantoni, who obligingly pilfered three exercise books from his primary school.[10] As well as recalling his flight towards Brindisi with Charlie, Ralph filled the *quaderni* with the poetry he'd learned as a boy: Wordsworth, Tennyson, Yeats and Longfellow, and composed Kiplingesque verse of his own about leading men to safety in hot desert sands, including the line: 'So into youth I passed, so into daydreams'. For a man remembered by his own family as remote and reserved, he had a curiously mystical sense of himself.[11]

Once the maize was in, men ploughed under fine, cloudless skies; on the hillside the oak leaves were turning brown. When it rained, they rubbed kernels from maize cobs and dried chestnuts to grind into flour. As warm afternoons faded to dusk, families sat outside reminiscing, the scent of wet earth and woodsmoke on the breeze.[12]

After that, everyone in Paitone gathered for the *vendemmia*. Armed with stepladders and secateurs, they heaped baskets with grapes to be carted off for pressing. 'It was as though something had happened that let people just enjoy themselves and forget there was still a war going on,' recalled one POW in hiding. Tastings followed: the nectar-like *mosto*, the unboiled *crudo* and the potent *cotto*. The wine mash became fodder, maize husks and stalks kindling for the fire.[13] Halcyon days were nonetheless marred by the horrors Doro heard on the resistance grapevine. In October, ten fighters of the Giustizia e Libertà formation were burned alive in Bagolino, thirty miles north of Paitone, and further north every house in the town of Case di Viso was razed to the ground.[14]

The winter of 1944–5 hit many families hard. In Prevalle some were forced to subsist on pumpkins after the local Brigate Nere stole their livestock. Meat, milk, eggs, sugar, soap and wool were all scarce, and leather only available on the black market.[15] Paitone was mercifully spared the worst of it. The ten-year-old Piero Garletti would remember only frosty evenings by a roaring fire, with roasted chestnuts and wild stories. In December, as word of the *rastrellamenti* and reprisals spread, so Ralph took stock. Christmas had come again, marking a year in Paitone. The Maccarinelli house was decorated with candles and 'window', strips of aluminium dropped by the RAF to confuse German radar.[16]

On Christmas Eve, two feet of snow fell. In the morning, clearing paths from their doors, people heard the drone of bombers over Prevalle, their target the rail track. Even though there was little damage and no serious injury, the war had come closer. A month later, a squadron of US P-47 Thunderbolts attacked the railway again, this time at nearby Gavardo, killing fifty-two civilians and injuring many others. Thereafter, the sound of approaching aircraft made people in Paitone nervous, sending them scrambling for the caves a short distance up Monte Budellone.[17]

Apart from working the land and writing in his *quaderni*, what had Ralph been doing all this time? Four years earlier, he had gone to fight, first in France, then Libya, after which he was taken prisoner, escaped and after that somehow slipped out of gear. There were so many mountain exit routes with reliable guides, and even some MI9 evacuation missions led by the Parachute Regiment and other elite British units. Even local Fiamme Verdi partisans helped evading prisoners get away.[18] By October 1944, some 6,500 POWs had reached Allied lines, and another 4,000 made it to Switzerland.[19] Ralph could have left Paitone – surely Doro raised the possibility – but he didn't.

His memoir was no help, but clues lay elsewhere. Transported to a world of friendship and freedom, one evader described how 'a warm peace entered my soul', blurring the past into meaningless abstraction. Ralph was humbled, not just because these were the people of a nation he'd been taught to despise but because it proved everyone was capable of what another ex-POW called 'a transformation that endows them with courage and virtues beyond all possible expectation'. Therein lay hope for the postwar world.[20]

The miracle of the 'strange alliance' was an enlightening therapy for men who knew little and had been through a lot. Its historian, Roger Absalom, called this rite of passage 'a revelation of their secret selves as much as of a country and a people of whose existence they had previously been scarcely aware'.[21] One soldier regressed to a life of medieval simplicity, where he 'learned that time can be accepted with the passing of the seasons, that birth, life and death can be seen calmly as part of a great rhythm of blossom and decay'. Tomorrow ceased to matter. He came up with many justifications for taking time out of life, most of them, he realized later, dubious. 'What kept me in limbo was that I did not want to emerge from it . . . In the last analysis, I dawdled because I liked it.'[22]

What, then, of Flo? She had heard nothing from Ralph or even of him since his last letter from Chiavari, written in August 1943, when he called her the best wife in the world and said he was always thinking of her. She and the rest of the family must have assumed he was dead. In April 1944, Flo's brother George and his wife had a baby they named Ralph, either for luck or in memoriam. Ralph knew they would think he had died, but perhaps he chose to forget. Seduced by the good life, he may just have satisfied himself that his wife would still be there when he got home.

One Sunday afternoon, I was browsing a bookshelf at my in-laws' house when I found a memoir by a veteran named Ray Ellis. His escape from Camp 53 Sforzacosta was an ordeal, he said, quite unlike a war film – the same difference between Frank Sinatra escaping from a train in *Von Ryan's Express* and Ralph doing it for real. Ellis had hidden out in the Marche region, toiling from sunrise to sunset with an impoverished couple, who showed him such love he called them 'Mamma' and 'Babbo' – Mum and Dad.[23]

But what caught my eye was Ellis's time with the partisans, whom he described as untrustworthy, chaotic and naive, brandishing weapons they were untrained to use, and more like swaggering bandits than soldiers. Soon after he quit, German troops wiped them out, a few killed in action, the rest hanged from lampposts.[24]

However brief, guerrilla warfare was a gripping part of Ellis's story. Reading it in bed, I fell asleep wishing Ralph had done something similar – had been the fighting hero I'd craved association with when I was a child. But weirdly, the next morning, trawling through photos from Pauline's archive, I found a typewritten document in

Italian, hitherto overlooked. The author was Omodeo Cantoni, the date April 1946. I ran the words through Google Translate, half holding my breath as the meaning appeared on the screen. According to Cantoni, Ralph had indeed been a partisan with the Fiamme Verdi – the 'Green Flames' – and had risked his life in the face of great peril. I could immediately see Ralph wearing a green scarf, oiling a Sten gun somewhere in the Brescian hills, and was desperate to know more. It was this discovery that first sent me to the National Archives to hunt for the MI9 files that identified the people who had sheltered Ralph and Charlie.[25]

Three years later, I was sitting with Dom in a flat above a flower shop in Prevalle, sipping an espresso and listening to the florist's husband talk about partisans. His name was Paolo Catterina, a modest, gracious ex-mayor of the town. Also present was Paolo's friend Marco Maccarinelli – no relation – who shared his passion for this history.

Paolo and Marco were not only amazed that Ralph had stayed hidden so long, but, like me, wondered quite what he'd been doing. I showed them Cantoni's document, which they agreed was a testimonial stating that Ralph had been a member of the FFVV – the Fiamme Verdi. Paolo suggested he might have operated as some kind of liaison or bilingual messenger.

The resistance agent Doro Garletti was the obvious person to induct Ralph into the movement – but he hadn't belonged to the FFVV. What about Maestro Cantoni? Paolo thought that, like many people, this mild-mannered teacher wasn't actually a partisan but had a support role from his CLNAI work. Paolo had already contacted Omodeo's son – but he'd suffered a stroke and had no interest in his father's war. When Celestina showed us Omodeo's grave, she hinted at disquiet when, after his wife died in 1947, he married Celestina's cousin, eighteen years his junior and his niece. Omodeo's papers, which doubtless included letters from Ralph, had been thrown away. All I had were the photos he'd given Ralph, taken in 1937 when Omodeo was aged thirty. Marco, who had known him later in life, said he was always well turned out and lived on Via Bonsignori.

Having drawn a blank with Omodeo's son, Paolo had spoken with another local, an old man who as a boy had known of an Englishman hiding with elderly siblings in Via Valletta. This surely meant Ralph and the Chiodis. The siblings spoke English, he said, and, being advanced in years and childless, had less to lose than their neighbours if betrayed. He remembered parachutes over Monte Budellone, behind Via Valletta: supply drops to partisans on neighbouring Monte Tesio, packed canisters which they buried or hid in caves. Sadly, this man was too unwell to meet us, but his nephew had agreed to phone Dom. 'A very passionate young student of history', according to the uncle, he had discovered relics in the hills using a metal detector.

Thanking Paolo and Marco, Dom and I drove to Via Bonsignori to see Omodeo Cantoni's house. Assuming he'd felt confident enough, Ralph may have come here – a twenty-minute walk. Chafing at confinement, many POWs in hiding disobeyed instructions to stay put, even drinking in the *dopo lavoro* – the village pub, where everyone knew each other. An old man appeared from next door. He had known Cantoni and his second wife and had heard of the Chiodis, whom he referred to as *gli americani*. He also remembered the Brigate Nere, whose headquarters were just over the road: they'd made him sing fascist songs at gunpoint. Back then, he said, gesturing wistfully at the built-up street, this was all countryside.

The metal detectorist called, and we went to meet him. Indicating the line of hills where the Germans and the Italian SS used to skirmish with the rebels, he showed us a handful of ground-dug British buttons and bullets, which, he said, had to be partisan-related because Prevalle had been liberated by the Americans. He gave me a couple of buckles as souvenirs.

That evening we went for a pizza with a representative of ANPI, the left-leaning Associazione Nazionale Partigiani d'Italia, or National Partisans' Association, who spoke of the antipathy between the Fiamme Verdi and the communist Garibaldi Brigades. Dom, weary after another hectic day, expressed intolerance of left and right scrapping over Italy's past – he'd put up with enough of that at Camp 65 – adding that gun-toting partisans had no monopoly over the memory of the resistance.²⁶

Paitone, early 1945: everyone dared to hope the war would soon be over. As the Allied advance closed in, so all the elements of the resistance – partisans and helpers, those who fought and those who carried messages or gave food and shelter – came together to rid the land of fascism.

Across the region, the Germans were gradually pulling back, fragmenting, deserting. One stormy night, Ralph was at the Maccarinellis when there was a knock at the door. Instead of hiding, Ralph answered it. Standing there were two bedraggled German soldiers seeking shelter and sanctuary. Ralph told them to piss off and slammed the door. The boy Piero was thrilled by this display of contempt. But was contempt all Ralph had in him?²⁷

Omodeo Cantoni's testimonial said that Ralph had been dedicated to 'supporting and directing the partisans of Prevalle, sharing the serious risks and dangers they faced, given that Prevalle and its surroundings were swarming with German soldiers and members of the Brigate Nere'.²⁸ This activity, Cantoni claimed, had lasted for eighteen months, between November 1943 and April 1945 – clearly an exaggeration, if not a complete fabrication. For one thing, Ralph didn't arrive in Paitone until December 1943; besides which, although he'd never said much about his Italian experiences, he hadn't said anything at all to Nan, and by extension me, about being a partisan. I would surely have remembered that. It emerged, however, that in the briefest of pencilled notes he informed MI9 that he had joined the FFVV, although not until 20 March 1945. Had he done anything at all?

The Fiamme Verdi was not the only partisan group active in the region, nor, I'd come to see, was fighting the only means of resistance. Ralph may have been engaged in some other way, perhaps as a liaison agent, as Paolo Catterina had suggested. There was a final line of inquiry. Ralph's MI9 report mentioned a man named Andrea Baronchelli, another member of the national liberation committee, the CLNAI, for whom Ralph apparently did some kind of secret work. Digging around, I found a Dr Andrea Baronchelli, a maths lecturer in London and the CLNAI man's grandson. Andrea told me that Baronchelli Senior had studied economics in Turin, married a journalist, then served as an army officer until the Italian Armistice of September 1943, when he fled from Rome. Arrested by the Germans, he was freed thanks to a friend of his wife's in the Red Cross. From there he went first to the family home in Cremona, and then another forty miles north to Nuvolento, the small town next to Paitone.

Andrea sent photos of his grandfather's ASC certificate, identical to Doro Garletti's, as well as his Socialist Party membership card and some photos, including one of him in the uniform of a fascist soldier, holding Andrea's uncle as a baby. I subsequently found online a partisan membership card for the 7th Brigata Matteotti.[29] Like Doro, then, Baronchelli was not FFVV, yet still belonged to the world of armed rebellion into which Ralph may have strayed by the beginning of 1945.

Reading the ASC claims again, I noticed that Doro Garletti, who had supplied Ralph with fifty kilos of maize flour and twenty of dried potato, said that he had received help from the same Andrea Baronchelli. Baronchelli, too, had a file showing that he had given Ralph clothing and money, and in return had received a chit, photo and postcard. Four men, he continued, could corroborate his story: Angelo Maccarinelli, Augusto Chiodi, Omodeo Cantoni and Doro Garletti, Doro having introduced him to Ralph. The supporting documents were missing, perhaps never submitted. Baronchelli didn't want reimbursement. He valued his assistance at 7,000 lire, but asked for it to be given to the Maccarinelli and Chiodi families.

This discovery led Dom and me to a remarkable archive in the city of Brescia, housed at the Università Cattolica del Sacro Cuore. Across a cloistered court, the good-natured archivist led us up a winding stone staircase to a room where he produced several boxes crammed with FFVV documents. Dom said we were looking for any mention of Ralph's connection to the partisans. But where to begin? It was like searching for a needle in a haystack – when there might not be a needle in the first place.

Various minutes and memos, typed and handwritten on thin economy paper, revealed the Fiamme Verdi to be a disciplined if poorly armed military organization. There were also posters warning against harbouring POWs, editions of *Il Ribelle* and other clandestine newspapers, and coded messages about parachute supply drops. The partisans were optimistic, confident they would build a new life once fascism was defeated.

After an hour or so, we began finding references to Andrea Baronchelli's role in postwar reconstruction, and intriguingly to a mission to the hill town of Serle, which he had undertaken on 21 March 1945. Clearly he had not gone alone – and this was the day after Ralph said he had joined the partisans. Another document made its way into the pile. I found myself staring at an Intelligence Corps memo relating to the bona fides of Baronchelli and his connection to a British soldier: Warrant Officer Ralph Corps. We had run him to ground.

That evening, the Garletti family, Doro's descendants, showed us round the theatrically lit city. At the cathedral, Piero recalled an Allied air raid on 13 July when flames turned night into day, and a direct hit sent streams of molten lead rilling down the roof.[30] At dinner, Piero told me how much he had admired Rodolfo. It suddenly occurred to me that he would have entertained the children with his escapes. Of course, Piero replied: he cut a hole in the floor of a train! For the first time in fifty years, I was hearing the story from someone who had heard it directly from Ralph.

The next day we returned to Paitone to see Celestina Maccarinelli, the granddaughter of Angelo, who had first sheltered Ralph. This time, her son took us along a steep path at the end of the garden, which snaked through woodland up Monte Budellone all the way to Serle, the destination for Baronchelli's mission. It was one of thousands of hill routes in northern Italy known to partisans, and favoured by them precisely because they were unknown to the Germans or because the enemy rightly feared ambush there.

Plagued by mosquitoes, we climbed only a little of the way, as far as the caves where people in Paitone had sheltered from Allied bombing. Through a break in the trees, we were rewarded with a panoramic view of the countryside – the sort of view that made partisans and evaders feel safer. When we got back down, Celestina insisted on washing my muddy boots, an echo of the care Ralph had received from this remarkable family.

We spent the evening at Anna's. After our last visit, she had promised to have the vegetation cut back from the Chiodi house, but hadn't got round to it. She did, however, have a surprise for me: she had located the bench in the now-famous photo of Ralph and restored it. Sitting there brought me very close to Ralph. Yet the real communion across that span of time came with the warmth of friendship at the dinner table.

'All this,' said Dom, looking round at the company eating and chatting. 'This is what Ralph felt. *Incredibile.*'

In the spring of 1945, however, the war still had to be won, mile by mile, hill by hill, valley by valley. German troops, many of them veterans from Russia, Greece and France, may have been on the back foot, but their ruthless fury was unrelenting. The dangers faced by Ralph and the Brescian resistance were not yet at an end.

21.

A Hazardous Mission

By high summer 1944, Charlie West had spent nearly four months in Ceraino, the village in the Adige Valley where he and Ralph had hidden after escaping from the train a year earlier. There, the farmer Cirillo Fumaneri and, indirectly, Cirillo's boss at the quarry, Signor Radaelli, continued to provide for him and keep him from prying eyes. Radaelli's daughter Vittorina still visited him in the *casotto*, bringing food and improving his Italian. Like Ralph on the opposite side of Lake Garda, Charlie felt part of the Fumaneri family and a wider secret network of resisters he trusted and respected.

Also like Ralph's friends, the Fumaneris tuned in to *Radio Londra*. American and British forces had taken up positions behind the Gustav Line at Anzio, and on 4 June liberated Rome. Two days later, the Normandy landings opened a new western front; in the east the Germans had suffered shattering losses, after which the Red Army sped towards the Vistula within striking distance of Berlin. In mid-August, Charlie heard that the Allies had landed in southern France and were already near the Franco-Swiss border.

This was the news he'd been waiting for. His plan was to head for the mountains, expecting either to meet British troops or to find a partisan band to fight with until they arrived. Again, Charlie said goodbye to Vittorina, this time doubting he'd ever return.

Once Charlie had gathered his things, Cirillo ferried him across the Adige. He then walked north towards the mountain village of Spiazzi, which, as Ralph had found, took him longer than the few days he'd anticipated. By the end of the month, he had reached

Lake Garda, at Brenzone in the shadow of Monte Baldo. There he asked a woman how he might cross the water – but she was suspicious and alerted Giuseppe Marozin, commander of the Ateo Caremi assault unit of the Garibaldi Brigades. At gunpoint, Charlie managed to convince Marozin that he was an RAF pilot, and perhaps pretended to be a communist – something that had worked on the electrician back in Camp 65 when he needed radio components.[1]

Charlie joined the Ateo Caremi partisans, who continued to believe he was a spy and, but for Marozin's protection, would have shot him. Enemy infiltration of so many units had made them paranoid. 'How the hell can one be expected to retain one's sanity,' asked a former POW in a similar situation, 'when the people one meets may be Italian fascists masquerading as peasants, or German soldiers masquerading as English prisoners, or even Germans pretending to be British prisoners masquerading as Italian peasants?'[2]

In the crags and ravines of Monte Baldo, Charlie did everything he could to prove himself, fearlessly attacking patrols and single-handedly capturing eight Germans and three of their Italian allies. Of these miserably doomed men, Charlie executed two and buried their bodies; the rest he interrogated, probably brutally and certainly without regard for the Geneva Convention. This was the man war had made, a measure of new extremes of savagery on both sides. To partisans, prisoners were an encumbrance and a danger, and in many cases it had become normal to torture and shoot them without compunction.[3]

In October 1944, Field Marshal Kesselring sent hordes of ruthless troops into the hills and valleys, scattering many partisan bands. As winter set in, Charlie and his Ateo Caremi comrades ran very low on food – and everything else they needed to survive and fight. The partisans were in crisis. Then in mid-November General Alexander, the supreme Allied commander in Italy, stood them down, causing rancour and dismay – even among the British. According to one SOE agent, Alexander had 'as well as told the partisans to disband, and . . . the enemy to come and finish them off while they were doing it'.⁴

The Ateo Caremi struggled on until the heavy snows of January 1945 brought all movement to a halt. Morale hit rock bottom, and the men became very lean, digging for roots in the frozen earth. Every day they scanned the skies for supply planes, but all they got were the Luftwaffe dropping leaflets bearing the message: 'Poor Partisans. What are you doing on the mountains now that the Allies have given you up?' Lay down your arms, Kesselring promised, and you'll be given food, lodgings and liberty. It was unthinkable – and yet to famished, bone-chilled men diabolically tempting.⁵

Sensing it was time to move on, Charlie bade farewell to the men whose trust he had earned so dearly and with whom everything had been shared during that winter on the mountain. He would go to Switzerland. This was the destination that had possessed him like a fever dream since his first notion to fly there – the fantasy he'd indulged in with Ralph, who in Molina seems to have persuaded himself it was impossible.

Back in the valley, Charlie met smugglers at Lake Garda, who one moonlit night rowed him across. Even in the blackout, he would have seen the silhouette of the palace where the RSI's Presidency of the Council of Ministers met. For this region, the so-called 'Republic of Salò', was now the seat of fascism in Italy. Landing south of Gargnano, Charlie walked all day and night into the hills until he reached Lake Idro, then proceeded to a hamlet on the far shore, where he slept in a cattle shed. Next day, he hiked into the mountains, past Lavenone to the village of Presegno, where deep snowdrifts prevented his going any further. Various partisan bands operated in these parts: the Giustizia e Libertà and Garibaldi Brigades, as well as the Fiamme Verdi, mostly former soldiers evading military conscription.⁶

Charlie was accepted by the commander of an FFVV unit, with whom he was to remain until April 1945. Although victory in Italy now seemed certain, there was much difficult terrain to traverse and many German defenders to dislodge. After slogging up towards the Apennines in the autumn of 1944, intending to liberate the Po Valley, the US 5th Army, like the partisans, had spent the winter resting, rearming and regrouping. They were preparing to breach the Germans' final defensive barrier: the Gothic Line, which north of Florence bisected Italy coast to coast. January 1945 brought the 5th Army within ten miles of Bologna, but the way ahead was blocked by strongholds cut into the rock and minefields thick with concertina wire. And until the Americans reached Brescia, another 130 miles north of Bologna, the task of harrying the enemy back to the Brenner Pass fell to the partisans.[7]

German soldiers not dug in on the Gothic Line were by now in retreat, and scattered columns on the main roads cheered ordinary Italians. Mostly young conscripts, these troops were haggard and despondent, their kit bundled in ox and horse carts. In many cases, their officers had fled, and they plodded on alone, prey to red-hot rumours that the Russians were coming. Panic set in and men stampeded up hillsides and across the fields. Now it was the Allies' turn to drop leaflets, informing German soldiers that the Russians were in Berlin and asking why on earth *they* were still fighting. The FFVV sent a copy to HQ with a pencilled Italian translation, either for intelligence purposes or perhaps just for fun.[8]

The FFVV exploited the collapse in morale by painting north-pointing arrows on walls with the message: 'ZUR HEIMAT' – this way home.[9] Wehrmacht troops, many non-Germans pressed into service in Eastern Europe, needed no encouragement to leave. In Brescia, thousands of men stationed in the capital had begun trekking east towards Salò, from where they aimed to head north through the Val Sabbia. The first leg of this journey took them across the valley, right at the edge of the hills, through Mazzano, Nuvolento and Paitone.

One day, Piero Garletti and his cousin Annibale Zanola, son of the family fascist, decided to wander down to the main road to watch the retreating German soldiers. Maestro Cantoni had cycled from Prevalle to see Ralph, and the two men said they would come too, perhaps to stop the boys getting into trouble. Sitting next to me in the restaurant in Brescia, Piero recounted the story. He remembered seeing a column of some 300 Germans heading in the direction of Gavardo and Lake Garda. Their uniforms were tatty, and most travelled on foot. A few had battered bicycles, which they rode on the rims if the tyres had gone. One German noticed Cantoni's bike and grabbed it. 'Immediately Rodolfo took hold of the bicycle,' said Piero, still gleeful after all these years, 'and, gripping it tightly, pulled it towards him.' Ralph held the German's gaze until, visibly frightened, he let go of the bike and quickly rejoined the column. This was the moment when Piero knew, beyond all doubt, that the Germans would never win the war.

Ralph, too, was brimming with optimism and courage. Some weeks earlier, he had visited Andrea Baronchelli at his home in Cremona, a city some forty miles south-west of Paitone. They had first met in Paitone in May 1944 and had been in contact ever since. Ralph arrived at the railway station, which like all stations was heavily guarded, and strolled down the Corso Garibaldi. As instructed, he knocked at number 10, using a side entrance in case the front was under surveillance, and was greeted by Baronchelli, who led Ralph across a courtyard. If the Germans came, anything compromising could be dropped through a trap door into the Cremonella, an ancient stream that ran beneath the house.[10]

A Hazardous Mission

Baronchelli provided Ralph with a better hat, a proper suit, shirts, a pair of shoes (to wear instead of his rough work boots) and 1,000 lire. Ralph also received false papers, including a safe-conduct pass, forged using a blank document procured from the RSI's Finance Ministry by someone with access to the correct stamp. Printed in German and Italian, this authorized 'Rodolfo Corpi' to travel anywhere in Italy unimpeded. The photo was one I recognized from Ralph's album, taken when he was in the Coldstream Guards. The copy he gave to Baronchelli was cropped to remove incriminating traces of his military mess jacket.

Afterwards, Ralph caught the train back to Prevalle, perhaps with his head stuck in a newspaper or pretending to be asleep. Had he been challenged, the *salvacondotto* I'd discovered in Warmsworth may have saved him; his Italian could have fooled a German soldier. But travelling in civilian clothing with forged documents and posing as an RSI official was staggeringly risky. If exposed, Ralph would surely have been shot as a spy, and probably tortured to reveal his contacts. Furthermore, operating, as he did, right in the black heart of the Republic of Salò, a place of excessive and ghoulishly sadistic violence, raised the danger to an extreme level.[11]

So, what was Ralph to Baronchelli – some kind of go-between? Ralph told MI9 that he had worked with him into the spring of 1945, when he had been in 'personal communication' with US parachutists at Serle. Had this really been his role? It was absolutely vital to know, and yet this promised to be the hardest episode to recover from the archives. It was more frustrating than ever that I still hadn't been able to see Ralph's classified military service record at the National Archives, which might have shed some light on his resistance work. But staff were struggling with a huge backlog of Freedom of Information applications from people like me, curious about what their relatives had done during the war.

The parachutists Ralph referred to belonged to the Office of Strategic Services (OSS), which sent hundreds of agents of the 2677th Regiment of the US 5th Army into northern Italy in 1944 and 1945. Many were second-generation Italian immigrants to America – 'glorious amateurs', according to the OSS director, William Donovan. The creator of James Bond, Ian Fleming, then a British intelligence officer, advised Donovan to select middle-aged men replete with tact and experience; ignoring this, Donovan chose unstinting, reckless, aggressive youths – very much in Charlie West's mould.[12] The OSS supported the partisans and, in turn, were themselves supported by a large, loose network of Italian resisters leading double lives in the villages, towns and cities – men like Andrea Baronchelli, Doro Garletti and Omodeo Cantoni.[13]

The OSS men, all too often wantonly lawless, laid ambushes, cut telephone lines and harassed the enemy, and were mainly embedded in partisan groups, whom they trained and supplied by coordinating Allied supply drops. Weather permitting, hundreds of tons of materiel were dropped every month – everything from guns, TNT and wireless sets to margarine, toothpaste and razor blades.[14] Given the political differences among partisans, these drops required diplomacy, and also discretion, as one British report put it, 'to prevent uncontrolled expansion of the resistance movement'. A weapon fired at a German today might tomorrow be turned on a rival partisan or Allied soldier.[15]

Compared with the British, who were concerned about the postwar status quo, the OSS were focused on the job in hand, which meant throwing everything against the enemy as quickly and ruthlessly as possible. Supply was key, requiring partisans to find appropriate drop zones, mark them with fires, read flare signals and send coded messages by Morse and by hand: 'Ditta' meant FFVV, 'Funghi' parachutists, and 'Patate' hand grenades. All being well, after a tense wait, grey blobs would appear in the sky, the shapes expanding as the planes banked away, before the aluminium canisters landed with a thud beneath a subsiding silk cloud. It was a beautiful sight, both in itself and for what it signified. Joyous partisans would rush forward, sever the nylon cords, bundle away the parachute, then lug their booty to safety before an enemy patrol arrived.[16]

Early in 1945, the skies cleared, and drops increased, even though

A Hazardous Mission

snow lay thickly on the ground.[17] For many partisans this was the start of the war's most dangerous and demanding phase. The Allies were hammering away at the Gothic Line, enraging the German defenders, who responded bestially to civilian resistance. In the first week of the year, the Waffen-SS and Brigate Nere launched a devastating *rastrellamento* on Monte Tesio, the base of the FFVV's Perlasca Brigade, formed to coordinate operations between Brescia, the Val Sabbia and the Val Trompia, sabotage enemy vehicles and seize weapons.[18] With an eye on economic stability in northern Italy, the British relied on partisans to counter German scorched-earth tactics, especially the destruction of factories and electricity stations. Senior SS officers were already exploring how to trade 'anti-scorch' for a negotiated local peace to allow them to escape to Germany.

Meanwhile, the FFVV had been tenaciously fighting Germans, Italian SS, RSI troops and Brigate Nere. Back in December, a group from Bedizzole had raided the Prevalle headquarters of the Guardia Nazionale Repubblicana, the RSI's rebooted *carabinieri*, and grabbed a dozen rifles. Led by a Pole wearing a German uniform, a detachment of the Perlasca Brigade ambushed Wehrmacht trucks on the road between Prevalle and Gavardo. In response, the Germans deployed waves of sickeningly violent *rastrellamenti*. Then, the capture of a key Perlasca commander threw the unit into disarray. Early in March, a partisan from the Garibaldi Brigades was executed by GNR troops in the Val Sabbia along with nine others.[19] But they sensed they had the fascists on the ropes and fought on.

In the Fiamme Verdi archives at the Università Cattolica del Sacro Cuore in Brescia, Dom and I found an intriguing letter. On the last day of the war, a US army major, Vincent Abrignani, wrote to Andrea Baronchelli to express on behalf of the OSS and the United States of America 'our appreciation for your generous and sincere collaboration with a group entrusted with a special and hazardous mission, which [was] despatched into Enemy Occupied Territory by this Detachment'. What this mission entailed, Abrignani didn't say – but he did refer to a report submitted by the mission's leader, who was unnamed but presumably an OSS officer, in which Baronchelli had been praised for his contribution, made 'often at great risk and without personal interest'.[20]

I searched for a copy of this report in OSS records in the National Archives and Churchill Archives in Cambridge, and, sparing the archive staff at NARA, hired an independent researcher in Maryland to comb through its voluminous collection of OSS records. Many tantalizing documents came to light, edging closer in time and space to the critical moment – but no smoking gun.[21]

There was, however, another clue to suggest that Ralph had been part of Baronchelli's mission. Among the papers of the Brescia liberation committee, I'd found Baronchelli's own account of his anti-fascist activity. After his release from prison in 1943, he obtained a false declaration stating that he worked for a company in Cremona, then in December that year secured a job at the Brescia office of the Foreign Trade Institute. Beneath that cover, he worked with the resistance, collecting weapons and supplies and helping Allied POWs into the mountains. Andrea Baronchelli Jr told me that his grandmother had made her husband swear not to have anything to do with the resistance – but the cause compelled him, meaning he had to keep his war work secret even from his own wife.

After a spell in Rome, a work posting during which he sheltered rebels in his apartment, Baronchelli returned to Brescia, where, still behind his wife's back, he produced the underground newspapers distributed by Doro Garletti, intercepted military telephone calls and, based in Nuvolento, organized resistance committees in Paitone, Prevalle and Serle. He also liaised with what he described as 'English prisoners in hiding'. His boss at the Foreign Trade Institute not only provided money to help the Chiodi siblings look after Ralph but, as an official of the Finance Ministry, must have been responsible for forging his safe-conduct pass.[22]

The more I understood of Ralph's war in northern Italy, the more subtle the shades of the resistance seemed. It was not a secret army, as in Belgium or Holland, nor was it confined by politics or class. Resisters came from every walk of life – soldiers, priests, peasants, housewives, engineers, students, doctors, lawyers, civil servants, artisans and shopkeepers. Baronchelli was a trade envoy, Omodeo Cantoni a teacher, and Doro Garletti a machinist; the Maccarinellis and Chiodis were farmers. Nor were the partisans they supported any less varied. Although many were demobilized soldiers, a British report described 'an astonishing mixture' of young and old, women and men, conservative and radical, plus escaped Allied POWs and Axis deserters. 'Bands exist of every degree, down to gangs of thugs who don a partisan cloak of respectability to conceal the nakedness of their brigandage, and bands who bury their arms in their back gardens and only dig them up and festoon themselves in comic opera uniforms when the first Allied troops arrive.'[23]

In Brescia, the Fiamme Verdi was no place for poseurs, buffoons or bad apples. They were disciplined troops in a proud regiment, whose most distinguished unit was the Perlasca Brigade. The hill town of Serle, where the brigade was formed, was surrounded by dense woodland with a sweeping prospect of the valley. When Dom and I drove up there from Paitone, the location made perfect sense as a military vantage point. A brigade member named Caterina Rossi Tonni owned a barn on Monte Tesio, where, hidden in a forest of oak and beech, she gave shelter to partisans and fleeing POWs. In the summer months peasants climbed Tesio to pasture their cattle, living off the land and sleeping in haylofts. But no one else went there, making it a prime spot for resistance planning and drop zones.[24]

Baronchelli's action on 21 March 1945 had to be the 'special and hazardous mission' referred to by the OSS. There, in Serle, Baronchelli met American parachutists from the 2677th Regiment, who had landed a fortnight earlier, and drove the leader, 'Franco', fifty miles south to Cremona. In the car were a mobile radio transmitter and false papers for Franco, probably including a safe-conduct pass like Ralph's. From Cremona they went to Porto Polesine, a commercial river crossing on the Po.[25] It was the beginning of the end for the German occupation of Italy. Allied armies were approaching, the weather was dry, air supplies were plentiful, and intelligence traffic was brisk and reliable.[26]

Without the OSS report, it was impossible to know exactly what they'd been doing.²⁷ They may have been exfiltrating resistance leaders; probably the rendezvous had something to do with Allied planning for a spring push to drive the Germans north of the river. Porto Polesine was just eighty miles from the Adriatic coast where a week later British commandos, supported by partisans of the Brigate Garibaldi, landed to spearhead the offensive.²⁸

Whatever the reason, Ralph had been there, in his suit and hat, *salvacondotto* in his pocket. Other sources indicated that Franco had reported problems with his radio, which received signals but wouldn't send any. This made the partisans suspicious. They were already on edge after losing their commander some weeks earlier, betrayed by a traitor in their midst. It's possible, then, that Ralph travelled to Serle from Paitone to mend Franco's transmitter, which, according to the records, was soon in working order. He knew about wireless from the camps, and was a trained telegraphist from his time on the railways, so he was able to send and receive Morse code in English and Italian.²⁹ Ralph may also have been sent there to see whether Franco struck him as an authentic American or a spy. He was, I discovered, by no means the only Italian-speaking British POW to join an OSS mission at this time.³⁰

At last, the story gathered momentum. It was now possible to reconstruct the journey made by Baronchelli and the OSS man Franco, probably with Ralph, from the house in the Corso Garibaldi to the Po. An aunt of Andrea Baronchelli Jr recalled that Andrea Sr had once brought an Englishman, presumably Ralph, to the family's country retreat, Cascina Farisengo, a large fifteenth-century farmhouse five miles south-east of Cremona. This lay directly on the route to Stagno Lombardo, another two miles south, the old ferry station for Porto Polesine. A hundred miles from there lay La Spezia and other ports of departure along the Ligurian coast.

I also identified 'Franco'. His name was Lionello Levi Sandri, not an American per se, but an Italian recruited by the OSS and parachuted into Brescia. A copy of Major Abrignani's letter to Andrea

Baronchelli was sent to a young FFVV partisan named Sam Quillieri, co-opted as a liaison officer with the OSS.

In March 1945, at Serle, Quillieri met Sandri, whom he described as both American and Italian, dressed in alpine cap and knee socks, speaking slowly yet emphatically, his gestures both deliberate and calm. Quillieri had tried to catch 'the Famous Franco' out in conversation, but found nothing amiss. Sandri simply said that his task was to prepare the ground for subsequent missions. At Castello di Serle, west of the town, Sandri went to church one Sunday and began singing psalms, which moved locals. Quillieri was there in the pews and whispered to his neighbour: 'Nice guys, these Americans.'[31]

Soon afterwards, the Perlasca Brigade distributed the plentiful supplies that had arrived with Sandri and, well armed and newly confident, set about waylaying columns of withdrawing Germans. Among these partisans was a charismatic, brave, restless British airman, an escaped prisoner of war whose *nom de guerre* was 'Carlo'.

22.

Incipit Vita Nova

The gruelling winter of 1944–5 had left the Perlasca Brigade in bad shape, the men scrawny with long beards, threadbare clothing and worn-out shoes. Nerves were frayed from frequent alerts, sleepless nights and the constant threat of ambush. They had had to keep moving, burdened by kit, walking by starlight, sheltering in outhouses, subsisting on polenta, cheese and milk. Thick fogs descended suddenly, halting them in their tracks, deepening a sense of surreal isolation. To these men, some still in their teens, the enemy had come to seem less ideologically defined, more a fact of life in an unvarying, never-ending present. The past felt like a dream; the future – a new life – a fantastical mirage.[1]

The last person to call Charlie by his real name had been Ralph, in Molina, more than a year earlier. Since then, he had become Carlo, a fierce guerrilla so immersed in his partisan band that, like Ralph, he was essentially Italian – carrying himself like his comrades, speaking the same argot, sleeping among them, sharing fireside songs and stories and the same meagre rations. His cause was no longer just anti-fascist, and perhaps it never had been king and country. Charlie's staunch loyalty was to his brothers-in-arms.

Comprising just 100 men, his battalion was based in the Brescian Dolomites, overlooking the town of Pertica Alta. Its name was S4 – the 'S' standing for Val Sabbia, their zone of operations – and their headquarters, if it could be called that, was a stone shelter known as 'Malga Sacù', 5,000 feet above sea level on Corna Blacca.

In March 1945, they received a message saying that OSS parachutists had landed thirty-five miles away in Serle, so the commander sent a squad of men to see if it was true. After a ten-hour hike,

Incipit Vita Nova

they met up with the OSS operatives, who arranged for supplies to be dropped, conceivably using a radio repaired by an Allied POW known only as 'Rodolfo'. Ralph and Charlie could so easily have bumped into each other at Serle, yet otherwise wouldn't have known of each other's presence because partisans used generic code names: there were many Carlos and Rodolfos. Another coincidence almost reunited the old friends. The Perlasca Brigade was briefly part of the Tito Speri Division, whose deputy commander was none other than Lionello Levi Sandri – the OSS agent 'Franco'.[2]

After the particulars of the drop were confirmed, Charlie was sent to an area north-west of Lake Idro. From Presegno, a mountain path led to a valley on the border between Lombardy and South Tyrol. There Charlie laid out the drop zone as instructed: an isosceles triangle of three bonfires, the acute angle indicating the direction of the wind. A plane came into view, but the weather had deteriorated, and the sortie was aborted. Charlie hiked back to base with the disappointing news.

The following month, the *rastrellamenti* ceased, and the US 5th Army and British 8th Army set out from their bridgeheads to prevent the fleeing Germans regrouping in the Alps.[3] As peace settled across the province of Brescia, the partisans were emboldened to come down into the Val Sabbia. Charlie and his comrades stretched out in the spring sunshine, drank wine and were fêted by local *contadini*, who prayed now that sons missing in North Africa, Russia and Greece would come home. The Germans, however, especially the diehard Waffen-SS, remained extremely dangerous, ordering people to stay indoors as they passed through. Anyone in the streets or fields was liable to be shot as a bandit.

Thirty miles south-west of there, the war was also gradually coming to an end. On 25 April, the Fiamme Verdi liberated Brescia, long a fascist stronghold, at the cost of seventy men. During the uprising, many workers fell in with the partisans, some forming unofficial units like the Tempini Brigade at Doro Garletti's factory, which had been bombed but was still partly working.[4] Doro was issued with a rifle and a membership card (in his birth name of Umberto) and may have taken part in a victorious assault on the castle led by Andrea Baronchelli, during which a large sum of money was seized. Baronchelli had helped plan this insurrection, liaising with Lionello Levi Sandri at Serle, and afterwards took part in the surrender negotiations. The CLNAI, the liberation committee in northern Italy, then took control of Brescia's government and administration, a new mayor was appointed, and a motto chosen from Dante: 'Incipit Vita Nova' – a new life begins.[5]

There was much work to do: Italy was, in the words of one historian, 'a grievously wounded nation'.[6] And the threat to newfound peace and democracy from civil conflict was grave. As in many northern Italian cities, the British fretted about the revolutionary ambitions of Brescians like Garletti, considered to be 'the less disciplined elements of the population, who are anxious to reverse the old order'. But Baronchelli and his CLNAI comrades had everything in hand.[7] After all, the ethos of the Fiamme Verdi had always been: liberate Italians so that they can govern themselves.[8]

True to this ideal, a cross-party committee of twelve members set about governing Nuvolento, Prevalle and Paitone. Baronchelli reported to the socialists, who represented a quarter of the population, that anti-fascist feeling was widespread and loyal militias were keeping order. He also noted that the *contadini* needed money, and that those who had sheltered Allied servicemen should be prioritized. 'I would point to the case of an English warrant officer', Baronchelli continued, 'who for a year has been hosted by a poor peasant family, who have received only modest assistance from me and from some of my companions.'[9] He could only have been referring to Ralph.

The day after the liberation of Brescia, Thursday, 26 April, the Nuvolento subcommittee met in the town hall, with Andrea Baronchelli in the president's chair and Doro Garletti representing the communists, 'to assume and carry out necessary administrative and public order functions'.[10] The following day, the new Prevalle council assumed office and was addressed by their president, none other than Omodeo Cantoni, the primary school teacher and the third of Ralph's friends to be thrust into government. 'We extend our confident greetings to the population,' he began, 'calling on everyone to maintain discipline and harmony for the good of the country.' Looking optimistically towards the future, and 'the distant children of this land' returning to their homes, Cantoni also remembered the dead of all nations, drawn into 'this immense tragedy that has shocked the world'.[11]

Exultantly proud, the Fiamme Verdi distributed flyers throughout the region. 'The flags of freedom are unfolded and fly in the wind', these read, and the 'beautiful divisions' of partisans had come down from the mountains now their job as soldiers was over. 'Tomorrow each of us begins the task of becoming a citizen according to personal convictions and aspirations' – yet every sacrifice made to build a new life for Italy from the rubble of defeated fascism, the message continued, should never be forgotten.[12]

Elated to hear that Brescia had been liberated, twenty miles away Charlie and his partisan comrades had no choice but to keep on fighting. His MI9 evasion report contained a single eye-popping sentence on the subject: 'we managed to surround a German SS motorised column in Val Sabbia on their retreat towards Trento'. This claim, at first hard to believe, was supported by witness statements, including one from a partisan belonging to Charlie's S4 battalion of the Perlasca Brigade.[13] After coming down from Malga Sacù, by night they had sabotaged unattended enemy vehicles by putting soil in the fuel tanks – just as Charlie had done in Ceraino – but soon found there was real fighting to be done. In the last week of April, they and other partisans exchanged fire with a Waffen-SS rearguard at Lake Idro. Short of weapons and ammunition, on the 28th they raided a fascist RSI garrison, and by the end of the day had taken 600 prisoners, German and Italian.

That was Saturday. Not far from there German sappers, chased by US troops, were frantically demolishing bridges to cover the retreat, including the main crossing points at Nozza and Lavenone, south-west of the lake. What the Germans didn't know was that the exit towards Trento had already been blocked by the American 5th Army. The 34th Division had taken control of Brescia that same day, three days after the partisans liberated it, and was rapidly fanning out across the entire region.

The next day, Sunday the 29th, at around 8.30 a.m., S4 received a phone call from comrades in Salò warning that a motorized column of the 16th SS Panzergrenadier Division, around 750 men, had left Tormini near Gavardo heading for Riva del Garda, a rallying point on the lake's north side. This was the last contingent of German soldiers heading north through the Val Sabbia, rerouted after a landslide and rapidly approaching Nozza.

S4, who thought they'd seen the last of the Germans, were forced to take up defensive positions on the road south out of town. They waited tensely, outnumbered and outgunned. In fact, Charlie was one of only about twenty who knew how to fight, the remainder of S4 being inexperienced latecomers. They wheeled an abandoned German anti-aircraft gun into the road. But the sight was missing, so they had to aim by looking down the barrel.

At 10 a.m. the lookout spotted a truck crossing the River Chiese, and then another, as the column turned in their direction. Once the Germans saw the cannon pointing at them they stopped, unaware how weak the opposition was. Three SS men came up the road waving a white flag and two partisans went to meet them accompanied by the parish priest, Don Primo Alessio Leali, wearing both cassock and surplice. Meanwhile, locals on the hillside made noise to fool the Germans into thinking S4 was bigger than it was.

The six men saluted. The SS commander, a colonel, was plump and clean-shaven, with piercing blue eyes and sparse flaxen hair. The brown-faced partisans studied their enemy. When the colonel asked to be allowed to pass in return for the safety of Nozza, S4's leader, Paolo Pagliano, a former Italian army officer, informed him that the bridges ahead had been blown. Affronted, the colonel said his men could repair them. He added that the Germans had only come to save Mussolini's Italy, implying that the partisans had a

Incipit Vita Nova

funny way of showing gratitude. Besides, the colonel boasted, his men had already defeated the partisans at Tormini and elsewhere. Pagliano's response was simply that the Americans were in charge now, and gave the commander until 5 p.m. to surrender.

Pagliano then sent a messenger to Brescia, thirty miles southwest of Nozza, to request American air support. Duly informed of this, the German commander, believing it to be a bluff, burst out laughing – although his amusement turned to rage when a squadron of US Thunderbolts appeared on the horizon. The planes proceeded to fly menacingly up and down the SS column until the astonished commander gave in.

The colonel's request to bring up their wounded and field kitchens was granted, likewise lame soldiers were allowed to keep bicycles and officers their pistols provided they were unloaded. All other weapons were dumped at the roadside, and the prisoners proceeded into Nozza, where they were made to rip off the SS cuff bands they proudly wore and leave them in the dirt. An officer found to have kept bullets in his pistol was executed on the spot. (The partisans learned later that the division to which these men belonged, named in honour of the Reichsführer-SS, Heinrich Himmler, had committed a third of the atrocities in Italy, including the murder of 2,000 civilians.[14])

An hour later, a major and a captain of the US 135th Infantry Regiment of the 34th Division arrived from Brescia to take the surrender and relieve the Perlasca Brigade of their other 600 prisoners. That same Sunday, 100 miles north in Bolzano, Waffen-SS General Karl Wolff signed the instrument of surrender, thus ending the war in Italy.

The next day, Monday 30 April, Charlie's and Ralph's paths began to converge. They may never have known how close they were to being reunited. Ralph returned to Paitone to spend a few days with his friends – his adopted families. The end had finally come. The Maccarinellis, Garlettis and Chiodis gathered to see him off, lining up before their beloved English visitor. Doro may already have given him the photo of the children – it was dated the 19th – as well as the snap of Ralph as a *contadino*, on which he had written: 'For Rodolfo, a token of friendship'.

Omodeo Cantoni was also there to shake Ralph's hand and give him some of his own photos. Each written dedication appealed to posterity. Evidently, the Chiodis had nothing to give; perhaps this was the moment that Augusto instead wrote his autograph in Ralph's memoir in a bold, curvilinear hand. Then Ralph returned to the Fiamme Verdi in the hills. We can only imagine the feelings of the people he left behind. But upon the departure of their POW, a family in Turin said this: 'Everyone who knew him loved him . . . We love the British as if they were our brothers.' They marvelled to think that all Englishmen were like their guest: 'humble, discreet, well-behaved, polite and affectionate'.[15]

On 1 May, Italy celebrated workers' day, a festival banned by Mussolini, and the Nuvolento committee heard a report from an FFVV colonel, Edmondo Raimondi. He had fought alongside Baronchelli to liberate Brescia, and had been appointed by 'Commander Franco' – Lionello Levi Sandri – who himself was now liaison officer between the CLNAI Brescia and the US 5th Army. Raimondi gave an encouraging account of local policing, which included news that officers in Paitone had been issued with weapons taken from German prisoners in the Val Sabbia, conceivably from the haul Charlie West and his comrades had captured.[16] Afterwards, Ralph was taken into Brescia by 'the leader of the partisans', presumably Raimondi, where he reported to the headquarters of the 34th Division. Except for his forged pass, according to which he was an RSI finance official, he had no identification papers. But Raimondi would have confirmed his credentials.

The Americans escorted Ralph to the Hotel Brescia, where, two days earlier, 411 Field Security Section of the Intelligence Corps (FSS) had set up its headquarters, at that time the only British presence in the city. The work of 411 FSS included investigating rumours of both communist and fascist uprisings, and diffusing tension between armed factions, mainly the communist Garibaldi

Brigades and the Christian centrist Fiamme Verdi, until the Allied Control Commission managed to get a grip on law and order.[17]

There Ralph met up with Andrea Baronchelli, with whom over many months in Paitone and Cremona, he had enjoyed what Baronchelli called 'a relationship of true and cordial friendship'. Ralph vouched for his friend, who was eager to work with the Allies to strengthen political stability in the region. An FSS officer issued a pass stating that Baronchelli was 'engaged in intelligence work on behalf of this Section' and requesting for him every assistance. Ralph exaggerated, as Omodeo Cantoni would later exaggerate for him, claiming that Baronchelli had personally sheltered him since December 1943. This was the document that Dom and I had triumphantly found in the Fiamme Verdi archive in Brescia. Ralph's bona fides probably helped set Baronchelli up as an agent for the Polizia Militare di Sicurezza, a counter-espionage network whose members reported to the British through the FSS.[18]

On the same day Ralph and Baronchelli were there, another British ex-POW turned partisan showed up at the Hotel Brescia: Charlie West. Tantalizingly, he and Ralph passed like ships in the night. After the German surrender at Nozza, Charlie had returned with the Americans to the 34th Division's headquarters in Brescia. There, he'd informed intelligence officers about local roads and bridges and, ceasing to be Carlo, resumed his old identity as 565667 Warrant Officer C. E. West.

A fluent Italian speaker with a solid grasp of local politics, Charlie was eagerly co-opted by 411 FSS, and given a room in the hotel and a clean uniform. He would soon be having a proper bath, something he hadn't done since leaving England four years earlier. While he was being briefed, news arrived that Mussolini had been shot by partisans and Hitler had killed himself. The following day the bedraggled remnants of the German LXXV Corps of 40,000 men, including two Italian divisions, surrendered to the US 34th Division. Victory in Europe, when the challenges of peace would begin, was just days away.

*

Charlie's job with 411 FSS would consist of searching buildings, checking identities and questioning suspects. Now he, rather than Ralph, was the sleuth – and a real one. He was said to have hooked up with a small special forces unit, in the style of the SAS, led by the charismatic Vladimir 'Popski' Peniakoff, a British officer of Russian extraction. And while there's no firm evidence to support this, it is true that in May 1945 Popski's Private Army, as they were known, were looking for Himmler and that Charlie was engaged in similar detective work. He interrogated an Albanian crook caught by partisans in possession of two million lire, who took Charlie to a hoard of £1,445 – some £50,000 in today's money – in British banknotes. The Albanian admitted having been a courier for a man named Friedrich Schwend based in Merano near Bolzano, who, the FSS war diary records, had been despatching money to contacts in Italy, Romania and Holland.[19]

The banknotes were counterfeits, manufactured by Jewish engravers and printers in Sachsenhausen concentration camp as part of Operation Bernhard. This was Himmler's brainchild to undermine the British economy. Schwend, an honorary SS officer and money launderer, had been put in charge of distribution, using the forged five-pound notes to buy valuables and information, hiring spies and closing deals connected with an OSS plot code-named Operation Sunrise. Cooked up between the Americans and senior SS commanders looking to sue for peace in Italy, it was kept secret not only from Himmler, but also from Stalin, who would have been outraged by the prospect of a negotiated settlement.[20]

Meanwhile, British and American soldiers combed through the Italian countryside, rounding up stray German and Italian prisoners, disarming partisans and directing British fugitives towards military headquarters. Like Ralph and Charlie, absorbed by local culture, some men had mixed feelings. A British partisan leader nicknamed 'Giorgio' recalled, on the point of reunion with his countrymen, being held back by 'an unaccountable diffidence': a deep affinity with Italian comrades pulled him back towards the hills.[21] To the disgust of liberating Allied forces, many POWs seemed to have

Incipit Vita Nova

contributed nothing to the war after the Armistice. Vladimir Peniakoff was appalled to find that these servicemen:

> preferred a lazy country-house life – entertained as they were now in one farm, now in another – to the risks of escape and the rigours of military life. Some of them had married farmers' daughters and talked of their estates; all had acquired an oddly exaggerated Italian appearance and many affected difficulty in expressing themselves in English (forgetting that we knew that, at most, nine months had elapsed since they had been thrown into this strange way of life).

Whenever Peniakoff pointed them in the direction of Allied lines, they just shied away, protesting they first had to go 'home' – meaning their Italian families – to settle their affairs.[22] MI9's escape and evasion section also noted how difficult it was to dislodge POWs, who feared the open country and had comfortable billets in village communities where they were accepted. Some, fluent in Italian, brown as berries, with calloused hands and patched clothing, denied they were British at all, and claimed to have been there since birth. One in every twenty-five Allied prisoners who fled in September 1943 – about 2,000 men – was never accounted for. Some came to grief, of course, shot by the Germans or lost for ever in the mountains, but others, discovering new loves and new lives, simply melted into the landscape.[23]

On 3 May, Ralph travelled south by train via Florence, Rome and Naples, admiring sights last glimpsed on the journey from Gravina to Chiavari. At Naples, RASC lorries took him and other ex-POWs to the repatriation camp at Resina, where Vesuvius loomed. There wasn't much there, just a sprawl of dusty tents surrounded by palms, resembling a more sanitary version of Derna or Benghazi. The air reeked of Jeyes disinfectant, sprayed DDT and burning uniforms. Men received a hot shower, a medical and vaccinations against diphtheria and whooping cough, and were kitted out with battledress cut from smooth Canadian cloth and a woollen

American blanket. On each neatly made-up bed there were toiletries, chocolate, cigarettes and a 'welcome home' note.[24]

It was luxury – yet many felt confined, claustrophobic, bossed about. One Yorkshireman tried to think about home and his waiting fiancée. 'But nothing was real any more,' he said. 'I had left reality behind in the mountains.'[25]

The next day, Friday the 4th, Ralph was interviewed by intelligence officers from MI9, whose habit it was to ask why fleeing POWs had taken so long to reach Allied lines. To this, the standard response was to ask why the Allies had taken so long to reach them.[26] Ralph gave a brisk account of his capture at Gazala, escape from Camp 65, relocation to Camp 52, the second escape at Dolcè and the assistance he'd received.

After that, he was free to do as he pleased until a place on a ship became available. Carrying temporary ID, a chit to say he'd been debriefed and a couple of pounds sterling, he was allowed into Naples. There, the shops were empty, skinny barefoot children begged and half the women had been driven to prostitution. Otherwise, servicemen killed time on the beach, snoozing on the dark volcanic sand and watching the tide, where pumice stones bobbed among the scum and sewage.[27]

Then Ralph's number came up, and on the 17th he embarked at the port of Naples. Passengers were handed packets of corned beef sandwiches and crowded up on deck as the engines throbbed, for many a grim echo of the crossing from Benghazi three long years previously.

As the ship steamed out into the bay, Ralph leaned over the teak rail, inhaling the salt-spray tang and watching the Neapolitan coast shrink behind him. Soon they were steering north through the Tyrrhenian Sea surrounded only by waves and sky, lost in thought.

Reunion with Flo was no doubt uppermost in Ralph's mind, mixed with the queasy thrill of going home. Like every man on the cusp of repatriation, he sensed the impending collision of past and future, after which everything that had happened to him would either have to be forgotten or remade as memory.

PART SEVEN

Memory

23.

The South Country

Ralph docked at Southampton on 24 May 1945 after an unhurried voyage lasting eight days. Lumbering down the gangway shouldering kitbags issued at Resina, men were badgered by customs officials and escorted from the harbour. Ralph spent a few days at the Corps of Military Police base in Aldershot, where he was reinstated and granted eight weeks' accumulated leave.

On Monday the 28th, he arrived home in Wombwell. Flo, who had been notified of his return a fortnight earlier, was overcome with joy. Ralph struggled to hide his unease. They had been apart longer than they had been married, and some estrangement was inevitable. Nor were these awkward feelings entirely one-sided. Flo had adapted to life on her own – indeed, had herself been a police officer for nearly three years. All husbands and wives had to rediscover each other and knit together frayed threads.

England was greyer, rougher, diminished. People looked shabby and careworn, habituated to new ways. Ralph took the bus to his parents' home in Balby. Like the vow engraved on Pietro Maccarinelli's mess tin, he had kept his promise: 'Mamma ritorno' – Mum, I'll be back. But Gladys Corps had died a year earlier, having never lost hope that her son would make it home. Ralph, presumably, was deeply shocked. What passed between him and his father about Gladys, or anything else for that matter, is unknown. Returning servicemen were usually welcomed like heroes; few of them appreciated it. There were surprise parties and drinks in the pub, which men endured until they could get back to their brooding. Families thought returned menfolk had lost their minds, a suspicion shared by the men themselves. How could they have spent so long dreaming of home and yet feel so awful when the dream came true?

According to an official survey, almost all ex-prisoners from Italian camps described feeling restless and unhappy at home. Some experienced nightmares, panic attacks, and paranoia that people were laughing at them. Men felt 'out of the picture' – a sense of dislocation dubbed the 'Rip Van Winkle effect', as if after years of sleep they had woken up in a world they no longer recognized. Some wanted to escape. 'Yet where could you go?' wondered one RAF sergeant. 'Escape to the past was clearly impossible.'[1]

The shame of capture flooded back. The war had been won by free, valiant crusaders who had pushed on into the heart of Germany. This was an especially troubling thought for Ralph, given how he'd largely sat things out in Paitone. To counteract it, the memoir he brought home from Italy spoke mainly of his initiative, stamina and courage in trying to get back into the war. It was the story of himself he wanted others to believe.

Flo fussed, refusing to let Ralph leave her sight. The *Daily Mail* urged women to make their strained husbands feel they had 'lived an experience and not a tragedy'. But men were also expected to snap out of their gloom, an expectation that was a tragedy in itself. 'It is misguided and utterly useless to try to cheer them up,' lamented one medical officer, a former POW in Italy. 'The lack of the opportunity for shutting oneself off, unexplained and unheeded, till these spells passed is one of the chief difficulties of readjustment to normal life.' For everyone, getting used to peace was as hard as getting used to war had been. The victory that had gleamed so enticingly turned out to be a complicated business.[2]

Peace was even more complicated in Italy, where people felt the ambiguity of losing the war in 1943 and defeating Germany in 1945. This identity crisis was deepened by the plethora of political parties, on a spectrum from left to right, unfrozen from the 1920s first by the Armistice, then by the Allied occupation and the fall of Mussolini's RSI. The nation now had to avert the kind of civil strife that had afflicted Greece, outface communist takeover and resurgent fascism, and build stable government across the political landscape.

Italy did not get bogged down in recrimination. In Britain ex-POWs swore affidavits for the UN War Crimes Committee. Little came of it. The commandants of both Ralph's camps had breached the Geneva Convention but were never indicted. Attilio Coppola, from Camp 65, was already a police chief in Bari when questioned in 1946; he pleaded innocence and that was that.[3] At a tribunal in Bologna, Bill Strachan denounced Dino Castelli-Taddei and the Camp 52 *carabinieri* who beat him up, one of whom admitted striking Strachan for calling him 'a fucking bastard'. Strachan also implicated the deputy commandant Filippo Zavatteri for staying on at Chiavari after the arrival of political dissidents and Jews in transit to Nazi concentration camps. Yet Zavatteri was not culpable and faced no charges. The trigger-happy German sergeant, whose reckless burst from a sub-machine gun had broken a prisoner's arm, also escaped prosecution.[4] Whereas the memory of Nuremberg cast a shadow over postwar Germany, in Italy amnesty shaded into amnesia.[5]

For the Allies, there was a better use for the past: recognizing the Italian contribution to the defeat of fascism, on political as well as moral grounds. In October 1944 the British minister to the Holy See recorded his nation's gratitude for help given to POWs: 'We owe a debt to the Italian people in this respect that should not be forgotten and cannot be repaid.'[6] Now, with peace, the Allied Screening Commission pointed to the 'enormous possibility of a friendly Italy in a continent seething with unrest', which might be achieved with proper compensation. Yet there were problems. The Treasury paid out at the pre-Armistice rate of seventy-two lire to the pound, whereas by 1945 inflation had diminished the lira's value by a factor of twenty-five. This meant in real terms many families received next to nothing. The travel writer Eric Newby, then an ASC field officer, visited ordnance depots to scrounge blankets and tyres, more useful than debased banknotes.[7]

Inadequate remuneration, Newby predicted, would cause resentment – but greater offence loomed. 'The whole operation of recognizing the bravery of Italians who had helped prisoners-of-war turned out to be an utter disaster' – the words of ASC agent Vanda Škof, a Slovenian whose family had sheltered Newby in the Apennines and who later became his wife.[8] In theory, Italian helpers were eligible for the King's Medal for Courage in the Cause of Freedom, but the British government declined to decorate a former enemy. Lobbying for the *contadini*, with their 'great, unconcerned Homeric sense of the sacred right of the guest', came to nothing. When the foreign secretary Ernest Bevin suggested that anti-fascist Italians be honoured with a statue, an official regretted that 'we are so unpopular, that the erection of a monument might well be an opportunity for the Communists and other anti-British elements in Italy to cause a riot'.[9]

Instead of a medal, helpers were given what Vanda Škof described as 'a Roneoed sheet of paper bearing a type-written message and a completely unconvincing reproduction of Field Marshal Alexander's signature'. Her future husband thought Alexander would have been shocked to see recipients' reactions, concluding 'it would have been better to have given nothing at all'. Others believed it should simply have been a better certificate, publicly awarded because, they said, 'Italians love Pomp and Ceremony'.[10]

This was largely untrue of the *contadini*, who were quietly, humbly proud to have been resisters. And that's what the Chiodis, Maccarinellis and Garlettis were: brave, patriotic, selfless resisters. On 1 July 1945 the three household heads – Augusto, Angelo and Doro – gathered in Nuvolento, where the parish priest witnessed their statements. Augusto attested that he had opened his home to Ralph, where their English guest was visited by other enemies of fascism. The Chiodis and Rodolfo had developed 'una vera e schietta amicizia' – a true and sincere friendship.

Their claims were filed on the same day in January 1946 and settled a year later. If Italians couldn't go to the ASC, the ASC, briefed by MI9, came to them. Vanda Škof recalled rattling through the hills in an old army truck, equipped with sub-machine guns and a strongbox full of cash.[11] Angelo Maccarinelli received 8,000 lire and

Doro Garletti 3,000. Augusto Chiodi, who had taken a risk Ralph judged to be 'exceptional', was awarded 34,000 lire. Andrea Baronchelli attended the same session, his own claim filed immediately after theirs. Characteristically, his only concern was to pay tribute to everyone else.[12]

These virtuous men did not disdain their Alexander certificates. Baronchelli framed his, and the Garlettis were just as pleased with theirs – the document Federico Garletti showed me in Paitone. Over lunch that day, Federico's grandfather, whose memory was failing, was under the impression it was a personal letter of thanks from Churchill, which didn't seem a bad way to remember the recognition of their courage.[13]

Ralph was back with his family: his wife and bereaved father, brother George and his wife Ethel and their young daughter, Pauline. There was no escaping that Yorkshire was his home. Much as Flo in her police uniform represented war's transformations, a great deal was unchanged: predictable routines of work and leisure, meals of meat and two veg and listening to the wireless, the brown teapot on its trivet. Ralph would buy cigarettes at the newsagent on the corner and chat to the same old neighbours; visit the chip shop and, on a Saturday, the pub. Ralph was still a soldier, but he'd be back in the West Riding Constabulary soon enough. After all, that was who he was.

And yet Ralph's thoughts were undoubtedly of Italy. Unlike POWs repatriated from Germany, men who some time ago had left Italian camps were bewildered, their sense of themselves divided or drawn out between two worlds. Jim Wilde, the submariner who escaped from a train out of Chiavari, arrived home in Yorkshire a week after Ralph. After months living with partisans, he was at first unable to speak English, and upon seeing his fiancée asleep after a shift building Spitfires, he felt 'a great sadness . . . a great, indefinable sense of loss'. They married – but he was fidgety, irritable, 'mixed up'. Another returning POW regarded his time in Italy as hugely precious, yet 'now more like a dream than reality'.[14]

There was a poem Ralph knew, copied into one of his *quaderni*. It was Hilaire Belloc's 'The South Country', a nostalgic meditation that spoke to a northerner remembering Italy:

> When I am living in the Midlands
> That are sodden and unkind,
> I light my lamp in the evening:
> My work is left behind;
> And the great hills of the South Country
> Come back into my mind.[15]

Such was his regard for the people of Paitone, Ceraino and Molina, that Ralph may even have felt as one British officer did, that 'given the chance to be born again and to choose the place of my birth, Italy would be the country of my choice'.[16]

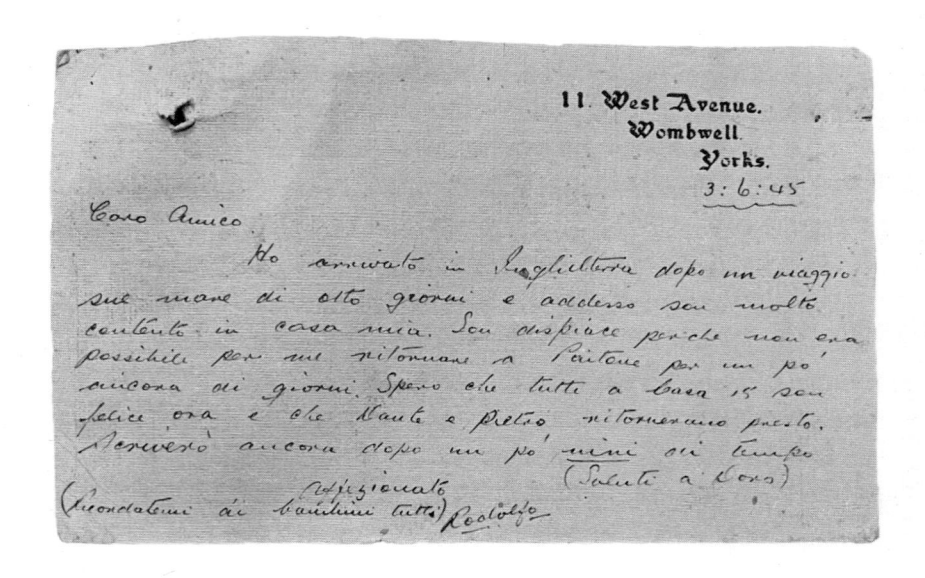

The best way for a serviceman to thank his hosts, critics of certificates believed, was to write a letter.[17] Many did just that. My most stunning discovery in the ASC archives was correspondence from Ralph to his friends, written in Italian, full of warmth, humour and concern. Six days after returning home, on 3 June 1945, he posted a card to Angelo Maccarinelli. Apologizing for not returning before his final departure, he hoped everyone in Paitone was well, and that the Maccarinelli boys would soon be home from the war. He promised to write again, and asked Angelo to say hello to Doro and to remember him, Rodolfo, to all the children – 'ricordatemi ai bambini tutti'.[18]

Even before this, he wrote a letter to Erminia, Augusto and Pietro Chiodi. He told a white lie about ending up in the Verona region, which, being further away than Brescia (where he had really been), was a better excuse for neglecting to say a last goodbye. Ralph claimed to have asked permission to go to Paitone but had been refused. He also told the Chiodis that Flo had gone 'macacco' – crazy, like a monkey – when he arrived home. Everyone was happy, he added, but his melancholy was etched between the lines:

> The weather here is insane, always raining and fog, very different from Italy. I received 56 days of leave and my wife said it is not possible to escape from her even for five minutes. Life here is a big contrast to life in Italy but I will always remember, and never forget, number 13 in Paitone and the Chiodi family . . . My wife said to give everyone her thanks and also said she will never forget what you did for me while I was in Italy. When you reply I want you to tell me the dates of your birthdays – my wife wants them for some reason!

Ralph also promised to send Augusto a little money each month, and something for the Maccarinellis and others by way of compensation.[19]

The letter also contained two pieces of emotional news, one true, one untrue. Ralph said that his mother had died while he was away, but 'fino l'ultimo giorno di sua vita sempre aveva fede che io era vivo in Italia' – to her last day she never lost faith that he was alive in Italy. The untruth was this: 'Mie bambini non conoscere loro padre' – my children didn't recognize their father, a bitter blow to many young families, but not to Ralph, because he had no children.

Back in December 1943, he had invented these offspring, presumably to persuade the Maccarinellis to let him go home, then kept it going either because he couldn't admit having lied or because he enjoyed the fantasy of being a complete man in Italian eyes. He may even have co-opted the two children he knew best: his nieces, Pauline and my mother Audrey.

Did the Italians write back? Did Ralph send money? Did Flo remember their birthdays? Piero Garletti recalls a parcel of goodies, which may have come from Ralph or Flo, or from Andrea Baronchelli using the 4,000 lire he reluctantly accepted, or directly from the ASC. But afterwards, to the best of his knowledge, no one in Paitone heard from Ralph again.

In July 1945, Ralph resumed his duties as a military policeman, albeit demoted to sergeant, his warrant officer rank merely a wartime arrangement. Flo was heartbroken to see him leave so soon after arriving home, yet knew he would soon be demobilized, a procedure already in motion. Returning from Italy, he'd been placed on the 'Y List' of dislocated servicemen and classed as 'non-effective': surplus to military requirements. He was then given a demob number: 22, based on his age and service since 1939, and as a married man placed in category C. Time served as a POW was also taken into consideration.[20] In August, the War Office caught up and entered him on their casualty lists as 'no longer POW', there being no official term for where or what he'd been for the past couple of years.[21]

In September, Ralph was sent back to the CMP depot at Mytchett in Surrey, where he was issued new kit from the quartermaster's stores, including a scarlet cap cover, arm band and police whistle. Routines and possessions restored some semblance of his old life. The previous month he had been surprised to receive a parcel containing three pairs of socks, a cigarette case and a watch case (the watch itself had been stolen), which he'd left behind when Rommel overran his position on the Gazala Line. A major of the 50th Division had stored these 'articles of intrinsic and sentimental value' so that they could be returned by the CMP.[22]

The South Country

In October, Ralph was given a discharge date, and, after serving desultorily for another three months, on 18 January 1946 once again became a civilian. He had declined a place on a civil resettlement course, preferring just to get on with what remained of his old life as best he could and in his own way.[23]

Ralph rejoined the police as an ordinary constable, essentially the same job Flo had done until the previous August. The work was dull. In September he qualified as an animal diseases inspector.[24] He was thirty-two and beginning to wonder if he'd ever make sergeant. The war had accelerated his promotion in the army; now, in the police, in peacetime, he was back at the bottom of the ladder. The rain and fog got him down. He started making plans to emigrate – somewhere warm, he told Flo, who liked the idea. There was nothing to stop them. They spent Christmas in Wombwell, then, on 27 December, Ralph resigned.

The past, however, was a drag on the future, specifically regarding what Ralph had been doing between December 1943 and May 1945. Both Military Intelligence and the West Riding Constabulary had wanted to know, and Flo was perhaps curious too. They may have suspected that he could have got home through the Alps had he really tried. He explained to MI9 that he had decided to wait for the arrival of the Allies – but he had waited a long time.[25]

Evidently, Omodeo Cantoni's testimonial of April 1946 was a reply to a request from Ralph to fill this lacuna in his CV. Why else would Cantoni have declared that Ralph was 'supporting and directing the partisans of Prevalle' for all of 1944 when Ralph himself told MI9 that he hadn't joined until 1945? Like so much about Ralph's life, Cantoni's letter implied pretence and self-reinvention, memory and the flight from memory.

Further self-reinvention lay ahead, out in the British Empire. After finding a job with the East African prison service, which employed many ex-Coldstream Guardsmen like Ralph, he and Flo set off for Tanganyika, a former German colony where three-quarters of the Europeans were British. A lot of Italians lived there, too. During the war as many as 15,000 had been interned – in Uganda and Southern

Rhodesia, as well as in Tanganyika itself – and in the 1950s many more settled there.[26] Mr and Mrs Corps, the liberated ex-pats, soon filled their album with happy photos.

This was not, however, Ralph's first African destination. Barely five years since he was captured at Gazala, he was drawn back to the Libyan desert. Whom he went with and for how long is unknown. Flo may have gone with him to see what he had seen. Surviving photos are few and indistinct, but Ralph seems to be dressed much as he was in Paitone. One shows him and some companions in front of the fifty-foot high Arco dei Fileni – or 'Marble Arch' as the British knew it – described by an SAS man as 'that ridiculous monument that Mussolini had built way out in the desert near the Tripolitanian frontier'.[27] (It remained a relic of Italian imperialism in Africa until 1973, when the Libyan dictator Colonel Gaddafi blew it up.)

Charlie West also had a difficult homecoming. He had spent the rest of May 1945 in Italy, chasing the SS forger Friedrich Schwend, who was finally picked up by the OSS and interrogated about resurgent Nazism. Charlie did get to arrest one of Schwend's top agents, who led him to Milan, where he found more forged banknotes. (Caches of money turned up all over the place: when, twenty years after the end of the war, the church organ at Merano was dismantled for maintenance it was found to be crammed full of them.) After the Field Security Section moved to Austria, Charlie was transferred to 75 Special Investigations Branch of the Military Police in Milan, where he investigated murders of prisoners of war and Italian civilians.[28] But his time was up. A few days later he was stood down and told to report to a repatriation centre in Turin, where he arrived on 1 June.

During his intense, often brutal time with the partisans, Charlie thought often of his family: his brother Syd, half-sisters Olga and Brenda and their beloved mother. Mabel Scoullar was just one of many thousands of women whose sons were missing in action. Like Ralph's mother, she could choose either to believe that Charlie was alive or to give in to the notion that he was dead. 'Mamma ritorno'

The South Country

had been Charlie's pledge, too, one he'd clung to at his lowest ebb in the mountains. After Germany surrendered, he had written saying he was 'one of the Partisan Leaders in the hills of Northern Italy'. Now he could keep his promise and go home.

From Turin, Charlie went by road to Genoa, then south to Rome and Resina, the transit camp where Ralph had been. After a spell of rest and a grilling by MI9 intelligence officers, on 10 June he was flown in a converted Lancaster bomber to the RAF reception centre at Cosford, near Wolverhampton. Driven from the runway to a hangar, he was registered and told that his next of kin would be notified by telegram. Charlie was relieved to think that his mother would know he was on British soil, even though the Air Ministry, informed about his 'special duties' with 411 FSS, had already written to her. After a hot bath, he was seen by a doctor and fed. Many of the airmen he met were in a bad way, eating slowly and saying little. Nor did they seem excited by victory, whereas the rest of the nation had gone wild.[29]

The hope on which Charlie had set his heart would soon turn to ashes. For his mother had died, like Ralph's mother, in the spring of 1944. Gladys and Mabel never knew their sons were alive, and the two friends came home unaware their mothers had died. Shortly before Mabel Scoullar's death, the Air Ministry wrote to say that they would be sending the possessions Charlie left in North Africa: a damaged leather case, a photographic light meter, a set of spanners and some roller skates. It was as though he were dead, and these sad things his effects. Mabel's daughter Olga informed the Ministry of her mother's death – but the information didn't reach Charlie, either in Brescia or at RAF Cosford.[30]

Nor had Charlie's letter from Italy arrived. Once Syd West heard his brother was alive, however, he asked to be put in touch with him to break the bad news himself. But nothing was done, and Charlie arrived in Plymouth to find Olga alone there. He was devastated. Syd complained to the Air Ministry that this was no way for a nation to reward a man who had already suffered so much. The Ministry apologized that they were trying to repatriate thousands of former

POWs, 'all naturally anxious to be on their way home and impatient of restraint or formalities'.³¹

During July and much of August, Charlie was on leave in Plymouth, mourning his dear mother. After that he reported for duty and was debriefed about Operation Squatter and the plane crash in 1941, although he remembered little about it. On 22 August, he was interviewed by an officer from IS9(W), the section of MI9 dedicated to learning from escapers and evaders. Charlie described his escapes with Ralph, the clandestine radio, fighting with the partisans and his field security work. A report sent to a half a dozen intelligence departments was filed then forgotten.³² He stayed in the RAF until August 1946, when he was transferred to the Reserve and entered civilian life for the first time since he was fifteen.³³

By now, Ralph and Flo had already embraced new lives. Arriving in Dar es Salaam in the spring of 1947, Ralph was appointed assistant superintendent of prisons. Boosted by his war service, his starting annual salary was £444, double his police pay.³⁴ And he and Flo could live more cheaply there than in England. His first posting was to Msasani Prison north of Dar es Salaam, where they settled at Oyster Bay. Two years later, they moved to Mwanza, a town on Lake Victoria, when Ralph was promoted to senior provincial superintendent at HMP Butimba. There he oversaw work schemes, including quarrying and land reclamation.

He was photographed in khaki shorts inspecting prisoners fishing at a water hole, looking every inch the imperial 'man on the spot'. Dozens of petty offences in that camp were punished with loss of remission, a penal diet and hard labour. All prisons held some Europeans, but they had better accommodation and tea, milk, butter and fruit, whereas Africans were given only beans and rice.³⁵

It was the mid-1950s. After passing the Higher Standard Kiswahili Examination, Ralph was promoted again and made a member of the Overseas Civil Service. He and Flo returned to England briefly – by air, yet sailing back on the SS *Uganda*, first class, which entitled them to use the promenade deck pool and smoking room decorated with tusks and trophies. By then they were living at the prison farm in Kingolwira, near Morogoro, in the foothills of the Uluguru Mountains, where coffee, tea and sisal grew on vast plantations. As ever, Europeans were at the top, Black people at the bottom, and Asians in the middle, a caste structure entrenched by the tripartite educational system.[36]

For white people, of course, it was paradise. Undemanding schedules, gin and whist in the evenings, perfect weather. The grass was tough, but there was abundant bougainvillea, hibiscus and frangipani. Grace-and-favour houses had electric fans, huge American fridges and gas stoves. Meat, fish and eggs were available, and mangos, pawpaw and guava grew everywhere. Window nets kept mosquitos out, and the tsetse fly had almost been eradicated. There were servants for everything. Europeans and Africans rarely mixed for any other reason: to do so would have invited alienation from polite society.[37]

There were dangers. Ralph knew an officer at Kingolwira named Basil Davis, who like him had joined the 2nd Battalion of the Coldstream Guards on his eighteenth birthday and been an exemplary NCO in North Africa. It's unclear exactly when Ralph and Flo settled in Kingolwira, but Davis, his wife Matty and their daughters had been there since 1946. In October 1948, Matty Davis was murdered, her grave on a hill near Morogoro a constant reminder for vigilance.[38] Ralph and Flo kept large, aggressive dogs.

Spread over 10,000 acres, the prison farm held nearly 2,000 prisoners, mostly serving long sentences. Like other East African prisons, it was an extension of the colonial state, directed by commercial profit. Working mostly by hoe and hand, the prisoners grew citrus fruits, maize, soya and vegetables; they also reared dairy cattle, collected eggs and were employed in the manufacture of sisal mats.[39]

Kingolwira had no walls, unlike HMP Butimba, to which Ralph would return later in the decade. Butimba surely reminded him of Italy. As well as bland rations, there were tedious routines, barbed wire, poor sanitation and escapes. The stone huts were overcrowded, and prisoners slept on the ground. By roll call at 5.30 a.m., the air stank from unwashed bodies and overflowing latrine cans. Prisoners cleaned until breakfast, then worked all day. There's no evidence that Ralph ever connected his own wartime privations to the hardships of his charges – but then he had lived a privileged existence as a POW. And whatever hopes for postwar humanity Italians had raised in him, they did not extend to Africans.[40]

Prison officers in Tanganyika applied a similar divide-and-rule principle as the authorities at Gravina and Chiavari had done. A 'prison aristocracy' ruled the rest and was rewarded with beds and sugar and soap; they were universally loathed.[41] As if to mark this strange reprise, Flo took the first volume of Ralph's memoir and beneath Augusto Chiodi's autograph on the inside cover wrote her name and address at Kingolwira Prison. This had been one of the first things I'd noticed in Pauline's kitchen in Warmsworth. At last, it made sense.

As an ambitious NCO, Ralph had surely thought himself worthy of a commission, and in the camps had played the part of an officer – living separately, making decisions, issuing orders and probably enjoying the services of a batman. Nor had it been unknown for junior ranks fighting with the partisans to feel that, through their leadership in battle, they had deserved to be treated as officers and promoted themselves accordingly – not that this counted for anything when they came home.[42] Tanganyika made this elevation in status real. A man of quasi-military substance now, Ralph got to wear a tailored uniform, leather Sam Browne cross-belt and flat-topped peaked cap.

Florence Corps made the most of her social ascent. She looked chic in well-cut frocks, perching hats and pearls, in a style reminiscent of Princess Margaret. In October 1956, Margaret toured Tanganyika. Ralph and Flo were invited to a tribal display put on for the visiting royal, 400 miles north-west at Tabora, where they sat in the VIP stand. They didn't meet the princess, who stuck to a safe itinerary. Nationalists staged strikes and boycotts, and protesting voices were heard in pro-independence newspapers. Margaret met as few Africans as possible, wore white gloves and ate no fish in case of typhoid.[43]

Two days after this, Ralph and Flo were back in Kingolwira. Ralph bought a copy of the *Rubaiyat of Omar Khayyam*, the long poem he knew from school:

> The Worldly Hope men set their Hearts upon
> Turns Ashes – or it prospers; and anon,
> Like Snow upon the Desert's dusty Face
> Lighting a little Hour or two – is gone.

The mood of the verse was exotic and elegiac, matching the creeping sense that royal visits were harbingers of imperial decline.[44]

A fortnight later, the Suez Crisis erupted in Egypt, a humiliation for Britain and France, and a victory for African nationalism. My father was a chief petty officer on the first Royal Navy ship into the battle, now seen as the last gasp of the British Empire's gunboat diplomacy as Cold War enmity set in between east and west. The old order was crumbling, and the twentieth-century lives that had sustained it were destined to change.

★

For Ralph, the 1950s were also a time for reacquaintance with his wartime experiences. After his father died in March 1958, he was granted leave to return to England, presumably to sort out his affairs. Ralph had inherited half of the modest estate, the other half going to Ethel, his now deceased brother's widow.

He and Flo flew from Tanganyika to Heathrow in April, arriving by coach at the new West London Terminal on the Cromwell Road. Mum's brother John, aged eleven, had met them off the plane with his mother Charlotte, who was Flo's sister and my Nan. He remembered seeing Ralph and Flo, the debonair jet-setters, crossing the BOAC arrivals hall, with its orange-brown façades and oval map of the world, the airline's destinations picked out in lights. Then, after visiting Doncaster, they set out overland, by car or train and boat, to Italy.

The reason for Ralph's pilgrimage to Ceraino is a mystery; likewise, his feelings about being there. Other accounts offer clues. In 1954, an ex-POW took his wife to Chiavari – where, four years later, Ralph may also have visited – only to find that Camp 52 had 'returned to agriculture', as if he'd hallucinated it all. 'As with many soldiers, that nostalgic longing to go back grew strong in me,' wrote a New Zealander who made the same trip, 'and from an enjoyable dream it became a disquieting restlessness bubbling up like a volcanic spring.' Thus compelled, he visited Filippo Zavatteri, the former adjutant, and found him much the same as he'd been in the camp, and later took a former guard out to dinner to thank him for the bread he'd given him when he was hungry.[45]

Ralph's advancement in Tanganyika had been primed by the war, his colonial status built on his military reputation. And yet he was dissatisfied. He believed he deserved as much credit as any other escaper, especially those who had joined the partisans, and surely heard stories about men he'd known. Hugh Owen, the RAF pilot who dimmed the lights at Gravina, escaped from a camp at Monte Urano and reached Allied lines, as did the Camp 52 train escaper Paddy Cullen, who walked over 500 miles. A transported prisoner who slipped down an alley in Chiavari made it all the way to Switzerland.[46] Most of these men, he was acutely aware, had been rewarded. Many received Mentions in Despatches, including James McBean, who escaped from Gravina the same night as Ralph and Charlie. In January 1947, Charlie himself was honoured 'for meritorious service'.[47] This seemed only fair. An inquiry found that without the partisans with whom these men had fought, 'there would have been no Allied victory in Italy so swift, so overwhelming or so inexpensive'.[48]

There were decorations for gallantry, too. Paddy Cullen was awarded the Military Medal, the citation for which demonstrates he did no more than Ralph. The rebellious Scot Bill Strachan also received an MM, as did another ex-Camp 52 partisan, Alexander Hoggan. Yet another MM went to a Coldstream Guardsman once called a 'country idiot' by Churchill while guarding Chequers but who as 'Major Rolando' had united the partisans of Piacenza, organized an escape route for POWs and did 'much to enhance the reputation of the British'.[49] Was Ralph jealous? Intriguingly, his medal box in Warmsworth contains a single loose ribbon for the Military Medal, which he had no legitimate reason to own. Perhaps he thought to add it to the row of ribbons on his prison officer's tunic, before getting cold feet. Ex-Coldstreamers in Tanganyika would have been impressed but were bound to ask how and where he'd won it. The answer would have been an untruth too far, and a criminal offence.

Even Ralph's campaign medals were dubious. Also in his box was the Defence Medal, to which he was not entitled – although he never actually wore it. He did, however, wear the France and Germany Star, awarded for fighting after the Normandy landings, in which Ralph took no part. Campaign stars were unnamed, and he most likely bought one from another veteran. This may have been to rebuff aspersions cast upon the men who *had* fought in Italy – the 'D-Day Dodgers' as an infamous slander put it. Soldiers of the Italian campaign had replied in an ironic song, sung to the tune of 'Lili Marlene', in which they owned the slur. I mentioned this to Mum, who amazed me by singing the entire first verse. How did she know this? No idea. Was it from Uncle Ralph? Maybe . . .⁵⁰ He also wore the Italy Star, for which, as a non-combatant prisoner, technically he was ineligible but was awarded. In exceptional circumstances POWs able to prove they had been partisans were given the medal, another reason for asking Omodeo Cantoni to vouch for him.⁵¹

Ralph should have counted his blessings. Hundreds of Italian civilians had died helping fugitives like him.⁵² Men he'd known had been killed or maimed at Dunkirk and Gazala; others had succumbed to disease in the camps. RSM Wilf Alderson, who had helped Ralph escape from Gravina, ended up in Stalag XVIII-A Wolfsberg and then in Klagenfurt, where he died in July 1944, possibly in a bombing raid. Many fleeing POWs had been recaptured, including his old friend Bill Barker, imprisoned in southern Bavaria. Evan Llewellyn Edwards, another soldier who fled the transport from Chiavari, was sent to Dachau.⁵³

Max Löw and Tom Butterworth, whose photos Ralph put in his album, both suffered at the hands of the Nazis. By pretending to be Australian, Max, a German Jew, did at least survive Wolfsberg; his gaolers even treated his rheumatic fever. I traced his grandson Marc in Berlin, who told me that Max returned to Haifa, where he became Moshe Lev and had a son, Marc's father. He fought for a Jewish homeland and died in a car accident in 1949.⁵⁴ Tom Butterworth was held in Stalag VIII-B Lamsdorf until March 1945, when, through one of the twentieth century's coldest winters, he was marched 700 miles to Fallingbostel, south of Hamburg. After the war he unloaded fish in Hull until foot and stomach problems caused by wartime privation forced him to stop, following which he ran a café.⁵⁵

The theatre director Eric Huggett and the artist Horace Wade ended up in Polish mines, where Huggett suffered permanent eye damage and Wade lost a leg in an accident.⁵⁶ After the war, both became teachers. Wade's daughter told me that as a child she assumed he'd lost his leg in battle. Few men wanted to talk. The artist Robert Lee was haunted by his experiences at Gravina, visible in his postwar paintings. In 1997, he completed a sculpture of an angel, which today hangs in the Frauenkirche in Dresden, a visual gesture of expiation for the Allied bombing he witnessed as a prisoner there.[57]

Lee lived to be ninety-two and Huggett eighty-five – but such longevity was exceptional. So many men died young: Tom Butterworth and Horace Wade, both from lung cancer in their mid-fifties; Paddy Cullen at fifty-two, from the long-term effects of incarceration and exposure.[58] Digestive and respiratory disorders were common among former POWs, as were sexual and emotional problems: depression, anxiety, irrational anger, poor concentration, dislike of strangers, a craving for solitude – and a more general, indefinable feeling of having missed out, the loss of precious time and slippage from reality.[59]

A friend's father, a tank commander at D-Day, wrote movingly of 'the frail predicament by which in the midst of the apparent stability of life we are always in the instability of possible immediate obliteration'.[60] Visceral experiences of combat and captivity – that frail predicament, of living so fully, yet so near to death – changed men like Ralph and Charlie for ever. The choice after the war was either to remain silent or to tell anodyne stories in pursuit of inner calm and perhaps, in time, redemption.

24.
Redeemed from Time

Charlie West vowed to live the rest of his life in peace. Through an RAF connection, he found a job with a firm in London that made Bakelite, Lucite and other plastics, and after a few years met Barbara Williams, a secretary at the Victoria Hospital for Children in Chelsea. She came from Bermondsey – the code name of his plane in the desert – and was the daughter of a policeman: his old companion Sleuth – Ralph Corps – would have approved. They married in July 1959 at Wandsworth Register Office, when Barbara was thirty-four and Charlie forty-three. Ralph didn't attend the ceremony: he was 7,000 miles away in Mwanza, worrying about the future of the colony he'd made his home.

Charlie and Barbara lived for the next twenty-five years in the South London suburb of Streatham, and like Ralph and Flo had no children. Charlie indulged a passion for fast, stylish cars: Bentleys and Daimlers, a Jowett Jupiter, an S-type Jaguar and a Triumph Roadster 2000. Every year he drove down to Ceraino to see his friend and saviour Cirillo Fumaneri and other good Italian people. He attended meetings of the RAF Escaping Society, and was present at St Clement Danes, the RAF church in London, when a commemorative plaque depicting a downed airman aided by a pair of brave civilians was unveiled.[1] Charlie also attended reunions of the Special Air Service, where he was revered as 'L' Detachment's first and favourite pilot. Everyone said what a gentleman he was, including the Wests' niece Emma Bassom, who today wishes she'd known him better.

I had Emma to thank for letting me see Charlie's address book, so full of Italian names, as well as a list of PO boxes for Ralph in Tanganyika. Evidently the former comrades had exchanged letters, perhaps the occasional Christmas card, but none of these have survived. I'd given up hope of knowing whether they were ever reunited, until one day I was looking at the 1958 photo of Ralph and Flo in Ceraino and had an epiphany. Returning to Charlie's holiday photos I realized the unidentified person was Barbara Williams – which meant the photographer had to be her fiancé Charlie West. Finally, there was proof that Ralph and Charlie had travelled to Italy together, and had taken Flo and Barbara with them so that the two women could see where the escapers had lived in the autumn of 1943.

By the early 1980s, Charlie was terminally ill. In June 1984 he made a will, and four months later was admitted to Charing Cross Hospital. On 31 October he died peacefully, aged sixty-eight. The funeral was held at Lewisham Crematorium, and instead of flowers well-wishers were invited to make donations to the RAF Escaping Society. 'For one of such a quiet, gentle and generous character, he had an abundance of courage and determination,' wrote Ernie Bond in his obituary. 'Of Charles Edwin West it can be truly said that having risen to eminence by merit, he lived respected and died regretted.'[2]

After Princess Margaret's visit to Tanganyika, Ralph and Flo spent the remainder of the 1950s watching the splendour of their imperial lives fade away. Independence became a question of when not if, and was answered by the elections of 1958–9, which resulted in a landslide for the Tanganyika African National Union. Its charismatic leader, Julius Nyerere, adhered to progressive socialism, preaching cooperation in the name of equality and harmony. 'We glorify human beings, not colour,' said Nyerere – otherwise, he added, TANU would be no better than the Nazis.[3]

By now Ralph was earning three times his starting salary, but was perturbed by this changing world. Correspondence with his friend Pat Manley, chief officer of prisons, makes this clear. Ever sensitive to matters of status, in January 1959, Ralph wrote seeking clarification about insignia of rank and the staffing required to preserve hierarchy. Manley replied pessimistically, fearing Tanganyika might go the way of Kenya, where Manley had worked before the war. Crime was increasing, as was prison indiscipline, which the British punished with floggings and the imposition of something like slavery. Many Europeans detected a defiant tone among Africans and started selling up.[4]

In 1960, a United Nations mission reported that the country was 'progressing smoothly and rapidly towards the ultimate goal'.[5] The following year, Ralph was granted five months of leave in England, where my parents were engaged to be married that December. But much as Flo wanted to stay for their wedding, her husband had to be back at his desk by 19 November. Three weeks later, Tanganyika was declared an independent country – Tanzania – and admitted as the 104th nation of the UN. Its prime minister was Julius Nyerere.

Ralph received a letter from the new minister for home affairs, appealing to his loyalty to the country. Nyerere's government favoured 'dependent development', harnessing the experience of long-established colonists.[6] But Ralph had no desire to work under Africans, nor did he and many other whites care for socialism, which they felt could only be to their disadvantage. So he handed in his notice and requested a letter of recommendation from Pat Manley. In his reply, Manley bemoaned that senior positions in the police and prison service were already being filled by indigenous candidates, adding that Ralph was leaving not a moment too soon. Manley himself retired that June and became warden of prisons in Bermuda, the last remaining British colony in the North Atlantic. In his reference, Manley praised Ralph's sound judgement and organizational skills, summing him up as 'a thoroughly reliable and steady type of man'.[7]

Ralph and Flo returned to England in the spring of 1962, and the following year used their post-independence compensation of £7,000 and Ralph's £500 annual pension to buy a detached house in Ampleforth, North Yorkshire. I received an email from a woman named Ruth White, whose Ancestry DNA test had matched my own. She turned out to be my cousin, her father the boy born to

Flo's brother George and his wife in 1944 and named Ralph after his missing uncle. Ruth's mother had known Ralph and Flo well and visited them in Ampleforth. She found them frosty, remote people, who allowed their muscular dogs to run at visitors before calling them off at the last moment. There were no insurgents or lions in North Yorkshire, but perhaps they kept the dogs to remind them of Tanganyika, where there had been.

After two years, Ralph and Flo moved to the Isle of Man, a Crown dependency in the Irish Sea. They had a fine view: perhaps open water felt like an escape route, a reassuring reminder that they could leave. They stayed seven years, during which Ralph was embroiled in a dispute with the RAF about jet aircraft disrupting the productivity of his hens, for which Ralph supplied meticulous records – a habit formed at the prison farm in Kingolwira.

Now in his mid-fifties, this tough, brave man was becoming a pedantic crank. In May 1972, he and Flo upped sticks again, this time sailing to Rhodesia on the SS *Angola* – always travelling, never really arriving. Pretending to be a farmer, Ralph was offered a job at an isolated station near Inyanga, but turned it down, baulking at the duties, which included castrating and dehorning cattle. Three years later, they were living in Fish Hoek, in South Africa's Western Cape, in another quiet house overlooking a bay.

By the mid-1970s, they were ailing. Flo's arthritis – long the justification for living in warm climates – was severe, and she may already have been displaying signs of dementia. With no one to care for them in South Africa, they returned to Doncaster, where they moved in with Pauline and John while looking for a house.

Accustomed to having servants in Africa, they were peevishly demanding. Flo was quick-tempered, impulsive, confused, and her jokey injunction from 1945 that Ralph wasn't to leave her sight turned into something more serious. One day, frantic not to be separated, she refused to let him fetch vegetables from the greenhouse and, when he demurred, threatened him with a kitchen knife. Everything was wrong. They were irritable and bored. Doncaster was too damp and cold. They didn't like the room Pauline gave them. One night, Flo screamed in panic because Ralph was bleeding from the rectum. Bowel cancer was suspected – but nothing came of it.

In the winter of 1980, they decided to spend Christmas and New Year on the Costa Brava. Booking a month in Lloret de Mar with Saga, a tour company for retired people, they were on the move again. Ralph was sixty-six, Flo sixty-five. Whether Ralph felt unwell is not known, but on 29 December, he died suddenly. It must have felt to Flo like a terrible dream. Two days later, she received a death certificate in Spanish, citing acute pulmonary oedema and congestive heart failure. There was no question of repatriating the body, nor even of anyone in the family flying out. The Església de Sant Romà, the main church in Lloret de Mar, has no record of a funeral service. So, with Flo the only mourner, Ralph was buried in the local cemetery. There's a photograph of Flo by the graveside, a mound of earth topped with flowers. Standing alone in cardigan and slacks, her hands twisted with arthritis, she looks utterly lost. 'Our years end like a sigh,' teaches the Psalm, and so they had.

Returning from Spain, Flo lived another eighteen years. In 1993, she bequeathed to Pauline and John the semi-detached house she and Ralph had bought in Doncaster, which they sold when she needed to go into a nursing home. In 1998, having lived for three-quarters of the twentieth century, Flo died from dementia and pneumonia. On her dressing table stood a hinged silver double-frame containing portraits of Ralph and her at the peak of their pomp and pride.

Most stories can be wound up wherever we choose – but those that reach into the present have other ideas, and whether we like it or not they just keep going.

After a wait of more than a year, I finally received Ralph's military service file, just as I'd nearly given up on my Freedom of Information application. It shed no light on Ralph's resistance work, but did confirm some hunches about his experiences prior to capture in 1942, including his employment as a wireless telegraphist, evacuation from Dunkirk and promotion to warrant officer after he arrived in

Camp 65. There was also a definitive list of the medals that Ralph was (and by implication wasn't) entitled to, where, it was poignant to note, the section headed 'Gallant Conduct' had been left blank.[8]

The file also contained some fascinating nuggets. A final report on his Coldstream Guards service, citing Ralph's lack of dynamism, expressed doubt that he would ever be 'a good leader of men'.[9] After sensing how far he'd followed Charlie's lead while on the run, pulled rank to get his way in the camps, and seized up in Paitone until energized by Andrea Baronchelli, this didn't really surprise me.

Perhaps the most bizarre revelation was the army's determination to reunite Ralph with his socks and other possessions recovered from the desert after he was taken prisoner. Astonishingly, a letter had even been sent to him in Camp 65 in June 1943, asking where he would like these articles to be delivered. By the time the letter arrived, he had been moved north to Chiavari, so the Italian authorities stamped it 'return to sender' and posted it back to England. It was then intercepted by the advancing Allies, who sent it on its way, back to the records department of the Corps of Military Police.[10]

Ralph's story continued to unfold in other ways. Gianni Fumaneri, the boy in the Ceraino photo, died before I could interview him. His widow Itala recalled him speaking of the fascist who would have had his father, Cirillo, shot had Ralph and Charlie been discovered. And though some details were confused – both POWs were thought to be downed airmen – Itala did say that the train taking them to Germany had halted at Dolcè, which was correct, and that this had been due to an air raid, which was plausible. Best, however, was Gianni's memory of that summer's day in 1958:

> My husband told me that when the English people arrived it came as a great surprise to him. They were loaded with gifts: a rocking horse and other toys, and delicious sweets including the famous toffees, which my Gianni loved. They had arrived in a beautiful right-hand-drive car – I think it was a Bentley. They were staying on Lake Garda.

The Glass Mountain

Colour and sound had been added to that washed-out photo. I checked Charlie's address book. He and Barbara had stayed at the Albergo Ideal at Brenzone, the small port where in 1943 Charlie had crossed the lake in a smuggler's boat, back when his future was measured out in a sequence of death-defying minutes.

From the lakes, Charlie had also revisited the mountains – perhaps not in 1958, but definitely in the 1960s or early 1970s. He had, in a sense, been haunting his former self, just as I would later haunt him at Sant'Anna d'Alfaedo. On that trip I had taken with me a photo, sent by his niece Emma, which showed him surveying the valley, lost in a dream of the past. Above the treeline, where vegetation turned to scrub, we found a view that fitted, and Dom recreated the photo with me in his place. I imagined Charlie standing there, remembering partisan friends, perhaps also enemies he'd left in the ground. It seemed the perfect counterpoint to the photo of Vittorina Radaelli in a similar pose. He may have been thinking of her, too.

What of Vittorina? Flavio Manzelli sent a postwar photo of her with his mother, looking dignified in a double-breasted coat. Had she and Charlie stayed in touch? I checked his address book: there she was, but all it said was Ostiglia, her family home. Perhaps she'd written to him, omitting by accident or design an address for him to write back. She married and moved to Milan, where she had two children before settling in Bologna. I tracked down her son there – but then: silence. 'We can remember', said the cultural historian of fascism Luisa Passerini, 'only thanks to fact that somebody has remembered before us, that other people in the past have challenged death and terror on the basis of their memory.'[11] Even so, like the descendants of Omodeo Cantoni, some people just want to forget or, for good reasons or none, simply aren't interested.

Fortunately, this hadn't been the case in Paitone, where everyone was keen to add links to the chain of memory. The Maccarinelli brothers, Pietro and Dante, returned to their mothers. The Chiodis lived to see their murdered nephew honoured with the Gold Medal of Military Valour.[12] Pietro died in 1947, Augusto in 1958. Their sister Erminia lived into the mid-1960s, when she sold the house to Anna Maccarinelli's family. A Maccarinelli cousin emigrated to Wales, where his son became an international boxing champion.[13]

Doro Garletti set up his own machine workshop. He kept the Beretta pistol he'd had as a partisan, and his membership card for the Tempini Brigade, a band so ephemeral I was told at the Brescia archives it had never formally existed.[14] Doro stayed in touch with a Russian named Yuri, whom he'd helped escape from the Germans and who visited Paitone in 1991.[15] Doro's son Piero, the living link to Ralph, became a semi-professional cyclist, and still mows his own lawn, though his eyesight is failing. His brother Ugo worked in a factory in England. They all got on with their lives, remembering the war without obsessing about it.

Similarly, Andrea Baronchelli returned to the Foreign Trade Institute, this time in Rome, and lived a quiet yet distinguished life. I met his affable namesake grandson in a pub in London, where he showed me a photo from the early 1960s of Andrea Senior posing with a pair of cheetah cubs, unsolicited gifts from Somalia, which he kept in the zoo and was allowed to take for walks. A brave man of parts, said the grandson, Andrea the ex-resister liked a drop of grappa in his coffee and was fond of the accordion.

The most striking remains of Ralph's life are the places he went, where now the membrane between present and past is thinnest. In 2025 Camp 65 was awarded €830,000 by the Municipality of Altamura to conserve key buildings and may yet acquire a European Heritage Label, denoting outstanding cultural importance. Once a place of isolation, the camp brings people together from all over the world. It is, as Doro Garletti's grandson Stefano says, truly 'a place without borders'. As for Camp 52, there may be nothing left, but the Genoese State Archives and the Superintendent of Archival Heritage in Liguria have judged Fabio Zavatteri's relics to be of potential 'national significance'. The Chiodi house continues to crumble, but the concrete *casotto* at Ceraino will probably be there for ever.

There wasn't time to retrace all Charlie's steps, though Dom and I had crossed Lake Garda and seen Monte Baldo, where he lived with the partisans. I didn't go to Nozza to envision the Perlasca Brigade's S4 battalion forcing an SS column to surrender, or visit the square named in 2021 after the priest Primo Alessio Leali, who was made a Knight of the Republic for his part in the victory. Malga Sacù, S4's mountain retreat, is still there – 'experienced hikers only', according to the Italian Alpine Club at Vestone – and has been restored as a memorial. Stefano Garletti sent photos from the opening ceremony, showing the entrance to the stone hut hung with the flag of the Fiamme Verdi Association.[16] Nor did I make it to Cascina Farisengo, the Baronchelli family home through which Ralph passed in March 1945. Today, like so many former homes of the *contadini*, it is a bed and breakfast for tourists who would never imagine the wartime dramas staged there.[17]

I made a final visit in the summer of 2024, not to Italy but to the last place Ralph ever saw: the Spanish resort of Lloret de Mar. I imagine it's changed a bit since 1980. My wife and I arrived late at night, when the streets were heaving with teenage Brits eating kebabs and queueing for night clubs. The next day we set off in close midday heat, away from the main strip to the cemetery, famous for its art nouveau memorials. We searched the winding lanes of marble walls. The registry had told me he was in 'fosa número dos' – grave two – but it was impossible to see what this meant.

The adjacent *cementeri civil*, an overgrown enclosure full of Arabic and other non-Catholic burials, looked promising – but the background scenery in the graveside photo of Flo didn't match. Once again, I was desperate to break the frame. I phoned the registry, but there was no one there. A site attendant with an ancient hand-drawn plan took us to the *fosas*, but they were unnumbered.

That night, I dreamed I was floating through the cemetery – a filmic cliché. But even in my dreams, Ralph refused to show himself. I woke up at dawn, however, startled to recall another map at the entrance. So back we went and, sure enough, on that plan the *fosas* were numbered. We went straight to number two, an untidy area of maybe twenty graves, abandoned like those in the civil cemetery. Only one grave, unmarked, just a rectangle of rough stones, aligned with the photo. I erected a small tin cross long parted from its own grave, and propped up copies of a couple of photos of Ralph.

On the back of one of the originals, Ralph, in his way, had copied out an eighteenth-century epitaph he'd come across somewhere:

> Time was I stood where thou dost now,
> And viewed the dead as thou dost me,
> E'er long you'll lie as low as I,
> And others stand and look on thee.

Hoping this was what he would have wanted, I'd typed it out before we left England. The photo was a group shot of policemen in the West Riding Constabulary. Ralph wears his medal ribbons, which dates it to 1946, when he was thirty-two. He looks like he's somewhere else in his mind, pruning Italian vines, perhaps, or eating polenta by the fireside, or dreaming of a new life in Africa . . . anywhere but South Yorkshire.

We left the cemetery. I felt at peace, and hoped Ralph had found peace too.

★

Ralph's memory lives on in Altamura. The portrait of him as a Coldstream Guardsman, the photo Nan gave me, now appears in a huge mural depicting people and scenes from Camp 65. Through Dom, local schoolchildren have been tasked with translating Ralph's memoir, creating graphic novels and even making a short film, *Il Diario di Ralph*, a screening of which I attended in Altamura. Hearing Ralph's words spoken in Italian, in the very place he was describing, reduced people to tears. Three years later, one of the students told me of his ongoing spiritual connection with the story. As well as working on the film, he had worked all night on the translation, feeling a torch of memory had been handed to him.[18]

Dom and I will always be close. He sends me photos of student visits to Gravina, one of which showed a girl holding an A4 print of Ralph's face that, set against the wasteland of the camp, looked like a portal ripped through to the past. Maybe one day we'll make a pilgrimage to Pescantina, where many Allied ex-prisoners would have brushed past Dom's father, as they all tried to get home. In Paitone and Brescia, the Maccarinellis and Garlettis have become our friends, as their forebears were to Uncle Ralph.

Camp 65 has never been more contested as a site of memory. Locals think of it as a former refugee camp, which it became postwar, rather than as a camp for POWs from Britain and the Commonwealth. 'It is not only the sleep of reason that produces monsters', says Dom, quoting Goya, 'but also the sleep of memory.'[19] Yet history and identity are fraught in Italy, and memory is distorted. Ordinary people have been portrayed as the victims of fascism rather than its perpetrators, and the resurgent right also sees them as the victims of Italy's former foreign enemies.[20] In 2023, a plaque inscribed with a nationalistic dedication was fixed to one of Camp 65's concrete gateposts. Soon afterwards, Dom sent me a message written by a young graduate on an online forum, which read: 'Why aren't Italians grateful to Mussolini, who in just a few years transformed a backward, miserable country into a great power?'[21] Il Duce's tomb in Predappio is a shrine for neo-fascists, its shops selling troubling souvenirs. In June 2024, the Brescia branch of ANPI, the left-wing partisan association, posted film showing portraits of Mussolini and his proclamations hanging in the municipal offices in Prevalle. Even if displayed out of historical interest, such things cause real offence.

And so the search for a *memoria condivisa*, an apolitical Italian history that can be shared in the name of humanity, has become desperately difficult. The weaponization of history, to strengthen difference not common ground, continues. And to an extent difference is fixed in the calendar of commemoration. Although 25 April evokes proud memories of national liberation in 1945, this is followed by 8 September – the anniversary of the 1943 Armistice – when Italy was defeated, saw fascism revived in the Republic of Salò, and then entered a long, dark era of political strife: civil war in all but name.

And what of Ralph's final legacy? However much his deeds have been cemented in public memory, elsewhere his reputation is still chequered. Mum still maintains that he and Flo were a pair of cold fishes. Pauline is more strident. 'You could be writing a book about a very gallant man,' she told me, 'but he wasn't one. He never did anything for anyone, except take Audrey on holiday.' Like Mum, Pauline knew nothing of Ralph's time in the resistance. 'We feel that if he was a partisan he would have done as little as possible,' she continued. 'Because we always felt as though he didn't like work.'

This didn't sit quite right with me. I neither liked nor disliked Ralph, nor did he disappoint me. And I certainly didn't wish that Charlie had been my great-uncle, though once I might have. But Philip James Bailey's aphorism, inscribed by Ralph in his notebook, seemed apt and fair: 'he most lives who thinks most, feels the noblest, acts the best'. Ralph was not always honest, yet he believed this and held himself to that standard. Furthermore, I'd discovered many sides to him: the rigid policeman and soldier, but also the boy in the man, the pretend father, the moralist, the romantic, the tender friend. 'To comprehend is to complicate,' a historian once said. And that's what I'd done, embracing his contradictions: for 'within the contradiction', Philip Roth writes, 'lies the tormented human being'.[22] I'd also seen how Ralph had changed over the course of his life. Inconsistencies of character had come to feel more like contrasts between phases of innocence and experience, as he aged and reacted to circumstance and event.

Finally, knowing Ralph had exposed all the things I could never know. In a way, I found myself back at the beginning, as in T. S. Eliot's 'Little Gidding', not fully enlightened yet seeing that place clearly for the first time.[23] Ralph's story now seemed less like a string of facts than a collage of brilliant, vanishing moments, the flashes and shadows of a dream. Historians are lured by the past only to be pulled up short by its deficiencies and otherness. What things were *really* like, we can't say. And there's no complete life – only fragments.[24]

Among the Warmsworth papers is a letter from my Nan, Charlotte, to her sister, Flo, written in the early summer of 1976. It was sent in a spirit of reconciliation after some rift and referred to Ralph and Flo's plans to return to England for good. Charlotte felt their deceased mother would have wanted them to be friends again. She also said how much 'the boy', meaning me, was thrilled to hear about Ralph's war. Stumbling upon this was a heart-stopping moment. For there I was, another fragment in the archive, somewhere in the middle of the story – or, if you prefer, at the beginning of the end. A passion dormant for fifty years had been awoken by Mum's dream, and one thing had led to another.

Archives are spectral places – but only because historians summon ghosts there. Ralph's papers were dead and dry in Pauline's attic until I started poking around, initiating a rite of conjuration from which then there was no escape. And like a crystal ball, the glass mountain through which the past is seen reflects as well as refracts, a reminder that the dead exist only in the minds of the living, where they strive to show us who we are. Entwined with Dom's hesitant search for his father, my strange invocation of Ralph in wartime Italy had led me to discover my own secret history encoded in his. This wasn't mawkish nostalgia: more an avid appreciation of life, both now and in prospect. It turns out there really is no time like the present. Ralph had pulled me, as he had Mum, back in time; but through friendship on my travels, he'd guided me home again.

Epilogue: Monte Generoso

Having deciding to end Ralph's story with his death and legacy, I found that I didn't, after all, want to leave him there. It surprised me how emotionally attached I'd become. The man I'd started out with had been so dead, and I'd spent seven years trying to see him live. Instead, it seemed more fitting that a story that began with a dream – Mum's dream of Ralph – should finish with one, too: Ralph's wartime vision of liberty, realized at last.

To prisoners of war, Switzerland had symbolized freedom, the exit from Italy and the way home. Charlie West's doomed plan to fly there came from a fantasy that sustained hope, in the prison camps and later on. Ralph had seen out the war in Paitone – but in his heart he knew he should have had another shot at getting through the Alps. Once I'd grasped this, a vision of white crests, sharp against a perfect cerulean sky, fixed itself in my mind.

Mum sent more holiday snaps she'd found. Here were Ralph and Flo on a mountain, larking around with snowballs; there, Mum and Flo at Lake Lugano – my son, a budding geolocator, identified a portion of cast-iron railing. So, assuming the mountain was near Lugano, which one was it? Another photo showed Mum and Flo leaving a railway carriage bearing a sign which, thanks to more internet sleuthing, identified it as the funicular train on Monte Generoso at the Italian–Swiss border.

I booked a flight to Milan, from where it was a ninety-minute drive to the mountain. Magically, this unlocked Mum's memory: a warm evening in the city, Flo with her amber cigarette holder (and missing finger), drifting music – 'Volare', or something similar. They saw *Madame Butterfly*, not at La Scala with Maria Callas as she'd hoped, but some lesser venue, where they also saw *La Bohème*, in which Rodolfo – how the name must have

Epilogue: Monte Generoso

touched Ralph – sings with Mimì 'Che gelida manina' and 'O soave fanciulla'.¹

But after that vivid flash of recall: nothing. Had Mum blanked it all out? Pauline said: who wouldn't want to forget a holiday with Ralph and Flo!² But then, on a hunch, I checked the date of her father's death, which she'd been sure was 1957. It was May 1955, just before the holiday. Guilt at leaving her mother and brother in a house drenched in grief, she supposed, explained her amnesia and, unconsciously, the altered date.³

I stayed with my family in a hotel on Monte Generoso itself, high up in the clouds. At Capolago, we took the funicular train – electric now, not steam – further up the mountain. The sky was a gauzy blue, the slopes and ridges of the valley folded into each other, and the peaks seemed divinely lit.

At the top lay the patchy snow from Mum's photos, but the hotels and souvenir shop are long gone. The path to the summit offers mesmerizing views of the Alps, Apennines and the lakes and valleys of Ticino. On the way down, my wife and I recreated the snowball photo, our children angling smartphones where once Mum had

Epilogue: Monte Generoso

stood with her Box Brownie. 'Tutto torna', as Dom likes to say: everything returns to its beginning.

Dar es Salaam, 1955. Ralph and Flo settle in their seats on a twin-propeller Douglas DC-3, a repurposed wartime Dakota. The flight, via Nairobi, Khartoum and Rome, takes two days. At London Airport, Ralph and Flo transfer by bus to Waterloo Air Terminal, and from there by taxi to King's Cross to catch the train to Doncaster, where they've arranged to stay with Ralph's father.

Ralph visits a Vauxhall showroom, where he pays £900 for a new six-cylinder Cresta E, the black model with chrome bumpers and whitewall tyres, red leather upholstery and cream steering wheel. After saying goodbye to his father, he and Flo drive 200 miles south to Gillingham in Kent. They'll soon see their niece, Audrey – the daughter they never had.

There are few cars on Gillingham Avenue, and none as glamorous as Ralph's Cresta. Flo wrote to her sister Charlotte to say when they were arriving, and now they are here, filling the hallway of the terraced house. It's only been a few weeks since Arch's funeral, and mourning hangs in the air.

Audrey has packed two main outfits: the jacket she wears with a pleated skirt and her sleeveless cotton dress; she also has sandals and flat shoes, her big coat and a couple of headscarves. Most of her wages from the Westminster Bank go to her mother, but she has saved up for a camera: a Kodak Brownie Cresta – like Ralph's car.

Ralph swings Audrey's case into the boot, and Charlotte and her son John wave limp farewells from the doorstep. Soon the Cresta is cruising east on the Dover road, and an hour later they are queueing for the novel 'roll-on-roll-off' car ferry.

Out in the Channel, choppy waves take Ralph back to his homecoming ten years ago. How their lives have changed since then! Audrey is daydreaming about Switzerland: alpine scenery, the chocolate missed during rationing and cuckoo clocks.

Skirting Paris, Ralph drives 500 miles to Lyon, where they spend the night in a hotel. Early the next morning, they continue south to

Epilogue: Monte Generoso

Provence, where everything is drier and brighter. By mid-afternoon they are in Nice, and picnic by a stream, making tea on a primus stove. Ralph tops up the tank with Esso while Flo and Audrey wash, then taking Audrey's camera captures them drying off in the Provençal sunshine.

Heading east along the Ligurian coastline, they peel off into the Italian *campagna* outside Genoa. Audrey cranes her neck from the car window. Some streets are still in ruins; postwar tourism has yet to flourish. Through Piedmont sails the Cresta, along the edge of the Alps, over the River Po into the plains of Lombardy as far as Milan. Scarred by bombing, the city nonetheless bounces with life.

They stay a couple of days, then continue their journey to Chiasso, where customs officials riffle through their passports before waving them on. It's almost too easy. They check into a hotel at Lugano, and the next day drive to Capolago.

On Monte Generoso, they peer down at the map-like stillness of the valley and visit the souvenir shop, where Audrey buys a cuckoo clock for her brother, John. It plays 'La Vie en Rose'. Taking the path to the top, Ralph unbuttons his jacket. The weather is warm, and it's been a decade since he climbed so high.

Audrey and Flo wander round the guard rail, arm-in-arm; Ralph is quiet, lost in a reverie, lifted from time. He stands 100 miles north of Sega di Ala, the green uplands that in 1943 pointed home and where he turned away. Now, finally, he has caught up with his dream, suspended between heaven and earth, where even the air smells like freedom.

And with this vista stretching before him he completes his story, and by conjuring that image seventy years on I complete mine.

Acknowledgements

My greatest pleasure writing this book has been falling in love with Italy and getting to know its people. Chief among them is Domenico Bolognese, a man of rare integrity, enthusiasm and generosity. This book is for him because he made it possible.

It's also dedicated to my mother, Audrey Gaskill. I owe so much to her and to my father, Eddie, who first nurtured my love of the past. I was privileged to have opportunities denied their generation, and was cheered on by inspirational teachers. But the greater part of who I am – and how I write – comes from my mum and dad.

Other family members have assisted. My first cousin-once-removed Pauline Kendell has been so helpful, likewise my cousin Ruth White. My sister, Sally Gardner, has been a staunch supporter, and since the death of our uncle John Davis we've been closer than ever. I'm glad I had the chance to talk to John about Ralph before he left us.

Gratitude to my in-laws, Roger and Rosina Peirse, rolls over year on year, as it does to many friends who have shown an interest in this book, to name but a few: Ros Roughton, Mike Farrar, Chris Jones, Edmund Slater, Spenser Frearson, Alan Sewell, Alice Feinstein, Fiona Bannatyne, Annabel Agace and my dear film agent Rebecca Watson. Ros kindly read a draft, and she and Mike turned their Yorkshire home into a writers' retreat for me.

In Altamura, I'm indebted to Tina Patella for her hospitality and allowing me to take her husband, Dom, on field trips. Giuliano De Felice taught me about the archaeology of Camp 65. I'm also grateful to Gennaro Zubbo, Laura Squicciarini, Francesca Zaccaria, Nunzia Cacciapaglia and the students of the Liceo Statale Classico e delle Scienze Umane 'Cagnazzi', the Liceo Scientifico e Linguistico 'Federico II di Svevia' and ITT 'Nervi-Galilei'. Thank you Matteo Berloco, who was perhaps most moved by Ralph's story.

Acknowledgements

Covering Ralph's ground led me to some amazing places and people. In Noci I would like to thank José Mottola, Cesareo Putignano, Vincenzo Sansonetti, Giulia Basile and Lorita Tinelli; in Paitone, the Maccarinelli family – Celestina, Anna, Ugo, Elena, Elsa, Mimma, Manuela and Celestina's son Maurizio Amadei; in Prevalle, Paolo Catterina, Jacopo Avanzi, Abele Ballerini, Marco Maccarinelli and Attilio Mendini; in Brescia, Stefano Garletti, his wife Rosa, their sons Federico and Alessandro, Stefano's father Ugo, and, above all, Ugo's extraordinary brother Piero Garletti.

I am indebted to others in Brescia: Carlo Gianuzzi, Carlo Susara, Lucio Pedroni, Vanni Massari and Professor Rolando Anni, who allowed me to consult the Fiamme Verdi archive at the Università Cattolica del Sacro Cuore. The archives in Bussolengo, Verona, were opened up to me by Matteo Zenari and Cristiano Girelli.

For valuable information about Ceraino, I'm grateful to Stella Manzelli, Claudio Manzelli, Flavio Manzelli, Barbara Calmasini and Arnaldo Testi. After Gianmaria Fumaneri sadly died, his widow Itala Poli Fumaneri shared memories. In Breonio and Molina, I appreciated the help of Alberto Antolini, Fioravante Bacilieri, Marco Bacilieri, Remo Sandri, Francesco Laiti and the Sega family, especially Raffaele. Special thanks go to Fabio Giacopuzzi and Rosangela Adamoli, and their children, who entertained us like honoured guests. Witnesses to war, Fioravante and Raffaele have since died – a generation fading away.

In Calvari, Fabio Zavatteri showed us relics from Camp 52, and we were entertained in the hills by Robert and his wife, who asked not to be identified. Elena Passalacqua sent a photo of a theatrical production. I would like to thank the staff of the cemetery at Lloret de Mar, and Rosa Sanchez Alba and Rosana Torres Gomes, who helped me find Ralph's grave.

For information about Charlie West, I am indebted to his family: Emma Bassom, Caroline Bloch, Jane Scott, Vanessa Steer and Katherine Rennie. I'm also grateful to Louise Bush of the Lincolnshire Aviation Heritage Centre, Claire Skinner of the Plymouth Archives and Charlotte MacKenzie. My private investigator uncle Malcolm

Acknowledgements

I. Gaskill gave tips on tracking Charlie down. Jo Foster helped me learn about the Camp 52 train-escaper Bill Barker. Tony Armstrong helped with Ralph's school days.

Staff at the Cambridge University Library delivered obscure war memoirs, as did their counterparts at the British Library. I am grateful to the Monte San Martino Trust for access to its archives, and for Anne Copley's advice about the Allied Screening Commission. Many ASC requests were handled by Suzanne Zoumbaris at the National Archives and Records Administration at College Park, Maryland, and Ann Trevor dug up OSS records there. Allen Packwood and Nicole Allen at the Churchill Archives Centre let me consult William J. Donovan's OSS papers on microfilm, and Thomas E. Buffenbarger of the US Army Heritage and Education Center in Pennsylvania checked their Donovan archive.

In the archives of the Imperial War Museum, Dominic Hewett, Zipporah Blake-Gravesande and Fiona Kelly were obliging. Tina Kilnan searched for records at the Royal Military Police Museum, as did Chelsea Taylor at the National Army Museum, and Marie Allemann at the International Committee of the Red Cross in Geneva.

At the National Archives in Kew, I am indebted to the keeper, Saul Nassé, and to Helen Potter and the Access Service Team of MOD Personnel Records, likewise Amanda Bevan and Will Butler. Clare Jackson also helped me to access Ralph's classified service record. Thanks, too, to Stephen Di Rosa at the Army Personnel Centre in Glasgow.

I incurred many debts tracing men who Ralph knew or had shared his experiences. I'm grateful to Andrea Baronchelli and, on the same trail, Paola Pettenella and Sabrina Bonato in Rovereto. Thanks are also due to the Butterworth family – Andrew, Tracey and Steve – and to Ian Brown, Marc Löw in Berlin, and in Israel Talya Klayner Dayagi. Thank you, Angela Hopper, daughter of Horace Wade, and Kate Hopper. Thanks, too, to Olivia Coughlin of the Tank Museum in Bovington, Dorset. Louis van Schaik and Eric Falletisch shed light on the relationship between a Camp 52 prisoner and his fiancée. I also exchanged emails with descendants of

Acknowledgements

POWs: Mike Churchill-Jones, Sarah Hattersley, Glynda Morrison, Pete Mallon, Dylan Murphy, Claire Edwards, John Dilworth, Tony Leversha, Lorraine Wheeler and Helen Snelson. Edward Finch informed me about the liberation of Altamura.

I am immensely grateful to Janet Kinrade Dethick, who shared her knowledge of Italian POW camps and located the Maccarinellis. This would have been a different and poorer book without her. Thanks, too, to Enzo Gilini, her amiable husband. Other helpful historians and writers include Tony Hopkins, Isabella Insolvibile, Nicola Cacciatore, Luke Turner, Murray Cox and Sir Stephen Sedley. Special thanks go to my friends Amy King, translator extraordinaire, and Kate Summerscale, who offered penetrating insights. Mervyn Foster and Steve Thomas commented on the secret radio, and Luisa Tammaro did her best to teach me some Italian.

I am, once again, fortunate to have a dream team to publish the book. Thank you, Natasha Fairweather, my literary agent at Rogers, Coleridge and White, for your constant support, likewise Ivy Pottinger-Glass. And thank you, Tom Penn, my ideal editor and friend, and everyone else at Penguin, principally Tom's assistant Olivia Kumar, editorial manager Ruth Pietroni, copy editor David Watson, proofreaders Stephen Ryan and Chris Shaw, and Maddie Watts and Gavin Read, who handled publicity and marketing respectively. Thanks, too, to Neil Gower, who drew the excellent maps.

My greatest debt is to my wife, Sheena Peirse, and our children Kate, Tom and Lily, who must often feel they're competing with a book for attention. Sheena is the most loving, encouraging and patient person, as well as an astute counsellor, and without her life is unimaginable. It's my most cherished good fortune, in what has been a charmed life, that we are together. Our house is full of affection and good humour: through thick and thin, someone always seems to have a joke about something.

Sources

The principal source for Ralph's early life was Pauline Kendell's archive in Warmsworth, Doncaster. Information about schools came from the 'Ossie through the Ages' project run by Tony Armstrong, another Warmsworth resident. Derek and Enid Holland, *A Yorkshire Town: The Making of Doncaster* (2013) helped set the scene.

Ancestry.com and Findmypast.co.uk provided details of births, marriages and deaths, and census records, especially the fascinating 1939 Register. There are also some military records there. Deborah Cohen's *Family Secrets* (2013) is an important reminder of the murky complexity of past lives and relationships.

Ralph's army service record is in the National Archives at Kew (TNA) – WO 423/436012. Also helpful were the war diaries of the 150th Infantry Brigade and the Provost Company of the 50th 'N' Division, both in TNA. For life in the desert, I used R. L. Crimp's *The Diary of a Desert Rat* (1971) and Sven Lindqvist's *Desert Divers*, trans. Joan Tate (2002). On Ralph's capture, Ken Ford's *Gazala 1942* (2008) was invaluable. Charlie's plane crash in 1941 is described in TNA, AIR 81/10384. Alan Allport, *Browned Off and Bloody-Minded* (2015) is excellent on the mentality of servicemen. Full publication details of all these works are given in the notes.

The star attraction at Warmsworth was Ralph's memoir, my first encounter with Camp 65 Gravina. Further insights came from TNA, mainly the files of the International Red Cross (WO 224/127 and WO 361/1898, and Domenico Bolognese et al., *Camp 65*, trans. Amy King (2024), especially the chapter by Nunzia Cacciapaglia. See also Giuliano De Felice's *Archeologia di un Paesaggio Contemporaneo* (2020). One of the best first-hand accounts is John Cheetham, *Italian Interlude* (2000).

Sources

There is a Red Cross file for Camp 52 Chiavari (TNA, WO 361/1890), and files on war crimes there (notably WO 311/1209, WO 311/317, TS 26/712 and TS 26/417). Overviews are provided by Massimo Minella's *Campo 52* (2019) and Silvano Benedetti and Stefano Schiappacasse, *La Caserma di Caperana* (n.d.). The best memoir is Robert Garioch, *Two Men and a Blanket* (1975), but most inspiring are Fabio Zavatteri's relics at Casa Sartù in Calvari, Comune di San Colombano Certenoli.

POW life in general is covered by Clare Makepeace, *Captives of War* (2017), Adrian Gilbert, *POW* (2006) and Charles Rollings, *Prisoner of War* (2007). A. J. Barker, *Behind Barbed Wire* (1974) explores the psychology of imprisonment. On Italian camps, see Isabella Insolvibile, *La Prigionia Alleata in Italia, 1940–1943* (2023).

Numerous diaries, memoirs and letters, some specific to Camps 65 and 52, are referenced in the notes. Published memoirs can be found in the British Library, manuscript accounts in the archives of the Imperial War Museum (IWM). For Camp 65, the diary of John Glass (Docs.3306) and a memoir by Bert Graham (Docs.17336) are especially revealing. For Camp 52, see the memoirs of Ernest Carter (Docs.460) and George Peacock (Docs.24671), the diary of Harold Rumsey (Docs.22675) and the letters of Fred Frost (Docs.20705). Letters to Camps 65 and 52 – never delivered – sleep in the Archivi del Campo di Lavoro PG 148 at the Biblioteca Civica in Bussolengo, Verona.

The Monte San Martino Trust (MSMT) preserves a valuable collection of memoirs, accessed online, but the originals are in the Cambridge University Library. Most significant are Frank Osborne's scabrous description of Tuturano and Gravina, and William Strachan on Camp 52. Many MSMT and IWM memoirs cover not only imprisonment in Italy but escape and evasion. The most useful primary sources are MI9's 'liberation reports' in TNA – Ralph's is WO 344/73/2, Charlie's WO 344/339/2 – now available in facsimile on Ancestry.com. On British Intelligence and escaped POWs, see Helen Fry, *MI9* (2020) and M. R. D. Foot and J. M. Langley, *MI9* (1979).

Sources

Liberation reports and other MI9 debriefs can be cross-referenced with the Allied Screening Commission records at the National Archives and Records Administration, College Park, Maryland. The ASC's enlightening final report is in TNA (WO 208/3397). There is an index on the NARA website, and digitization of the files is under way, partly funded by the Monte San Martino Trust. Facebook is an invaluable resource for tracing families who helped POWs, likewise Google Maps for understanding escape routes and resistance networks.

Roger Absalom's *Strange Alliance* (1991) is the classic history of POWs and the *contadini*, Eric Newby's *Love and War in the Apennines* (1971) the classic memoir. Recommendations for awards to helpers can be seen at TNA (WO 208/5451–60, 5479) and their voices heard in Janet Kinrade Dethick, *As If He Were My Brother* (2021).

On fascism and war, see Philip Morgan, *Italian Fascism, 1915–1945* (2003) and John Foot, *Blood and Power* (2022). See also memoirs by Wanda Newby, *Peace and War* (1991) and Iris Origo, *War in Val d'Orcia* (1947). I learned most about life in Paitone from Piero Garletti. I also benefitted from the stories in Nadia Massella's *Lessinia, 1943–1945* (2022) and Caterina Rossi Tonni's *I Giorni del Tesio* (1995).

John Gooch, *Mussolini's War* (2020) and Thomas X. Ferenczi, *Fascist Italy at War* (2024) describe Italy's defeat and ensuing civil conflict. On the Allied campaign and its impact on civilians, see James Holland's *The Savage Storm* (2023) and *Italy's Sorrow* (2008), David W. Ellwood, *Italy 1943–1945* (1985) and Richard Lamb, *War in Italy, 1943–1945* (1996).

On the resistance, see Roberto Battaglia, *The Story of the Italian Resistance* (1957) and Charles F. Delzell's 'The Italian Anti-Fascist Resistance in Retrospect', *Journal of Modern History*, 47 (1975). On resistance as civil war, see Claudio Pavone, *A Civil War*, trans. Peter Levy (2013), and for controversial revisionism Santo Peli, *Il Primo Anno della Resistenza* (2014).

On the experience of partisans: Ada Gobetti, *Partisan Diary*, trans. Jomarie Alano (2014) and Giovanni Pesce, *And No Quarter*, trans. Frederick M. Shaine (1972). See also *The Path to the Spiders' Nests* by

Italo Calvino, trans. Archibald Colquhoun (1998) and *A Private Affair* by Beppe Fenoglio, trans. Howard Curtis (2023). Primary source material came from the Archivio Storico della Resistenza Bresciana at the Università Cattolica del Sacro Cuore in Brescia, and the context from Rolando Anni, *Storia della Resistenza Bresciana* (2005) and Lodovico Galli, *Pagine di Verità* (1992).

For POWs and partisans see Malcolm Tudor, *Among the Italian Partisans* (2016), Gordon Lett, *Rossano: A Valley in Flames* (2011), Michael Ross, *From Liguria with Love* (1997) – republished in 2019 as *The British Partisan* – and C. E. T. Warren and James Benson, *The Broken Column* (1966), about a Camp 52 prisoner who escaped from a train. Darker memories haunt Stuart Hood's *Carlino* (1985).

The records of the Office of Strategic Services (OSS) are at NARA, with some microfilm copies in the Churchill Archives, Cambridge. OSS operational reports can be found in TNA (WO 204/11414–15, WO 219/40B, 5100). Many of these relate to collaboration with the Special Operations Executive (SOE), whose work in Italy is described in the papers of Martin Lam (IWM, Docs.16288).

On peace and reconstruction, see: Mark Gilbert, *Italy Reborn* (2024), Paul Ginsborg, *A History of Contemporary Italy* (1990) and Steven F. White, *Modern Italy's Founding Fathers* (2020). See also Philip Cooke, *The Legacy of the Italian Resistance* (2011). For the case of Brescia: *Quel Giorno, Che Giorno!* (n.d.), and Marcello Zane, *25 Aprile e Dintorni* (2004).

My knowledge of Tanzania came mostly from John Iliffe's *A Modern History of Tanganyika* (1979), and Godfrey Mwakikagile, *Life in Tanganyika in the Fifties* (2010). Also useful were articles by G. G. Hadjivayanis, 'Prisons in Tanzania', *East Africa Law Review*, 7 (1974), and David Williams, 'The Role of Prisons in Tanzania: An Historical Perspective', *Crime and Social Justice*, 13 (1980).

Combining past narratives and narratives of discovery is tricky. Howard Reid's *Dad's War* (2003) follows his father in Italy, a POW evader who left a memoir. A memoir by Gabrielle Ayers's father inspired her to do the same in *Luigi* (2020). Tom Carver explores his own father's trek in *Where the Hell Have You Been?* (2009). Wartime investigations unrelated to Italy also helped – full references here, since these aren't mentioned in the notes. Philippe Sands's *East West Street: On the Origins of Genocide and Crimes against Humanity* (London, 2016) and *The Rat Line: Love, Lies and Justice on the Trail of a Nazi Fugitive* (London, 2020) are outstanding. See also Bart van Es, *The Cut Out Girl: A Story of War and Family, Lost and Found* (London, 2018); Hadley Freeman, *House of Glass: The Story and Secrets of a Twentieth-Century Jewish Family* (London, 2020); Daniel Lee, *The SS Officer's Armchair: Uncovering the Hidden Life of a Nazi* (London, 2020); Angela Findlay, *In My Grandfather's Shadow: A Story of War, Trauma, and the Legacy of Silence* (London, 2022); and Joe Dunthorne, *Children of Radium: A Buried Inheritance* (London, 2025). Like me, Dunthorne took a few liberties with the chronology of his research 'for the sake of narrative progression' (p. 297).

On the subjectivity of research, see: Katie Barclay, 'Falling in Love with the Dead', *Rethinking History*, 22 (2018); Emily Robinson, 'Touching the Void: Affective History and the Impossible', *Rethinking History*, 14 (2010); and Sarah Fox, 'Archival Intimacies', *Transactions of the RHS*, 1 (2023). See also Michael Roper's 'The Unconscious Work of History', *Cultural and Social History*, 11 (2014) and, for some words of caution, David A. Bell, 'Ego-Histories', *New York Review of Books*, 70 (June 2023). On the uses of photos, see Susan Sontag, *On Photography* (1978) and Roland Barthes, *Camera Lucida*, trans. Richard Howard (1993). Wendy Lower's *The Ravine* (2021) inspired me to 'break the frame'.

Two articles – Michael Mayerfield Bell, 'The Ghosts of Place', *Theory and Society*, 26 (1997) and Tina Paphitis, 'Haunted Landscapes: Place, Past and Presence', *Time and Mind*, 13 (2020) – attuned me to 'hauntology' and the eeriness of landscape. My most penetrating insight into the 'spectral turn', however, came from psychoanalysis. 'What haunts us are not the dead,' suggests Nicolas Abraham, quoted by Philippe Sands in *East West Street* (p. xxv), 'but the gaps left within us by the secrets of others.'

Notes

Abbreviations

ASC	Allied Screening Commission
ASR	Archivio Storico della Resistenza Bresciana, Brescia
CMP	Corps of Military Police
ICRC	International Committee of the Red Cross, Geneva
IWM	Imperial War Museum, London
MSMT	Monte San Martino Trust archives, Cambridge University Library
NARA	National Archives and Records Administration, Maryland
RCP	Ralph Corps papers, private archive, Doncaster
TNA	The National Archives, Kew
TTM	The Tank Museum, Bovington, Dorset
WO	War Office, London

Prologue: The Dream

1 *Hansard*, UK Parliament, vol. 234 (Aug. 1961); John Whiteclay Chambers II (ed.), *The Oxford Companion to American Military History* (Oxford, 2000), p. 849.
2 On the pain of POWs returning home, see Alan Allport, *Demobbed: Coming Home after the Second World War* (New Haven, CT, 2009), pp. 90–91, 199–203, 205–6.

Chapter 1: War Relics

1 *Von Ryan's Express* (1965), dir. Mark Robson, based on a 1964 novel of the same name by David Westheimer. Shot down in 1942, Westheimer

was a POW in Stalag Luft III, and later wrote a television pilot set in Italy entitled *Campo 44*.

2 Luke Turner describes similar memories in *Men at War: Loving, Lusting, Fighting, Remembering, 1939–1945* (London, 2023).

3 P. R. Reid, *Colditz: The Colditz Story and The Latter Days* (London, 1972). On Reid's remaking of the story as his own, see Ben Macintyre, *Colditz: Prisoners of the Castle* (London, 2022), pp. 306–7.

4 *One Hundred Great Lives* (London, n.d. [1948]). I have it still. My sister wrote our names in the front, suggesting that this book mattered to us.

5 Arlette Farge, *The Allure of the Archives*, trans. Thomas Scott-Railton (New Haven, CT, 2013), p. 31: 'The archive is an excess of meaning, where the reader experiences beauty, amazement, and a certain affective tremor.' See also: Carolyn Steedman, *Dust* (Manchester, 2001), ch. 2, and Jacques Derrida, 'Archive Fever: A Freudian Impression', trans. Eric Prenowitz, *Diacritics*, 25 (1995), p. 57, where the 'compulsive, repetitive, and nostalgic desire for the archive' is likened to homesickness.

6 Tolstoy (1908) quoted in Isaiah Berlin, *The Hedgehog and the Fox* (New York, 1957), p. 25; Felix Gilbert, 'What Ranke Meant', *The American Scholar*, 56 (1987), pp. 393–7.

7 So said the great historian Raphael Samuel in 1990, quoted by Florence Sutcliffe-Braithwaite in the *London Review of Books*, 46 (May 2024), p. 20.

8 *The Glass Mountain* (1949), dir. Henry Cass, starring Michael Denison and Dulcie Gray, a box office hit, partly shot on location in Italy. See BFI Film Forever archive: https://web.archive.org/web/20120712175042/http://explore.bfi.org.uk/4ce2b71f35d7e.

Chapter 2: A Perfect Gentleman

1 Tony Armstrong, personal correspondence, 5 Apr. 2024; Winifred M. Renshaw, *An Ordinary Life: Memoirs of a Balby Childhood* (Doncaster, 1984); Derek and Enid Holland, *A Yorkshire Town: The Making of Doncaster* (n.p., 2013), esp. pp. 34, 57–64.

2 TNA, WO 423/436012, pp. 52–3; Tony Armstrong, personal correspondence, 5 Apr. and 19 Nov. 2024.

3 RCP, Certified Copy of Attestation, 9 May 1932; TNA, WO 423/436012, pp. 2, 16, 36.
4 TNA, WO 423/436012, pp. 2, 16, 36; RCP, Army Certificates of Education (20 Jul. 1932 and 15 Mar. 1933).
5 RCP, Regular Army Certificate of Service, 1932–5; TNA, WO 423/436012, pp. 2, 4.
6 Susan Sontag, *On Photography* (1978; London, 2019 edn), esp. pp. 24, 72, 121, 165–7. On deconstructing photographic 'reality', see also Roland Barthes, *Camera Lucida*, trans. Richard Howard (London, 1993); John Berger, *Understanding a Photograph*, ed. Geoff Dyer (London, 2013).
7 RCP, Royal Life Saving Society Elementary Certificate (Nov. 1935); St John's Ambulance Association, 'First Aid to the Injured' Certificates (Dec. 1935, re-examined Feb. 1936).
8 Mark Simner, 'Ancestors at Work: Military Police', *Who Do You Think You Are?*, 4 (2019).
9 Uys Krige, *The Way Out (Italian Intermezzo)* (London, 1946), p. 307.

Chapter 3: The Cauldron

1 TNA, WO 423/436012, pp. 2, 7.
2 Lionel F. Ellis, *The War in France and Flanders, 1939–1940*, ed. J. R. M. Butler (London, 1954), pp. 83, 87–92, 132–3, 196; H. F. Joslen, *Orders of Battle: Second World War, 1939–1945* (Uckfield, 2003), pp. 299, 301; N. H. Gibbs, *Grand Strategy: History of the Second World War*, vol. 1 (London, 1976), pp. 507, 514–15.
3 TNA, WO 166/605/1, minutes of conference, Divisional HQ (17 Mar. 1941); WO 423/436012, pp. 2, 4.
4 TNA, WO 423/436012, pp. 2, 4, 48.
5 See, for example: TNA, WO 166/5902–9 (1940–41).
6 TNA, WO 166/605/1; WO 166/617.
7 TNA, WO 423/436012, pp. 2, 8, 42; WO 169/4163, War Diary (Jan. 1942); photo at Transjordan border in RCP.
8 TNA, WO 169/4163, War Diary (Jan. 1942).
9 Ibid. Ralph's name appears at the entry for 20 Jan. 1942.

10 Ibid.; R. L. Crimp, *The Diary of a Desert Rat*, ed. Alex Bowlby (London, 1971), p. 38.
11 See the 1942 watercolour painting: https://www.iwm.org.uk/collections/item/object/4765.
12 Crimp, *Diary of a Desert Rat*, p. 35; Sven Lindqvist, *Desert Divers*, trans. Joan Tate (London, 2000), pp. 28–9, 65; Denis Avey with Rob Broomby, *The Man Who Broke into Auschwitz* (London, 2011), pp. 22–3.
13 TNA, WO 169/4163, War Diary (Feb.–Mar. 1942).
14 Lindqvist, *Desert Divers*, p. 52; John Cowtan, *From the Gazala Line to Behind the Lines*, ed. Jane Meredith (Milton Keynes, 2011), p. 25.
15 Crimp, *Diary of a Desert Rat*, pp. 73–9; Avey, *Man Who Broke into Auschwitz*, p. 50.
16 Lindqvist, *Desert Divers*, pp. 29, 49–51, 68–9; Crimp, *Diary of a Desert Rat*, pp. 22, 29–30, 35–9; Cowtan, *From the Gazala Line*, pp. 26–8; Alan Caillou, *The World Is Six Feet Square* (London, 1954), p. 1.
17 James Ambrose Brown, *Retreat to Victory: A Springbok's Diary in North Africa, Gazala to El Alamein, 1942* (Johannesburg, 1991), p. 89; Albert Winter, *Behind the Wire: Life as a POW during WWII* (Leeds, 2005), pp. 45, 50–51.
18 John Gooch, *Mussolini's War: Fascist Italy from Triumph to Collapse, 1935–1943* (London, 2020), p. 307; TNA, WO 169/4163, War Diary Pt. 2 – 229/10 (May 1942); IWM, Documents.22675 (Harold Rumsey), pp. 67–73.
19 Vivian Milroy, *Alpine Partisan* (London, 1957), pp. 7–8; Alan John Flederman, *And Direction Was Given: A Daring Escape from a POW Camp and a Dramatic Journey to Neutral Switzerland* (London, 2008), pp. 20–23.
20 Roy Farran, *Winged Dagger: Adventures on Special Service* (London, 1948), p. 141. See also Ken Ford, *Gazala 1942: Rommel's Greatest Victory* (Oxford, 2008), pp. 47–64.
21 Gordon Horner, *For You the War Is Over* (n.p., 1948), no page nos.; Cowtan, *From the Gazala Line*, pp. 41–2; IWM, Documents.4284 (G. A. Braithwait), pp. 1–2.
22 B. H. Liddell Hart (ed.), *The Rommel Papers* (New York, 1953), p. 212; Winter, *Behind the Wire*, pp. 48–50, 58.
23 Ford, *Gazala*, pp. 47–52; Ambrose Brown, *Retreat to Victory*, pp. 137–8.
24 Churchill quoted in Ben Reynolds, *Call Me Corp* (London, 2015), p. 16.

Chapter 4: In the Bag

1 Adrian Carton De Wiart, *Happy Odyssey* (Barnsley, 2007), p. 183. On the shame of capture, see A. J. Barker, *Behind Barbed Wire* (London, 1974), ch. 3. 'Defeat, grief, loss . . . so overwhelming a disaster that for a little while one's mind fails to grasp its significance': James Hargest, *Farewell Campo 12* (London, 1945; 1950 edn), pp. 17–18.
2 See Michael Ross, quoted in David M. Guss, *The 21 Escapes of Lt Alastair Cram: A Compelling Story of Courage and Endurance in the Second World War* (London, 2018), p. 13: 'I felt guilty and ashamed . . . I was suddenly a useless, almost helpless being, a parasite destined to be fed and housed until some day, mercifully, I should be set free.'
3 Quoted in James Holland, *The Savage Storm: The Battle for Italy 1943* (London, 2023), p. 57.
4 See film footage in IWM: AYY 191/1–2, AYY 283/2. See also IWM, Documents.25624 (Richard Hamilton Jones), pp. 13–14; IWM, Documents.24671 (George Peacock), pp. 67–8; Ian Murray, *Another Time, Another Life: My Life as a POW* (Cape Town, 2012), no page nos.; Eric Moss, *Solvitur Ambulando* (Swanage, 1990), p. 71.
5 IWM, Documents.17336 (A. J. Graham), p. 82; Pat Spooner, *A Talent for Adventure: The Remarkable Wartime Exploits of Lt Col Pat Spooner MBE* (Barnsley, 2012), p. 25; IWM, Documents.1755 (Abbie Jones), diary, July 1942; G. Norman Davison, *In the Prison of His Days: The Memoirs of a Captured World War II Gunner* (Leeds, 2009), p. 110; J. C. Mustardé, *The Sun Stood Still* (London, 1944), pp. 49–51; Alfred Nisbett, *Always Tomorrow – Sempre Domani* (London, 2008), pp. 31–2; R. G. W. Vasey, 'Prison Life in Italy', *Blackwood's Magazine*, 257 (Mar. 1945), p. 196.
6 John Bosman, *Providence Was My Guide* (n.p., n.d.), p. 83; IWM, Documents.17336 (A. J. Graham), pp. 83–5; Ian Bell, *And Strength Was Given* (Lowestoft, 1989), pp. 73–4; Harold Denny, *Behind Both Lines* (London, 1943), pp. 40–41; Hazel Spencer (ed.), *Till We Meet Again: Gunner Bert Martin, 1941–1945* (n.p., 2017), pp. 42–54; Hargest, *Farewell Campo 12*, p. 35. On the shit wagon, see Robert Briggs, *A Funny Kind of War: A Wartime Log* (London, 1985), pp. 42–4.

7 Robert Garioch, *Two Men and a Blanket: Memoirs of Captivity* (Edinburgh, 1975), pp. 17–18; Davison, *In the Prison of His Days*, p. 114; Denny, *Behind Both Lines*, p. 46.

8 TNA, WO 311/1206, testimony of Dennis Fuller, 30 May 1946; IWM, Documents.17336 (A. J. Graham), pp. 88–9; Dallas Allardice, *Friendship in a Time of War, 1939–46* (Dundee, 2004), pp. 196–9; G. C. Bateman, *Diary of a Temporary Soldier* (Guildford, 1986), pp. 61–2; Robert Dick, *I Was Not Alone* (Edinburgh, 1997), pp. 132–3; Bosman, *Providence Was My Guide*, pp. 85–6.

9 MSMT, Frank Osborne, p. 10. See also: Frank Unwin, *Escaping Has Ceased to Be a Sport: A Soldier's Memoir of Captivity and Escape in Italy and Germany* (Barnsley, 2018), pp. 10–12; Ken de Souza, *Escape from Ascoli: Story of Evasion and Escape* (Kent, 1989), pp. 64–6. For a terrifying account of being torpedoed, see Newman Robinson and Peter Ogilvie, *In the Bag* (Johannesburg, 1975), pp. 31–6.

10 IWM, Documents.3589 (W. Asquith), p. 83; Dick, *I Was Not Alone*, p. 133; Bell, *And Strength Was Given*, p. 77.

11 Fred Hirst, *A Green Hill Far Away* (Stockport, 1998), p. 51.

12 IWM, Documents.3589 (W. Asquith), pp. 85–6; MSMT, Frank Osborne, p. 12; Joan Chambers, *For You the War Is Over: The Story of H. R. (Aussie) Hammond* (Cape Town, 1967), ch. 6; Cyril Crompton and Peter Johnson, *Luck's Favours: Two South African Second World War Memoirs* (Fish Hoek, SA, 2010), pp. 144–5; Edward Ward, *Give Me Air* (London, 1946), pp. 23–9; Bosman, *Providence Was My Guide*, pp. 88–9; W. Wynne Mason, *Prisoners of War* (Wellington, NZ, 1954), p. 112.

13 John Cheetham, *Italian Interlude: The Experiences of a Prisoner-of-War in Italy, July 1942–June 1944* (n.p., 2000), p. 3.

14 RCP, Memoir, Book 1, p. 1.

Chapter 5: The Beehive

1 M. R. D. Foot and J. M. Langley, *MI9: Escape and Evasion 1939–1945* (London, 1979), p. 128.

2 It turned out the memoir had already been transcribed by a journalist,

Bill Ross, and published online for the BBC's *WW2 People's War* archive of memories. See https://www.bbc.co.uk/history/ww2peopleswar/stories/05/a4121605.shtml.

3 Domenico Bolognese et al., *Campo 65: La Memoria Che Resta* (Altamura, 2020), now available as *Camp 65: The Memory That Remains*, trans. Amy King (Altamura, 2024).

4 Bolognese et al., *Camp 65*, pp. 47–8, 110–12. For a strong photographic sense of the region, see Piero Castoro et al., *Guida al Parco Nazionale dell'Alta Murgia* (Altamura, 2005).

5 'È brutto ... È brutale regione': Francis S. Jones, *Escape to Nowhere* (1952; repr. St Albans, 1977), p. 132.

6 Statistics from the table at the 'Allies in Italy' website (English version), pp. 3–4: https://www.alleatiinitalia.it/en/camps/camp-tab/?ricerca=14.

7 TNA, WO 361/1898: visits 8 Apr. 1942 and 12 May 1942 (quotation). See also TNA, WO 224/127.

8 RCP Memoir, Book 1, p. 13.

9 Bosman, *Providence Was My Guide*, p. 96; IWM, Documents.17336 (A. J. Graham), p. 92.

10 IWM, Documents.17336 (A. J. Graham), pp. 92–3; IWM, Documents.3306 (John K. Glass), Diary Book 1, p. 36.

11 TNA, WO 361/1898; MSMT, Frank Osborne, p. 15; Cheetham, *Italian Interlude*, pp. 5, 10; IWM, Documents.3306 (John K. Glass), Diary Book 1, pp. 164–5. The Red Cross noted that the whitewashed walls were 'decorated by well-chosen pictures': TNA, WO 361/1898 (ICRC visit, 14 May 1943).

12 IWM, Documents.3306 (John K. Glass), Diary Book 1, p. 61.

13 RCP, Memoir, Book 3, p. 13.

14 Geoffrey D. Vaughan, *The Way It Really Was: A Prisoner of War During World War II Recounts* (Budleigh Salterton, 1985), pp. 17–18; IWM, Documents.3306 (John K. Glass), Diary Book 1, p. 31.

15 Avey, *Man Who Broke into Auschwitz*, p. 94.

16 On Cione's appearance, see TNA, WO 311/1211, assault on Silas Hickman (Jun. 1942).

17 Anthony Deane-Drummond, *Return Ticket* (London, 1953), pp. 43–6; George Clifton, *The Happy Hunted* (London, 1952), p. 257.
18 TNA, TS 26/744 (abuse of prisoner Dronfield).
19 RCP, Memoir, Book I, p. 2.
20 IWM, Documents.3306 (John K. Glass), Diary Book I, p. 65.
21 Ibid., pp. 69–70, 86.
22 IWM, LBY E. 16808, *Domani Griff*. Mentioned in IWM, Documents.3306 (John K. Glass), Diary Book I, p. 65.
23 Martin Schou, *Mountains of Freedom* (n.p., 2000), pp. 7–8.
24 IWM, Documents.3306 (John K. Glass), Diary Book I, pp. 28–30, 40, 46–7; Vaughan, *The Way It Really Was*, pp. 32–3; IWM, Documents.1050 (G. A. Puplett), no page nos. 'We were not in a position to covet our neighbour's wife,' wrote a POW in another camp, 'he had not got one with him': Deane-Drummond, *Return Ticket*, p. 78.
25 TNA, WO 423/436012, pp. 4, 5, 40–41.
26 TNA, WO 417/45, 48–9, Casualty Lists Nos. 865, 904, 925 (1942); Personal correspondence with ICRC, 15 Mar. 2023.
27 Noel Barber, *Prisoner of War: The Story of British Prisoners Held by the Enemy* (London, 1944), pp. 13–16.
28 *The Prisoner of War*, vol. I (May 1942–April 1943), blanket pattern in issue no. 3, July 1942, p. 15. See also Bateman, *Diary of a Temporary Soldier*, p. 53.
29 George Millar, *Horned Pigeon* (London, 1946), pp. 98–9.
30 Cheetham, *Italian Interlude*, p. 20; Clare Makepeace, *Captives of War: British Prisoners of War in Europe in the Second World War* (Cambridge, 2017), pp. 79, 111.
31 Harold Robinson letter, 9 Oct. 1942, personal archive of Sarah Hattersley.
32 Robinson and Ogilvie, *In the Bag*, p. 70.
33 Adrian Gilbert, *POW: Allied Prisoners in Europe, 1939–1945* (London, 2006), p. 94; Makepeace, *Captives of War*, pp. 102–4; Cheetham, *Italian Interlude*, p. 31.
34 Brian Stone, *Prisoner from Alamein* (London, 1944), pp. 120–21; Guss, *Alastair Cram*, p. 13; Barker, *Behind Barbed Wire*, pp. 78–80; Millar, *Horned Pigeon*, pp. 94–5; Makepeace, *Captives of War*, pp. 156, 161, 163–5.
35 Jack Rossiter, *'You'll Never Make It': The Escape Diary of Pte Jack Rossiter*,

August–September 1943 (Cirencester, 1992), p. 18; Vaughan, *The Way it Really Was*, pp. 17, 30; Winter, *Behind the Wire*, pp. 71–2; Eric Bull, *Go Right, Young Man*, 2nd edn (Bedale, 1997), p. 69; Robert H. Lee, 'The Enemy, My Friend', IWM, Documents.8017, vol. 1, p. 136.

36 Rossiter, *'You'll Never Make It'*, p. 18; Avey, *Man Who Broke into Auschwitz*, p. 98.

37 Winter, *Behind the Wire*, pp. 75, 80–81. 'While prisoners' memories often evoke the spirit of camaraderie . . . they also recount sectarian antagonism and hostility': Nunzia Cacciapaglia in Bolognese et al., *Camp 65*, p. 67.

38 Alex Franks quoted in Bolognese et al., *Camp 65*, p. 80.

39 IWM, Documents.3306 (John K. Glass), Diary Book 1, pp. 143–4; Vaughan, *The Way It Really Was*, pp. 30–31; Jones, *Escape to Nowhere*, p. 138.

40 Schou, *Mountains of Freedom*, pp. 7, 12–14; IWM, Documents.254 (Robert Heath).

41 Jones, *Escape to Nowhere*, pp. 138–9; IWM, Documents.17336 (A. J. Graham), pp. 94–5; Vaughan, *The Way It Really Was*, p. 31.

42 TNA, WO 310/13, Ill-treatment of POWs, Gravina; WO 311/1206, testimony of Dennis Fuller, 30 May 1946. On the arrival of medics and a padre in Camp 65, see IWM, Documents.3306 (John K. Glass), Diary Book 1, p. 94. The prisoner was Henry Williams, see his German POW registration card at TNA, WO 416/393/185, where in the photo he appears to be covering the scar on his neck.

43 Robinson and Ogilvie, *In the Bag*, pp. 54–6.

44 N. I. Robinson, *Missing, Believed Prisoner: The Story of a South African Prisoner of War* (Durban, 1944), pp. 61–2; IWM, Documents.3306 (John K. Glass), Diary Book 1, p. 68.

45 IWM, Documents.25624 (Richard Hamilton Jones), pp. 35, 37.

46 TNA, WO 208/5447/15, John Rossouw MI9 affidavit, p. 4; RCP, Memoir, Book 1, pp. 3–4.

47 Jones, *Escape to Nowhere*, pp. 135, 141. Coppola is described at TNA, WO 311/1206, testimony of Siro Gemelli, 27 Mar. 1946.

48 TNA, WO 423/436012, pp. 4, 5, 8.

49 Gilbert, *POW*, pp. 131–2; 'Allies in Italy', p. 8.

50 Bolognese et al., *Camp 65*, pp. 54–8; 'Allies in Italy', pp. 5–7; IWM, Documents.3306 (John K. Glass), Diary Book 1, pp, 79, 90.
51 Jones, *Escape to Nowhere*, p. 139.
52 Janet Kinrade Dethick, *Some Corner of a Foreign Field: Deaths behind the Lines in Italy, 1942–3* (London, 2022), pp. 14–15; Avey, *Man Who Broke into Auschwitz*, pp. 97–8; 'Allies in Italy', pp. 6–9.
53 TNA, TS 26/713, testimony of Arnold Lazarus, 23 Aug. 1945; IWM, Documents.3306 (John K. Glass), Diary Book 1, p. 54.
54 IWM, Documents.25624 (Richard Hamilton Jones), p. 36; IWM, LBY E. 16808, *Domani Griff* (16 Jun. 1942), p. 2; TNA, TS 26/713, testimony of John Gilmour, 19 Jul. 1945; WO 311/1206, testimonies of Leslie Boult, Ernest Eagan, Charles Brown, Joseph Caldwell and Wallace Murdoch; Winter, *Behind the Wire*, pp. 68, 79; IWM, Documents.17336 (A. J. Graham), pp. 93–4.
55 *The Prisoner of War*, vol. 1, no. 9 (Jan. 1943), p. 1.
56 IWM, Documents.17336 (A. J. Graham), pp. 105–6.
57 Bull, *Go Right, Young Man*, p. 54.
58 Winter, *Behind the Wire*, pp. 87–90.
59 Bolognese et al., *Camp 65*, p. 47.
60 Royden Henry Halse, 'My WWII Prisoner-of-War Escape' (2010), pp. 6, 8 – samilitaryhistory.org/diaries/halse.html.
61 IWM, Documents.3306 (John K. Glass), Diary Book 1, pp. 30, 124, 152; Cheetham, *Italian Interlude*, p. 31; Winter, *Behind the Wire*, pp. 72–3, 75.
62 Cheetham, *Italian Interlude*, pp. 31–2; Vaughan, *The Way It Really Was*, p. 30; TNA, TS 26/744 (abuse of prisoner Dronfield); Bosman, *Providence Was My Guide*, p. 97.

Chapter 6: Charlie

1 See S. P. MacKenzie, *The Colditz Myth: British and Commonwealth Prisoners of War in Nazi Germany* (Oxford, 2004); Macintyre, *Colditz*, pp. 21–4 and passim.
2 Vaughan, *The Way It Really Was*, p. 9.
3 Michael Ross, *From Liguria with Love: Capture, Imprisonment and Escape*

in *Wartime Italy* (London, 1997), p. 100; Clifton, *The Happy Hunted*, pp. 256–7; Deane-Drummond, *Return Ticket*, pp. 67–8, 70, 80. One POW thought that only 1 per cent of POWs even got the chance to escape: James B. Chutter, *Captivity Captive* (London, 1954), p. 9.

4 Barker, *Behind Barbed Wire*, ch. 11, quotation at p. 147; Gilbert, *POW*, pp. 262–3. For similar remarks, see Paul Brickhill, *Escape – or Die: Authentic Stories of the RAF Escaping Society* (London, 1952), p. 10 (introduction by H. E. Bates).

5 RCP, Memoir, Book 1, pp. 4–5.

6 TNA, WO 208/5583; International Bomber Command Centre Digital Archive, University of Lincoln, A.P. 1548, 'Instructions and guidance to all officers and men of the RAF regarding the precautions to be taken in the event of falling into the hands of the enemy', see https://ibccdigitalarchive.lincoln.ac.uk/omeka/collections/document/23599.

7 The Wests, like every other family, met scandal and shame with secrecy and deception, see Deborah Cohen, *Family Secrets: Living with Shame from the Victorians to the Present Day* (London, 2013), chs. 3–5.

8 TNA, MH 106/2257/674.

9 TNA, WO 363, 'Burnt Documents' (Archibald West).

10 TNA, AIR 79/2005/222512; *Western Morning News and Mercury* (23 Jul. 1931), p. 4; Ernie Bond, 'Charles Edwin West', *Mars & Minerva: The Journal of the Special Air Service*, vol. 6, no. 4 (1984), pp. 47–8.

11 *Hampshire Telegraph & Post* (31 May 1935), p. 5.

12 Tom Carver, *Where the Hell Have You Been? Monty, Italy and One Man's Incredible Escape* (London, 2009), pp. 9, 13.

13 See Gavin Mortimer, *The SAS in World War II* (Oxford, 2011), chs. 1–2; Ben Macintyre, *SAS: Rogue Heroes* (London, 2016), chs. 1–4.

14 Oliver Clutton-Brock and Raymond Crompton, *The Long Road: Trials and Tribulations of Airmen Prisoners from Stalag Luft VII (Bankau) to Berlin, June 1944–May 1945* (London, 2013), p. 350.

15 IWM, Documents.3306 (John K. Glass), Diary Book 1, p. 117.

16 Virginia Cowles, *The Phantom Major: The Story of David Stirling and the SAS Regiment* (London, 1958), p. 38.

17 For a full account of Operation Squatter, see Michael Asher, *The Regiment: The Real Story of the SAS* (London, 2008), pp. 45–7, 67–9.

18 Clutton-Brock and Crompton, *The Long Road*, pp. 127–8. Details vary between accounts.
19 Roger Stanton, 'Charles West – Airman with the SAS', *WW2 Escape Lines Memorial Society Newsletter*, 25 (2021).
20 'Of One Company: The Remarkable Story of the Birth of the SAS', BBC Radio 4, *Archive Hour*, presented by Gordon Stevens, broadcast 3 Feb. 2007.
21 Asher, *The Regiment*, pp. 66–7.
22 Clutton-Brock and Crompton, *The Long Road*, pp. 126–30, 357; Sir Chris Bonington in the *Mail on Sunday*, 2017 – https://www.dailymail.co.uk/femail/article-4937000/How-two-risk-taking-parents-inspired-SIR-CHRIS-BONINGTON.html.
23 Clutton-Brock and Crompton, *The Long Road*, pp. 128–9; Bond, 'Charles Edwin West', p. 48.
24 Stanton, 'Charles West'.
25 TNA, AIR 81/10384.
26 Jochen Prien et al., *Die Jagdfliegerverbände der Deutschen Luftwaffe, 1934 bis 1945*, 9 vols., viii (Eutin, 2004), p. 282. His name was Otto Schulz.
27 TNA, WO 208/3327/3078; Stanton, 'Charles West'.
28 Mustardé, *The Sun Stood Still*, pp. 63–9, quotation at p. 67; Spencer (ed.), *Till We Meet Again*, pp. 42–54.
29 Ward, *Give Me Air*, pp. 19–21; Spencer (ed.), *Till We Meet Again*, p. 51; IWM, Documents.24671 (George Peacock), pp. 69–70; de Souza, *Escape from Ascoli*, pp. 61–2; MSMT, Frank Osborne, pp. 8–9; Bosman, *Providence Was My Guide*, pp. 83–4; Spooner, *Talent for Adventure*, p. 25; Wynne Mason, *Prisoners of War*, pp. 107–9; Lee, 'The Enemy, My Friend', vol. 1, p. 121. For the use of kitbags as air raid protection, see TNA, WO 208/5447/15, John Rossouw MI9 affidavit, p. 1.
30 TNA, WO 392/21, Directorate of POWs, Italy Section 8, RAF, p. 3; John F. Leeming, *Always To-Morrow* (London, 1951), p. 64.
31 On Camp 85 Tuturano, see Wynne Mason, *Prisoners of War*, pp. 111–12; Ward, *Give Me Air*, pp. 2–9.
32 John K. Soper, 'War Time Memories, 1939–1945', in IWM, Documents.16771; Halse, 'My WWII Prisoner-of-War Escape', p. 7. For a

description of a Camp 65 blower, see Vincent van Reenen, 'A Soldier Remembers' (1992), IWM, Documents.3164, p. 42.
33 Quoted in Simon Schama, *Landscape and Memory* (London, 2004), p. 24.
34 Donald Pleasence had been shot down in an RAF bomber in 1944 and held captive in Stalag Luft I in Western Pomerania until the end of the war.

Chapter 7: Flashes and Sparks

1 IWM, Documents.3306 (John K. Glass), Diary Book 1, pp. 150–51, 154.
2 TNA, WO 416/3/417 (Alderson); RCP, Memoir, Book 1, p. 6. On the importance of food, see Jones, *Escape to Nowhere*, p. 135.
3 Winter, *Behind the Wire*, p. 88.
4 Bernard Foyster, aged twenty-six, from Kessingland, Lowestoft: TNA, 310/13. By then, diphtheria was endemic, see TNA, WO 361/1898 (ICRC visit, 14 May 1943).
5 IWM, Documents.19045 (Victor A. Long), diary entry for 21 Dec. 1942.
6 IWM, Documents.3306 (John K. Glass), Diary Book 1, p. 157; IWM, Documents.19045 (Victor A. Long), diary entry for 12 Jan. 1943; RCP, Memoir, Book 1, pp. 6–7.
7 Halse, 'My WWII Prisoner-of-War Escape', p. 7; IWM, Documents.3306 (John K. Glass), Diary Book 1, pp. 157–60; Documents.19045 (Victor A. Long), diary entries for 24–25 Dec. 1942; Documents.17336 (A. J. Graham), pp. 101–2, 110; Documents.4284 (G. A. Braithwaite), p. 3; Documents.1050 (G. A. Puplett), no page nos.; Leslie Williams, *Letters to My Daughter: Reminiscences of a POW* (Stockport, 2004), p. 61.
8 IWM, Documents.3306 (John K. Glass), Diary Book 1, pp. 46–7; Diary Book 2, pp. 1–2; Bosman, *Providence Was My Guide*, p. 99; TNA, WO 361/1898 (ICRC visit, 5 Mar. 1943).
9 TNA, WO 361/1898 (ICRC visit, 5 Mar. 1943). See also WO 224/127.
10 IWM, Documents.3306 (John K. Glass), Diary Book 2, p. 2; TNA, WO 361/1898 (ICRC visit, 5 Mar. 1943); RCP, Memoir, Book 1, p. 5.
11 TNA, TS 26/713, testimony of David Corcoran, 25 Jun. 1945. On

mepacrine, see: Lee, 'The Enemy, My Friend', vol. 1, p. 139; TNA, WO 361/1898 (ICRC visit, 14 May 1943).

12 Van Reenen, 'A Soldier Remembers', p. 41; IWM, Documents.3306 (John K. Glass), Diary Book 2, pp. 3–5, 9.

13 Rossiter, *'You'll Never Make It'*, p. 11.

14 TNA, WO 208/5447/15, John Rossouw MI9 affidavit, p. 3.

15 TNA, TS 26/713, testimony of Alan Bagnall, 23 Aug. 1945; Winter, *Behind the Wire*, pp. 82, 92.

16 Schou, *Mountains of Freedom*, pp. 15–17; Rossiter, *'You'll Never Make It'*, pp. 20–22; Williams, *Letters to My Daughter*, p. 59.

17 IWM, Documents.3306 (John K. Glass), Diary, 'Blocco per Note', p. 18; IWM, Documents.17336 (A. J. Graham), p. 105; Jones, *Escape to Nowhere*, p. 137; Vaughan, *The Way It Really Was*, p. 23; MSMT, Frank Osborne, pp. 15–16.

18 John Glass, *Memories of a POW* (Cirencester, 1994), pp. 17–18; Gilbert, *POW*, pp. 168–9.

19 IWM, Documents.3306 (John K. Glass), Diary Book 1, p. 62; Robinson and Ogilvie, *In the Bag*, pp. 72–3; TNA, 310/14 (Peden and Cruickshank, re. escape of 8 Jul. 1942).

20 Jones, *Escape to Nowhere*, p. 141; IWM, Documents.3306 (John K. Glass), Diary Book 1, pp. 130–31; Williams, *Letters to My Daughter*, pp. 57–8. On the Sector 5 escape, see TNA, WO 208/5447/15, John Rossouw MI9 affidavit, p. 4. This was probably the same escape where, according to another account, two men fled from *Sector 3* and were caught *twenty* miles away: Cheetham, *Italian Interlude*, p. 30.

21 RCP, Memoir, Book 1, pp. 8–9.

22 Ibid., pp. 9–10.

23 Ibid., pp. 10–11. 'Some pilots thought of stealing a plane, but this was beyond most of us and, so far as I know, was not successfully carried out': Douglas Flowerdew, *Finding the Way: Wartime Adventures in Italy 1942–43* (n.p., 1988), p. 29. See also Millar, *Horned Pigeon*, pp. 112–21. There were in fact several attempts, but only one was successful – by a Norwegian who made off in a German seaplane: Barker, *Behind Barbed Wire*, pp. 160–61.

24 RCP, Memoir, Book 1, pp. 15–16.

Chapter 8: Pursued Hares

1. The account of the escape comes from RCP, Memoir, Book 1, pp. 19–33.
2. Quotation at ibid., p. 23.
3. Ibid., pp. 25–6.
4. *Danger Within* (1959), dir. Don Chaffey and based on a 1952 novel, *Death in Captivity*, by Michael Gilbert, who had been a POW in PG 49 Fontanellato.

Chapter 9: Chi Va La!

1. RCP, Memoir, Book 1, p. 49.
2. Ibid., pp. 50–53.
3. Ross, *From Liguria with Love*, p. 77. See also Gilbert, *POW*, p. 122.
4. See Geoffrey P. Megargee et al., *The United States Holocaust Memorial Museum Encyclopedia of Camps and Ghettos, 1933–45*, 4 vols. (Washington, DC, 2018), iii, pp. 431–2.
5. RCP, Memoir, Book 1, pp. 58–64.
6. Ibid., pp. 69–70.
7. RCP, Memoir, Book 2, pp. 88–9.

Chapter 10: Noci

1. The arrest at Noci is described in detail in RCP, Memoir, Book 2, pp. 84–91.
2. In all, 230,000 Italian soldiers were sent to Russia, half of whom were killed or went missing, including 70,000 taken prisoner: John Foot, *Blood and Power: The Rise and Fall of Italian Fascism* (London, 2022), p. 246.
3. 'I am a mother of six children and I am poor but I have done everything I possibly could, as I was thinking of the anxiety those mothers

deprived of their children would be suffering.' So said one POW helper quoted in Janet Kinrade Dethick, *As If He Were My Brother: Italians and Escapers in Piedmont, 1943–1945* (n.p., 2021), p. 120.
4 RCP, Memoir, Book 2, pp. 91–2.
5 Ibid., p. 105.

Chapter 11: Passing Time

1 The return to Gravina is covered by RCP, Memoir, Book 2, pp. 124–36.
2 Robinson, *Missing, Believed Prisoner*, p. 73.
3 Ibid., p. 73; Robinson and Ogilvie, *In the Bag*, p. 73.
4 TNA, WO 361/1898 (5 Mar. 1943).
5 Italian War Ministry (17 Jul. 1942), see http://campifascisti.it/documento_doc.php?n=973.
6 TNA, WO 208/3324/64 (John Langdon).
7 *The Prisoner of War*, vol. 2, no. 15 (Jul. 1943), p. 3; TNA, WO 208/5447/15, John Rossouw MI9 affidavit, p. 4.
8 Macintyre, *Colditz*, ch. 7; Fry, *MI9*, pp. 148–9; Carver, *Where the Hell Have You Been?*, pp. 125–6.
9 RCP, Memoir, Book 3, pp. 3ff.
10 Ibid., pp. 20–21.
11 IWM, Documents.19045 (Victor A. Long), diary entry for 17 Mar. 1943, Bolognese et al., *Camp 65*, 'Violations of the Geneva Convention', pp. 84–6.
12 TNA, WO 311/1206, testimony of Attilio Coppola, 27 Mar. 1946; Peter Medd and Frank Simms, *The Long Walk Home: An Escape in Wartime Italy* (1951; expanded edn, London, 2019), p. 79. On the alleged 'order from Rome' to confiscate rings, see TNA, TS 26/713, testimonies of Alan Bagnall and Arnold Lazarus, 23 Aug. 1945.
13 TNA, WO 208/5447/15, John Rossouw MI9 affidavit, pp. 3–4.
14 'Allies in Italy', p. 10.
15 Clifton, *The Happy Hunted*, p. 276.
16 TNA, WO 416/228/418.

Chapter 12: The Bread Palace

1. TNA, TS 26/713, testimony of Ernest Riddell; WO 311/1206, testimonies of Ernest Riddell and Attilio Coppola; WO 310/13, Ill-treatment of POWs, Gravina; 'Allies in Italy', p. 10. The incident was reported to the Red Cross, see TNA, WO 361/1898 (ICRC visit, 14 May 1943).
2. TNA, TS 26/713, testimony of Major Hunter, SAMC.
3. Rossiter, *'You'll Never Make It'*, pp. 9, 11. See also William Lawson's liberation report, accessed via Ancestry.com, not found in TNA (though see WO 416/218/336).
4. TNA, WO 208/3324/64 (John Langdon). In his liberation report, Private David Kidd claimed not even to have attempted escape, perhaps ashamed about having twice failed – accessed via Ancestry.com, not found in TNA (but see WO 416/208/416).
5. RCP, Memoir, Book 3, p. 11.
6. Robinson and Ogilvie, *In the Bag*, p. 65.
7. Gilbert, *POW*, p. 112.
8. R. A. Radford, 'The Economic Organisation of a POW Camp', *Economica*, 12 (1945), pp. 189–201, quotation at p. 189.
9. Radford, 'Economic Organisation of a POW Camp', p. 199; Bosman, *Providence Was My Guide*, p. 96; IWM, Documents.17336 (A. J. Graham), p. 96; Vaughan, *The Way it Really Was*, p. 21; Alex Franks, quoted in Bolognese et al., *Camp 65*, pp. 71–2.
10. Robinson and Ogilvie, *In the Bag*, pp. 53–4.
11. Ibid., pp. 64–5; IWM, Documents.23373 (Christopher W. M. Wynes), pp. 32–3.
12. Cheetham, *Italian Interlude*, pp. 13–14; Lee, 'The Enemy, My Friend', vol. 1, pp. 139–40.
13. IWM, Documents.17336 (A. J. Graham), p. 96; Lee, 'The Enemy, My Friend', vol. 1, p. 140; Robinson and Ogilvie, *In the Bag*, p. 65.
14. Lee, 'The Enemy, My Friend', vol. 1, p. 144.
15. Max Löw, liberation report accessed via Ancestry.com, not found in TNA (but see WO 416/228/418).
16. Lee, 'The Enemy, My Friend', vol. 1, pp. 139–40.

17 Cheetham, *Italian Interlude*, pp. 13–14; Van Reenen, 'A Soldier Remembers', p. 43; MSMT, Frank Osborne, pp. 4–5, 21.
18 IWM, Documents.17336 (A. J. Graham), p. 95.
19 Raymond Andrew, *Survive for Tomorrow: Early Days to Prisoner of War* (n.p., n.d.), p. 50 – accessed via MSMT website.
20 Cheetham, *Italian Interlude*, p. 35; Jones, *Escape to Nowhere*, pp. 132–3, 135; Halse, 'My WWII Prisoner-of-War Escape', p. 7.
21 RCP, Memoir, Book 1, pp. 2–3.
22 IWM, Documents.23373 (Christopher W. M. Wynes), p. 30; Cheetham, *Italian Interlude*, p. 35; TNA, WO 310/14 (David Cruikshank).
23 TNA, WO 208/5447/15, John Rossouw MI9 affidavit, p. 7; TNA, WO 416/73/124. The accused man was Sergeant James Collins (235860, WO2, South African Land Forces, ended up in Stalag VIII-B Teschen).
24 TNA, WO 208/5447/15, John Rossouw MI9 affidavit, pp. 4, 7; Cheetham, *Italian Interlude*, p. 35; IWM, LBY E. 16808, *Domani Griff* (16 Jun. 1942), p. 3.
25 Robinson and Ogilvie, *In the Bag*, p. 70; Cheetham, *Italian Interlude*, p. 35. See also Makepeace, *Captives of War*, pp. 107–9. One POW recorded that the WOs in the huts at the top of each sector 'had their own batmen and by all accounts lived well': IWM, Documents.23373 (Christopher M. Wynes), p. 30.
26 Warrant Officers were not NCOs. As RSMs and CSMs, they did not hold commissions but unlike NCOs were addressed as 'sir': Alan Allport, *Browned Off and Bloody-Minded: The British Soldier Goes to War 1939–1945* (New Haven, CT, 2015), p. 328.
27 Halse, 'My WWII Prisoner-of-War Escape', p. 8; Cheetham, *Italian Interlude*, pp. 40–41. On free movement between sectors, see TNA, WO 361/1898 (ICRC visit, 14 May 1943).
28 Winter, *Behind the Wire*, pp. 82–5, 92–3.
29 TNA, WO 361/1898 (ICRC visit, 14 May 1943).
30 Cheetham, *Italian Interlude*, pp. 40–41.
31 RCP, Memoir, Book 1, pp. 6–7; Cheetham, *Italian Interlude*, p. 41.
32 RCP, Memoir, Book 1, p. 7.
33 Halse, 'My WWII Prisoner-of-War Escape', p. 8; Cheetham, *Italian*

Interlude, pp. 26–7. On POWs exploring boundaries of sexuality and gender, see Turner, *Men at War*, pp. 231–4.
34 Barker, *Behind Barbed Wire*, p. 134; Gilbert, *POW*, p. 119; Makepeace, *Captives of War*, pp. 114–22.
35 Dan Billany and David Dowie, *The Cage* (London, 1949). For a summary and analysis of their story, see Turner, *Men at War*, pp. 248–60.
36 Lee, 'The Enemy, My Friend', vol. 1, p. 149; IWM, Documents.17336 (A. J. Graham), p. 96; Robinson and Ogilvie, *In the Bag*, p. 70; IWM, Documents.23373 (Christopher W. M. Wynes), p. 32.
37 RCP, Memoir, Book 3, p. 32.

Chapter 13: Amapola

1 Philip Roth, *American Pastoral* (London, 1997), p. 35.
2 Italo Calvino, quoted by James Butler in the *London Review of Books*, 45 (Jun. 2023), p. 9.
3 Andrew, *Survive for Tomorrow*, pp. 44–5.
4 Jones, *Escape to Nowhere*, pp. 145–6; Roger Absalom, 'Allied Escapers and the *Contadini* in Occupied Italy (1943–5)', *Journal of Modern Italian Studies*, 10 (2005), p. 416.
5 *The Prisoner of War*, vol. 2, no. 16 (Aug. 1943), p. 7; Garioch, *Two Men and a Blanket*, p. 55.
6 Garioch, *Two Men and a Blanket*, p. 56; Jones, *Escape to Nowhere*, p. 147.
7 Chambers, *For You the War Is Over*, p. 40; Garioch, *Two Men and a Blanket*, p. 56.
8 RCP, Memoir, Book 3, p. 39.
9 'Allies in Italy', pp. 5–6; Jones, *Escape to Nowhere*, pp. 146–7; Herbert C. Macey, 'Life as an Italian POW' (1967), IWM, Documents.3282, p. 1; IWM, Documents.24671 (George Peacock), p. 78; TNA, WO 361/1890, summary of visits Apr.–Oct. 1942; Edwin N. Broomhead, *Barbed Wire in the Sunset* (Melbourne, 1945), p. 115.
10 Murray, *Another Time, Another Life*, no page nos.; Garioch, *Two Men and a Blanket*, p. 97.
11 Macey, 'Life as an Italian POW', p. 1.

12 Garioch, *Two Men and a Blanket*, p. 56.
13 Broomhead, *Barbed Wire in the Sunset*, pp. 113–14; Murray, *Another Time, Another Life*, no page nos.; Andrew, *Survive for Tomorrow*, p. 52. On peach and apple blossom, see *The Prisoner of War*, vol. 2, no. 14 (Jun. 1943), p. 2.
14 IWM, Documents.3238 (Herbert C. Macey), wartime log. See also Macey's liberation report, accessed via Ancestry.com.
15 On the history of the camp, see Massimo Minella, *Campo 52: Pian di Coreglia, 1941–1944* (Milan, 2019), chs. 5–7.
16 See data at https://www.alleatiinitalia.it/en/camps/camp-tab/?ricerca=50.
17 Murray, *Another Time, Another Life*, no page nos.
18 Macey, 'Life as an Italian POW', p. 2; IWM, Documents.17518 (D. Troop), p. 55.
19 Garioch, *Two Men and a Blanket*, pp. 55, 74; Chambers, *For You the War Is Over*, pp. 45–6; IWM, Documents.3189 (Stanley J. Doughty), p. 28; *The Prisoner of War*, vol. 2, no. 13 (May 1943), p. 1.
20 Broomhead, *Barbed Wire in the Sunset*, p. 127. For a photo of the shoes, see Minella, *Campo 52*, plates section.
21 Macey, 'Life as an Italian POW', p. 2; Murray, *Another Time, Another Life*, no page nos.; Chambers, *For You the War Is Over*, p. 44; TTM, Horace Wade archive, see https://www.lovefromscotland.co.uk/campo-52/.
22 William Cullen, *Italy – The Hard Way: Paddy Cullen's War Memoirs* (n.p., 2004), p. 14. Camp 65 Gravina, meanwhile, had also improved, see the telegram sent by the ICRC to London, 26 Jun. 1943: TNA, WO 336/1898.
23 IWM, Documents.8246 (E. C. Stirling), p. 35; Silvano Benedetti and Stefano Schiappacasse, *La Caserma di Caperana* (n.p., n.d.), pp. 33–4.
24 Macey, 'Life as an Italian POW', p. 1; Garioch, *Two Men and a Blanket*, pp. 62–3; Francis S. Jones, *Hit or Miss: Being the Adventures of Driver Randle Barlow* (London, 1954), pp. 133–8; Chambers, *For You the War Is Over*, pp. 51–3; Murray, *Another Time, Another Life*, no page nos.; IWM, Documents.17518 (D. Troop), p. 55; Jim Henderson, *Gunner Inglorious* (Wellington, NZ, 1945), pp. 149, 171–2.
25 Jones, *Escape to Nowhere*, pp. 150, 154–6; Chambers, *For You the War Is Over*, pp. 60–61.

26 Macey, 'Life as an Italian POW', p. 2; *The Prisoner of War*, vol. 1, no. 11 (Mar. 1943), p. 6; MSMT, Les Hutty; TNA, WO 361/1890 (ICRC visits, 20 Jan. and 21 Apr. 1943); Broomhead, *Barbed Wire in the Sunset*, p. 115.

27 IWM, Documents.460 (Ernest Carter), pp. 44–5; Documents.3238 (Herbert C. Macey), wartime log; Documents.3189 (Stanley J. Doughty), p. 30; Documents.16202 (Arthur Pailin), diary transcription, p. 7; Documents.22675 (Harold G. Rumsey), war diary, no. 7, p. 76; MSMT, Les Hutty; *The Prisoner of War*, vol. 2, no. 16 (Aug. 1943), p. 10.

28 IWM, Documents.24671 (George Peacock), p. 81.

29 Chambers, *For You the War Is Over*, p. 49; IWM, Documents.3238 (Herbert C. Macey), wartime log; Harold. G. Rumsey, 'Behind the Wire', IWM, Documents.22675, p. 78; IWM, Documents.16202 (Arthur Pailin), diary transcription, pp. 4–6.

30 *The Prisoner of War*, vol. 1, no. 11 (Mar. 1943), pp. 7–8; IWM, Documents.3238 (Herbert C. Macey), wartime log; Barber, *Prisoner of War*, pp. 87–8. Rumsey claimed this play was *Pygmalion*, but Elena Passalacqua has shown it was *The Importance of Being Earnest*: personal correspondence, 22 Nov. 2024.

31 Macey, 'Life as an Italian POW', p. 2. See also IWM, Documents.3238 (Herbert C. Macey), wartime log; Documents.24671 (George Peacock), p. 81.

32 Macey, 'Life as an Italian POW', introduction; IWM, Documents.3189 (Stanley J. Doughty), p. 29; Documents.20342 (R. K. Kinton), p. 31; Cyril Medley, 'The Day the War Began', IWM, Documents.12337, p. 24; Murray, *Another Time, Another Life*, no page nos.; Chambers, *For You the War Is Over*, pp. 45, 56–7.

33 IWM, Documents.22675 (Harold G. Rumsey), war diary, no. 7, p. 77.

34 Fred Frost, 'There and Back, 1939–1945' (1996), no page nos., IWM Documents.20705. In 1950 Reg Allen was transferred to Manchester United for £11,000 – a new world record for the transfer of a goalkeeper.

35 Murray, *Another Time, Another Life*, no page nos.

36 Macey, 'Life as an Italian POW', p. 2.

37 TNA, WO 311/317, testimony of Daniel Paul, 1946.

38 *The Prisoner of War*, vol. 2, no. 16 (Aug. 1943), p. 7. For similar letters, see IWM, Documents.20705 (Fred. C. Frost); *The Prisoner of War*, vol. 1, no. 1 (May 1942), p. 10.

39 Basil Brudenell-Woods, *Four Packs to Freedom* (East Roseville, NSW, 1998), p. 25.
40 IWM, Documents.8246 (E. C. Stirling), p. 36; Garioch, *Two Men and a Blanket*, pp. 90–91.
41 Broomhead, *Barbed Wire in the Sunset*, pp. 113, 128; Chambers, *For You the War Is Over*, p. 57; Benedetti and Schiappacasse, *Caserma di Caperana*, p. 34; Macey, 'Life as an Italian POW', p. 2. The Red Cross described these walks as happy, healthy excursions 'during which there is occasion to climb hills and enjoy a fine view on the coast and on the sea': TNA, WO 361/1890 (ICRC visit, 21 Apr. 1943).
42 IWM, Documents.22675 (Harold G. Rumsey), war diary, no. 7, p. 76; Documents.460 (Ernest Carter), p. 44; Chambers, *For You the War Is Over*, pp. 49–50; Broomhead, *Barbed Wire in the Sunset*, p. 121.
43 IWM, Documents.22675 (Harold G. Rumsey), war diary, no. 7, p. 77; Broomhead, *Barbed Wire in the Sunset*, p. 120; Andrew, *Survive for Tomorrow*, p. 48; Frost, 'There and Back', no page nos.
44 IWM, Documents.460 (Ernest Carter), p. 46; Documents.17518 (D. Troop), p. 57. 'Lili Marlene' was also played in POW camps, filling men with romantic nostalgia, see Guy Weymouth, *A.W.O.L.: In an Italian Prison Camp and Subsequent Adventures on the Run in Italy 1943–1944* (London, 1993), pp. 41–2.
45 Chambers, *For You the War Is Over*, p. 40.
46 Rumsey, 'Behind the Wire', pp. 78–80.
47 See https://nzetc.victoria.ac.nz/etexts/WH2-1Epi/WH2-1Epi-1012b.jpg.
48 TNA, WO 344/17/1 (William Barker).
49 TNA, WO 311/317, war crimes affidavit of R. K. Bates, 5 Feb. 1946.
50 RCP, Memoir, Book 3, pp. 39, 41.

Chapter 14: Days of Hope

1 I am indebted to Janet Kinrade Dethick for making this introduction. See her *An Insatiable Curiosity: A Personal Journey through Wartime Italy* (n.p., 2024), ch. 14.

2. An annual ceremony is held, see 'Calvari: Camp 52 Commemorates the Victims of the Deportations', *Levante News* (21 Jan. 2022) – www.levantenews.it.
3. MSMT, William Strachan, pp. 2–9; IWM, Documents.17518 (D. Troop), pp. 57–60.
4. MSMT, William Strachan, pp. 9–10; TNA, WO 311/317, 311/1209, 311/1243; TS 26/417; TS 26/712, testimony of William Strachan, 8 Jun. 1945.
5. Macey, 'Life as an Italian POW', p. 2; Chambers, *For You the War Is Over*, pp. 46–7; TNA, TS 26/712, testimony of James Downey (24 Jul. 1945) and Walter Bindon (23 Apr. 1945); WO 311/1206, testimony of Glyn Sells, 1945; WO 311/317, testimony of John Shimmin (12 Jun. 1946).
6. Van Reenen, 'A Soldier Remembers', p. 41. See also Eric Garrad-Cole, *Single to Rome* (London, 1955), pp. 61–3; Macintyre, *Colditz*, pp. 150–51, 173–4.
7. IWM, Documents.460 (Ernest Carter), pp. 46–7; IWM, Documents.3189 (Stanley J. Doughty), p. 29.
8. Garioch, *Two Men and a Blanket*, pp. 92–3, 95.
9. Victor Emmanuel III quoted in Thomas X. Ferenczi, *Fascist Italy at War, 1939–1943* (Stroud, 2024), p. 222. This episode is covered well in Gooch, *Mussolini's War*, pp. 390–410.
10. See the illustration in Marco Minardi, *Bugle Call to Freedom: The POW Escape from Camp PG 49, Fontanellato 1943*, trans. John Simkins (London, 2020), p. 51.
11. Barber, *Prisoner of War*, pp. 40–44; *The Prisoner of War*, vol. 1, no. 1 (May 1942), p. 10. On anxiety about returning to a changed world, see ibid., vol. 2, no. 15 (Jul. 1943), p. 1.
12. John Verney, *Going to the Wars: A Journey in Various Directions* (London, 1955), p. 121.
13. For a POW returning from Italy to find that his wife hardly recognized him and their daughter not all, see Jack Bishop, *In Pursuit of Freedom* (London, 1977), p. 126.
14. Frost, 'There and Back', no page nos.; IWM, Documents.460 (Ernest Carter), pp. 46–7.
15. Cullen, *Italy – The Hard Way*, p. 7.
16. Fabio Zavatteri, personal communication, 8 Sept. 2023.

17 Archivi del Campo di Lavoro PG 148, Biblioteca Civica, Bussolengo, Verona, letter from Doris Angus to William H. Angus, 26 Jun. 1943. On this archive, see Mauro V. Quattrina, *Da Prigionieri ad Alleati: Bussolengo, dal Campo di Lavoro per Prigionieri di Guerra no. 148 al 25 Aprile 1945* (Bussolengo, 2007); Rosamond Roughton, 'The Bussolengo Letters', in Bolognese et al., *Camp 65*, pp. 133–51.
18 Ibid., Herma Falletisch to Ian Murray, 17 May 1943.
19 TTM, Horace Wade archive, see https://www.lovefromscotland.co.uk/campo-52/.
20 *The Prisoner of War*, vol. 2, no. 16 (Aug. 1943), p. 8; IWM, Documents.20705 (Fred C. Frost), letter of 21 Jul. 1943; Documents.15477 (Charles Saunders), postcard, 18 Aug. 1943.
21 IWM, Documents.16202 (Arthur Pailin), diary transcription, p. 8; Documents.8246 (E. C. Stirling), p. 36; Documents.3238 (Herbert C. Macey), wartime log.

Chapter 15: A Hole in the Floor

1 Murray, *Another Time, Another Life*, no page nos.; Jones, *Hit or Miss*, pp. 145–50.
2 Jones, *Escape to Nowhere*, p. 167.
3 On the weather and the mood that day, see Ian English (ed.), *Home by Christmas?* (n.p., 1997), pp. 33–4.
4 RCP, Memoir, Book 3, pp. 46–7.
5 Carver, *Where the Hell Have You Been?*, p. 134.
6 Benedetti and Schiappacasse, *Caserma di Caperana*, p. 37.
7 Dominick Graham, *The Escapes and Evasions of 'An Obstinate Bastard'* (York, 2000), pp. 152–3; Ian Reid, *Prisoner at Large: The Story of Five Escapes* (London, 1947; 1976 edn), p. 12.
8 Jones, *Escape to Nowhere*, pp. 163–4; Cullen, *Italy – The Hard Way*, p. 8; IWM, Documents.460 (Ernest Carter), p. 47.
9 Carver, *Where the Hell Have You Been?*, pp. 133–5; Rex Woods, *Special Commando: The Wartime Adventures of Lt-Col Robert Wilson, DSO and Bar* (London, 1985), pp. 91–4.

10 TNA, WO 208/5447/15, John Rossouw MI9 affidavit, p. 5; WO 311/317, testimony of Ernesto Ramezzano, 16 May 1946; Jones, *Escape to Nowhere*, pp. 164–5.
11 Jones, *Hit or Miss*, pp. 145–50; Cullen, *Italy – the Hard Way*, pp. 8–9.
12 Jones, *Escape to Nowhere*, p. 167; IWM, Documents.460 (Ernest Carter), pp. 47–8.
13 IWM, Documents.3189 (Stanley J. Doughty), p. 30.
14 IWM, Documents.460 (Ernest Carter), p. 48.
15 Foot, *Blood and Power*, pp. 261–6; Foot and Langley, *MI9*, pp. 169–76, 239; Carver, *Where the Hell Have You Been?*, pp. 136–41.
16 Absalom, 'Allied Escapers and the *Contadini*', p. 413; Holland, *Savage Storm*, p. 195.
17 Bolognese et al., *Camp 65*, p. 63, footnote 11.
18 RCP, Memoir, Book 3, p. 43.
19 Frost, 'There and Back', no page nos.; Karen Horn, 'South African Prisoner-of-War Experience during and after World War II: 1939–c.1950', PhD thesis, Stellenbosch University, 2012, p. 146. See also the testimony of Ronald Myburgh at https://powcamp52.weebly.com/the-armistice.html. The German note is reproduced in Benedetti and Schiappacasse, *Caserma di Caperana*, p. 69.
20 Cullen, *Italy – The Hard Way*, pp. 10–11; Jones, *Escape to Nowhere*, pp. 165–6.
21 Jones, *Escape to Nowhere*, p. 166; Cullen, *Italy – The Hard Way*, p. 13.
22 Roger Absalom, 'Hiding History: The Allies, the Resistance and the Others in Occupied Italy 1943–1945', *Historical Journal*, 38 (1995), pp. 111–12. See also idem, 'Allied Escapers and the *Contadini*', pp. 413–17 and p. 413 for quotation (paraphrased in Holland, *Savage Storm*, p. 195); Gilbert, *POW*, pp. 283–8; Foot and Langley, *MI9*, pp. 171, 176–7.
23 Brudenell-Woods, *Four Packs to Freedom*, pp. 30–31.
24 Frost, 'There and Back', no page nos.; IWM, Documents.460 (Ernest Carter), pp. 48–9; Documents.24671 (George Peacock), p. 92; Documents.3189 (Stanley J. Doughty), p. 30.
25 W. H. Strachan, 'Farewell Camp Fifty-Two!', MSMT, pp. 1, 3.
26 W. H. Strachan, 'Escape from Camp 52', MSMT, p. 10; idem, 'Farewell Camp Fifty-Two!', pp. 2–4; idem, 'Disaster at Sesta Godano', MSMT, pp. 1–2; TNA, TS 26/712, testimony of William Strachan, 8 Jun. 1945.

27 Cullen, *Italy – The Hard Way*, p. 12.
28 Ibid., pp. 12–14.
29 TNA, TS 26/417; WO 311/1243.
30 There's confusion about dates of departure. Ralph said they left on 12 September, Charlie on the 11th – but William Barker's liberation report says he escaped on the 14th, so the 12th must be right. Harold Rumsey left Camp 52 that day: Sunday 12th, at 2.30pm. Cross-referencing other memoirs suggests there were four batches: 11, 12, 13, 14 September.
31 Macey, 'Life as an Italian POW', introduction.
32 Jones, *Escape to Nowhere*, p. 168; Cullen, *Italy – The Hard Way*, pp. 14–15; Rumsey, 'Behind the Wire', p. 82; IWM, Documents.460 (Ernest Carter), pp. 50–52, 54–62, 64.
33 Minella, *Campo 52*, pp. 73–4; Cullen, *Italy – The Hard Way*, pp. 14–15; Jones, *Escape to Nowhere*, p. 168; Medley, 'The Day the War Began', p. 25; IWM, Documents.24671 (George Peacock), p. 93.
34 Cullen, *Italy – The Hard Way*, pp. 15–17; IWM, Fred Frost, 'There and Back', no page nos.; Medley, 'The Day the War Began', p. 25.
35 Rumsey, 'Behind the Wire', p. 82; Cullen, *Italy – The Hard Way*, pp. 18–19.
36 See, for example, Briggs, *Funny Kind of War*, p. 121; Millar, *Horned Pigeon*, p. 158; Ward, *Give Me Air*, p. 106; Guss, *Alastair Cram*, p. 176. As with the sea crossing, men stressed that they had been transported like livestock.
37 Described in IWM, Documents.18136 (Albert H. Brown), pp. 9–10. For the photo, see: www.awm.gov.au/collection/C56078.
38 IWM, Documents.24671 (George Peacock), pp. 93–4; Cullen, *Italy – The Hard Way*, p. 21; IWM, Documents.17518 (D. Troop), p. 62; Frost, 'There and Back', no page nos.
39 C. E. T. Warren and James Benson, *The Broken Column: The Story of James Frederick Wilde's Adventures with the Italian Partisans* (London, 1966), pp. 24–9. See also Jim Wilde's liberation report, accessed via Ancestry.com, which states that he escaped on 13 September.
40 TNA, WO 208/3324/64 (John Langdon); Medd and Simms, *Long Walk Home*, pp. 76–7.
41 Cullen, *Italy – The Hard Way*, pp. 18–19, 22–4.
42 Evan Llewellyn Edwards, liberation report, accessed via Ancestry.com.
43 RCP, Memoir, Book 3, p. 47.

44 IWM, Documents.3189 (Stanley J. Doughty), p. 31.
45 TNA, WO 208/5447/15, John Rossouw MI9 affidavit, p. 5; Garrad-Cole, *Single to Rome*, pp. 7–10; IWM, Documents.17518 (D. Troop), p. 62; Robinson and Ogilvie, *In the Bag*, pp. 79–80; Brudenell-Woods, *Four Packs to Freedom*, p. 32; Guss, *Alastair Cram*, p. 182.
46 Rumsey, 'Behind the Wire', p. 82.
47 Rex Woods, *Night Train to Innsbruck: A Commando's Escape to Freedom* (London, 1983), pp. 77–8.
48 TNA, WO 344/73/2 (Corps); WO 344/339/2 (West).
49 Cullen, *Italy – The Hard Way*, pp. 18–19, 20; Jan Bolwell, *Milord Goffredo: A Daughter Rediscovers Her Father's War in Italy* (Wellington, NZ, 2002), no page nos.; Warren and Benson, *The Broken Column*, p. 23.
50 TNA, WO 311/317, war crimes affidavit of R. K. Bates, 5 Feb. 1946; WO 208/5447/15, John Rossouw MI9 affidavit, p. 6.
51 Woods, *Special Commando*, pp. 133–5. For Desmond Haslehust's remarkable story, see also http://www.worcestershireregiment.com/pow_haslehust.php.
52 TNA, WO 344/17/1 (William Barker).
53 Warren and Benson, *The Broken Column*, p. 28.
54 On the mid-September moon: Laurie du Preez, *Inside the Cage* (Cape Town, 1973), p. 131.

Chapter 16: The Fig Tree

1 TNA, WO 344/73/2 (Corps); WO 344/339/2 (West).
2 Philip Morgan, *Italian Fascism, 1915–1945*, 2nd edn (Basingstoke, 2004), ch. 8. Mussolini resided there in a state of 'resigned and depressed impotence': ibid., p. 229.
3 On the world of the *contadini*, see Paul Ginsborg, *A History of Contemporary Italy: Society and Politics, 1943–1988* (London, 1990), pp. 23–8; Iris Origo, *War in Val d'Orcia: An Italian War Diary, 1943–1944* (London, 1947; 2003 edn), pp. 22–4; Howard Reid, *Dad's War* (London, 2003), pp. 44–5, 72, 81–2, 100.
4 Medd and Simms, *Long Walk Home*, p. 57. See also Stuart Hood, *Carlino* (Manchester, 1985), p. 69.

5. Les Dann, *Laughing We Ran* (Heighington, 1995), p. 76; Tony Davies, *When the Moon Rises: An Escape through Wartime Italy* (London, 1973), pp. 40–41; Medd and Simms, *Long Walk Home*, p. 112; Reid, *Prisoner at Large*, p. 53; Gordon Lett, *Rossano: A Valley in Flames, An Adventure of the Italian Resistance* (Barnsley, 2011), p. 19.
6. Absalom, 'Allied Escapers and the *Contadini*', p. 413; idem, 'Hiding History', pp. 111–12.
7. Roger Absalom, *A Strange Alliance: Aspects of Escape and Survival in Italy, 1943–45* (Florence, 1991), quotation at p. 7; Hood, *Carlino*, pp. 135–6; Absalom, 'Allied Escapers and the *Contadini*', p. 421. On amity between POWs and Italians, see also: Gabreille Ayers, *Luigi: A True Story of a Journey through Time* (Tolworth, 2020); Anne Copley, *The Girl with a Peach: Courage and Compassion in Wartime Italy* (London, 2024); Susan Jacobs, *Fighting with the Enemy: New Zealand POWs and the Italian Resistance* (Auckland, NZ, 2003).
8. Minardi, *Bugle Call to Freedom*, p. 79.
9. Dethick, *As If He Were My Brother*, p. 10; Malcolm Tudor, *Beyond the Wire: A True Story of Allied POWs in Italy 1943–1945* (Powys, 2009), pp. 3–8.
10. TNA, FO 371/73168; Tudor, *Beyond the Wire*, pp. 7–8; Absalom, 'Hiding History', pp. 128–9; Absalom, *Strange Alliance*, pp. 317–20. The NARA website surveys the ASC's work: www.archives.gov – Records of the Allied Screening Commission within Records of Allied Operational and Occupation HQ, WW2 (Record Group 331): Helper Claims, 7/1944 – 4/1947.
11. Anne Copley, an MSMT trustee (and author of *The Girl with a Peach*), personal communication, 21 Aug. 2022.

Chapter 17: Farewell at Molina

1. NARA, ASC, Vittorina Radaelli, claim 75,614. Cirillo Fumaneri's file was numbered 75,613, suggesting that in 1946 he and Vittorina submitted their claims together and were paid at the same time, as the receipts are also consecutively numbered.
2. Arnaldo Testi, personal communication, 31 Oct. 2022.

3 Hood, *Carlino*, p. 45.
4 Mentioned by many POWs in hiding, see Donald I. Jones, *Escape from Sulmona* (New York, 1980), p. 111; Krige, *The Way Out*, pp. 25–3.
5 Absalom, 'Hiding History', pp. 118–19; Reid, *Dad's War*, p. 142; Medd and Simms, *Long Walk Home*, p. 44; Eric Newby, *Love and War in the Apennines* (London, 1971), p. 94 (quotation); Bull, *Go Right, Young Man*, p. 322; Hirst, *A Green Hill Far Away*, p. 87.
6 Joseph Orna, *The Escaping Habit: The Most Audacious Escape Saga of WW2* (London, 1975), p. 135.
7 On the change in weather in October 1943, see Davies, *When the Moon Rises*, pp. 142–3; Philip Kindersley, *For You the War Is Over* (New York, 1983), p. 93.
8 Ronald Mann, *Moving the Mountain* (London, 1995), pp. 35–6.
9 Flederman, *And Direction Was Given*, p. 57.
10 NARA, ASC, Francesco Sega, claim 34,650. Francesco's son Battista also submitted a form, but his claim, no. 34,650, was added to his father's.
11 Cullen, *Italy – The Hard Way*, pp. 102–10.
12 NARA, ASC, Emilio Assogna, claim 34,652.
13 TNA, WO 344/73/2.
14 T. S. Eliot, 'Little Gidding', *Four Quartets* (New York, 1943), v. 5.

Chapter 18: Sega di Ala

1 On Cardinal Bartolomeo Bacilieri and his distinguished family, see https://archiviostorico.diocesiverona.it/images/Immagini_articoli/Pubblicazioni_on_line/documenti/CRONOTASSI/BACILIERI.pdf.
2 NARA, ASC, Domenico Veronesi, claim 35,151. See also Woods, *Special Commando*, ch. 17.
3 For the full story, see Nadia Massella, *Lessinia, 1943–1945* (Verona, 2022), pp. 218–19.
4 NARA, ASC, Gino Antolini, claim 34,656.
5 This was Desmond Haslehust: Woods, *Special Commando*, pp. 178–9.
6 See here a receipt for 10,000 lire, 2 May 1946: NARA, ASC, Emilio Assogna, claim 34,652. However, Assogna pleaded with the ASC for

over a year, seen in the extensive correspondence here. Cf. claim 35,179 (Pietro Marogna).

Chapter 19: Rodolfo

1 Origo, *War in Val d'Orcia*, p. 10.
2 NARA, ASC, Francesco Sega, claim 34,650.
3 TNA, WO 208/3327/3078.
4 John Verney, *A Dinner of Herbs* (London, 1966), p. 67.
5 Peter Stainforth, *Wings of the Wind* (London, 1952), p. 189.
6 Reid, *Prisoner at Large*, p. 75.
7 Ralph told MI9: 'People in this area were very afraid of the Germans and I could obtain very little assistance': TNA, WO 344/73/2. See also Foot and Langley, *MI9*, p. 268.
8 Sam Derry, *The Rome Escape Line: The Story of the British Organization in Rome for Assisting Escaped Prisoners-of-War, 1943–44* (London, 1960), pp. 196–7.
9 G. H. Harris, *Prisoner of War and Fugitive* (Aldershot, 1947), chs. 11–13.
10 Described in Kindersley, *For You the War Is Over*, p. 112.
11 TNA, WO 344/73/2; NARA, ASC, Angelo Maccarinelli, claim 54,907 ('Pro-Memoria').
12 R. G. W. Vasey, 'Escape', *Blackwood's Magazine*, 256 (Nov. 1944), p. 304; Hood, *Carlino*, pp. 28–9; English (ed.), *Home by Christmas?*, pp. 42–3, 74–9.
13 Malcolm J. Mason, *The Way Out: A Kiwi Escapes in Italy* (Hamilton, NZ, 1946), p. 22; Mann, *Moving the Mountain*, p. 29; Krige, *The Way Out*, pp. 65–6.
14 Krige, *The Way Out*, p. 86. On Christmas 1943, see Milroy, *Alpine Partisan*, p. 93.
15 Allardice, *Friendship in a Time of War*, pp. 236–7.
16 Moss, *Solvitur Ambulando*, pp. 113–14; Unwin, *Escaping Has Ceased to Be a Sport*, pp. 110–11. For a description of a typical peasant house, see John Esmond Fox, *Spaghetti and Barbed Wire* (Derbyshire, 1988), p. 90.
17 Mann, *Moving the Mountain*, pp. 29–30; Roy Marlow, *Beyond the Wire* (London, 1983), p. 66.

18 TNA, WO 344/73/2, General Questionnaire Pt. III. See also Kindersley, *For You the War Is Over*, p. 89.
19 Arthur Page, *Una Bella Passeggiata: Or a Walk in Wartime Italy* (Swindon, 1995), p. 40; Gilbert, *POW*, pp. 279–80; Halik Kochanski, *Resistance: The Underground War in Europe, 1939–45* (London, 2022), pp. 81–2. See Robert Briggs's cartoon of three stereotypically English evaders with moustaches and pipes, wearing peasant clothes, stranded on a mountain: *Funny Kind of War*, p. 73.
20 The dedication actually said *January* 1944 – but this was probably a mistake on Doro Garletti's part, since Ralph wasn't installed at the house until February.
21 On breaking the frame, see Wendy Lower, *The Ravine: A Family, a Photograph, a Holocaust Massacre Revealed* (London, 2021), esp. p. 6.
22 A story told by Janet Kinrade Dethick in *An Insatiable Curiosity*, pp. 124–5.
23 Augusto and Pietro Chiodi appear on the manifest of the *Prinzess Irene* out of Genoa, arriving in New York on 7 Apr. 1910, see https://heritage.statueofliberty.org/passenger-details/czoxMjoiMTAoNTM3MDQwMDE3Ijs=/czo4OiJtYW5pZmVzdCI7.
24 Celestina Maccarinelli, personal communication, 14 Nov. 2022. The nephew's name was Giovanni Venturini – see www.fiammeverdibrescia.it/personaggi.
25 Flederman, *And Direction Was Given*, pp. 58–9; Hood, *Carlino*, pp. 28–9.
26 NARA, ASC, Angelo Maccarinelli, claim 54,907 ('Pro-Memoria').

Chapter 20: Green Flames

1 Unwin, *Escaping Has Ceased to Be a Sport*, pp. 107, 129–30; Moss, *Solvitur Ambulando*, pp. 138–9.
2 Dann, *Laughing We Ran*, pp. 37–8; Moss, *Solvitur Ambulando*, p. 137; Ian English, *Assisted Passage: Walking to Freedom, Italy 1943* (n.p., 1994), p. 96; Gilbert Broadbent, *Behind Enemy Lines* (Bognor Regis, 1985), p. 145; Vasey, 'Escape', p. 303. The best accounts of the polenta ritual are Michael Blackman, *By the Hunter's Moon* (London, 1956), p. 83, and George Dunning, *Where Bleed the Many* (London, 1955), pp. 163–4.

3 Interview with Piero Garletti, 2 Dec. 2022.
4 NARA, ASC, Umberto 'Doro' Garletti, claim 54,906 ('Pro-Memoria') – 'le razioni delle mietessere (di fumare)'.
5 The complexity of partisan allegiance is covered well by Rolando Anni, *Storia della Resistenza Bresciana, 1943–1945* (Brescia, 2005). See also Lodovico Galli, *Pagine di Verità . . . Brescia, 1943–1945* (Brescia, 1992); Santo Peli, *Il Primo Anno della Resistenza: Brescia, 1943–1944* (Brescia, 2014).
6 Kochanski, *Resistance*, p. 457.
7 Moss, *Solvitur Ambulando*, pp. 121–2.
8 Paolo Catterina, *La Resistenza a Prevalle* (Prevalle, 2003), p. 4.
9 Roberto Battaglia, *The Story of the Italian Resistance* (London, 1957), pp. 162–6; Charles Macintosh, *From Cloak to Dagger: An SOE Agent in Italy 1943–45* (London, 1982), p. 92; Richard Lamb, *War in Italy, 1943–1945: A Brutal Story* (London, 1995), pp. 73–5.
10 The memoir must have been written in the second half of 1944, as Ralph refers to 'Musso's black brigade[s]' – the Brigate Nere – which was not formed until 30 June that year. See RCP, Memoir, Book 1, p. 73.
11 RCP, Memoir, Book 2, pp. 138–45.
12 See Blackman, *By the Hunter's Moon*, pp. 82–3.
13 Milroy, *Alpine Partisan*, ch. 10; Archie Baird, *Family of Four* (Edinburgh, 1989), pp. 44–9; Unwin, *Escaping Has Ceased to Be a Sport*, p. 115 (quotation); Mason, *The Way Out*, pp. 29, 34–5.
14 Catterina, *Resistenza a Prevalle*, p. 5.
15 *Quel Giorno, Che Giorno! Il 25 Aprile 1945 nel ricordo di prevallesi che a quell'epoca erano bambini* (n.p., n.d.), p. 87; Origo, *War in Val d'Orcia*, pp. 19–20.
16 Interview with Piero Garletti, 2 Dec. 2022.
17 Caterina Rossi Tonni, *I Giorni del Tesio* (Salò, 1995), pp. 49–52, 71; *Quel Giorno, Che Giorno!*, pp. 89–90; Marcello Zane, *25 Aprile e Dintorni: Il Faticoso Cammino dalla Resistenza alla Democrazia nella Bassa Valle Sabbia* (Brescia, 2004), pp. 36–44.
18 See ASR, Fondo Morelli, Q III.1a – CVL – Quartier Generale del Raggruppamento FFVV, Nr. 1 (1943–6), Busta 31, Fascicolo 2, entries for 19 Nov. 1943, 17 Jan. 1944 and 16 Mar. 1944.

19 Foot and Langley, *MI9*, pp. 262–6; Absalom, 'Allied Escapers and the *Contadini*', pp. 417–18; J. E. Cameron, 'Prisoner-snatching in Italy', *Blackwood's Magazine*, 259 (Feb. 1946), pp. 109–14; Ettore Damini, *A Boy at War*, trans. Philip Vaughan (n.p., 1999), pp. 67, 68, 85.
20 Hargest, *Farewell Campo 12*, p. 149; Hood, *Carlino*, p. 144.
21 Quotation from Absalom, 'Hiding History', p. 112. To one POW it was 'an opportunity that comes the way of very few . . . education in its fullest and richest sense': Davies, *When the Moon Rises*, p. 99.
22 Hood, *Carlino*, pp. 129–31.
23 Ray Ellis, *Once a Hussar: A Memoir of Battle, Capture and Escape in the Second World War* (Barnsley, 2013), pp. 171–4, 207–22. See also MSMT, Ray Ellis.
24 Ellis, *Once a Hussar*, pp. 201–4. In general, see Malcolm Tudor, *Among the Italian Partisans: The Allied Contribution to the Resistance* (Stroud, 2016).
25 RCP, Omodeo Cantoni testimonial, 29 Apr. 1946.
26 On the memory of *contadini* bravery being stronger in Britain than in Italy, see Damini, *Boy at War*, p. 68.
27 Interview with Piero Garletti, 2 Dec. 2022.
28 RCP, Omodeo Cantoni testimonial, 29 Apr. 1946.
29 See https://partigianiditalia.cultura.gov.it/commissione/commissione-riconoscimento-qualifiche-partigiani-lombardia/.
30 On the bombing of Brescia, see Roberto Chiarini and Elena Pala, *Brescia Sotto le Bombe, 1940–1945* (Brescia, 2018).

Chapter 21: A Hazardous Mission

1 TNA, WO 208/3327/3078.
2 Briggs, *Funny Kind of War*, p. 107.
3 TNA, WO 208/3327/3078; Claudio Pavone, *A Civil War: A History of the Italian Resistance*, trans. Peter Levy (London, 2013), pp. 558–62. On this life, see also Ada Gobetti, *Partisan Diary: A Woman's Life in the Italian Resistance*, trans. Jomarie Alano (Oxford, 2014); Giovanni Pesce, *And No Quarter: An Italian Partisan in World War II*, trans. Frederick M. Shaine

(Athens, OH, 1972); Italo Calvino, *The Path to the Spiders' Nests*, trans. Archibald Colquhoun (London, 1998).

4 Ginsborg, *History of Contemporary Italy*, p. 56; Basil Davidson, quoted in David W. Ellwood, *Italy, 1943–1945* (Leicester, 1985), p. 163.

5 TNA, WO 204/11415 (OSS G-3 report, Jan. 1945). On the winter crisis in northern Italy, see Ginsborg, *History of Contemporary Italy*, pp. 54–9; Pier Paolo Battistelli and Piero Crociani, *World War II Partisan Warfare in Italy* (Oxford, 2015), pp. 73–4.

6 TNA, WO 208/3327/3078.

7 James Holland, *Italy's Sorrow: A Year of War, 1944–1945* (London, 2008), chs. 29–36.

8 Vladimir Peniakoff, *Popski's Private Army* (London, 1950), p. 425; ASR, Fondo Morelli, T I.1: Propaganda Alleata (1944–5), Busta 60, Fascicolo 1.

9 ASR, Fondo Morelli, P.I.1, Missione Anticer, 1944–5, Busta 28, Fascicolo 5.

10 TNA, WO 344/73/2; Andrea Baronchelli, personal communication, 31 Dec. 2022.

11 Mark Gilbert, *Italy Reborn: From Fascism to Democracy* (London, 2024), pp. 110–20, 125–7; Foot, *Blood and Power*, pp. 263–4; Pavone, *Civil War*, pp. 520–22. See also Pier Paolo Pasolini's film *Salò, or the 120 Days of Sodom* (1975).

12 Albert Lulushi, *Donovan's Devils: OSS Commandos behind Enemy Lines – Europe, World War II* (New York, 2016), p. xv; R. Harris Smith, *OSS: The Secret History of America's First Central Intelligence Agency* (Berkeley, CA, 1972), p. 35.

13 Raimondo Craveri, *La Campagna d'Italia e i Servizi Segreti: La Storia dell'ORI, 1943–1945* (Milan, 1980), pp. 32ff.

14 Lulushi, *Donovan's Devils*, chs. 5, 10–13; Max Corvo, 'The OSS and the Italian Campaign', in George C. Chalou (ed.), *The Secrets War: The Office of Strategic Services in World War II*, 2nd edn (Washington, DC, 2002), pp. 183–93; Anthony Cave Brown, *The Last Hero: Wild Bill Donovan* (London, 1982), esp. pp. 474–8.

15 TNA, WO 204/11414, report of 15 Mar. 1945.

16 ASR, Fondo Morelli, P.I.1, Missione Anticer, 1944–5, Busta 28, Fascicolo 5; Milroy, *Alpine Partisan*, p. 98.

17 Max Corvo, *The OSS in Italy, 1942–1945: A Personal Memoir* (New York, 1990), pp. 249–52; Lulushi, *Donovan's Devils*, pp. 241–5.
18 NARA, RG 226/99/33–4, Mar. 1945, pp. 19, 21–2; Tonni, *I Giorni del Tesio*, pp. 53–60.
19 Catterina, *Resistenza a Prevalle*, pp. 4–7; Tonni, *I Giorni del Tesio*, pp. 75–81; Zane, *25 Aprile e Dintorni*, pp. 25–6, 34.
20 ASR, Archive of the Provincial CLN of Brescia, 93. CLN Comunale di Nuvolento: Amministrazione (Aprile–Ottobre 1945), Busta 16, Fascicolo 182, letter from Major Vincent A. Abrignani to Dr Andrea Baronchelli, 8 May 1945.
21 For Abrignani's files, see NARA, RG 226/92A/71 and RG 226/224/2.
22 Baronchelli's boss was Silvio Raile, see ASR, Archive of the Provincial CLN of Brescia, 93. CLN Comunale di Nuvolento: Amministrazione (Aprile–Ottobre 1945), Busta 16, Fascicolo 182, Structure of the Foreign Trade Institute, 3 May 1945. Baronchelli reported to the Allied Screening Commission that Raile had provided money and comforts, for example 'liquers': NARA, ASC, Baronchelli, claim 54,908 (see also claim 77,005).
23 Macintosh, *From Cloak to Dagger*, pp. 176–7; Lamb, *War in Italy*, pp. 206–7. For a portrait of a partisan with an ironed jumpsuit, polished jackboots, brilliantined hair, stick grenades in his belt and a girl on his arm, see Ben Owen, *With Popski's Private Army* (Cambridge, 2011), p. 101. See also Adrian Gallegos, *From Capri into Oblivion* (London, 1959), p. 221.
24 Tonni, *I Giorni del Tesio*, pp. 7–8.
25 ASR, Archive of the Provincial CLN of Brescia, 93. CLN Comunale di Nuvolento: Amministrazione (Aprile–Ottobre 1945), Busta 16, Fascicolo 182, letter from Major Vincent A. Abrignani to Dr Andrea Baronchelli, 8 May 1945.
26 Corvo, *OSS in Italy*, pp. 253–8; Churchill Archives, Churchill College, Cambridge, Donovan Papers, Box 15, Microfilm Reel 106, report for Mar. 1945.
27 OSS's Mission Franconia, led by 'Franco', began on 13 February 1945, and received a British SOE team on 21 March: Corvo, *OSS in Italy*, pp. 251–2, 260–61. A report (15 Apr. 1945) by 'Franco' is at NARA, see RG 226 UD 190-B, 'Report on the partisan formations in the province of Brescia', pp. 1–10. The detailed report of 2671st OSS Special

Reconnaissance Battalion for 21 March didn't mention it: NARA, RG 226/99/45.
28. This was Operation Roast, and the landing was known as the Battle of the Argenta Gap, see Sir William Jackson et al., *History of the Second World War: The Mediterranean and Middle East . . . November 1944 to May 1945* (London, 2009), pp. 267–84.
29. Max Corvo, head of the Italian secret intelligence section of OSS, recalled grave shortages of radio equipment and operators: *OSS in Italy*, pp. 160, 163–5.
30. Zane, *25 Aprile e Dintorni*, pp. 25–6. Jim Wilde, the submariner POW from Camp 52, took part in the OSS Roanoke mission and was mentioned in their reports: Dethick, *An Insatiable Curiosity*, pp. 21–2.
31. Giannetto Valzelli (ed.), *Brescia Ribelle, 1943–1945* (Brescia, 1966), pp. 117–18. Later, some partisans downplayed the importance of the OSS, emphasizing that many 'Americans' were in fact Italian, see Claudia Nasini, 'The OSS in the Italian Resistance: A Post Cold War Interpretation', *EuroStudium³ʷ*, 24 (2012), pp. 46–82.

Chapter 22: Incipit Vita Nova

1. Rolando Anni, *Storia della Brigata 'Giacomo Perlasca'* (Brescia, 1980), pp. 156–69. The OSS described the winter as 'particularly rigid': NARA, RG 226 UD 190-B, 'Report on the partisan formations in the province of Brescia', p. 1. On fog, see Beppe Fenoglio, *A Private Affair*, trans. Howard Curtis (New York, 2023), ch. 6.
2. NARA, RG 226 UD 190-B, 'Report on the partisan formations in the province of Brescia', p. 2. Later the Perlasca Brigade moved from Tito Speri to the Astolfo Lunardi Division. This may have been the same 'Franco', who in 1944 commanded the Pasubiana (later Pablo) Brigade, from which the Ateo Caremi group evolved: IWM, Documents.1130.
3. Lulushi, *Donovan's Devils*, p. 263.
4. TNA, WO 170/7134, Security Survey for Rimini and Brescia, Apr. 1945. For a Tempini worker's memory of the liberation, see Roberto

Cucchini et al., *Le Vie della Libertà: Un Percorso della Memoria (Brescia 1938–1945)* (Brescia, 2005), pp. 91–2.
5 Catterina, *Resistenza a Prevalle*, pp. 5, 7–8.
6 Gilbert, *Italy Reborn*, p. 144.
7 TNA, WO 170/7134, Security Report for Brescia–Bergamo, 28 Apr.–14 May 1945. See also ibid., (1 Feb.–31 Dec. 1945), which reported cooperation by the Fiamme Verdi, and in the Garibaldi Brigades the weeding out of 'last minute partisans, mainly communist, who took up arms either for the opportunity of plunder or for use in political strife later'.
8 See ASR, Fondo Morelli, Q III.1: CVL – Commando raggruppamento divisioni Fiamme Verdi (1944–5), Busta 31, Fascicolo 1, regulation of 8 Nov. 1944. On the complexity of this political shift postwar, see Steven F. White, *Modern Italy's Founding Fathers: The Making of a Postwar Republic* (London, 2020); Gilbert, *Italy Reborn*, chs. 4–7.
9 ASR, Archive of the Provincial CLN of Brescia, 93. CLN Comunale di Nuvolento: Amministrazione (Aprile–Ottobre 1945), Busta 16, Fascicolo 182, report from Comrade 'Silvio' (Andrea Baronchelli) for the Socialist Party *c.* spring 1945.
10 ASR, Archive of the Provincial CLN of Brescia, 93. CLN Comunale di Nuvolento: Amministrazione (Aprile–Ottobre 1945), Busta 16, Fascicolo 182, meeting, City Hall of Nuvolento regarding the appointment of a mayor and the function of the CLN, 26 Apr. 1945.
11 Zane, *25 Aprile e Dintorni*, pp. 66–8.
12 ASR, Fondo Morelli, Q III.1: CVL – Commando raggruppamento divisioni Fiamme Verdi (1944–5), Busta 31, Fascicolo 1, FFVV printed flyer, 28 Apr. 1945.
13 This episode comes from Gianpaolo Capelli, 'The Last Days of the Second World War in the Memories of Andrea Bonardi "el Berto" of Anfo', *Valle Sabbia News* (2 May 2022); Emilio Arduino, *Brigata Perlasca* (Brescia, 1946), pp. 160–66, 202–6, 212–40; Vincenzo Chiesa, 'The surrender of 750 German SS soldiers to the partisans of the *Fiamme Verdi* at Nozza di Vestone' (2002), accessed at www.rsapralboino.net/vincenzo-chiesa-i-miei-ricordi-di-vita-partigiana/; 'Emiliano Rinaldini: Deputy

Commander of S4 Perlasca Brigade', accessed at www.ccdc.it/documento/emiliano-rinaldini-cristiano-maestro-ribelle-per-amore/.
14 See, in general, Christian Jennings, *Anatomy of a Massacre: How the SS Got Away with War Crimes in Italy* (Cheltenham, 2021), esp. chs. 4–8, 11, 16.
15 Dethick, *As If He Were My Brother*, p. 42.
16 ASR, Fondo Morelli, Q III.2am – Attività Partigiana nel Comune di Nuvolento, 1945, Busta 46, Fascicolo 10, statement by Col. Edmondo Raimondi, 1 May 1945.
17 See the FSS war diaries at TNA, WO 170/7134, esp. report of 30 May 1945.
18 ASR, Archive of the Provincial CLN of Brescia, 93. CLN Communale di Nuvolento: Amministrazione (Aprile–Ottobre 1945), Busta 16, Fascicolo 182, 3 or 4 May 1945. Baronchelli's devotion to this work is reflected in the fact that he soon resigned as president of the Nuvolento council, explaining that he was fully occupied as 'a liaison official with the Intelligence Corps of Brescia': ibid., minutes, 5 May 1945.
19 TNA, WO 170/7134 (1 Feb.–31 Dec. 1945), especially the entry for 12 May 1945. See also WO 170/8949. On the supposed link to PPA, see Stanton, 'Charles West'. For a memoir of an ex-POW hunting SS and Brigate Nere, see Ian Bell, *No Place to Hide* (London, 1998). See also IWM, Documents.467 (Robert Ian Bell).
20 NARA, RG 226/99/33-4, April 1945; Churchill Archives, Churchill College, Cambridge, Donovan Papers, Box 12, Microfilm Reel 76, pp. 45–8, 66–7, 71. See also Smith, *OSS*, pp. 115–20; Corvo, *OSS in Italy*, pp. 173, 245, 251–2, 260–61, 281; Holland, *Italy's Sorrow*, pp. 500–501, 516, 519–24; Dennis Whitehead, 'In the Shadow of Sunrise: The Secret Surrender of Italy', *WWII History*, 7 (2008), pp. 28–33; Allen Dulles, *The Secret Surrender* (New York, 1966). For the SS counterfeiting scheme, see Anthony Pirie, *Operation Bernhard: The Greatest Forgery of All Time* (London, 1961).
21 Dunning, *Where Bleed the Many*, pp. 253–4.
22 Peniakoff, *Popski's Private Army*, pp. 390–91.
23 Foot and Langley, *MI9*, p. 262; Absalom, 'Hiding History', p. 117. In *The Long Walk Out* (n.p., 1994) – accessed via MSMT website – John Langrishe wrote: 'understandably no one was anxious to leave their comfortable billets for the uncertainty of the open country' (p. 16). On POWs' reticence, see also Lamb, *War in Italy*, pp. 163–4.

24 Hood, *Carlino*, pp. 127–8; Moss, *Solvitur Ambulando*, pp. 152–3; Dann, *Laughing We Ran*, pp. 89–91.
25 Warren and Benson, *The Broken Column*, p. 204.
26 Moss, *Solvitur Ambulando*, pp. 152–3; Warren and Benson, *The Broken Column*, pp. 203–4.
27 Dann, *Laughing We Ran*, pp. 89–91; Moss, *Solvitur Ambulando*, pp. 153–5; Hood, *Carlino*, p. 128. See also Norman Lewis, *Naples '44: An Intelligence Officer in the Italian Labyrinth* (London, 1978; 1983 edn), esp. p. 105.

Chapter 23: The South Country

1 Allport, *Demobbed*, p. 203; Makepeace, *Captives of War*, pp. 201–2, 205, 210–11; Gilbert, *POW*, pp. 316–21, quotation at p. 320. See also Joanna Bourke, *An Intimate History of Killing* (London, 1999), ch. 11.
2 Barber, *Prisoner of War*, p. 20; Mustardé, *The Sun Stood Still*, pp. 204–5.
3 TNA, WO 311/1206, testimony of Attilio Coppola, 27 Mar. 1946. See also WO 311/1211, assault on Silas Hickman (Jun. 1942).
4 TNA, WO 311/317, testimony of Guido Ottria, 15 May 1946; TNA, TS 27/712; TS 311/1209. On Feldwebel Heinz Böhle, the accused German (a POW in the US), see TS 311/1243; TS 26/417.
5 See Luigi Prosperi, 'The Missed Italian Nuremberg: The History of an Internationally-Sponsored Amnesty', *Social Science Research Network* (25 Nov. 2016) – https://ssrn.com/abstract=2887267 or http://dx.doi.org/10.2139/ssrn.2887267.
6 TNA, WO 204/1012, Sir D'Arcy Osborne, 17 Oct. 1944.
7 TNA, WO 208/3397, p. 2; Wanda Newby, *Peace and War: Growing up in Fascist Italy* (London, 1991), pp. 186–7; John Miller, *Friends and Romans: On the Run in Wartime Italy* (London, 1987), pp. 260–61; Lucy de Burgh, *My Italian Adventures: An English Girl at War 1943–47*, ed. Mary Hodge (Stroud, 2013), pp. 270–71; Newby, *Love and War in the Apennines*, p. 221.
8 Newby, *Peace and War*, p. 186.
9 TNA, WO 208/5451–60; WO 208/5479 (Guido Calogero, 'The Handful of Flour'); WO 208/3397, ASC Final Report, 1947; FO 372/4902,

Minutes of the Treaty Department, 1947–8; William C. Simpson, *A Vatican Lifeline* (London, 1995), p. 222; de Burgh, *My Italian Adventures*, p. 273–4.

10 Newby, *Peace and War*, pp. 186–7; Newby, *Love and War in the Apennines*, p. 221. See the comments in TNA, WO 208/3397, p. 1.

11 Newby, *Peace and War*, p. 186. 'Many were the stories of excitement,' wrote one ex-POW, 'with which the peasants of remote mountain villagers had greeted the arrival of someone connected with the dangers which they had endured': Miller, *Friends and Romans*, p. 260.

12 NARA, ASC, claims 54,905–54,908 (Chiodi, Garletti, Maccarinelli, Baronchelli).

13 Simpson, *Vatican Lifeline*, pp. 219–20.

14 Warren and Benson, *The Broken Column*, pp. 204–5; Carol Mather, *When the Grass Stops Growing: A War Memoir* (London, 1997), p. 240.

15 RCP, Memoir, Book 2, p. 143. Perhaps Ralph knew of Hilaire Belloc's great walk from England through the Alps: *The Path to Rome* (London, 1902).

16 Lewis, *Naples '44*, p. 183. See also Farran, *Winged Dagger*, p. 198: 'This was a land of peace. If war is civilisation, you can keep your flush lavatories, your nylon tooth-brushes and your vulgar motor cars. Give me rather a two-roomed casa with a strong wife, salami sausages hung from the rafters and strings of onions from the windows; two pigs in a sty, three oxen in my stable and a plot of land which is my own.'

17 Newby, *Love and War in the Apennines*, p. 221.

18 NARA, ASC, Angelo Maccarinelli, claim 54,907, postcard from 'Rodolfo' to Maccarinelli, 3 Jun. 1945.

19 Ibid., Augusto Chiodi, claim 54,905, letter from 'Rodolfo' to 'Chiodi Fratelli', 1 Jun. 1945.

20 TNA, WO 423/436012, pp. 3, 7.

21 TNA, WO 417/96/1, Casualty List No. 1838 (23 Aug. 1945).

22 TNA, WO 423/436012, pp. 14, 20, 24–6, 28–33, 34–5.

23 Ibid., pp. 3, 8, 9, 17.

24 RCP, 'Diseases of Animals, Acts and Orders', 12 Sept. 1946.

25 TNA, WO 344/73/2.

26 Godfrey Mwakikagile, *Life in Tanganyika in the Fifties*, 3rd edn (Dar es Salaam, 2010), pp. 32, 41–3. See also John Iliffe, *A Modern History of Tanganyika* (Cambridge, 1979), especially chs. 8–11.
27 Farran, *Winged Dagger*, p. 172.
28 See TNA, WO 170/7062, 75 Section SIB, CMP, 5th Army (Milan), Jan.–Oct. 1945.
29 TNA, AIR 29/1102, RAF No. 106 Personnel and Reception Centre, Cosford.
30 TNA, AIR 81/10384, correspondence between Olga Burford and the Air Ministry, 10–26 May 1944.
31 Ibid., correspondence between Syd West and the Air Ministry, May–July 1945.
32 TNA, AIR 81/10384; WO 208/3327/3078; WO 208/5583. See also Foot, and Langley, *MI9*, pp. 224–5; Fry, *MI9*, pp. 54–5, 145–50.
33 Bond, 'Charles Edwin West', p. 48.
34 See pay scales in *Tanganyika Territory Blue Book* (1947) – copy in RCP.
35 See G. G. Hadjivayanis, 'Prisons in Tanzania', *East Africa Law Review*, 7 (1974), pp. 247–73, and David Williams, 'The Role of Prisons in Tanzania: An Historical Perspective', *Crime and Social Justice*, 13 (1980), pp. 27–38.
36 Mwakikagile, *Life in Tanganyika*, pp. 28–31, 43–4, 50; Iliffe, *Tanganyika*, chs. 9, 12.
37 Mwakikagile, *Life in Tanganyika*, pp. 25, 180–82; Joyce Thackeray, *The Woven Basket* (London, 2001), pp. 1–16.
38 Thackeray, *Woven Basket*, pp. 9–12, 21. See also Mwakikagile, *Life in Tanganyika*, pp. 202–3.
39 Hadjivayanis, 'Prisons in Tanzania', pp. 248–9; Williams, 'Role of Prisons in Tanzania', pp. 28–30.
40 Hadjivayanis, 'Prisons in Tanzania', pp. 254, 264–5.
41 Ibid., pp. 265–6.
42 Owen, *With Popski's Private Army*, p. 59.
43 RCP, letter from the Provincial Commissioner, Dar es Salaam, to Ralph Corps, 23 Jun. 1947; Mwakikagile, *Life in Tanganyika*, pp. 412–13; S. L. Chachage, 'Socialist Ideology and the Reality of Tanzania', PhD thesis, Glasgow University, 1986, pp. 312–13.

44 RCP. This was Edward Fitzgerald's translation, ed. George F. Maine (London, 1953), which Ralph inscribed with his name and 'Prisons Service, Tanganyika, 15.10.56'.

45 Medley, 'The Day the War Began', pp. 25–6; E. S. Allison, *Kiwi at Large* (London, 1961), pp. 12, 147–53, quotation at p. 12. There are many accounts of POWs returning to Italy, testifying to enduring friendship, see, for example, Fox, *Spaghetti and Barbed Wire*, pp. 167–8.

46 Jones, *Escape to Nowhere*, pp. 169–70.

47 *London Gazette* (15 Jun. 1944), p. 2856 (James McBean); ibid. (31 Jan. 1947), p. 559 (C. E. West); Bond, 'Charles Edwin West', p. 48. At least one other ex-Camp 65 prisoner, the improbably named Randolph Churchill, was Mentioned in Despatches for escaping from a train: Mike Churchill-Jones, personal communication, 18 Jun. 2025.

48 Quoted in Ginsborg, *History of Contemporary Italy*, p. 70.

49 TNA, WO 373/63/136 (William Cullen); WO 373/64/192 (William Strachan); IWM, Documents.22656 (Rowland Hewson) – see also MSMT, Rowland Hewson.

50 Allport, *Browned Off and Bloody-Minded*, p. 58; Dethick, *An Insatiable Curiosity*, pp. 24–5.

51 Katrina Kittel, 'Chasing a Star: The Evidence for the Posthumous Issue of the Italy Star', *Sabretache*, 64 (2023), pp. 10–18.

52 In November 1945, the ASC informed the British government that over 500 Italians had died helping escaped POWs: Krige, *The Way Out*, p. 373n.

53 See his testimony of 8 Dec. 1945: http://iwasindachau.blogspot.com. See also TNA, FO 950/1927–1.

54 TNA, WO 416/228/418; Marc Löw, personal correspondence, 1 and 8 Feb. 2023. See also Max's memorial at https://honorisraelsfallen.com/fallen/lev-moshe-max/.

55 TNA, WO 416/53/119; interview with Steve Butterworth, 15 Dec. 2023.

56 TNA, WO 416/187/1 (Eric Huggett); WO 416/374/308 (Horace Wade); interview and correspondence with Angela Hopper, May 2024.

57 TNA, WO 416/220/66; Lee, 'The Enemy, My Friend', vol. 4 (paintings and photos). See also https://artuk.org/discover/artists/lee-robert-henry-19152007.

58 Cullen, *Italy – The Hard Way*, p. 207.

59 Barker, *Behind Barbed Wire*, p. 191; Gilbert, *POW*, pp. 321–3.
60 David Holbrook, *Flesh Wounds* (London, 1966; 2007 edn), p. 115.

Chapter 24: Redeemed from Time

1 Christopher Long, 'The Great Escaping Society Meet to Remember the Brave' (1981) – London Newspaper Group CN/WPN 08-05-1981; Bond, 'Charles Edwin West', pp. 48–9. On the RAF Escaping Society's foundation, see *The Times* (17 Jan. 1947), p. 8. Personal information from Charlie's nieces, Emma Bassom and Vanessa Steer. On the work of RAFES, see IWM, LBY K.36974, Chairman's Report, 1956.
2 *The Times* (2 Nov. 1984), p. 28; Bond, 'Charles Edwin West', p. 49.
3 Mwakikagile, *Life in Tanganyika*, pp. 11–14, 16, 53–4, 79, 92; Erika Johnston, *The Other Side of Kilimanjaro* (London, 1971), pp. 154, 212–13. Nyerere quoted in Ronald Aminzade, *Race, Nation and Citizenship in Postcolonial Africa* (Cambridge, 2013), ch. 4. On these changes, see also Iliffe, *Tanganyika*, chs. 15–16.
4 Hadjivayanis, 'Prisons in Tanzania', p. 251; Johnston, *Other Side of Kilimanjaro*, pp. 39, 154, 212–14; Thackeray, *Woven Basket*, p. 170.
5 *United Nations Visiting Mission to Trust Territories in East Africa, 1960: Report on Tanganyika* (New York, 1960), p. 36.
6 Cranford Pratt, *The Critical Phase in Tanzania, 1945–1968: Nyerere and the Emergence of a Socialist Strategy* (Cambridge, 1976). See also Paul Bjerk, *Building a Peaceful Nation: Julius Nyerere and the Establishment of Sovereignty in Tanzania, 1960–1964* (Rochester, NY, 2015), ch. 3.
7 RCP, letter from Pat Manley to Ralph Corps, 29 May 1962. On Manley, see the database at www.europeansineastafrica.co.uk.
8 TNA, WO 423/436012: FOI application 21 Dec. 2023; file received 10 Jan. 2025.
9 Ibid., p. 36: the report of 12 Sept. 1934 said he 'lacks go in his work'.
10 Ibid., pp. 20–33, esp. p. 24.
11 Luisa Passerini (ed.), *Memory and Totalitarianism* (Oxford, 1992), p. 2.
12 Stefano Garletti sent me a copy of *Valcamonica Libera* (3 Jun. 1945) – a newspaper 'dedicated to the fallen rebels for liberty' – found among

his grandfather Doro's papers. On the front page was the story of Giovanni Venturini, the Chiodis' nephew.
13 Enzo Maccarinelli (born Swansea, 1980).
14 'The Tempini Brigade did not exist . . . Probably just a fantasy of the war!': Rolando Anni, personal communication, 18 Nov. 2022.
15 Yuri Radcenko of Krasnodar Krai. Two of his letters to Doro Garletti survive, written in Italian, undated but probably late 1980s. Radcenko laments the demise of their shared socialist dream, with 'the old Stalinists still in power . . . stoking inflation but looking after themselves'.
16 Stefano Garletti, personal communication, 26 Aug. 2024. On the restoration of Malga Sacù, see https://www.facebook.com/100063699870428/posts/1007788108021176/?rdid=ysUDnkUpyM3yKCJM.
17 Andrea Baronchelli, personal communication, 12 Dec. 2024. On Cascina Farisengo, see https://cascinafarisengo.it/en/home-en/history/.
18 Matteo Berloco, personal communication, 26 Nov. 2024.
19 Giuliano De Felice, 'Camp 65: Archaeology of the Contemporary Past', in Bolognese et al., *Camp 65*, pp. 111–12; Domenico Bolognese, 'Shaping the Future of the Camp: A Challenge for our Community', ibid., p. 130.
20 Foot, *Blood and Power*, pp. 299–321; Filippo Focardi, *The Bad German and the Good Italian: Removing the Guilt of the Second World War*, trans. Paul Barnaby (Manchester, 2023); Philip Cooke, *The Legacy of the Italian Resistance* (Basingstoke, 2011), pp. 23–6; Pavone, *Civil War*, ch. 8; Morgan, *Italian Fascism*, pp. 229–32. For the effect on politics, see Pier Paolo Pasolini, 'Il Vuoto del Potere', *Corriere della Sera* (1 Feb. 1975).
21 Giovanni Dal Mas, *Quora* online forum, 2022, Domenico Bolognese, personal communication, 29 Aug. 2023.
22 Lucien Febvre, *Combats pour L'Histoire* (Paris, 1952), p. 96; Philip Roth: *I Married a Communist* (London, 1998), p. 223.
23 Eliot, 'Little Gidding', v. 5.
24 James Salter, *Light Years* (1975; London, 2007 edn), pp. 35, 187. Emily Robinson asks why historians 'pursue a past they know to be unreachable and unpresentable' in 'Touching the Void: Affective History and the Impossible', *Rethinking History*, 14 (2010), p. 504. See also Andrew Michael Hurley, *Starve Acre* (London, 2019), pp. 176–7.

Epilogue: Monte Generoso

1. That summer, 1955, EMI made a classic recording of Maria Callas singing *Madame Butterfly*, conducted by Herbert von Karajan. It's likely that Ralph, Flo and Audrey went to the Sala Puccini at the Milan Conservatory, which had opened three years earlier. The Sala Verdi, bombed during the war, didn't re-open until 1958.
2. 'Poor old Audrey having to sit in that car with them all that way, it must have been awful!': Interview with Pauline Kendell, 15 Jul. 2022.
3. Evocative colour cine film from the mid-1950s is available online, showing tourists leaving the funicular for the mountain. Even this evoked no memories in my mother: https://lanostrastoria.ch/entries/EDknOGwnp24.

Picture Credits

Every effort has been made to contact copyright holders. The author and publisher would be glad to amend in future editions errors or omissions brought to their attention.

Author's Collection (pages 6, 176, 201, 260, 236, 243, 314); Pauline Kendell (pages 19, 20, 24, 30, 34, 136, 139, 202, 294, endpapers); The National Archives, Kew, WO 310/13 (pages 76, 100); Imperial War Museum, London, LBY E.16808 (page 54); The Tank Museum, Bovington, Horace Wade Collection (pages 157, 160, 178); National Archives and Records Administration, College Park, MD, Maccarinelli RG 331 Entry UD 1003-A Box 648 File 54907 (page 286); Emma Bassom (page 306); Flavio Manzelli (page 210); Fabio Zavaterri (page 168); Newman Robinson and Peter Ogilvie, *In the Bag*, Johannesburg, 1975 (page 51); *Mars & Minerva: The Journal of the SAS*, 6, 1984 (page 69); Australian War Memorial, Accession No. 129002, public domain (page 191)

Index

Abrignani, Maj. Vincent A., 263, 266–7
Absalom, Roger, 204, 248, 323
Acroma Fort, 29
Aden, 26
Adige, River (and valley), 193, 194, 206, 219, 222, 224
   see also Fumaneri, Cirillo
'affective tremor', see archives, experience of
Afghanistan, 14, 15
Afrika Korps, 25, 33, 35, 39, 40, 145
   see also Rommel, Gen. Erwin
Air Ministry, 73, 291–2
aircraft (British):
   Bristol Bombay, 67–8, 70, 72, 300
   Hurricane, 32, 71
   Lancaster, 291
   Spitfire, 32, 285
aircraft (German):
   Junkers 52, 44, 75, 89–90
   Junkers 87 (Stuka), 32, 35, 95
   Junkers 88, 187
   Messerschmitt 109, 71, 72
   V-1 (flying bomb), 5
aircraft (US):
   Douglas DC-3, 315
   B-24 Liberator, 183
   P-47 Thunderbolt, 248, 273
Al-Mafraq, 28
Albania, 82
Alderson, RSM Wilf, 84, 90, 94–6, 132, 137, 150, 298
Alexander, Gen. Sir Harold, 257–8

'Alexander certificates', 239–40, 253, 284–5
All Quiet on the Western Front, 102
Allen, Reg (footballer), 163, 347
Allied Control Commission, 275
Allied Screening Commission, 206, 211, 216, 219, 221, 237, 240, 253, 283, 286
   pays compensation to Italians, 204–5, 210, 214, 224, 238, 284–5, 288
   issues certificates, see Alexander, Gen Sir Harold
Alps, see: Apuan Alps; Dolomites; Monte Generoso; Switzerland
Altamura, 10, 12, 46–7, 69, 76–7, 82, 97, 98, 101, 116, 144, 221, 310
   residents from visit Gravina, 52, 69, 139, 149
   POWs buried in, 62, 84
Altopiano delle Murge, 81, 102
'Amapola' (song), 158, 161, 165
Ampleforth (N. Yorkshire), 302, 303
Ancestry.com, 13, 66, 302–3, 321
'Anti-Boredom Committee', see Gravina (Camp 65), pastimes, music and sport
'anti-scorch', see sabotage, by Germans
Antolini, Alberto, 221–2, 224–5
Antolini, Gino, 221–2
Anzio, landings at (1944), 256
Apennine mountains, 223, 230, 259, 284, 314

Index

Apuan Alps, 155
archives, experience of, 7–8, 154, 170, 193–4, 208, 253–4, 312, 328
Arco dei Fileni ('Marble Arch'), 290
Argentina, 86
Ariosto (Italian ship), 43
Armistice, Italian (1943), 184–5, 201, 211, 245, 253, 282, 311
   mass walk-out of prisoners after, 187, 204, 276–7
   see also Chiavari (Camp 52)
Arras, BEF at, 24
Associazione Nazionale Partigiani d'Italia (ANPI), 251, 310
Assogna, Emilio, 214, 222, 223–4
Ateo Caremi (assault unit), see Garibaldi Brigades
Auchinleck, Gen. Sir Claude, 68, 70, 71, 73
Auschwitz, 170
Australians, 28, 30, 41, 49
   prisoners, 48
   see also Löw, Max
Austria, 20, 290
Auxiliary Territorial Service, 148

Baalbek, 28
Bacilieri, Cardinal Bartolomeo, 218, 355
Bacilieri, Fioravante, 215–16, 217, 220, 318
Bacilieri, Marco, 218–19
Bader, Douglas, 70
Badoglio, Gen. Pietro, 175, 176, 186
Bagolino, 247
Bailey, Philip James, 8, 311
Balby, 14, 18, 19, 20, 281
   bombing of (1941), 26–7
'barbed wire fever', 57, 111
Bari, 47, 77, 81, 109, 116, 283
   Banca d'Italia, gold allegedly stored at, 138

Barker, RSM W. J. ('Bill'), 149, 166, 171, 173, 190
   escapes from train, 194, 195, 352
Barnsley (S. Yorkshire), xviii, 17, 124
Baronchelli, Andrea, Jr, 253, 264, 266, 307–8
Baronchelli, Andrea, Sr, 252–3, 262, 285
   friendship with Ralph, 254, 275, 305
   supplies clothes and money, 253, 260–1
   mission with Ralph (1945), 254, 263–4, 265–7
   trade envoy, 264–5, 307
   socialist partisan, 253, 270, 274
   intelligence agent, 275
   president of Nuvolento sub-committee, 270
   gives credit to others, 253, 285, 288
   gifted cheetah cubs, 307–8
   see also: Cremona; *salvacondotto*
Bartlett, RSM S. V., 173, 190, 194
Bassom, Emma, 69, 72, 75, 205–6, 212, 300, 306
Bates, H. E. (novelist), 337
Bates, Sgt Ron, 166–7, 171, 172, 190, 194
batmen, see warrant officers, privileges of
Battle of the Argenta Gap (1945), see Operation Roast
Bedale (N. Yorkshire), 14, 17
Bedizzole, 263
Beeton, Mrs (Isabella), 164
Bekaa Valley, see Syria
Belloc, Hilaire, 286, 366
Benghazi, 42–3
   POW camp, 43, 49, 74–5, 137, 197, 277
   sea passage from, 43–4, 75, 278
   war cemetery, 73
Bentley (Doncaster), 14, 17
Berlin, 140, 256, 259, 298

Index

Berlusconi, Silvio, 224
Bersaglieri, 40, 110
Berti, Remo, 205
Bevin, Ernest, 284
'Big Nanny', *see* White, Florence Mary
Billany, Dan, *see Cage, The* (1949)
Bir Hakeim, *see* Gazala, defensive line at
Bismarck (German battleship), 26
Blandford, 25
'blower' stoves, *see* Gravina (Camp 65), tea ritual
Bodleian Library, Oxford, 134, 175
Böhle, Feldwebel Heinz, 189, 283, 365
Bologna, 246, 259, 283, 307
Bolognese, Domenico, 10, 17, 27, 47, 48, 69, 77, 125, 139, 154, 177, 306
   attitudes and character, 41, 81–2, 98–9, 101–2, 168, 207, 220, 251–2
   friendship with, 12, 76, 99, 214, 225, 255, 310
   road trips with, 98–102, 106–7, 109, 115–18, 122–3, 133, 168–71, 206–9, 214–25, 239–43, 250–2, 253–5, 265, 308
   in the archives, 133, 177, 253–4, 263, 275
   rediscovery of his father's story, 221–2, 225, 310, 312
   see also Camp 65 Association
Bolognese, Michele, 82, 99, 101, 221, 225, 310
Bolzano, 193, 273, 276
Bond, Ernie, 69, 72, 73, 74, 301
Bonington, Lieut. Charles, 70–2
Bonington, Sir Chris, 72
Brenner Pass, 184, 185–6, 190, 206, 259
Brenzone, 257, 306
Breonio, 215, 219–3, 229
   see also: Giacopuzzi, Fabio; 'Le Rive'
Brescia (city), 9, 214, 237, 242, 259, 260, 287, 310

   bombing of, 234, 254
   resistance in, 233, 245–6, 255, 263, 264–5
   Foreign Trade Institute, 264, 307
   liberation of, 269–70, 274
   see also Università Cattolica del Sacro Cuore
Brescia Libera (resistance newspaper), 245
Brigate Nere ('Black Brigades'), 246, 247, 251, 252, 263, 358
Brindisi, 44, 75, 89–90, 102, 104, 114, 117, 247
British Broadcasting Corporation (BBC), 166, 174, 194
   secret messages to POWs, 173, 184
   Radio Londra, 212, 245, 256
British 8th Army, 31, 68, 183–4, 231, 269
British Expeditionary Force (1939–40), 23, 24
Buckingham Palace, Ralph on guard at, 6, 240–1
Burford, Olga (*née* Scoullar), 67, 290, 291
Bussolengo, 195
   Camp 148, 149
   POW letters at, 177
Butterworth, Steve, 140, 148–9
Butterworth, Tom, 139, 140, 142–3, 148–9, 166, 174, 186–7
   gives Ralph his photo, 139, 145, 149
   postwar, 298, 299

Cage, The (1949), 151
Cagney, James (actor), 52
Cairo, 29, 67, 71
   leave taken in, 30–1, 61
Callas, Maria, 313, 371
Calvari, 163, 168, 171
Calvino, Italo, 154
Cambridge University Library, 51

Index

Camp 52, *see* Chiavari
Camp 53 Sforzacosta, 249
Camp 65, *see* Gravina
Camp 65 Association, 10, 47, 77, 82, 99
Camp 85, *see* Tuturano
Camp 148, *see* Bussolengo
Cantoni, Omodeo, 241, 245, 250–1, 274, 307
   resistance work, 235, 237, 245–6, 262, 265
   supplies exercise books, 247
   bicycle saved by Ralph, 259–60
   president of Prevalle council, 270–1
   writes testimonial for Ralph, 249–50, 252, 275, 289, 298
Capolago, 314, 316
carabinieri, 27, 44, 198, 202
   in Camp 65, 52–3, 59, 90, 126, 129–31, 134–8, 141–2, 146, 149, 152–3
   in Camp 52, 156–7, 159, 165, 166, 172, 176, 179, 185–8, 283
   at Noci, 120, 121–3, 124, 125, 126
   Ralph's opinion of, 53, 157
   see also Guardia Nazionale Repubblicana
Casa Scariotti, 213–14, 215–17, 218, 219, 223, 229
Cascina Farisengo, 266, 308
Case di Viso, destroyed, 247
Castelli-Taddei, Col. Dino, 162, 164, 169, 172, 184, 186
   POWs' affection for, 160, 163
   surrenders to Germans, 186–7
   as fugitive, 188
   accused of war crimes, 283
'Cauldron, the', *see* Gazala, defensive line at
Ceraino, 198, 202–3, 207–9, 210–11, 212–13, 229, 230, 256, 286
   casotto at, 200, 206, 207–9, 211, 256, 308

   pilgrimage to (1958), 205–6, 296, 300, 301, 305–6
Chatham Dockyard, 4
Chiavari (Camp 52):
   appearance, 156–7, 158, 165, 168, 169–70
   hard early days, 161
   favourable conditions, 158–61, 175–6, 179
   cultural life, 162–5, 169, 175, 179
   brutality of *carabinieri*, 165, 166, 172, 283
   tunnels and escape attempts, 165–6, 171–2, 183, 186, 188, 296–7, 298
   sexual reawakening, 164–5
   Armistice announced, 174–5, 183–5
   'stay put' order and arrival of Germans, 184–9
   card index of POWs, 169
   transports from, 189–92, 305
   relics, 169, 308
   legacy, 170–1, 283, 296
   see also: Castelli-Taddei, Col. Dino; Zavatteri, Lieut. Filippo; Shimmin, RSM John; wireless set; theatrical productions by POWs
Chiavari (town), 155–6
Chiese, River, 231, 272
Chiodi, Augusto ('Agostino'), 235, 238, 251, 253, 264–5, 307, 357
   writes in Ralph's notebook, 8, 9, 236, 294
   friendship with Ralph, 239, 273–4, 284, 287–8
   rewarded, 284–5, 307
Chiodi, Erminia, 235, 237, 238–9, 244–5, 251, 287, 307
Chiodi family graves, 241, 243
Chiodi house (13 Via Valletta), 235, 237–8, 240, 241–3, 246, 255, 308

Index

Chiodi, Pietro, 235, 237, 238, 251, 287, 307, 357
Church, Sgt Albert, 133, 134
Churchill, Winston, 35, 55, 124, 161, 285, 297
Ciano, Count Galeazzo, 138
Cicagna, 163
Cione, Col. Vincenzo, 52, 59, 186
Clifton, Brig. George, 138–9
Colditz, 4
  myth of, 64, 138
Coldstream Guards, 15, 17, 171, 261, 289, 297, 305, 310
  Caterham Barracks, 16, 21, 123
  Pirbright Barracks, 16, 17
  Wellington Barracks, 21
Comitato di Liberazione Nazionale Alta Italia (CLNAI), 245, 252–3, 270, 274
communism, 205, 270, 274–5, 283, 284
  among partisans, 233, 245, 251, 363
  Charlie feigns allegiance to, 135, 257
Como, 138, 171
contadini, 232, 269, 270, 308
  mentality and culture, 203, 248–5, 284
  female sympathy for POWs, 120, 198, 203–4, 274, 341–2
  Ralph adopts manners of, 235, 239, 249
  'strange alliance', 204, 205, 248
  see also Italians
cooks, corruption in camps, 61, 144–5, 147, 161, 163
Coppola Lieut. Col. Attilio, 59–60, 87, 129–30, 133–4, 137–8, 141, 149–50, 283
Corna Blacca, 268
Corps, Ethel, *née* White, 18, 21, 285, 296

Corps, Florence, *née* White ('Flo'), xviii, 8, 34, 54, 201, 239, 249, 278, 296
  sense of ambition, 19–20, 198–9, 294–5
  job at Peglers, 18, 19, 198
  letters and parcels to Ralph, 54–56, 90, 176–8
  Women's Auxiliary Police Corps, 54–5, 175, 285, 289
  in Switzerland, xviii, 10, 313–14, 316
  married life, 20–1, 23, 175, 200, 203, 239, 300
  reunited with Ralph, 281–2, 285, 287, 288
  in Africa, 289–90, 292–5, 301–2, 303
  threatens Ralph with knife, 303
  declining health, 303–4
  left alone in Spain, 304
Corps, George (Ralph's brother), xviii, 7
Corps, George (Ralph's uncle), 14, 22, 24
Corps, Gladys (*née* Catherall), 14, 281, 287, 291
Corps, Ralph:
  character, xviii, 14–15, 16, 21–2, 24, 59, 65–6, 94–5, 99, 154, 199–200, 252, 340, 247, 274, 282, 287, 301–2, 305, 311–12
  early life, 13–15
  LNER telegraphist, 15, 266, 304
  joins army, 15–17, 21–2
  as policeman, 17–18, 20, 21, 26, 49, 124, 129, 157, 285, 289, 309
  meets and marries Flo, 18–21
  at war, 21–35
  taken prisoner, 35–46
  in Camp 65, 47–63
  meets Charlie West, 63, 65–6

Corps, Ralph – *cont.*
  head of Sector 2 police, 59–60, 62, 63, 84, 87, 92, 130, 132, 148
  escape (Gravina), 88–115
  recapture and detention, 115–26
  leaves Gravina, 152–3, 155
  escape (Dolcè), 193–6
  evasion in northern Italy, 197–216
  parts company with Charlie, 217
  turns away at Alps, 229–30
  trek to River Po, 230–1
  arrives Paitone, 232–3
  reborn as 'Rodolfo', 235–6, 239, 240–1, 243, 244, 248–9
  stands up to Germans, 252, 259–60
  knowledge of Italian, 8–9, 123, 211, 230, 232, 239, 261, 286
  love of classical music, 27, 126, 162, 314
  love of poetry, 8, 14–15, 34, 199, 247, 286, 295
  memoir ('diary'), xviii, 7–9, 12–13, 41, 47, 64, 65, 99, 109, 116, 125, 154–5, 190–3, 209, 246–5, 282, 310, 332–3
  undercover in Cremona, 260–1
  as FFVV partisan, 249–50, 252–3, 254, 274
  mission with Andrea Baronchelli (1945), 254, 263–4, 265–7
  leaves Italy, 273–4, 277–8
  reunited with Flo, 279–82, 285, 287
  death of mother, 281
  writes to Paitone, 286–8
  rejoins CMP and demobilization, 288–9
  medals and dubious entitlement, 6, 297–8, 305, 309
  emigrates to Africa, 289–90, 292–5
  as prison governor, 292–4, 301–2
  return to Italy (1958), 202–3, 296, 301, 305–6
  retirement and death, 8, 27, 302–4
  grave in Spain, 304, 308–9
  remembered, 310, 311–12
Corps, Thomas, xviii, 13–14, 15, 24, 281, 296
Corps of Military Police (CMP), 21, 23, 26, 31, 53, 61, 213, 305
  Aldershot, 281
  Kidderminster, 214, 224
  Mytchett, 288
  75 Special Investigations Branch, 290
Corsica, 21
Corteno, 238, 246
counterfeit banknotes, 276, 290
Covid-19 pandemic, 76–7, 102, 235
Coward, Noël, *see* theatrical productions by POWs
Cremona, 193, 253, 265, 266, 275
Crete, 68, 75, 240
Cullen, Gnr Paddy:
  escapes from train, 192, 194
  with partisans, 296, 297
Cyprus, 26, 27, 46, 162
  see also Gravina (Camp 65), Greek Cypriots in
Czechoslovakia, 20, 21

D-Day, *see* Normandy landings
'D-Day Dodgers' slur, 297
Dachau concentration camp, 298
Daily Mail, 55, 58, 282
Damascus, 28
Danger Within (1959), 99
Dar es Salaam, 292, 315
Davis, Archibald ('Arch'), xviii, 20, 159, 199, 201, 315
Davis, Audrey, *see* Gaskill, Audrey

Davis, Basil, 293
Davis, Charlotte (*née* White, 'Nan'), xviii, 5–6, 7, 9, 16, 18, 20, 123, 159, 193, 201, 252, 296, 310, 312, 314, 315
Davis, John, xviii, 296, 315, 314, 316
Davis, Matty, murder of, 293
Derna, 29, 41
   POW camp, 42, 43, 49, 137, 277
   hospital, 73, 74
Dethick, Janet Kinrade, 237, 320, 323, 348, 357
diphtheria, 61, 84, 277, 339
Dolcè, 194, 206, 207, 278, 305
Dolomites, 11, 222, 268
Domani Griff, 53–4, 61–2
Doncaster, 13, 15, 18, 19, 108, 177, 296, 303, 304, 315
   see also: Balby; Bentley; Mexborough; Oswin Avenue School; Warmsworth
Donovan, William, 262
Dowie, David, see *Cage, The* (1949)
D'Oyly Carte Opera Company, 162
Dresden, 194, 299
Duke and Duchess of Windsor, 42
Dunkirk, evacuation from (1940), 24, 25, 34, 35, 298, 304
dysentery, 42, 43, 61, 74, 86

East Yorkshire Regt, 25, 140
Edward VIII, King, 240–1
   see *also* Duke and Duchess of Windsor
Edwards, Sgt Evan Llewellyn, 192, 298
Egypt, 25, 26, 28–9, 46, 67
   see also: Cairo; El Alamein; Mersa Matruh; Port Said; Suez Canal
Eisenhower, Gen. Dwight D., 175, 205
El Alamein, 29
Eliot, T. S., 'Little Gidding', 217, 312

Ellis, Ray (escaper and partisan), 249
escape lines, 217, 219, 221–2, 248, 297
escapers:
   POWs' hostility towards, 64, 88, 137, 194
   minority unlike 'keepers', 64–5, 87, 88, 138
   from trains, 3, 4–5, 191–5, 249, 285
   (see also: Barker, RSM W. J.; Cullen, Gnr Paddy; Haslehust, Capt. Desmond; Wilde, Able Seaman Jim)
Església de Sant Romà, see Lloret de Mar
Ethiopia, 18, 20

Facebook, 10, 12, 98, 203, 205, 237
Famagusta, see Cyprus
Fiamme Verdi (FFVV), 246, 248, 250, 252–3, 267, 274–5, 308
   ethos and composition, 245, 254, 265, 270
   fighting, 258–9, 262–3
   liberate Brescia, 269–70, 271, 274
   see also: Perlasca Brigade; Tito Speri Division; Raimondi, Col. Edmondo
50th (Northumbrian) Division, 23, 24, 25–6, 27, 31, 288
First World War, 14, 24, 31, 44, 66–7, 216
Fleming, Ian, 262
Florence, 233, 259, 277
Foggia, 141
Forrest, Helen (jazz singer), 165
Fort Widley, Portsmouth, 148
Fosse, 219, 222
Foster, Percy (wrestler), 163
411 Field Security Section, Intelligence Corps (FSS), 274–5
   Charlie's work with, 275–6, 291

Index

France, 18, 23, 25, 66, 173, 188, 192, 248, 255, 256, 295
Frauenkirche, Dresden, *see* Lee, Robert H.
'Franco' (Lionello Levi Sandri), 265, 266–7, 269, 270, 274, 361, 362
Fumaneri, Cirillo, 198, 205–6, 210–11, 212, 229, 300, 354
  rows POWs across the Adige, 200, 230, 256
Fumaneri, Gianmaria ('Gianni'), 206, 305–6
Fumaneri, Itala Poli, 305
Fumaneri, Lisetta, 205

Gaddafi, Col. Muammar, 290
Gargnano, 258
Garibaldi Brigades (Brigate Garibaldi), 245, 251, 258, 263, 266, 274–5, 363
  Ateo Caremi (assault unit), 257–8, 362
Garioch, Robert (poet), 158, 174
Garletti, Federico, 239–40, 241, 285
Garletti, Isodoro ('Doro'), 234, 235, 238, 242, 248, 254, 273–4, 287
  resistance work, 233, 237, 245, 247, 250, 262, 264–5
  supplies Ralph, 244–5, 246, 253
  helps Russian POW, 307, 370
  representative at Nuvolento, 270
  postwar reward, 239–40, 253, 284–5
  see also: Tempini metalworks; Tempini Brigade
Garletti, Piero, 239, 247, 288, 307
  memories of Ralph, 240–1, 252, 254, 259–60
Garletti, Stefano, 308
Garletti, Ugo, 239, 307
Garner, James (actor), 77
Gaskill, Audrey (*née* Davis), 4–5, 7, 8, 20, 159, 198, 201, 238, 288
  dream about Ralph, xvii, 6–7, 11, 154, 312, 313
  opinion of Ralph and Flo, xviii, 27, 83, 311
  in Switzerland, xvii–xviii, 10, 311, 314, 315–16
  war memories, xviii, 5, 232, 297–8
  strange amnesia of, xvii, 5, 13, 314
Gaskill, Eddie (my father), 4, 5, 41, 295
Gavardo, 206, 209, 248, 260, 263, 272
Gazala, 29, 31, 46, 49, 70, 71, 73
  defensive line at, 31, 40, 43, 84, 95, 278, 288, 290, 298
Geneva Convention, 84, 133, 141, 257, 283
Genoa, 155, 168, 170, 172, 183, 184, 193, 291, 316
German army, 23–5, 152, 195, 256
  6th Army, 86–7
  retreating in Italy, 185, 219, 220, 246, 252, 255, 259–60, 265–6, 269–73
  deserters in Brescia, 252, 259, 265
  LXXV Corps, surrender of, 275
  see also: Afrika Korps; Gothic Line; Gustav Line; Stalingrad, German defeat at
German POW camps:
  Stalag VIII-A (Görlitz), 194
  Stalag VIII-B (Lamsdorf & Teschen), 298, 344
  Stalag X-1B (Fallingbostel), 298
  Stalag XVIII-A (Wolfsberg), 298
  Stalag Luft I (Barth), 339
  Stalag Luft III (Sagan), 77, 328
Gestapo, 53
ghosts, *see* history, ghostliness of
Giacopuzzi, Fabio, 214, 215–16, 218–20, 222–5
Giacopuzzi, Rosangela, 215, 220
Gioia del Colle, 102, 107–11, 116, 117, 126, 200

Index

Gillingham (Kent), 4, 5, 7, 20, 159, 315
  'Fifty-Pee Brian', 4, 6
Giustizia e Libertà (partisans), 247, 258
Glass Mountain, The (1949), 11
Google:
  Maps, 10, 116, 206, 213, 214
  Translate: 47, 125, 250
Gothic Line, 259, 263
Gravina (Camp 65):
  appearance and organization of, 47–9, 81, 82–4, 100–1
  conditions and routines, 46, 49–52, 56, 59–61, 62–3, 85–6, 133–4, 142–3, 149
  as 'hell camp', 142
  palazzina comando, 48, 49, 75, 129, 133, 147
  varied nationalities, 48–9, 149
  Greek Cypriots in, 48, 59, 88, 91, 94, 135–6, 144–6, 150, 152
  closed world of, 46, 52, 55, 56, 58, 142, 146–7
  guards and officers, 48, 51, 52–3, 59–60, 65, 87, 129–32, 146
  food, 50, 53–4, 56, 60–1, 62, 85, 86–7, 89, 143, 144–5, 147
  exchange-and-mart system, 143–4
  tea ritual, 65, 75–6, 85, 89, 136
  importance of firewood, 49, 50, 85, 86, 87
  news and letters, 53–4, 54–6, 69, 84, 160, 162, 175, 176–9
  photography in, 51, 52, 69, 99–101, 139, 145, 149
  doctors and padres, 49, 58, 146
  filth and infestation, 51–2, 86, 133–4, 143
  sickness and death, 58, 61–2, 84, 86
  depression and suicide, 57–8
  gangs, 'barons' and bullying, 57, 143–4, 144–5
  brutal treatment of prisoners, 52–3, 88, 134, 138, 141
  escaping from, 52, 87, 88–92, 93–101, 132–5, 138–8, 146
  Christmas in (1942), 84–5
  pastimes, music and sport, 53, 58–9, 85, 88, 149–50 (*see also*: 'tin-bashers'; theatrical productions by POWs)
  Welfare and Social Committee, 58, 146
  homosexuality and cross-dressing, 150–2
  masturbation, 151
  confiscation of gold rings, 137–8
  work parties from, 141–2
  evacuation of, 149, 152–3
  postwar memory, 10, 12, 82, 139, 308, 310
  see also: Domani Griff; Camp 65 Association; prisoners of war
Great Escape, The (1963), 77
Greece, 140, 144, 145, 255, 269, 283
Greek Cypriots, *see* Gravina (Camp 65)
Green Howards (Alexandra, Princess of Wales's Own Yorkshire Regt), 25, 26
Guardia Nazionale Repubblicana (GNR), 263
Guernica (1937), *see* Spanish Civil War
Gulf of Aqaba, 28
Gustav Line, 245, 256

Hackett, William, 13
Haifa, 27, 28, 140, 298
Hamburg, 221, 298
Haslehust, Capt. Desmond, 194–5, 222, 353, 355
Haydon, Brig. Cecil, 31, 34, 35
Heaney, Seamus, 225

Index

Heliopolis, *see* Baalbek
'Hellfire Pass' (Halfaya), 29
Himmler, Heinrich, 273, 276
history:
    definitions of, 11, 170
    myths, 3, 138, 146
    family lore, 4–5, 6, 11, 13, 18
    as mirror as well as window, 221, 312
    as storytelling, 7, 304
    ghostliness of, xix, 4, 11, 76–7, 84, 125, 129, 170, 198, 209, 223, 309, 312, 325
    see also archives, experience of; photographs, as sources; Italy, contested history
Hitler, Adolf, 3, 18, 20–1, 25, 44, 152, 165
    death of, 275
HMP Butimba, 292
    echoes of Camp 65, 293–4
HMS *Bedouin*, 159, 179
HMS *Exeter*, 26
HMS *Hood*, 26
HMS *Thetis*, 164
Hoggan, Tpr Alexander, 297
Holbrook, David, 299
Holland, 264, 276
Holocaust, the, *see* Jews, persecution of,
homosexuality, *see* Gravina (Camp 65)
Hotel Brescia (FSS HQ), 274–5
Howard, Trevor (actor), 3
Huggett, Eric, 162, 179, 185, 298, 299
Hull (E. Yorkshire), 139, 140, 298
Humphries, Bill, 72, 73
150th Infantry Brigade, 26, 140
    defensive 'box', 31, 33–5, 39, 84

Il Diario di Ralph (film), 310
Il Ribelle (FFVV newspaper), 246, 254
Imperial War Museum, 41, 53, 54, 68, 147, 170, 192

India, 14, 84
    POWs from in Italy, 45
Indian Army Ordnance Corps, 166
Intelligence Corps, *see* 411 Field Security Section
International Committee of the Red Cross (ICRC), 55, 73, 131, 148, 253
    camp inspections, 48, 55, 133–4
    food parcels, 53, 60–1, 62, 63, 65, 76, 84–5, 86, 134, 143, 145, 146, 160, 169, 171
    other supplies, 150, 161, 162, 163, 175
    see also Prisoner of War, The
Iraq, 28
    see also Kirkuk
IS9(W), *see* MI9 (Military Intelligence),
Isle of Man, 303
Ismailia, 28–9, 68
Italian army, 18, 20, 25, 134, 152, 186
    8th Army, 87
    9th Army, 52
    jokes about, 40–1
    prisoners of war, 31, 72–3, 137, 276
    see also: Bersaglieri; Waffen-SS
Italians:
    Allied opinion of (negative), 9, 40–1, 44, 145
    Allied opinion of (positive), 40–1, 222, 248, 286, 366
    attitude towards Allies, 44, 88–9, 90, 176, 204, 274
    civilian fear of Germans, 172, 197, 230, 232, 246
    penalties for helping POWs, 212, 213, 214, 234, 242, 269
    myths about the British, 124, 233, 238–9
    evading POWs morph into, 276–7, 278, 285

Index

reparations and rewards for, 204–5, 210, 270, 283–5
see also: contadini; Allied Screening Commission
Italy:
   food, 101, 170, 215, 220, 224–5, 244–5
   geography, 47, 81, 155, 222, 229, 230, 259
   weather, 62–3, 102, 212, 229, 287
   postwar challenges, 270–1, 282–3
   contested history, 10, 220, 223–4, 225, 251–2, 310–11
   see also: Armistice, Italian (1943); Mussolini, Benito; *memoria condivisa*

Jews, persecution of, 109, 140, 170–1, 192, 283
Jordan, 28

Kendell, John, 200, 303, 304
Kendell, Pauline, 7, 14, 193, 203, 235, 237, 285, 288, 294, 303–4
   Warmsworth archive, 7–8, 10, 13, 16, 19, 46, 139, 198, 201–2, 249–50, 312
   opinion of Ralph and Flo, 8, 15, 198–200, 311
Kenya, 302
Kesselring, Field Marshal Albert, 246, 257, 258
Khartoum, 315
Kidd, Sgt David, 134, 343
Kingolwira Prison Farm, 8, 293, 294, 295, 303
King's Medal for Courage in the Cause of Freedom, 284
Kipling, Rudyard, 14, 33, 247
Kirkuk, 28, 39
Klagenfurt, 298
Klim (powdered milk), 75, 88

Knaresborough (N. Yorkshire), 17, 26, 124
Knowles, Sgt Jack, 192

'L' Detachment, *see* Special Air Service (SAS)
La Bohème, 314
La Spezia, 155, 184
Lake Como, *see* Como
Lake Garda, 8, 9, 193, 198, 202, 214–15, 222, 231, 260, 305
   Charlie attempts to cross, 256–7, 258, 308
Lake Idro, 258, 269, 271
Lake Iseo, 238, 246
Lake Lugano, 313, 316
Lake Victoria, 292
Langdon, Sgt John, 134, 142, 192
Lavenone, 258, 271–2
Lawrence, D. H., 188
League of Nations, 18
'Le Rive' (POW safe house), 214, 219, 222, 223–4
Leali, Don Primo Alessio, 272, 308
Lebanon, 28
Lee, Robert H. (artist), 57, 83
   friendship with Greek Cypriots and Palestinian Jews, 144–5
   on cross-dressing in Camp 65, 151–2
   artwork in Frauenkirche, Dresden, 298–9
Lefkonico church, *see* Cyprus
Lessini Mountains (Lessinia), 222, 225
Levantine Sea, 27
liberation reports (POW), 145, 148, 195, 205
   of Ralph and Charlie, 193–4, 199, 204, 212, 322
Libya, 25, 40, 48, 87, 133, 137, 230, 290
   see also: Benghazi; Derna; Timimi; Tripoli

Ligurian Sea, 155, 158, 164, 266, 316
'Lili Marlene' (song), 297, 348
Livorno, 155, 184, 186
Lloret de Mar, 304, 308–9
lockdowns, *see* Covid 19 pandemic
Lombardy, 190, 231, 269, 316
London North Eastern Railway (LNER), 15–16, 17, 21, 304
Longfellow, Henry Wadsworth, 14, 247
Loro, Albina, 205, 206
Löw, Marc, 298
Löw, Sgt Max (Moshe Lev), 139–40, 144, 145, 148
  pretends to be Australian, 140, 298
Luftwaffe, 26, 29, 32, 71–2, 206–7, 212, 258
Lugano, *see* Lake Lugano

Maccarinelli, Angelo, 232–5, 236–7, 238–40, 241, 244, 254
  compensation for, 253, 284–5
  Ralph writes to, 286–7
Maccarinelli, Anna, 238, 240, 242, 255, 307
Maccarinelli, Celestina, 237, 239, 241, 242, 250, 254–5
Maccarinelli, Dante, 234, 240, 241, 307
Maccarinelli, Enzo (boxer), 307, 369
Maccarinelli, Marco, 250–1
Maccarinelli, Pietro, 240, 281, 307
Macey, PO Bert, 159, 161, 162, 163, 179, 189
Madagascar, 26
Madame Butterfly, 27, 313, 371
'Major Rolando' (escaper and partisan), 297
malaria, 61, 86, 156
  Charlie suffers from, 86, 89, 93, 104, 111, 135, 193, 195, 200, 208, 229
Malga Sacù (partisan hut), 268, 271, 308

Manley, Pat, 301–2
Mantua (Mantova), 193, 231
Manzelli, Claudio, 205,
Manzelli, Flavio, 211, 306
Manzelli, Stella, 205
Marche region, 249
Marconi, Guglielmo, 164
Marozin, Giuseppe, 257
Mason, J. P., 17
Massa, 155
massacres, Nazi, *see* partisans, reprisals for activity
Masseria Casabolicchio, 116–21
Matteotti Brigades (Brigate Matteotti), 253
Mazzano, 259
McBean, Pte James, 133, 134, 297
McGonigal, Lieut. Eoin, 70
memoria condivisa, 311
mepacrine, *see* malaria
Merano, 276, 290
Mersa Matruh, 29, 70
Mexborough, 13–14, 19, 59
Mexborough Adwick Road School, 14
MI9 (Military Intelligence), 134, 173, 185, 277, 284
  secret POW escape kit, 134–5, 184
  Ralph and Charlie debriefed by, 193–4, 195, 200, 209, 210, 212, 213, 236, 250, 252, 261, 271, 278, 289, 291, 292
Milan, 184, 225, 290, 307, 313, 316
Miles, Jasper (comedian), 164
Ministry of Defence, 27
Miranda, Carmen, 165
Molina, 213–14, 215–17, 218–19, 223, 229, 230, 232, 258, 268, 286
  il roccolo at, 218, 222, 223
Mombasa, 26
Montallegro, 164

Index

Monte (village), 230
Monte Baldo, 222, 224, 225, 229, 257, 308
Monte Budellone, 237, 248, 251, 254
Monte Generoso, 313–16
Monte San Martino Trust, 205, 322
Monte Tesio, 251, 263, 265
Monte Urano, 296
Monte Vesuvius, 155, 277
Montgomery, Gen. Bernard, 40, 161, 183, 185, 245
More, Kenneth (actor), 70
Morea, Onofrio Rocco, 123–4, 126
Morogoro, 293
Mottola, 142
Mottola, José, 116, 117–20, 125
Msasani Prison, 292
Munday, RSM Les, 59, 62, 84
Munich Crisis (1938), 21
Mussolini, Benito, 41, 44, 113, 122, 126, 138, 172, 274, 282
    colonial ambitions, 18, 20, 21, 25, 290
    economic and military woes, 25, 87, 134, 152, 272
    dismissed by king, 175
    as puppet at Salò, 201–2, 282
    death of, 275
    lingering respect for, 82, 223–4, 310–11
Mwanza, 292, 300

Nairobi, 315
Naples, 47, 155, 230, 277, 278
National Archives (Kew), The, 47, 48, 67, 73, 140
    Ralph's service record at, 27, 261, 304–5
    war diaries, 25–6, 27, 28
    see also liberation reports
National Archives and Records Administration (NARA), 205, 206, 210, 213, 237, 264, 323

New Zealand, 30, 67, 84, 166
    prisoners from, 12, 48, 62, 138–9, 159, 169, 170, 173, 194, 296
Newby, Eric, 283–4
Newby, Vanda (*née* Škof), 284
Nice, 21, 316
Nino Bixio (Italian ship), 43
Noci, 116, 120, 121–6, 129, 172, 197, 203, 230
Normandy landings (1944), 4, 256, 297
North Africa:
    campaign, xvii, 25, 41, 68
    desert life, 27–30, 31–2
    see also: Benghazi; Derna; Libya; Gazala; Tobruk
nostalgia, *see* Second World War, memory of
Nozza, 271–3, 275, 308
Nuremberg trials (1945–6), 283
Nuvolento, 231, 253, 259, 264, 270–1, 274, 284
Nyerere, Julius, 301, 302

Office of Strategic Services (OSS), 261–2, 263–4, 265, 266–7, 276, 290
    Mission Franco, 268–9
    Mission Franconia, 361
    Mission Roanoke, 362
    2671st Special Reconnaissance Battalion, 361–2
    2677th Regt, 261, 265
    see also: partisans; Donovan, William; 'Franco'
Operation Bernhard, *see* counterfeit banknotes
Operation Roast, 362
Operation Squatter (SAS), 70–3, 111, 292
Operation Sunrise, 276
Organisation Todt, 216

Index

O.S.B.R. (sugar, oatmeal, biscuits and raisins), 91–2, 93, 94, 104–5, 106
Ostiglia, 210, 231, 307
Oswin Avenue School, 14, 17
Ouija boards, 88
Owen, Fl.-Sgt Hugh, 90, 93, 95–7, 133, 296

Pagliano, Paolo, 272–3
Paitone, 8–10, 233–4, 236, 238, 241, 243, 254–5, 259, 264, 266, 273, 275, 285, 307
   rhythms of life, 234–5, 237, 244–5, 247–8
   Ralph settled in, 235, 239, 243, 247–8, 252, 282, 305, 313
   vendemmia, 247
   fear of bombing, 248, 254–5
   Christmas 1943, 234
   Christmas 1944, 247–8
   Ralph leaves, 273–4, 287
   restoration of order in, 270, 274
   see also: Maccarinelli, Angelo; Maccarinelli, Celestina; Garletti, Piero
Palestine, 28
Palestine Pioneer Corps, 140
Palestinian Jews, 48, 144
   as entrepreneurs in Camp 65, 144–5, 148, 150, 152
   see also Löw, Max
Parachute Regiment, 248
partisans:
   POWs join, 188, 191–2, 212, 225, 229, 246, 294–7
   negative stereotype, 249, 265, 316
   political variety, 220, 245, 251–2, 258, 265, 274–5
   morale of, 229, 252, 254, 257–8, 263, 269
   supply drops to, 251, 254, 262–3, 269
   Allied reliance upon, 248, 259, 263, 271–2, 297
   reprisals for activity, 206–7, 212, 222, 238, 244, 246
   truce with fleeing Germans, 219
   see also: Fiamme Verdi; Garibaldi Brigades; Matteotti Brigades; Giustizia e Libertà; Tempini Brigade; *rastrellamenti*; sabotage; Marozin, Giuseppe; Pagliano, Paolo; Ellis, Ray; 'Giorgio'; 'Major Rolando'
Passerini, Luisa (historian), 307
Patella, Tina, 101
Penguin Books, supplies POWs, 134
Peniakoff, Lieut. Col. Vladimir, 276, 277
Perlasca Brigade (FFVV), 263, 265, 267, 268, 308
   S4 battalion, defeats Germans at Nozza, 268–73
Persian Gulf, 25
Pertica Alta, 268
Pescantina, 193, 221, 222, 310
Pescara, 230
'Phoney War', *see* Second World War, early stages
photographs, as sources, 6, 8, 17, 19, 28, 68, 100–1, 202–3, 236, 301, 309, 313
Piacenza, 193, 297
Pian di Coreglia, *see* Chiavari (Camp 52)
Piedmont, 316
Pisa, 155
Pleasence, Donald (actor), 77, 339
Plymouth, 66, 67, 94, 291
Plymouth Public Secondary School for Boys, 67
Po, River (and valley), 210, 229–30, 231, 259, 316

Index

Poland, 21, 230, 298
polenta ritual ('the yellow peril'), 244
Polizia Militare di Sicurezza, 275
Pope Pius XII, 75
Popski's Private Army, see Peniakoff, Lieut. Col. Vladimir,
Port Said, 26
Porto Polesine, 265–6
Predappio, see Mussolini, Benito
Prevalle, 9, 231, 235, 241, 242, 247, 250, 251, 260, 261, 264, 311
   resistance in, 245, 252, 264, 289
   raids on fascists in, 263
   bombing of, 248
   new government of, 270–1
Presegno, 258, 269
Princess Margaret, see Tanganyika
Prisoner of War, The (Red Cross newspaper), 55, 160, 177
prisoners of war:
   psychology, 39–40, 56–7, 58–9, 64, 87, 88–9
   comforts of home, 54, 56, 65–6, 75–6, 102, 106, 161
   parcels from home, 55, 56, 62, 86, 90, 143, 147
   rumours among, 53, 143, 147, 152, 165, 174–5, 183–4
   secret radios, 173–4
   informers among, 90, 134, 159, 185
   depression and insanity, 57–8, 161, 174–5
   interest in sex, 54, 151–2, 164–5
   difficult return to civilian life, 281–2, 285, 290
   pilgrimages to Italy, 163, 203, 296 (*see also* Ceraino)
   later ill-health, 298–9
   see also: Chiavari (Camp 52); Gravina (Camp 65); 'escapers' and keepers'; theatrical productions by POWs; German POW camps
propaganda, 8, 41, 47, 53, 74, 122, 124, 238–9
   leaflets dropped by Germans, 212, 258
   leaflets dropped on Germans, 259
Puglia (Apulia), 10, 12, 44, 62, 81, 101–2, 149
   see also Altopiano delle Murge
Putignano, Cesareo, 117–18, 120, 123

Quillieri, Sam, 267
quinine, see malaria

Radaelli, Signor, 200, 210–11, 212, 256
Radaelli, Vittorina, 200, 210, 211, 229, 256, 306–7, 354
Radcenko, Yuri, 307, 370
Radford, Richard (economist), 143
Radio Londra, see British Broadcasting Corporation
Raimondi, Col. Edmondo (FFVV), 274
Rapallo, 164, 172, 188
rastrellamenti, 233, 244, 246, 247, 257, 263, 269
Rawmarsh (S. Yorkshire), 18, 19, 198
Reach for the Sky (1956), 70
Red Army, see Russia
Red Cross, see International Committee of the Red Cross
'Redcaps', see Corps of Military Police
Reid, Pat, see Colditz, myth of
Repubblica Sociale Italiana (RSI), 201–2, 211, 258, 311
   brutality of regime, 261
   Finance Ministry, Ralph posing as official of, 202, 261, 264, 274
   Presidency of the Council of Ministers, 258

Index

Repubblica Sociale Italiana (RSI) – *cont.*
  fall of, 282–3
  see also: Brigate Nere; Guardia Nazionale Repubblicana,
'Republic of Salò', *see* Repubblica Sociale Italiana
Resina (repatriation camp), 277–8, 281, 291
Rhodesia (Zimbabwe), 290, 303
Rimini, 184
Riva del Garda, 272
Rivetta, Augusta, 234, 244
Robinson, Billy (died 1945), 5
Robinson, Emily (historian), 370
Rogers, Ginger, 164
Romania, 276
Rome, 99, 133, 137, 172, 186, 253, 264, 277, 291, 307, 315
  liberation of (1944), 204, 256
Rommel, Gen. Erwin, 29, 32–5, 39, 40, 48, 95, 288
Rossouw, RSM John, 87, 138, 147–8, 192
Roth, Philip, 154, 311
Royal Air Force (RAF), 11, 33, 67, 70, 292, 303
  216 Squadron, 67–8
  Cosford, 291
  Cranwell, 67
  Fuka aerodrome, 70, 71
  Heliopolis aerodrome, 67
  Kabrit, 68
  Kinloss, 66, 67
  bombing raids, 43, 155, 173, 188
  use of 'window', 248
  see also partisans, supply drops to
Royal Air Force Escaping Society (RAFES), 300, 301
Royal Army Medical Corps, 49, 58, 61, 74, 214, 219, 282
Royal Artillery, POWs from, 88, 134, 145, 192
Royal Engineers, help hide radio, 137, 153
Royal Horticultural Society, 175
Royal Navy, 26, 43, 140, 295
  POWs from, 88, 159, 179, 188, 191–2
Rubaiyat of Omar Khayyam, The, 14, 295
Russia, 23, 86–7, 133, 152, 255
  Italians lost in, 120, 122, 269, 341
sabotage:
  by Germans, 263
  against Germans, 212, 229, 246, 263, 271
Sachsenhausen concentration camp, 276
Saint Joan (George Bernard Shaw), 179, 185
SAS, *see* Special Air Service
Salford Blitz (1940), 5
Salò, 202, 206, 258, 259, 261, 272, 311
  see also Repubblica Sociale Italiana (RSI)
salvacondotto (Ralph's forged pass), 201–2, 206, 261, 264, 265, 266
Sandrà, 195
Sandri, Lionello Levi, *see* 'Franco'
Sandri, Remo, 223–4
Sansonetti, Vincenzo, 116, 118, 123, 125
Sant'Anna d'Alfaedo, 224–5, 306
Santeramo, 108, 200
Sartre, Jean-Paul, 57
scabies, *see* Gravina (Camp 65), infestation and sickness
Schwend, Friedrich (money launderer), 276, 290
Scots Guards, 68, 93, 95
Scoullar, Brenda, 67
Scoullar, Frank, 67
Scoullar, Mabel, 66–7, 290–1

Index

Scoullar, Olga, *see* Burford, Olga
Sebald, W. G., *Austerlitz* (2001), 10, 11
Second World War:
   early stages, 21–2, 23
   course of, 24–5, 31–5, 86–7, 152, 165, 173, 174–5, 183–5, 256, 259, 275
   impact of, xix, 22, 175–6, 281, 290–1
   as source of stories, 22, 82, 117, 170
   myths and memory of, 3–4, 64, 107, 170–1, 138, 170, 241
   see also: war films and comics; war relics, power of; VE Day (1945)
Sega, Battista, 213, 215, 219, 223–4, 229, 230, 355
Sega di Ala, 222, 229, 316
Sega, Francesco, 213, 215, 223–4, 229, 230, 355
Sega, Raffaele, 219, 220, 318
Selby Wright, Rev. Ronnie (the 'Radio Padre'), 184
Serle, 254, 261, 264, 265–7, 268–9, 270
Shaw, George Bernard, *see Saint Joan*
Sheffield, 15, 17
Shimmin, RSM John, 159, 172, 174, 176, 184–7, 189
Shropshire, xvii, 7
'skilly', *see:* Gravina (Camp 65), food; Chiavari (Camp 52), food
Škof, Vanda, *see* Newby, Vanda
Sicily, 27, 159, 165
   invasion of (1943), 174, 176, 178
Simpson, Mrs Wallace, 240–1
   see also Duke and Duchess of Windsor
Sinatra, Frank, *see Von Ryan's Express* (1965)
Sontag, Susan, 17
South Africa, 12, 84, 164
   prisoners from, 48, 63, 86, 89, 91, 142, 144, 149, 159, 193, 194

POW bayonetted, 141
POW claims diabolic possession, 58
'the Hippo', 148
Afrikaner stooges in Camp 52, 186
Ralph and Flo at Fish Hoek, 303
see also: Rossouw, RSM John; Bates, Sgt Ron; Bartlett, RSM S. V.; Foster, Percy
'South Country, The', *see* Belloc, Hilaire
'South of the Border' (song), 188
South Tyrol, 269
Southampton, 281
Spanish Civil War, 18
Special Air Service (SAS), 68–9, 70, 72–3, 276, 290
   Charlie credited as founder member of, 69, 300
   see also Operation Squatter
Special Operations Executive (SOE), 257
Spiazzi, 256
spiritualism, *see* Ouija boards
sport, POW, *see:* Chiavari (Camp 52); Gravina (Camp 65)
SS *Angola*, 303
SS *Duchess of Bedford*, 26
SS *Uganda*, 292–3
stalags, *see* German POW camps
Stalin, Josef, 152, 165, 276
Stalingrad, German defeat at (1943), 86–7, 133
Stallone, Sylvester, 109
Steer, Vanessa, 69
Stirling, Col. David, 68, 70, 72
Strachan, Sgt Bill, 171–2, 183, 188, 297
   testifies against Italians, 283
'strange alliance', *see contadini*
Sturges, John, *see Great Escape, The* (1963)

Suez Canal, 25, 26, 28, 68
    see also Ismailia
Suez Crisis (1956), 295
Switzerland, 52, 222
    POWs' dream of, 3, 66, 77, 88–9, 111, 217, 229, 231, 233, 258, 313
    successful escapes to, 248, 296–7
    see also Gaskill, Audrey
Syria, 28, 46

Tanganyika, 8, 289–90, 292–6, 297, 301
    racial divisions, 292–3, 294, 302
    Italian settlers in, 289
    visit by Princess Margaret, 295
    gains independence (Tanzania), 301–2
Tanganyika African National Union (TANU), 301
Tank Museum, The, Bovington, 171, 177
Tanzania, see Tanganyika
telepathy, 131, 132, 200, 214
Tempini Brigade, 269–70, 307
Tempini metalworks, 234, 269, 245, 362
Tennyson, Alfred Lord, 14, 247
Testi, Arnaldo, 206
theatrical productions by POWs:
    'Aladdin and His Magic Embers' (Camp 65), 85
    Blithe Spirit (Camp 65), 88
    Of Mice and Men (Camp 52), 162
    The Importance of Being Earnest (Camp 52), 162, 347
    The Mikado, 97, 159, 162, 179, 185
    as source of sexual titillation, 151, 164–5
    see also Huggett, Eric
Tiberia, 28
Ticino, 314
Timimi, 41, 70

'tin-bashers', 62, 63, 75, 88
Tito Speri Division (FFVV), 269, 362
Tobruk, 25, 49, 68, 71, 84
Tolstoy, Leo, 11
Tonni, Caterina Rossi, 265
Tormini, 272
trains, escape from, see escapers, from trains
Transjordan Frontier Force, 28
Treaty of Versailles, 18
Trentino, 222
Trento, 192, 193, 195, 206, 271, 272
Tripoli, 87
Tripolitania, 290
trulli, 102, 103–4, 105–6, 112–13, 117, 200
tuberculosis, 221
Tunisia, 21, 133, 152, 165
Turin, 172, 188, 192, 253, 274, 290, 291
Tuturano (Camp 85), 44–5, 55, 75, 137, 322
Tyrrhenian Sea, 230, 278

Uganda, 289
Uluguru Mountains, 293
United Nations:
    mission to Tanganyika (1960), 302
    War Crimes Committee, see war crimes, accusations of
Università Cattolica del Sacro Cuore, 253–4
University of London, 175
US 5th Army, 265, 274
    advance of 1944–5, 259, 269, 272
    34th Division (incl. 135th Infantry Regt), 272, 273
    see also Office of Strategic Services (OSS)

Val d'Adige, see Adige, River
Val Fontanabuona, 163, 169–70

Index

Val Sabbia, 259, 263, 268, 269, 271–2, 274
Val Trompia, 263
Vatican, the, 85
   see also Pope Pius XII
VE Day (1945), 4, 291
Venosa, 142
Venturini, Giovanni (murdered partisan), 238, 307, 357, 369
Verona, 192, 193, 194, 206, 210, 215, 222, 224, 230
   railway station bombed, 221
   see also: Breonio; Bussolengo; Ceraino, Dolcè; Molina; Sandrà
Veronesi, Don Domenico, 219, 221, 222
Via Appia Antica, 102, 106
Victoria Cross, 5, 13
Voghera, 193
von Ranke, Leopold, 11
Von Ryan's Express (1965), 3, 5–6, 193, 249

Wade, Horace (artist), 156–7, 160, 169, 171, 177, 179
   loses leg in mining accident, 298
Waffen-SS, 263, 269, 271–3
   Italian Division, 251, 263
   16th SS Panzergrenadier Division, 272
   massacres in Italy by, 273
   see also Operation Sunrise
war crimes, accusations of, 138, 147, 283
war films, comics and toys, 3–4, 39, 77, 192, 249
   see also: *Glass Mountain, The* (1949); *Reach for the Sky* (1956); *Danger Within* (1959); *Great Escape, The* (1963); *Von Ryan's Express* (1965)
war relics, power of, 4, 5, 6, 170, 171, 242, 251
   see also Zavatteri, Fabio

War Ministry (Rome), 133, 134
War Office (London), 60, 185, 186, 288
Warmsworth (Doncaster), 7, 39, 46, 177, 198, 200, 294, 297, 312
warrant officers, privileges of, 58, 85, 122, 138, 141, 142–3, 147–9, 156, 159, 164, 172, 174
Warren, Billy (drummer), 173
Welfare and Social Committee, *see* Gravina (Camp 65), pastimes and entertainment
West, Archie, 66–7
West, Barbara (*née* Williams), 69, 300, 301, 306
West, Charlie:
   character and appearance, 63, 64–6, 69–70, 75, 93, 96, 99, 111, 114, 262
   early life, 66–7
   joins RAF, 67
   fined for speeding, 67
   shot down and injured, 70–3
   captivity, 74–5
   dims camp lights, 90–1
   escape (Gravina), 66, 93–8, 100–1, 147
   recapture and detention, 119–21, 124–5, 125–6
   returns to Gravina, 126, 129–33
   leaves Gravina, 152–3, 155
   escape (Dolcè) and evasion, 194–5, 197–8, 205–6, 212–13, 221–3, 229
   parts company with Ralph, 216–17
   reborn as 'Carlo', 200, 205, 211, 267, 268
   knowledge of Italian, 94, 109–110, 119, 211, 268, 275
   leaves Ceraino for good, 256
   as partisan, 256–8, 268–9, 290
   executes prisoners, 257, 306
   defence of Nozza, 271–3

West, Charlie – *cont.*
   work with FSS and CMP, 275–6, 290
   repatriation and leaves RAF, 290–2
   death of mother, 291–2
   love of cars, 69, 206, 300, 305
   mentioned in despatches, 297
   postwar life, 300
   address book entries, 206, 219–20, 300–1
   visits to Italy, 205–6, 300, 301
   death and obituary, 69, 301
   see also Special Air Service (SAS); malaria; wireless set
West, Mabel, *see* Scoullar, Mabel
West, Syd, 66, 290, 291–2
West Riding Constabulary, 17–18, 20, 199, 285, 289, 309
White, Florence Mary, 18–19, 33, 177
White, George, 18, 249
White, James Arthur, 18–19
White, Ralph, 249, 303
White, Ruth, 302–3
Wilde, Able Seaman Jim, 191–2, 194, 195, 352, 362
Williams, Barbara, *see* West, Barbara
Williams, Henry (attempted suicide), 58, 335

Windsor Castle, 15
wireless set (Camps 65 and 52), 135–6, 138, 142, 165–7, 172–4, 176, 194
   construction of, 136–7, 152–3
   smuggling and hiding of, 136–7, 155, 156–7, 166, 189, 192
Wolff, SS-Gen. Karl, 273
Wolseley Barracks, *see* Cyprus
Wombwell, xviii, 20–2, 33, 55, 94, 177, 199, 281, 289
Wordsworth, William, 247

Yeats, W. B., 247
Ypres, 24
Yugoslavia, 225

Zanola, Annibale, 259–60
Zanola, Caterina, 232–3, 234, 235, 239, 241, 244
Zanola, Domenico (fascist), 234, 241, 244
Zanoni, Giuseppe, 205, 206
Zavatteri, Fabio, 169, 170, 176, 308
Zavatteri, Lieut. Filippo, 160, 162, 169, 172, 176, 186, 187
   after the war, 283, 296
Zoagli, 172

any movement. The place might just as well have been dead. Wasting no time we scuttled across the road, continued along for a short distance, and turned down the first turning. It was another minor road. Our intention now was to get as far as possible from the main part of the Town. We walked briskly along, and were just about to congratulate ourselves on having negotiated the Town successfully when, from out of the darkness ahead, an Italian voice snapped "CHI VA LA?" My spine rocketed up through the top of my head, and my hair stood on end. I stood transfixed. The braccole under my arm fell to the ground almost un-noticed. I could see nothing of the hidden speaker but the way that command was pushed out left me in no doubt as to what it meant. Visualising a rifle pointing at my middle I looked round for some avenue of escape. There was none.

"What shall we do?" whispered my friend. I didn't know. Escape now was out of the